PERSPECTIVES ON WRITING
Series Editor, Susan H. McLeod

PERSPECTIVES ON WRITING
Series Editor, Susan H. McLeod

The Perspectives on Writing series addresses writing studies in a broad sense. Consistent with the wide ranging approaches characteristic of teaching and scholarship in writing across the curriculum, the series presents works that take divergent perspectives on working as a writer, teaching writing, administering writing programs, and studying writing in its various forms.

The WAC Clearinghouse and Parlor Press are collaborating so that these books will be widely available through free digital distribution and low-cost print editions. The publishers and the Series editor are teachers and researchers of writing, committed to the principle that knowledge should freely circulate. We see the opportunities that new technologies have for further democratizing knowledge. And we see that to share the power of writing is to share the means for all to articulate their needs, interest, and learning into the great experiment of literacy.

OTHER BOOKS IN THE SERIES

Charles Bazerman and David R. Russell (Eds.), *Writing Selves/Writing Societies* (2003)

Gerald P. Delahunty and James Garvey, *The English Language: from Sound to Sense* (2009)

Charles Bazerman, Adair Bonini, and Débora Figueiredo (Eds.), *Genre in a Changing World* (2009)

David Franke, Alex Reid, and Anthony Di Renzo (Eds.), *Design Discourse: Composing and Revising Programs in Professional and Technical Writing* (2010)

Doreen Starke-Meyerring, Anthony Paré, Natasha Artemeva, Miriam Horne, and Larissa Yousoubova (Eds.), *Writing in Knowledge Societies* (2011)

COPY(WRITE): INTELLECTUAL PROPERTY IN THE WRITING CLASSROOM

Edited by

Martine Courant Rife
Shaun Slattery
Dànielle Nicole DeVoss

The WAC Clearinghouse
wac.colostate.edu
Fort Collins, Colorado

Parlor Press
www.parlorpress.com
Anderson, South Carolina

The WAC Clearinghouse, Fort Collins, Colorado 80523-1052
Parlor Press, 3015 Brackenberry Drive, Anderson, South Carolina 29621

© 2011 by Martine Courant Rife, Shaun Slattery, and Dànielle Nicole DeVoss. This work is licensed under a Creative Commons Attribution-Noncommercial-No Derivative Works 3.0 United States License. All other rights reserved.

Printed in the United States of America

Library of Congress Cataloging-in-Publication Data

Copy(write) : intellectual property in the writing classroom / edited by Martine Courant Rife, Shaun Slattery, Danielle Nicole DeVoss.
   p. cm. -- (Perspectives on writing)
Includes bibliographical references and index.
 ISBN 978-1-60235-263-6 (hardcover : alk. paper) -- ISBN 978-1-60235-262-9 (pbk. : alk. paper) -- ISBN 978-1-60235-264-3 (adobe ebook : alk. paper) -- ISBN 978-1-60235-265-0 (epub : alk. paper)
 1. Fair use (Copyright)--United States. 2. Rhetoric--Study and teaching (Higher)--United States. 3. Universities and colleges--Law and legislation--United States. I. Rife, Martine Courant. II. Slattery, Shaun. III. DeVoss, Dànielle Nicole. IV. Title: Copyright.
 KF3030.1.C67 2011
 346.7304'82--dc23
                    2011036344

Copyeditor: Daisy Levy
Designer: Jeremy Harder
Series Editor: Susan H. McLeod

This book is printed on acid-free paper.

The WAC Clearinghouse supports teachers of writing across the disciplines. Hosted by Colorado State University, it brings together scholarly journals and book series as well as resources for teachers who use writing in their courses. This book is available in digital format for free download at http://wac.colostate.edu.

Parlor Press, LLC is an independent publisher of scholarly and trade titles in print and multimedia formats. This book is available in paperback, cloth, and Adobe eBook formats from Parlor Press at http://www.parlorpress.com. For submission information or to find out about Parlor Press publications, write to Parlor Press, 3015 Brackenberry Drive, Anderson, South Carolina 29621, or e-mail editor@parlorpress.com.

The editors dedicate this collection to the late Russ Wiebe. We miss you, friend and collaborator.

CONTENTS

Preface . . . . *xi*
    Martine Courant Rife, Shaun Slattery, and Dànielle Nicole DeVoss

Part I: The Law, the Landscape *1*

1 The Fair Use Battle for Scholarly Works *3*
    Jeffrey Galin

2 Plagiarism and Promiscuity, Authors and Plagiarisms *29*
    Russel Wiebe

3 Authoring Academic Agency: Charting the Tensions between
    Work-for-Hire University Copyright Policies *49*
    Timothy R. Amidon

4 Soul Remedy: Turnitin and the Visual Design of
    End User License Agreements *79*
    Barclay Barrios

5 Images, the Commonplace Book, and Digital Self-Fashioning *99*
    Bob Whipple

6 Intellectual Properties in Multimodal 21st-Century
    Composition Classrooms *107*
    Tharon W. Howard

7 Is Digital the New Digital? Pedagogical Frames of Reference and
    Their Implications in Theory and Practice *131*
    Robert Dornsife

8 Response to Part I—"An Act for the Encouragement of
  Learning" vs. Copyright 2.0 .... *149*
  John Logie

Part II: The Tools *157*

9 What We Talk About When We Talk About Fair Use: Conversations
  on Writing Pedagogy, New Media, and Copyright Law *159*
  Steve Westbrook

10 Parody, Penalty, and Pedagogy *179*
   E. Ashley Hall, Kathie Gossett, and Elizabeth Vincelette

11 Copy-rights and Copy-wrong: Intellectual Property
   in the Classroom Revisited *205*
   Janice R. Walker

12 Rhetorical Velocity and Copyright: A Case Study on Strategies of
   Rhetorical Delivery *223*
   Jim Ridolfo and Martine Courant Rife

13 Following the Framers: Choosing Pedagogy to Further
   Fair Use and Free Speech *245*
   TyAnna Herrington

14 Response to Part II—Being Rhetorical When We Teach
   Intellectual Property and Fair Use *263*
   James E. Porter

Part III: The Pedagogy *273*

15 Toward a Pedagogy of Fair Use for Multimedia Composition ... *275*
   Renee Hobbs and Katie Donnelly

16 Intellectual Property Teaching Practices in Introductory
   Writing Courses *295*
   Nicole Nguyen

17 Moving Beyond Plagiarized / Not Plagiarized in a Point,
   Click, and Copy World *309*
   Leslie Johnson-Farris

18 *Couture et Écriture*: What the Fashion Industry Can Teach
   the World of Writing *327*
   Brian Ballentine

19 The Role of Authorship in the Practice and Teaching of
   Technical Communication *347*
   Jessica Reyman

20 Response to Part III—Fair Use: Teaching Three Key IP Concepts ... *369*
   Rebecca Moore Howard

21 Afterword *375*
   Clancy Ratliff

Biographical Notes... *381*
Index *387*

PREFACE

MARTINE COURANT RIFE, SHAUN SLATTERY,
AND DÀNIELLE NICOLE DEVOSS

You have been invited to participate on a college-wide committee to examine work-for-hire policies at your institution. During your first meeting, a committee member boldly claims that all work faculty and students create during their tenure at the institution should rightly be the property of the institution—especially considering the economic hardship and budget cuts facing most institutions of higher education. What is your response to this claim?

An undergraduate student has accepted work doing freelance web authoring and design. She comes to you to ask what materials produced in a freelance capacity can be included in her professional portfolio. As both professor and professional mentor to this student, how might you advise her?

You serve on an advisory committee for your college's library. A library representative and faculty member co-present their proposal to adopt a college-wide media use policy. The policy includes requirements such as "faculty can use 30 seconds of a 5-minute song" in their teaching, or "faculty can post 10 minutes of a 90-minute film on the college's streaming server" for class use. How might you advise in this situation?

While working with a departmental curriculum committee, a committee member claims that there is no need to revise a writing course to include copyright and fair use because "there's not enough time to teach that, too." What might your response be?

Intellectual property, more and more, rubs up against the work we do in our classrooms, libraries, and offices and in our curricula, teaching, and policies. When we craft teaching materials that include visuals, audio, and video, we implicate ourselves in intellectual property issues. When we ask students to craft multimodal compositions, we implicate them in intellectual property issues. What intellectual property issues are involved depend on each composition, audience, context, purpose, and use. Intellectual property is an inherently rhetorical set of laws and practices, worthy of our attention as researchers, teachers, colleagues, and members of our institutional communities.

Appropriately, more and more rhetoric and composition studies scholars have entered into the conversation about intellectual property issues, especially as these issues orbit around digital writing practices and new media texts. However, very, very few of us are lawyers; few of us have had formal training in U.S. law. The purpose of this edited collection is to gather together stories, theories, and research that can further inform the ways in which we situate and address intellectual property issues in our writing classrooms. We focus in this introduction on the motivations for this collection and the intellectual backdrop for the work presented here, we include an overview of the collection's contents, and, in the appendix to this introduction, we provide a brief discussion of the foundational laws and legal precedents that frame our work.

WHY NOW?

We want to call attention to one tiny moment, one that might seem mundane but is incredibly important in terms of understanding our current cultural and political time and what changes we may foresee to intellectual property in the United States. That moment is this: One of the last acts President George W. Bush took as he planned to vacate the presidency in fall of 2008 was to create a cabinet-level position of intellectual property enforcement coordinator, or "copyright czar," as the position came to be referred to in the press. The position was created by the Prioritizing Resources and Organization for Intellectual Property Act of 2008, designed to coordinate the anti-piracy and intellectual property protection work of agencies including (but not limited to) the Department of Justice and the Patent and Trademark Office. Not only did this Act provide for the appointment of a copyright czar, but it also created a requirement that the czar chair an "interagency intellectual property enforcement advisory committee" and that this committee develop an administrative strategy to increase "enforcement against intellectual property infringement."

Preface

In April 2, 2009, a consortium—including the American Library Association, EDUCAUSE, the Internet Archive, Wikimedia Foundation, and others—delivered a letter to President Obama, encouraging him to break from the direction being pursued by the copyright czar. This consortium asked the president instead to "create offices devoted to promoting innovation and free expression" (American Association of Law Libraries, et al., 2009). The letter raised concern about Obama's potential candidates for copyright czar, noting that in the past almost all had close ties with or served as representatives for copyright industries. The letter warned, "we ask you to consider that individuals who support overly broad IP protection might favor established distribution models at the expense of technological innovators, creative artists, writers, musicians, filmmakers, and an increasingly participatory public." Potential implications noted by the consortium ranged from constraints to technology innovation to barriers being established to citizen use of cultural heritage materials. The key argument made in the letter is that although the government has established and adopted a range of copyright protection positions and acts, the government has not balanced such action by establishing any positions, acts, or offices devoted to encouraging technology innovation and intellectual property distribution.

In an April 20, 2009 response letter, a group representing copyright protection argued against the creation of a false dichotomy between control and innovation and noted that "intellectual property drives innovation and creativity" (Copyright Alliance, 2009). In a smart move—given the current economy in the U.S. and in the world—the authors called attention to the employment of some 38 million U.S. workers in the creative industries.

On September 25, 2009, President Obama appointed Victoria A. Espinel as the first U.S. Intellectual Property Enforcement Coordinator. Prior to the appointment, Vice President Joe Biden, a staunch intellectual property protectionist, promised industry groups—including the Motion Picture Association of America—that they'd be pleased by Obama's pick.

On February 23, 2010, the *Federal Register* published a notice authored by Espinel. The notice invited public input and participation in the larger process described in the document:

> The Federal Government is currently undertaking a landmark effort to develop an intellectual property enforcement strategy building on the immense knowledge and expertise of the agencies charged with enforcing intellectual property rights. By committing to common goals, the Government

will more effectively and efficiently combat intellectual property infringement. (Espinel, 2010)

Public comments were specifically requested to document the "costs to the U.S. economy resulting from intellectual property violations, and the threats to public health and safety created by infringement" and to provide "detailed recommendations ... for improving the Government's intellectual property enforcement efforts." The *Federal Register* notice further outlined twenty areas where additional public comments were sought, including, for example:

> Describe existing technology that could or should be used by the U.S. Government or a particular agency or department to more easily identify infringing goods or other products ... Suggest how state and local law enforcement authorities could more effectively assist in intellectual property enforcement efforts, including whether coordination could be improved, if necessary, and whether they should be vested with additional authority to more actively participate in prosecutions involving intellectual property enforcement ... Describe the adequacy and effectiveness of the reporting by the various agencies responsible for enforcing intellectual property infringements, such as the reporting of investigations, seizures of infringing goods or products, prosecutions, the results of prosecutions, including whether any further voluntary reporting of activities should be made, in keeping with other federal law ... Suggest specific methods to limit or prevent use of the Internet to sell and/or otherwise distribute or disseminate infringing products (physical goods or digital content) ... Provide information on the various types of entities that are involved, directly or indirectly, in the distribution or dissemination of infringing products and a brief description of their various roles and responsibilities ... Discuss the effectiveness of recent efforts by educational institutions to reduce or eliminate illegal downloading over their networks. (Espinel, 2010)

The call clearly focuses on documenting intellectual property violations and suggesting enforcement strategies; increased governmental oversight and enforcement of intellectual property thus continues to move forward.

In response to the call for comments on the joint strategic plan, the Conference on College Composition and Communication—with support from the

National Council of Teachers of English (NCTE), and with the endorsements of over 80 academics across the U.S. as well as organizational support from the Association of Teachers of Technical Writing and the Writing in Digital Environments Research Center—submitted a letter to the copyright czar reflecting the concerns of writing teachers in preserving fair use in teaching and learning (Conference on College Composition and Communication, 2010). Over 1,600 comments were received by Intellectual Property Enforcement Coordinator Espinel, and the 2010 Joint Strategic Plan on Intellectual Property Enforcement was issued in June 2010. Writing teachers have started to mobilize in their efforts to be heard regarding the continued development of copyright law and policy. The contributors to this collection drive that point further home as they detail the concerns and strategies that we face in our day-to-day responsibilities as teachers and researchers of writing.

We think that this particular cultural, historical, and technological moment offers us the opportunity to make unique contributions to educating students, teachers, and others about the rights they currently have and about the issues they will face due to what clearly appears to be a government-backed "enforcement" mode in the area of intellectual property protection. If we want to be part of the conversations that craft fair work-for-hire policies at our institutions, and position ourselves as experts to teach copyright and fair use to writing students and to raise the legal issues professional writers will face in their work lives, now is the time to act. As a small move toward this, we offer a collection of writing that we hope will be just the beginning of the additional larger conversations we need to have about copyright and writing in the digital age.

COPYWRITE SCHOLARSHIP: 1994 TO PRESENT

This collection builds on a body of scholarship over a decade old. We summarize this foundation of pioneering scholarship to contextualize and scaffold the contributions in this collection. Of particular interest here are those questions that endure—that remain points of contention from our field's earliest examinations of the intersection of composition and copyright—and those issues that arise anew. One of the most compelling emergent issues is the changing nature of composition through the proliferation of digital content production technologies and the development of a popular culture of media participation.

In 1994, Andrea Lunsford and Lisa Ede began publishing on their explorations of collaborative authorship and the teaching of writing, laying the groundwork for further copyright discussions in the context of teaching writing. It's also been a decade since Tharon Howard (1996) originally published

"Who 'Owns' Electronic Texts?," urging the field to attend to copyright and fair use issues as they intersect with technical communication. The conversation was continued in the 1997 special intellectual property issue of *Kairos*, in which TyAnna Herrington explained the fair use doctrine and its importance to the teaching of writing in online environments. In her article, Herrington argued that, contrary to popular belief, copyright laws do apply to digital communication, the public does have fair use rights, and fair use is necessary to protect freedom of speech. In an interview included in the same issue of *Kairos*, Johndan Johnson-Eilola (1997) characterized intellectual property as a social and economic construct existing to maximize profits for capitalists. Johnson-Eilola was asked during the interview where fair use should begin on the web, because everything is "published." The question was as interesting to the field in 1997 as it is still, and yet the question remains without a clear answer, even from legal scholars.

Interest and inquiry within composition studies on fair use, copyright, and their relevance to the teaching of writing was further expanded in a special issue of *Computers and Composition* (1998) edited by Laura Gurak and Johnson-Eilola. In this issue, Herrington, Henrietta Nickels Shirk and Howard Taylor Smith, John Logie, and Janice Walker discussed positions on copyright, fair use, and implications for the teaching of writing. Herrington connected free speech to fair use; Shirk and Howard discussed the implications of the Conference on Fair Use (CONFU) guidelines on writing pedagogy; Logie reminded us of intellectual property law's history and connections to developing technologies, calling for teaching copyright issues; and Walker argued that, because the Internet changes what writing teachers do in the classroom, we should develop theories that show differences and similarities between plagiarism and copyright.

It was in these earlier years that Jim Porter (1997) addressed the need for developing an ethical stance toward Web writing. He argued that if the law is unethical to follow, we can break it. Several years later, Logie (2005) addressed Porter's argument, stating that if we are going to engage in civil disobedience, it needs to be organized and public so our behaviors aren't mistaken for ignorance—or, even worse, seen as active theft.

More recent scholarship has emphasized the need to teach writers basic copyright law and fair use (DeVoss & Porter, 2006; DeVoss & Webb, 2008; Dush, 2009; Herrington, 2003; Howard, 1996; Juillet, 2004; Logie, 2005, 2006b; Reyman, 2006, 2010; Rife, 2006, 2007, 2010; Rife & Hart-Davidson, 2006; Waller, 2006a, 2006b). Because most research and writing is done on computers and in networked environments, reliance on the fair use doctrine has become crucial for the educational community. We live in a cut-and-paste world where remix is commonplace (Grabill & Hicks, 2005; Lessig, 2004, 2008; Ridolfo & DeVoss, 2009; Westbrook, 2006); however, it is unknown how (or if) composition teachers are teaching copyright. Thus far, only one collection in our field focuses on copyright law and its pedagogical implications—Steve Westbrook's (2009) excellent *Composition & Copyright: Perspectives on Teaching, Text-making, and Fair Use*.

Recent media coverage of peer-to-peer (P2P) file sharing cases—coupled with lawsuits against hundreds of schools, individuals (including students), and peer-to-peer software distributors—has understandably kindled disciplinary interest. In the context of P2P file sharing and teaching, writing pedagogy pieces have appeared by Porter and Martine Courant Rife (2005), Dànielle Nicole DeVoss and Porter (2006), and Rife (2006). Following Porter and Rife's short position paper on the U.S. Supreme Court's decision that Grokster was secondarily liable for the copyright-infringing behaviors of users of its software, the Caucus on Intellectual Property and Composition/Communication Studies (CCCC-IP) began a yearly publication, "Top IP Events," published on the NCTE Web site. In 2009, the CCCC-IP also began publishing a monthly report on the NCTE Web site and an announcement in the NCTE email list. In 2010, the Top Intellectual Property Developments annual, currently coordinated by Clancy Ratliff, one of the contributors here, contained the largest number of contributions (nine) in the 5 years since its inception.

In *Controlling Voices: Intellectual Property, Humanistic Studies, and the Internet* (2001), Herrington examined how intellectual property law impacts educators, including those in rhetoric and technical communication. Two years later, she produced *A Legal Primer for the Digital Age* (2003), a short textbook covering a wide range of laws relevant in the everyday practice of technical communicators. The text contains a section on intellectual property issues, where Herrington noted that copyright law is applied in conjunction with other laws and discussed basic work-for-hire issues.

Lunsford (1999) and Sarah Robbins (2003) combined feminist rhetorical theory with discussions of intellectual property. Lunsford's concern was with corporate authorship. Robbins argued that, as we try to understand intellectual property, we should look at cases and issues of authorship involving women's ways of making knowledge, particularly via collaboration.

Logie (2005) provided a broad overview of copyright laws (including a bit of history), and argued for the importance of teaching copyright in technical communication. In a short position paper a year later, Logie (2006b) argued that copyright instruction should have a central place in the writing classroom. He included a 1790s view of copyright in the U.S., explicitly arguing for the "importance of scholarly access" (p. 1). Copyright law was originally invented to assist learning, he noted, "and we, as educators, have failed in our obligation to embed this simple fact in the public's consciousness" (p. 1). To address this problem, Logie urged us to include a focus on copyright within our pedagogy.

Steve Westbrook (2006) made an important move by connecting visual rhetoric and copyright in a very pragmatic context—a student's multimedia piece, which was unable to be published because the requisite permissions were denied by the copyright holder. Pointing to the missing student piece in his article, Westbrook wrote that copyright affects composition teachers and students "on the level of daily practice" and threatens to silence both teachers and students. The author suggested using Lessig's Creative Commons licensing as an immediate practical solution to the copyright problem. Westbrook's 2009 collection includes a chapter where he continues this discussion, pushing further at issues of visual rhetoric and copyright in the context of writing pedagogy.

Jessica Reyman (2006) championed teacher awareness and activism, noting that the Technology, Education, and Copyright Harmonization (TEACH) Act of 2002 was developed to update copyright law to accommodate the uses of copyrighted materials in distance-education environments. And, yet, pursuant to her analysis of the TEACH Act and its implications for teaching writing, the act fails to offer the same protections for online teaching as it offers in face-to-face environments. Reyman argued that the TEACH Act provides an opportunity for faculty and their institutions to become more involved in the conversations about copyright and to influence law and policies. In Reyman's (2010) recent book, she discusses the narratives and metaphors within the intellectual property debate in a rhetorical context.

This rich base of existing work in the field is the conversation we enter with this collection. Our collection is timely because we have some evidence from the legal and media literacy fields that teachers tend to misunderstand copyright and fair use and pass that misunderstanding on to their students (Hobbs, Jaszi, & Aufderheide, 2007). In September 2007, the Center for Social Media at the School of Communication at American University released a report stating that the key goals of teaching media literacy are "compromised by unnecessary copyright restrictions and lack of understanding about copyright law" (Hobbs, Jaszi, & Aufderheide, p. 1). In another study, Marjorie Heins and Tricia Beckles (2005) found that artists and scholars have only a vague sense of what fair use means, and this uncertain knowledge circumscribes composing practices. An additional study, "The Digital Learning Challenge," reported that undue fear about copyright infringement liability has constricted exchanges of valuable information across social network spaces (Fisher & McGeveran, 2006). William Fisher and William McGeveran found that because of digital rights management (DRM) technologies, the only way certain media can be accessed even for purely educational uses is for teachers and individuals to knowingly violate copyright law by circumventing anti-access measures.

This collection, more generally, also emerges from recent pedagogy-focused scholarship that argues that, because of the changed nature of writing in digital environments, teachers need to recalculate what they teach. On a broad level, the argument in favor of teaching intellectual property derives from the growing body of scholarship on informational literacy, multiliteracies, and digital literacies (American Library Association, 2004; New London Group, 1996; Sorapure, Inglesby, & Yatchisin, 1998). The teaching of digital literacies imbricates the teaching of copyright because it relates to how one might legally use others' materials, and vice versa (see also Digital Rhetoric Collective, 2006; Grabill & Hicks, 2005; Henning, 2003; Selber, 2004; WIDE Research Center Collective, 2005).

COPY(WRITE): PREFACE AND PREVIEW

Copy(write) includes a range of voices and perspectives on copyright, fair use, and related topics such as originality, authorship, cultural participation, and institutional authority and power. We include several chapters by "copy-write" pioneers—composition and rhetoric scholars among the first to bring discussion of copyright to our scholarship, many of whom are revisiting the conversations they helped start—as well as the voices of new scholars and students, whose experience with and reflection on copyright issues are now shaping our scholarly conversations. *Copy(write)* includes a mix of traditional scholarship, original research, and personal reflection to engage the copyright issues we experience as university workers and participants in contemporary digital culture. The book is divided into three topic areas: Part I focuses on the law and legal landscape; Part II focuses on the tools and resources available to researchers and teachers; and Part III focuses on pedagogical practices and approaches for addressing intellectual property in the writing classroom. Each part concludes with a response by a notable scholar who helps highlight connections among the chapters and identifies enduring questions and future directions for scholarship and action.

Part I: The Law, the Landscape

In Part I: The Law, the Landscape, contributing authors explore the laws and institutional structures and policies that make up the scene of our copyright practices. We begin Part I with Jeffrey Galin's "The Fair Use Battle for

Scholarly Works," in which he revisits and extends the discussion of academics' rights and responsibilities in using scholarly work which he, along with several other scholars, began a decade ago. Galin examines the key issues and emergent transformations that educators face with respect to copyright practices and fair use advocacy. He also offers advice for how we as academics can reassert our fair use rights.

Through an engaging combination of scholarly discussion and personal reflection, Russel Wiebe examines the nature of plagiarism and cheating by complicating the concepts of authorship and originality in "Plagiarism and Promiscuity, Authors and Plagiarisms." His discussion resonates with our field's struggles with plagiarism and the origin of ideas. Alternately entertaining taxonomies of plagiarism and the impossibility of "some single, stable author," Wiebe advises teachers to engage students in conversations about intertextuality and plagiarism rather than acting as police.

In "Authoring Academic Agency: Charting the Tensions between Work-for-hire University Copyright Policies," Timothy Amidon explores the ambiguities and tensions that exist between university IP policies, Title 17 of U.S. Code, and various kinds of academic authorship. Amidon first describes his struggle in his institution as he tried to license his Master's thesis under a Creative Commons License and then discusses "work-for-hire" as defined by U.S. Code before providing an insightful analysis of the IP policies of 14 universities. He concludes with suggesting actions for academic authors to strengthen our ownership of the works we create.

A different kind of copyright policy is studied in Barclay Barrios' "Soul Remedy: Turnitin and the Visual Design of End User License Agreements." EULAs, as they are commonly known, are legal contracts that specify the rights and responsibilities of a company offering a service or software and its end users. In this chapter, Barrios analyzes the wording and design of these contracts and of the plagiarism-detection service Turnitin in particular, and discusses their implications for instructors and students. As opposed to the unreflective clicking of "I Agree" that we and students may engage in, Barrios suggests using EULAs as a teachable moment, and as documents that can be put to use to discover and question how these agreements position the user's work.

Bob Whipple contributes a reflection on collecting digital images as an important part of the construction of self. In "Images, the Commonplace Book, and Digital Self-Fashioning," Whipple compares image downloading and posting to the keeping of "commonplace books"—collections of texts and clippings used by men and women from the late medieval and renaissance periods through the mid-19th century. Often overlooked as frivolous, these catchall spaces, Whipple argues, are important for the development of our ideas and ourselves.

Composition and IP scholarship pioneer Tharon Howard revisits ideas first raised in his 1996 work, "Who Owns Electronic Texts?" In "Intellectual Properties in Multimodal, 21st-Century Composition Classrooms," Howard examines the origins of copyright law to challenge the commonly held view that authors have a "natural right" to their work that supersedes all other potential claims on how the public may rightfully use the work. Ultimately, he sees copyrights not as "rights" but instead as privileges granted by the State to balance the needs of society with the needs of the individual. Howard argues that today's students need a robust understanding of copyright laws in order to negotiate the complexities of digital authorship and IP laws and policies. To model this understanding, Howard poses five copyright conundrums from his teaching and professional experience and provides a lucid discussion of the legalities and rights at work in each.

In "Is Digital the New Digital?: Pedagogical Frames of Reference and Their Implications in Theory and Practice", Rob Dornsife explores the challenges of moving between analog and digital forms of media. He reflects on the incompatibility of their rules and aesthetics and, therefore, the problems of writing assignments that fail to acknowledge these differences. Through a fascinating discussion of recording and production technologies, Dornsife arrives at the problems with the concepts of "the copy" and "the original" in the digital world, and, thus, problems with copyrights and notions of plagiarism based solely on these concepts. To address analog bias, he proposes an ethic of "digital stewardship" and "artistic license."

We conclude Part I with a response by John Logie, author of the influential *Peers, Pirates, and Persuasion* (2006a) as well as numerous articles and chapters on copyright issues in the writing classroom.

Part II: The Tools

Part II: The Tools explores copyright and fair use in practice, through scenes of use and through techniques and tools for responding productively in moments when copyright is implicated. The authors provide stories, struggles, and solutions for the challenges of navigating authorial decision-making. Steve Westbrook begins Part II with a reflection on the nature of our field's conversation about fair use. "What We Talk About When We Talk About Fair Use: Conversations on Writing Pedagogy, New Media, and Copyright Law" is an examination of our scholarship, textbooks, and pedagogy. In addition to advocating that we teach students the four factors for determining fair use, Westbrook uses the case of *Online Policy Group v. Diebold, Inc.* (2004) to model the kind of rich, complex analysis of the fair use of digital material that we might engage in with our students.

To further complicate print-based notions of authorship and originality, E. Ashley Hall, Kathie Gossett, and Elizabeth Vincelette analyze YouTube's interface and examine parody videos posted there to explore practices of sampling, remixing, and appropriation in the composing process. "Parody, Penalty, and Pedagogy" reveals the complicated motives and composing decisions made in this important form of expression and cultural participation. They suggest strategies for helping students to thoughtfully and legally engage in digital discourse.

In "Copyrights and Copywrongs: Intellectual Property in the Classroom Revisited," copywrite pioneer Janice Walker returns to some of the questions she first raised in 1998. In light of the recent proliferation of digital production technologies and the increase in online teaching and digital pedagogy, Walker finds the majority of the textbooks and style guides of our field unhelpful for students and teachers in their treatment of copyright, often ignoring multimodal compositions or the use of copyrighted work in the classroom. In examining the use of IP in classrooms, she discusses the law, policies, practice, and responsibilities of various players in our educational systems. Walker's discussion of the evolution of her own IP pedagogy offers numerous examples of what we can do as teachers to inform, challenge, and empower students in relation to their own work. She closes with guidance for what we can do for our students, our peers, and ourselves to productively engage these complex issues.

Jim Ridolfo and Martine Rife untangle the Gordian knot of free speech, privacy, orphan works, *in loco parentis*, publicity/contractual rights, and fair use issues raised in the case of a student whose picture was taken at a protest but remixed and reused by her university for promotional materials. "Rhetorical Velocity and Copyright: A Case Study on the Strategies of Rhetorical Delivery" explores the copyright implications and unanticipated possibilities of rhetorical delivery in the mix-mash-merge age of digital rhetoric. Through a cogent analysis of the legalities of the use of Maggie Ryan's image, Ridolfo and Rife tease out the rights of and implications for the student and the actions of the university. Maggie's case is a rich source for discussion of ethical, cultural, and other issues in copyright, intellectual property, and rhetoric, and the authors include generative questions for use in the classroom.

TyAnna Herrington expands our discussion of fair use to include free speech in "Following the Framers: Choosing Pedagogy to Further Fair Use and

Free Speech." In this chapter, Herrington broadens her original work on fair use and free speech, drawing upon the spirit of the law drafted by the original framers of the U.S. Constitution to present a moving argument for the necessity of access to information and protected fair use for enacting free speech. Herrington argues that educators must choose pedagogies that support free speech and fair use to prepare students to participate in the democratic process as digital citizens.

We conclude Part II with a response by Jim Porter of Miami University, whose early work on networked spaces and ethical issues is considered landmark in the field (Porter, 1998) and whose recent work has addressed issues of digital delivery and research practices and copyright implications in digital spaces (McKee & Porter, 2008, 2009).

Part III: The Pedagogy

In Part III: The Pedagogy, contributing authors share their responses to the challenges of teaching students about copyright and fair use in the digital age.

In "Toward a Pedagogy of Fair Use for Multimedia Composition" Renee Hobbs and Katie Donnelly review the ongoing dialogue about fair use within the media literacy community, which has worked to reduce copyright confusion among educators through the development of the Code of Best Practices in Fair Use for Media Literacy Education. Hobbs and Donnelly discuss the fair use implications of two practices that specifically concern student multimedia composition: using copyrighted materials in creative work and sharing that work with authentic audiences as part of the teaching and learning process. Their chapter provides clear suggestions for negotiating classroom and student use of IP from a wide range of media.

To learn how teachers and students from introductory writing courses understand IP issues, Nicole Nguyen—an undergraduate student when she conducted her study and now a law student at DePaul University—conducted surveys and interviews. "Intellectual Property Teaching Practices in Introductory Writing Courses" presents Nguyen's findings, illustrating the shared concern among students for IP issues both in and out of the classroom and their sometimes limited exposure to and understanding of IP issues. Nguyen's study helps us see, in part through her inclusion of student participants' voices, the importance of instilling "a spirit of curiosity, awareness, and ethics" to prepare students for authorial decisions in the classroom, in their workplaces, and as participants in digital culture.

In "Moving Beyond Plagiarized/Not Plagiarized in a Point, Click, and Copy World," Leslie Johnson-Farris documents her "journey from ordinary, average community college composition instructor to intellectual property rights pedagogical philosopher." Her journey involves the realization that typical writing assignments automatically implicate copyright issues—issues some of us have not attended to as much as we might. Johnson-Farris turns to the institutional policies at her college and discusses how her understanding of these policies evolved in the context of her classroom teaching experiences. She outlines tensions present in the very infrastructure of community college teaching and the increasing need to produce students sophisticated about copyright and plagiarism issues in a digital world.

In "*Couture et Écriture*: What the Fashion Industry Can Teach the World of Writing," Brian Ballentine discusses the "piracy paradox" within the fashion industry. Ballentine describes this paradox as founded on the idea that "profits and productivity are greater due to an absence of copyright protection for fashion designs." In this chapter, he discusses an attempt at addressing this paradox through a now-defunct bill, the Design Piracy Prohibition Act, and issues around the piracy paradox are layered into Ballentine's experience teaching a writing course in which the students were all fashion industry majors.

In "The Role of Authorship in the Practice and Teaching of Technical Communication," Jessica Reyman discusses issues of authorship and attribution for working technical communicators. She offers specific suggestions for the teaching of technical writing, as we support students in making the transition from the educational setting to the workplace in the context of copyright, authorship, and ownership issues.

Rebecca Moore Howard, a key scholar in issues of plagiarism, intellectual property, and authorship in our field, provides a response to the Part III chapters. We are delighted to include an afterword by Clancy Ratliff, editor of the CCCC-IP Annual: Top Intellectual Property Developments.

Our initial goal in crafting this collection was to situate the need to identify and describe pedagogical strategies for addressing intellectual property in the teaching of writing. The authors in this collection offer theories, research, approaches, cautionary tales, and local and contextual successes that can further inform the ways in which we situate and address intellectual property issues in our writing classrooms. Because the law is a living entity, laws will of course evolve, as will digital tools, technologies, and networks. We hope that readers find in this collection both established landmark cases *and* current and predicted changes to our technologies, our laws, and our teaching. We hope readers will find relevance, resonance, and broad strategies that transcend specific cases and that are nimble enough for application at our wide range of institutional and disciplinary homes, and in the diversity of spaces in which we teach, research, serve, participate, and live.

REFERENCES

American Association of Law Libraries, et al. (2009, April 2). Letter to President Barack Obama. http://www.librarycopyrightalliance.org/bm-doc/ip_adminltr2009.pdf

American Library Association (ALA). (2004). Information literacy competency standards for higher education. http://www.ala.org/ala/acrl/acrlstandards/informationliteracycompetency.htm

Band, Jonathan. (2005). The Google print library project: A copyright analysis. http://www.policybandwidth.com/doc/googleprint.pdf

Conference on College Composition and Communication Intellectual Property Caucus (CCCC-IP). (2010, March 24). Re: Public comment on FR Doc. 2010-3539; The Joint Strategic Plan. http://www.ncte.org/library/NCTEFiles/Groups/CCCC/Committees/cccc-ip_caucus-committee-ltr-03-24-10.pdf

Copyright Alliance. (2009, April 20). Letter to President Barack Obama. http://www.copyrightalliance.org/files/ip_community_april_20_letter_to_president_obama.pdf

DeVoss, Dànielle Nicole, & Porter, James E. (2006). Why Napster matters to writing: Filesharing as a new ethic of digital delivery. *Computers and Composition, 23*, 178-210.

DeVoss, Dànielle Nicole, & Webb, Suzanne. (2008). Media convergence: Grand theft audio: Negotiating copyright as composers. *Computers and Composition, 25*, 79-103.

Digital Rhetoric Collective. (2006). Teaching digital rhetoric: Community, critical engagement, and application. *Pedagogy: Critical approaches to Teaching Literature, Language, Composition, and Culture, 2* (1), 231-259.

Dush, Lisa. (2009). Beyond the wake-up call: Learning what students know about copyright. In Steve Westbrook (Ed.), *Composition and copyright: Perspectives on teaching, text-making, and fair use* (pp. 114-132). New York: SUNY Press.

Espinel, Victoria. (2010, February 18). Coordination and strategic planning of the federal effort against intellectual property infringement: Request of the Intellectual Property Enforcement Coordinator for public comments regarding the joint strategic plan. *Federal Register, 75* (35). http://edocket.access.gpo.gov/2010/2010-3539.htm

Fisher, William W., & McGeveran, William. (2006, Aug.). The digital learning challenge: Obstacles to educational uses of copyright material in the digital age. A Foundational White Paper. The Berkman Center for Internet & Society at Harvard Law School. Research Publication No. 2006-09. http://cyber.law.harvard.edu/ home/research_publication_series

Grabill, Jeffrey T., & Hicks, Troy. (2005, July). Multiliteracies meet methods: The case for digital writing in English education. *English Education*, 301-311.

Gurak, Laura J., & Johnson-Eilola, Johndan. (Eds.). (1998). Introduction to the special issue on intellectual property. *Computers and Composition, 15* (2), 121-123.

Henning, Kathleen. (2003). Writing 2003: Shifting boundaries and the implications for college teaching. *Teaching English in the Two-Year College, 30*, 306-316.

Heins, Marjorie, & Beckles, Tricia. (2005, December). Will fair use survive? Free expression in the age of copyright control. A public policy report. Brennan Center for Justice. http://www.fepproject.org/issues/copyright.html

Herrington, TyAnna K. (1997). The unseen "other" of intellectual property law or intellectual property is not property: Debunking the myths of IP law. *Kairos: A Journal of Rhetoric, Technology, and Pedagogy, 3* (1). http://kairos.technorhetoric.net/3.1/coverweb/ty/kip.html

Herrington, TyAnna K. (1998). The interdependency of fair use and the first amendment *Computers and Composition, 15*, 125-143.

Herrington, TyAnna K. (2001). *Controlling voices: intellectual property, humanistic studies, and Internet.* Carbondale: Southern Illinois University Press.

Herrington, TyAnna K. (2003). *A legal primer for the digital age.* New York: Pearson Longman.

Hobbs, Renee; Jaszi, Peter; & Aufderheide, Patricia. (2007, October). The cost of copyright confusion for media literacy. http://www.centerforsocialmedia.org/resources/publications/the_cost_of_copyright_confusion_for_media_literacy/

Howard, Tharon W. (2004/1996). Who "owns" electronic texts? In Johndan Johnson-Eilola & Stuart A. Selber (Eds.), *Central works in technical communication* (pp. 397-406). New York: Oxford University Press.

Johnson-Eilola, Johndan. (1997, Spring). Intellectual property: Questions and answers. *Kairos: A Journal of Rhetoric, Technology, and Pedagogy, 3* (1). http://kairos.technorhetoric.net/3.1 /binder2.html?coverweb/johndan.html

Juillet, Christopher. (2004, November). Protect your web site from legal land mines. *Intercom*, pp. 6-7.

Katz, Zachary. (2006). Pitfalls of open licensing: An analysis of Creative Commons licensing. *IDEA: The Intellectual Property Law Review, 46*, 391-413.

Lessig, Lawrence. (2004). *Free culture how big media uses technology and the law to lock down culture and control creativity.* New York: The Penguin Press.

Lessig, Lawrence. (2008). *Remix: Making art and commerce thrive in the hybrid economy.* London: Bloomsbury.

Logie, John. (1998). Champing at the bits: Computers, copyright, and the composition classroom. *Computers and Composition, 15*, 201-214.

Logie, John. (2005). Parsing codes: intellectual property, technical communication, and the World Wide Web. In Michael Day & Carol Lipson (Eds.), *Technical communication and the World Wide Web*. (pp. 223-241). New Jersey: Lawrence Erlbaum Associates.

Logie, John. (2006a). *Peers, pirates, & persuasion: Rhetoric in the peer-to-peer debates*. Indiana: Parlor Press.

Logie, John. (2006b). Copyright in increasingly digital academic contexts: What it takes. WIDEpaper #7. http://www.wide.msu.edu/widepapers

Lunsford, Andrea. (1999). Rhetoric, feminism, and the politics of textual ownership. *College English, 61* (5), 1-16.

Lunsford, Andrea. & Ede, Lisa. (1994). Collaborative authorship and the teaching of writing. In Martha Woodmansee & Peter Jaszi (Eds.), *The construction of authorship: textual appropriation in law and literature* (pp. 417-438). Durham, NC: Duke University Press.

McKee, Heidi A., & Porter, James E. (2008). The ethics of digital writing research: A rhetorical approach. *College Composition and Communication, 59*, 711-749.

McKee, Heidi A., & Porter, James E. (2009). *The ethics of Internet research: A rhetorical, case-based approach*. New York: Peter Lang.

New London Group. (1996). A pedagogy of multiliteracies: designing social futures. *Harvard Educational Review, 66* (1), 60-92.

Porter, James E. (1997). Legal realities and ethical hyperrealities; A critical approach toward cyberwriting. In Stuart Selber (Ed.), *Computers and technical communication; pedagogical and programmatic perspective s* (pp. 45-73). Greenwich, CT: Ablex.

Porter, James E. (1998). *Rhetorical ethics and Internetworked writing*. Greenwich, CT: Ablex.

Porter, James E., & Rife, Martine C. (2005). WIDE PAPER #1 *MGM v. Grokster*: Implications for educators and writing teachers. http://www.wide.msu.edu/widepapers/grokster/ republished on NCTE-CCCC

Prioritizing Resources and Organization for Intellectual Property Act of 2008. http://www.gpo.gov/fdsys/pkg/PLAW-110publ403/content-detail.html.

Reyman, Jessica. (2006). Copyright, distance education, and the TEACH Act: Implications for teaching writing. *College Composition and Communication, 58*, 30-45.

Reyman, Jessica. (2008). Rethinking plagiarism for technical communication. *Technical Communication, 55*, 61-67.

Reyman, Jessica. (2010). *The rhetoric of intellectual property: Copyright law and the regulation of digital culture*. New York: Routledge.

Ridolfo, Jim, & DeVoss, Dànielle Nicole. (2009). Composing for recomposition: Rhetorical velocity and delivery. *Kairos: A Journal of Rhetoric, Technology, and Pedagogy, 13* (2). http://www.technorhetoric.net/13.2/topoi/ridolfo_devoss/intro.html

Rife, Martine C. (2006). Why Kairos matters to writing: A reflection on our intellectual property conversation during the last ten years. *Kairos: A Journal of Rhetoric, Technology, and Pedagogy, 11* (1). http://english.ttu.edu/KAIROS/ 11.1/

Rife, Martine C. (2007). The fair use doctrine: History, application, implications for (new media) writing teachers. *Computers and Composition, 24,* 105-226.

Rife, Martine C. (2008). A brief history of U.S. fair use. In Caroline Eisner & Martha Vicinus (Eds.), *Originality, imitation, and plagiarism* (pp. 145-156). Ann Arbor: University of Michigan Press.

Rife, Martine C. (2010, February) Copyright law as mediational means: Report on a mixed-methods study of U.S. professional writers. *Technical Communication.* Forthcoming.

Rife, Martine C., & Hart-Davidson, William. (2006). Digital composing and fair use: exploring knowledge and understanding of fair use among teachers and students in a university professional writing program. Pilot study report. SSRN Working Paper Series. http://papers.ssrn.com/sol3/papers.cfm?abstract_id=918822

Robbins, Sarah. (2003). Distributed authorship: a feminist case-study framework for studying intellectual property. *College English, 66,* 155-171.

Selber, Stuart. (2004). *Multiliteracies for a digital age.* Carbondale: Southern Illinois University Press.

Shirk, Henrietta Nickels, & Smith, Howard Taylor. (1998). Emerging fair use guidelines for multimedia: Applications for the writing classroom. *Computers and Composition, 15,* 229-241.

Sorapure, Madeline; Inglesby, Patricia; & Yatchisin, George. (1998). Web literacy: Challenges and opportunities for research in a new medium. *Computers and Composition, 15,* 409-424.

Wakefield, Sarah. (2006). Using music sampling to teach research skills. *Teaching English in the Two-Year College, 33,* 357-360.

Walker, Janice R. (1998). Copyrights and conversations: Intellectual property in the classroom. *Computers and Composition, 15,* 243-251.

Waller, Robert D. (2006a, April). Fair use. *Intercom,* p. 40.

Waller, Robert D. (2006b). Responses to "fair use." *Intercom.*

Westbrook, Steve. (2006). Visual rhetoric in a culture of fear: Impediments to multimedia production. *College English, 68,* 457-480.

APPENDIX: EXPLANATIONS OF LEGAL CONCEPTS RELATING TO COPYRIGHT

In the educational setting, in some ways the risks are great for inaccurate intellectual property knowledge, but in other ways the risks are low. The risks are great because the average cost of defending a copyright infringement lawsuit is just under one million dollars, but the risks are low in the academy because—until very recently—educators weren't often being sued (Fisher & McGeveran, 2006); this, however, may be changing (Rife, 2008). The complex writing lives of students are not completely encompassed in the space of our classrooms. Yet, the teaching of copyright issues in the writing classroom may be the only formal instruction many students ever receive. This knowledge will have to carry them forward in their jobs and future careers.

Four main areas of copyright law often arise in the teaching of writing: 1) the basic protections of copyright law; 2) exceptions to that protection as provided in the fair use statute; 3) the work-for-hire provisions within Title 17; and 4) authorized or licensed use (use with permission). We summarize these concepts here to help those unfamiliar with copyright law understand the legally based arguments of the chapters included in this collection.

The Basic Protections of Copyright Law

U.S. copyright law, enacted through Congress' constitutionally granted power under Article 1, Section 8 of the U.S. Constitution, is applicable to the teaching of composition because this law provides automatic protection to any work fixed and original at the moment of its fixation. For example, any original text, visual, sound, etc., published to the Web (or elsewhere) is copyright protected. Because of copyright law's broad application, virtually all digital publishing—whether or not it incorporates another's text, visuals, sounds, or movie clips—will invoke copyright law. Protected works include notes, webpages, software, computer code, emails, reports, patterns, tutorials, instructions, manuals, visuals, video, audio, and all other "fixed" media. Under current law, a copyright holder has the exclusive right to copy, distribute, perform/display, and create derivative works.

The Fair Use Statute

The fair use doctrine, as codified in Section 107 of the U.S. Copyright Act, provides relief from copyright holder monopoly. This doctrine provides an exception to the copyright holder's exclusive rights and is heavily relied upon in educational environments as students and teachers complete remixes, perform critical analysis, generate research, and compose mash-ups for purposes of teaching and learning (DeVoss & Porter, 2006; Grabill & Hicks, 2005; Lessig, 2004; Westbrook, 2006). Fair use is, essentially, unauthorized use—use that does not require authorization (in the form of permissions or licensing).

Section 107, Title 17 defines fair use as "reproduction in copies ... or by any other means" for uses including "criticism, comment, news reporting, teaching (including multiple copies for classroom use), scholarship, or research." The four factors that courts use to make legal determinations regarding infringement are listed in the statute, and function as a legal heuristic guiding not only judges, but also attorneys, users, authors, and others who attempt to make and justify everyday composing decisions. The four factors ask that one consider:

1. the purpose and character of the use including whether such use is of a commercial nature or is for nonprofit educational purposes;

2. the nature of the copyrighted;

3. the amount and substantiality of the portion used in relation to the copyrighted work as a whole; and

4. the effect of the use upon the potential market.

Although not often acknowledged, reliance on fair use is even alive and well in the business sector. For those of us teaching technical and professional writing, or for those of us using a service-learning component in our curriculum, fair use has continued utility outside the educational institution.

Further, everyday activities on the Internet rely on fair use. Search engines send out "spiders" that crawl the Web, copying increasingly vast amounts of data then stored in the search engines' databases (Band, 2005). This copying is completed without direct permission of Web site owners. Jonathan Band notes that "the billions of dollars of market capital represented by the search engine companies are based primarily on the fair use doctrine" (Band, p.5). Another example of for-profit reliance on fair use is the invention and sales of software that records screens or captures images on the web or from software applications (for instance, TechSmith Camtasia, a screen-casting tool, or Adobe Photoshop, image-editing software). If such uses were not deemed potentially fair, this software could be outlawed due, in part, to charges similar to those raised in cases against peer-to-peer software—its potential to "induce" users to infringe.

Work-for-hire Provisions

Just like copyright protections and fair use exceptions try to control or organize how texts can be appropriated and circulated, the work-for-hire provisions of Title 17 provide a default author in employer–employee contexts. Under copyright law, the default in employer–employee situations is that an employee's creations made within the scope of employment are technically "authored" by the employer, who thus owns all copyrights:

In the case of a work made for hire, the employer or other person for whom the work was prepared is considered the author for purposes of this title, and, unless the parties have expressly agreed otherwise in a written instrument signed by them, owns all of the rights comprised in the copyright. (Title 17, 201 (b): Works Made for Hire)

Many of us have become familiar with work-for-hire through our attempts to change default policies at our institutions so that policies better preserve faculty and/or student authorship in individual creations. Some institutions for example, allow faculty to retain ownership over their teaching materials and/or books and other materials they produce while employees—employees who, most often, rely on the institution's library databases, network connections, computers, and other resources to do their work. The most faculty-friendly work-for-hire policies are often won after hard-fought battles. Work-for-hire issues are also relevant for student writers, who will very quickly leave educational settings and become employees at organizations where their notions of individual authorship may be seriously challenged (Reyman, 2008; Rife, 2010).

Authorized or Licensed Use

Sometimes writers do not need to worry about whether or not they are within the perimeters of fair use because they receive express permission from a copyright holder, or they use work within the confines of a pre-attached license. Creative Commons and ccmixter, for example, provide a number of boilerplate copyright licenses that writers and musicians can affix to their work, allowing future authors and composers to appropriate under certain conditions as stated in the license. Creative Commons is a "major player shaping the production and distribution of creative works" (Katz, 2006, p. 391). Creative Commons licenses do not enhance nor detract from fair use; rather, they simply allow users to avoid fair use determinations in most cases (Rife, 2007).

Martine Rife, Shaun Slattery, and Dànielle Nicole DeVoss

More Information

The U.S. copyright web site, copyright.gov, is perhaps the best reference for the law itself and also plain-language discussion of the law. Many, many other helpful online resources exist, offering access to the full-text of various governmental statues, proposed laws, enacted policies, copyleft advocacy information and support, and more. The combined references cited in the chapters of this collection offer an abundance of work from fields with stake in and interesting perspectives on intellectual property issues.

PART I: THE LAW, THE LANDSCAPE

1 THE FAIR USE BATTLE FOR SCHOLARLY WORKS

Jeffrey Galin

> "Lobbying by special interests would invariably ensure that copyright and patent law favors private interests over public ones. That is not to say that politicians are always corrupt or that democracies always fail; it means simply that politicians respond to the same incentives as the rest of us and that consequently, democracies tend toward predictably biased outcomes."
>
> Bell, 2002, p. 7

Writing faculty and administrators might be surprised to discover how much the focus on fair use has changed in the decade since several of us in the Conference on College Composition and Communication Intellectual Property Caucus (CCCC-IP, 2000) published a short piece in *College Composition and Communication* titled "Use Your Fair Use: Strategies toward Action." In that piece, we presented an overview of fair use and identified application strategies for academic settings. That piece emerged in the wake of two highly publicized cases—*Basic Books, Inc. v. Kinko's Graphics Corp.* (1991) and *Princeton University Press v. Michigan Documents Services* (1996)—which dramatically limited faculty rights to produce course packets for students. Around the same time, the Copyright Clearance Center established its online presence—in 1995, just as the Web was becoming commercially viable. The Center's mission grew dramatically as blanket licensing practices became the norm for publishers who eagerly sought new revenue streams and the means to hold greater copyright control. The Digital Millennium Copyright Act (DMCA) emerged in 1998, making it a crime to circumvent anti-piracy measures in digital works and to build, sell, or distribute code-cracking devices, and, more importantly to educators, made many previously fair uses no longer legal. Furthermore, in late 1997, the Conference on Fair Use (CONFU) sought to achieve consensus on a new set of copyright guidelines for clarifying fair use practices and to achieve more input and buy-in than the 1976 guidelines that emerged from the Commission on New Technology Uses of Copyrighted Works (CONTU). Neither report reached consensus or legal status, but both have been influential. Publishers, libraries, university policies, and even courts use these guidelines on fair use as if they were legal standards. The CCCC-IP caucus was eager to encourage faculty to resist the chilling effects of overly zealous legislation, increasing corporate control, and over-reliance on guidelines. We wanted faculty to explore and exploit the extent of their fair use rights.

Although we still support these goals, the complexities of fair use have grown significantly. Since 2000, fair use has been subjected to important legislative changes, tested in several high-profile cases, and supported by the formation of new organizations championing fair use causes; new statements of best practices have also emerged. Fair use has been directly attacked and narrowed in some contexts, while it has expanded in other contexts as a result of, for instance, peer-to-peer technologies, online reserve policies at universities, corporate copyright control, and, conversely, the emergence of new open-source and open-access practices and policies. Although the struggle has been waged from many sides, corporate interests have achieved a decided advantage; Carol Silberberg (2001) argued that such changes "have reduced the scope of fair use in the educational setting," and that these trends "will eventually eliminate fair use for schools, colleges, and universities" altogether (p. 617). Whether fair use will be eliminated is difficult to assess, given the emergence of a strong open-source movement, legal professionals who champion fair use causes, and legislative and legal momentum, but there is little doubt we are moving in that direction and the impact on educators and scholars will intensify and likely fundamentally change how we conduct our work in higher education.

In the face of these changes, faculty must understand fair use and how it will continue to impact our scholarly work, particularly as more and more of us integrate a range of digital media into our teaching and research. To introduce the basic tenets of fair use and to explore the complexities posed by digital media, this chapter opens with the examples of Jane Caputi and Sut Jhally. These two cultural theorists are documentary filmmakers whose cultural critiques of corporate and commercial images expose the chilling effects of corporate copyright controls. I then examine the heightened rhetoric of copyright controls fostered by high-profile file-sharing cases like those involving Napster and Grokster, which further lead to hyper-control of copyright through legislative action. I also consider the literary estates of T.S. Eliot, Marianne Moore, and James Joyce, which would, arguably, charge for each cited word in scholarly works if able to do so. To restore the constitutional balance on which copyright was formed and provide Caputi, Jhally, and those who wish to draw upon the work of Eliot, Moore, and Joyce a fighting chance against corporate and estate copyright control, I then turn to copyright advocacy organizations such as Harvard's Berkman Center for Internet and Society, the Chilling Effects Project, and the Electronic Frontier Foundation. I conclude by describing the most likely means by which faculty can reassert fair use rights and better control scholarly works with a discussion of the history, accelerated growth, and reception of the open-access movement, and by suggesting disciplinary open-access archives.

My aim is not to provide legal advice or a comprehensive history of fair use in higher education. Rather, as a scholar who has studied and written about intellectual property concerns for over a decade, served as co-chair of the CCCC-IP, co-drafted IP policies at two different universities, and served as a member of the union bargaining team for IP at my current institution, I hope to provide a clear picture of the forces currently driving academic fair use and how we can play a significant role in averting the fate that Silberberg (2001) predicted.

SCHOLARLY PRODUCTION

Jane Caputi has been giving presentations on the pornography of everyday life for over 11 years. Her work examines about 130 images mostly drawn from contemporary advertising and other popular cultural images, including some drawn from ancient and contemporary art. These images often juxtapose imagery from mainstream media showing, for example, cropped torsos and images representing hierarchal gender roles with graphic depictions from actual pornography showing women's bodies in similar or nearly identical sexually explicit positions. Caputi (2004) uses the term pornography to signify a world view based in gendered ideas and practices of sexualized inequality and draws upon circulating imagery to support her claims. The impact of her insightful cultural critiques is magnified by the images she presents. Several years ago, Caputi received an unsolicited grant from a progressive foundation in New Mexico to make a documentary based on her illustrated lectures. Because of the funding structure, her contract with the filmmaker and her plans for the film had to be approved by her academic institution's legal counsel. She discussed issues with the campus attorney off and on for 2 years as she struggled with the producer to begin the project. University council was concerned that she needed permission from the copyright holders of the popular press images she was discussing in the film, even though the uses were for educational purposes.

An earlier case inspired Caputi to contact a copyright specialist: In 1991, Sut Jhally, a communications professor at the University of Massachusetts, successfully thwarted MTV's (and its parent company, media giant Viacom's) attempts to prevent him from showing his documentary, which critiqued sexist images in music videos (Jhally, 1990, 1992, 1995, 2007). Attorneys for MTV threatened to sue him and the university for the use of their trademarked logo and copyrighted broadcasts if he did not stop distributing *Dreamworlds*. Kembrew McLeod (2001) detailed Jhally's game of legal chicken with the major media conglomerate, explaining that even though his "appropriations of the music network's intellectual property fit the very definition of 'fair use'" and his university's attorneys acknowledge as much, they still advised him to back down. When he didn't, they told him he was on his own because the legal liability for the university was too great. Jhally established the Media Education Foundation to distribute the film and to bear the brunt of any legal battle. He then managed to get press releases picked up by many major news outlets. (MTV never responded, presumably because MTV's lawyers knew his work qualified as fair use.)

With this important precedent in mind, Caputi knew she should be able to produce her documentary, but she had to convince legal counsel and her producer to allow her to do so. She sought external consultation and learned that the public is entitled to use copyrighted material without permission or payment in certain circumstances, particularly for "criticism, comment, news reporting, teaching (including multiple copies for classroom use), scholarship, or research" (Title 17 U.S.C., Section 107). Caputi also learned that if a copyright owner sues and wins in court, then the defendant may be responsible for damages and court fees. Although her copyright attorney explained that there was no precise "right way" to proceed, the fair use four-factor analysis favored her use of the material:

1. the purpose and character of the use, whether such use is of a commercial nature or is for nonprofit educational purposes;

2. the nature of the copyrighted work, whether factual or creative;

3. the amount and substantiality of the portion used in relation to the copyrighted work as a whole; and

4. the effect of the use upon the potential market for or value of the copyrighted work.

The circumstances for fair use mentioned above, including educational use and teaching, do not guarantee fair use; however, such uses are favored, especially when there are cultural or social benefits involved. Kenneth Crews (2000) explained that although fair use "is intended to apply to teaching, research, and other such activities ... educational purpose alone does not make a use fair." Purpose is only one of four factors, and each factor is subject to interpretation by courts and must be reviewed within the specific facts of each case. Some policy-makers have incorrectly concluded that if a work is commercial, then the factor dealing with the nature of the work weighs against fair use. If this were true, no clip from a video production or a trade book could ever prevail for that factor. Other commentators have argued that if a viable license is easily available, "the action will directly conflict with the market for licensing the original" (Crews) and thereby tip the effect factor against fair use. Neither of these simplistic constructions of fair use is a valid generalization, even though they are rooted in "some truths under certain circumstances" (Crews). A reasoned analysis of all four factors must be conducted for a reliable evaluation. Furthermore, not all factors must lean in one direction for a given finding. A fifth moral factor is also often applied: Judges have evaluated the four criteria to find against fair use if the user acted either in bad faith (i.e., not being able to demonstrate that s/he reasonably believed that the use was a fair use) or in an offensive manner.

Caputi's and Jhally's cases make good demonstrations of how the factors are applied:

> **Purpose:** In both cases, the images and video clips are part of academic arguments for educational purposes, which weighs in favor of fair use. The courts also favor transformative uses that do not merely reproduce but transform the work into something new of new utility. Clearly both documentaries are transformative; the purpose factor weighs unambiguously in favor of fair use.
>
> **Nature:** The nature of the work examines characteristics of the work being used. The more factual and less creative the original work is, the more likely courts find for fair use. Because commercial, audiovisual, creative works are more strongly protected than factual works in print, this factor may

weigh more in favor of copyright holders like MTV and commercial advertisers. Yet, the transformative purpose for scholarly critique may mitigate the focus on this factor.

Amount: The two cases differ on this factor. Caputi utilized entire print ads, photographic representations or etchings from online sources and archeological texts, and single frame comics. Jhally edited clips of music videos, removing the music and dubbing a lecture track over the music. For Caputi, the amount factor could weigh in favor of the copyright holder in certain instances, particularly if many of the images were taken from the same source. But the court also takes into consideration whether the entire work is necessary for the educational purpose. Because her images come from so many sources and are clearly necessary for her analysis, this factor is likely to weigh in favor of fair use. Few courts would consider Jhally's use excessive unless he drew upon a large percentage of individual videos or excerpted the "heart" of a particular video. The latter would be hard to claim since no music track was included.

Market effect: In neither case is there likely to be any confusion of the cultural critiques of the commercial images with the originals, nor is it likely that a court will find that a purchase of the original should have been necessary for the use. When the purpose is research or scholarship for non-commercial uses, market effect may be difficult to prove. Courts are unlikely to find in either case that the limited circulation of these documentaries for dramatically different audiences and purposes is likely to compete with the original advertisements or music videos.

Although copyright owners might object to their products being critiqued in these ways, the very purpose of the fair use exemption for critical commentary is to prevent copyright holders from silencing critical voices. In this way, the fair use defense is often aligned with freedom of speech. Although there is no guarantee that fair use would be determined for Caputi or Jhally, assessment suggests fair use. Furthermore, if both scholars could prove that they completed this four-factor assessment prior to the actual production of their work, both would likely to be deemed to have acted in good faith, which could help their cases.

Even if both Caputi and Jhally prevailed, however, they have both risked being sued and being held responsible for damages and court fees. Unlike Jhally, most professors do not have the resources or audacity to take on potential lawsuits. Caputi, for example, took into consideration questions of which images to use, whether to use video clips, whether to obscure corporate logos, and how best to distribute her work. Some faculty, given the potential consequences, would simply give up the project.

INFLAMMATORY RHETORIC SHIFTS COPYRIGHT BALANCE

The examples of Caputi and Jhally shed light on several additional issues that concern faculty research. These cases expose a much broader problem that impacts scholarly work: Inflammatory copyright rhetoric leads corporate copyright holders to assert greater pressure on all markets they can control. To understand how this market pressure impacts our work, we must understand the role of fair use in the copyright regime.

Few of us realize how recently (1999) Shawn Fanning first conceived of Napster, which initiated grand-scale peer-to-peer music sharing (Lessig, 2004). Within 9 months of its launch, the tool claimed 10 million users. In another 9 months, there were 80 million registered users. The cultural, technological, and legal terrains were poised to change dramatically, in large part due to Napster. Tolerance for fair use plummeted, cease and desist letters proliferated, and the Recording Industry Association of America (RIAA) prosecuted users who "shared" files across the spectrum of peer-to-peer services that emerged between 2000 and 2002—Kazaa, Aimster, Morpheus, Musiccity, and Grokster, to name a few. One need only visit Grokster's Web site to find a permanent memorial to illegal peer-to-peer sharing of music files. The page, still emblazoned with the Grokster trademark, reads:

> The United States Supreme Court unanimously confirmed that using this service to trade copyrighted material is illegal. Copying copyrighted motion picture and music files using unauthorized peer-to-peer services is illegal and is prosecuted by copyright owners.
>
> There are legal services for downloading music and movies. This service is not one of them.

> YOUR IP ADDRESS IS <your ip address here> AND HAS BEEN LOGGED. Don't think you can't get caught. You are not anonymous.

Lawrence Lessig (2004) explained the various forms of trading files and the recording industry's understandable reaction to it and posed the fundamental question that lies at the core of copyright law: "While the recording industry understandably says, 'This is how much we've lost,' we must also ask, 'How much has society gained from p2p sharing?'"

Copyright law was designed to protect creative works and foster the creation of new culture. The U.S. Constitution provides the mandate for fair use by promoting "the progress of science and the useful arts, by securing for limited times to authors and inventors the exclusive right to their respective writing and discoveries" (U.S. Const., art. 1, sec. 8., cl. 8). This limited monopoly of rights was designed to balance the needs of creators to make a reasonable return on their works and inventions for a limited period of time, with the work then turning toward the public domain to serve as fodder for the development of future creative works. Thus, as Jessica Litman (2001) argued, "copyright was a bargain between the public and the author, whereby the public bribed the author to create new works in return for limited commercial control over the new expression the author brought to their works" (p. 78). The delicate balance on which this bargain was struck, however, has shifted in favor of copyright holders. Bell (2002) noted that "the influence of ... rough-and-tumble politics merely ensures that copyright and patent law put public and private interests into an *indelicate imbalance*" (p. 8).

We can see the impact of this imbalance in copyright legislation over the course of the past 220 years. The first federal copyright legislation of 1790 set the maximum copyright term of 14 years with one 14-year renewal available. Over the course of the next 110 years, both the initial and renewal terms doubled. In 1961, the maximum length of a copyright term was 56 years. From 1962 to the present, the term has changed three times, extending copyright protection to 70 years, then life of all authors plus 50 years, and now life plus 70 years or a total of 95 years for commercial owners (Bell, 2007).

Perhaps the escalation of copyright term extension encouraged Congress in 1976 to codify the common law concept of fair use from the 1909 Copyright Act. With a delay of about 100 years before works move into the public domain, the codification provides a loose framework to ensure that copyright holders do not have absolute monopolies on their works. Furthermore, the "Supreme Court has described fair use as 'the guarantee of breathing space for new expression within the confines of Copyright law'" (Electronic Frontier Foundation, 2002).

SCHOLARSHIP ON CREATIVE WORKS

As Caputi learned, creative works are more protected than factual works. We see the implications of such a practice in the miniscule word count limits and rigid standards that publishers and literary estates have placed on fair use citation of published materials. Boynton Cook/Heinemann/Greenwood Press, for example, set a 300-word maximum for the use of any text (excluding illustrations) before permission is required and fees are paid; Peter Lang follows the same standard for citing poetry. Literary estates vary widely in what they will allow to be published and how much permissions cost. There are several particularly notorious estates that so regularly threaten lawsuits for what amounts to fair use citation that publishers typically would rather consent to arbitrary and sometimes outlandish demands rather than risk a lawsuit based on a fair use defense.

Anyone who has sought to publish a biography on T.S. Eliot has been thwarted by his widow for the past 40 years. D. T. Max (2006) noted the distaste the Eliot estate has for academics, recalling Eliot's widow Valerie's "distaste for members of the 'Ph.D. industry' and her 'dry, formal, excessively polite notes giving them the least help possible.'" Max also mentioned the niece of Marianne Moore, who "has been unusually strict with permissions; in 1989, she demanded that a biographer remove all quotations from the poet's unpublished letters." By far, however, the most notorious estate executor is Stephen James Joyce, grandson of James Joyce. Nate Anderson (2006) noted that "Stephen James Joyce has proved himself extraordinarily unwilling to allow scholars access to Joyce's private letters and writings, and has even objected to their use of passages from his grandfather's works." The difficulties of dealing with Stephen Joyce became so notorious that a special panel was formed to help scholars deal with him: The International James Joyce Foundation Special Panel on Intellectual Property has developed a lengthy online FAQ for scholars seeking permission from the Joyce estate. The FAQ notes that, contrary to common practice by many publishers and estates, "fair use cannot be reduced to a certain quantity of words or number of lines." This outlook is aligned with the multi-factor analysis that I use to discuss Caputi's and Jhally's work, which is flexible and depends on case circumstances. Nonetheless, publishers can and typically do insist on extremely conservative rules to avoid any possibilities of litigation.

One of the only cases to ever challenge and prevail against the Joyce estate was settled in June 2007. Carol Loeb Shloss, a Stanford professor, had been working on a biography of Lucia Joyce, Stephen's mentally ill aunt, and was about to publish *Lucia Joyce: To Dance in the Wake*. Stephen Joyce wrote her and implied that he might sue if she quoted from copyrighted material. According to D. T. Max (2006), "Stephen pressured her publisher, Farrar, Straus & Giroux, which asked Shloss to cut many quotations." With great angst and frustration, she complied, cutting her use from 10,000 words to 7,000. When an attorney wrote to Stephen to explain the cuts and how they followed the provisions of fair use, Stephen responded, "this sounds like a bad joke." Copyright, he wrote, was meant "to protect the author's rights as well as those who inherited them, which is my case with respect to James Joyce." He noted, "You should be aware of the fact that over the past decade the James Joyce Estate's 'record,' in legal terms, is crystal clear and we have proven on a number of occasions that we are prepared to put our money where our mouth is."

Such disregard for the balance of rights set forth in the U.S. Constitution is not uncommon. The shift in metaphors from bargain to incentive that Litman (2001) discussed has emboldened corporate and estate owners alike. Taking is taking from the owners' perspective, a belief strengthened in the post-Napster era. Soon after the publication of her book, Shloss met the copyright lawyer Lawrence Lessig. After Shloss shared with him her correspondence with Stephen Joyce, Lessig decided to take her case pro bono. In March 2005, he suggested that she gather the material that she had purged from the book and post it on the Web "to aid scholars and researchers." Although much of the material that Shloss sought to publish online was previously unpublished work, the fair use statute states specifically that unpublished work will not bar the finding of fair use if the case details warrant such a finding. Furthermore, when scholars or publishers ask permission to use material in ways that would normally be understood as fair use, they typically do so to avoid litigation or threats of legal action. Even if permission is denied, fair use is not negated under U.S. copyright law. With this knowledge in mind, Lessig crafted a letter to the Joyce estate and explained that even though Farrar, Strauss, & Giroux had asked Shloss to remove the material, the quotations did in fact fall under the fair use doctrine. Joyce's lawyers responded, as one might imagine, with surprise and veiled threats. In response, Lessig joined forces with Robert Spoo, a Joyce scholar turned copyright lawyer, and David Olson, a Stanford associate, to prepare a lawsuit for a declaratory judgment and injunctive relief to allow Shloss to publish the materials online without the threat of being sued by the defendants. After additional posturing, the estate realized it would likely lose the case if it went to trial and settled out of court; Shloss was granted attorney fees in a separate settlement hearing. Although the estate's attorney called the result "more of a nuisance settlement," the Fair Use Project saw the "case more broadly, as part of its ongoing efforts to loosen the tightening grip of copyright holders' intent on discouraging new creative works" (Cavanaugh, 2007). The atmosphere of intimidation that Napster and Grokster spawned in the music world had already been brewing in estate permission practices, but finally came to a head in this example.

If the case had been litigated and decided in favor of Shloss, it would have had more legal impact. Also, had Stephen Joyce not pursued rights well beyond those made available in the U.S. copyright statute—including calls to librarians to prevent Shloss from viewing unpublished Joyce letters or publishing Lucia Joyce's medical records (which he did not own)—the case would have had a wider impact. Although the settlement does not offer litigants great leverage for future cases, it does frame the set of issues that scholars who work primarily with creative works must face in order to publish their scholarly works. Furthermore, it sets an important precedent that literary estates and publishers need to heed.

EMERGENCE OF STRONG FAIR USE ADVOCATES

If no strong and vocal advocates had emerged to fight for fair use over the past 10 years, Silberberg's (2001) proclamation that fair use was doomed for schools might have already come true. These issues are further represented in another recent, high-profile case. In October 2008, J. K. Rowling won a decision against RDR Books for copyright infringement for an encyclopedic work entitled *The Lexicon* that Steven Vander Ark wrote based on his comprehensive Web site of all things Harry Potter. For 10 years, the site had been growing and serving as a resource for fans and even J. K. Rowling, her publisher, Bloomsbury, and her film producer, Warner Bros. When Vander Ark began to pursue a book project, Rowling and Warner Bros. sued, claiming copyright violations (*Warner Bros. Entertainment Inc. and J. K. Rowling v. RDR Books et al.*, 2008). J. K. Rowling is known for her desire to control all aspects of productions concerning Harry Potter. Most of the materials for the book had been posted online for many years; thus the Stanford Law School and its affiliated Fair Use Project joined forces with RDR's legal team to defend the case. Here was an opportunity to win a strategic case against both the movie industry and a huge publishing conglomerate—and to gain high-profile notoriety by taking on J. K. Rowling. The drama of the case was impressive. The popular press set up a battle between media giant Warner Bros. and famously wealthy J. K. Rowling, and the little publisher RDR Books and librarian Stephen Vander Ark.

The judge's decision was, in the end, even-handed and significant for both copyright holders and creators who do scholarship on creative works. Judge Patterson found that *The Lexicon* used too much of Rowlings' creative language and descriptions, often without citation. He also found that although the encyclopedic text was transformative enough not to infringe upon the novels, it was not considered transformative enough of the two companion books Rowling has published, *Quidditch Through the Ages* and *Fantastic Beasts & Where to Find Them*, themselves encyclopedic in nature. The court also found that *The Lexicon* was not derivative because it was mostly transformative; the fact that Rowling planned to write her own encyclopedia thus had no bearing on the case.

Even though Vander Ark and RDR lost their fair use defense, the case was as much a win for creators as a win for fair use advocates. It set useful standards for future encyclopedic works and other non-creative works that faculty may produce if they follow a few clear rules: 1) use all copyrighted material carefully; 2) use only as much from the work as necessary—do not include full songs, poems, or creative language that could be rephrased or summarized; and 3) ensure the work is consistently transformative—include additional scholarly reflection that does not appear in the original works. The judge concluded that *The Lexicon* was not fair use "in its current state," but he did leave the door open not only for a revision and resubmission of the work but also future works by stating that "reference works that share the Lexicon's purpose of aiding readers of literature generally should be encouraged rather than stifled" (*Warner Bros. Entertainment Inc. and J. K. Rowling v. RDR Books et al.*, 2008). RDR Books withdrew its initial appeal when Vander Ark completed a substantial revision. *The Lexicon: An Unauthorized Guide to Harry Potter Fiction and Related Materials* has now been on sale since January 2009.

Both the Shloss and Vander Art cases demonstrate a dramatic shift in copyright litigation within the past few years. Prior to the emergence of strong advocate organizations like the Fair Use Project, the Berkman Center of the Harvard Law School, and the Electronic Frontier Foundation, publishers, authors, and professors like Caputi and Jhally were left to their own resources if challenged by a copyright holder. Almost no fair use cases have gone to court concerning faculty work because faculty typically have not been able to pay the legal costs. Furthermore, scholars usually agree to unreasonable and overly restrictive publishing contracts to get published, and without much reflection. Little attention is paid to increasing copyright restrictions, citation limitations, and the insistence by publishers to garner permissions for nearly all cited work. Faculty are not often aware of what Bell (1998) identified as *fared use*—the increased expectations of publishers that all uses of copyrighted work should be licensed. We see the impact of this thinking in the dramatic growth of the Copyright Clearance Center and the increased emphasis in the courts on the harm to existing markets in fair use cases concerning use of scholarly works. Most faculty do not realize that the courts recognize customary practices as evidence for shifting markets and business models. Perhaps most important of all, faculty do not seem to realize that these chilling effects on scholarship, teaching, and creation are not inevitable, even though they are currently tipping the delicate balance on which copyright is constitutionally founded in the favor of copyright holders. This quiet acquiescence will lead to greater copyright restrictions unless faculty learn more about advocacy organizations, consciously assert their rights, and play an active role in advocating for alternative disciplinary practices.

Since 1998, when the Berkman Center for Internet and Society at Harvard Law School was officially named, increasing numbers of fair use advocacy groups have emerged to counter these chilling effects. Wendy Seltzer originally envisioned the Chilling Effects Project as a clearinghouse to vet cease and desist letters—like the ones that Sut Jhally received from MTV—which are often sent to intimidate scholars and other users. The Electronic Frontier Foundation, with which the Chilling Effects Project is affiliated, provides legal support to important fair use cases. But the Berkman Center for Internet and Society at Harvard Law School, the Electronic Frontier Foundation, the Future of Music Foundation, Digitalconsumers.org, Creative Commons, and Stanford's Center for Internet and Society and the Fair Use Project, among others, have limited resources and must be selective in the cases they support.

Each new, high-profile copyright case and each piece of legislation that carves out exceptions and exemptions for corporate interests or further restricts educational or public use of copyrighted works (like the Copyright Term Extension Act and the Digital Millennium Copyright Act) inspires fair use advocates to explore new options. To pay for its litigation with J. K. Rowling and Warner Bros, RDR Books created the Right to Write Fund. The nonprofit Berkman Center's Citizen Media Law Project pledged to work with the Right to Write Fund's mission of serving as "an educational repository and clearinghouse for freedom of expression and 'fair use' issues that writers, filmmakers, professors, recording artists, and publishers encounter when moving among the worlds of print, Internet, film, the fine arts, and new media" (Reidy, 2008). As these resources continue to grow and proliferate, more faculty who find themselves in need of legal support or advice will benefit from them. In the interim, faculty must be aware of the ways in which affirmative fair use rights are shrinking and must become advocates for alternative management practices.

ADVOCATING FOR AFFIRMATIVE FAIR USE RIGHTS

Faculty have a range of ways to advocate for affirmative fair use rights for their scholarly works. Knowing and understanding rights is the first step toward protecting them. There are many resources available for helping faculty better understand the nuances of copyright law and the role of fair use. In 2008, the MLA Style Manual and Guide to Scholarly Publishing published a chapter on copyright, providing a clear and concise summary of each facet of the U.S. copyright law. Although this chapter makes few recommendations on how to interpret the statute, it is easily accessible and provides a useful framework for understanding the complex copyright landscape. Stanford's Copyright and Fair Use Web site is an excellent resource; its FAQs for copyright and fair use pose the questions we need to ask, provide brief but accurate summaries of copyright principles, offer brief summaries of key case law examples, and address all forms of media. The Berkman Center for Internet and Society provides an extensive list of advocacy projects including the Center for Citizen Media, Chilling Effects, Citizen Media Law, Cooperation, Copyright for Librarians, Creative Commons, Cyberlaw Clinic, Freedom To Teach: an Educational Fair Use, and many others. Each of these projects provides its own unique set of resources, all worth exploring.

Faculty can also pay attention to the rhetorics of control and free access that drive most public debates over access to academic works. Understanding the impact of examples like those described earlier in this chapter provides important guidance. Furthermore, faculty can seek university copyright policies. In another collection, I (2009) provide a careful analysis of university intellectual property policies and strategies for faculty for reading these policies; in the appendix to that chapter, I offer fifteen recommendations that all faculty should consider when reading intellectual property policies at their institutions.

Among the possible strategies that faculty can pursue to extend public access to work and even the playing field with corporate interests that control copyright, the most significant are publishing in open-access journals and participating in university institutional repositories (IRs). The open-access (OA) movement has been building for about two decades, but has expanded dramatically in the past 5 years or so. Participation in OA practices provide faculty ways to resist over-control of scholarly work and to change the ways in which new knowledge is produced and disseminated. Institutional repositories proliferated beginning around 2003; although related to open-access initiatives, institutional repositories are typically university-based and have not been as successful as open-access initiatives as a whole. I close this chapter with a brief explanation and history of OA and IR initiatives, the reception these initiatives have had by faculty, and a set of strategies that faculty can use to guide their publishing practices.

THE OPEN-ACCESS MOVEMENT AND INSTITUTIONAL REPOSITORIES

Peter Suber (2007b) explained in his blog that open-access works are "digital, online, free of charge, and free of most copyright and licensing restrictions," and are "compatible with copyright, peer review, revenue (even profit), print, preservation, prestige, career-advancement, indexing, and other features and supportive services associated with conventional scholarly literature." There are two primary standards of OA publishing: gold and green. Gold OA journals are peer-reviewed, allow authors to retain copyrights, and typically provide open access to research titles without delay. The green standard represents non-peer-reviewed works in archives or repositories that are often pre- or postprint reproductions of journal articles. Faculty have a choice of where they publish and can influence journal editors to participate in open-access practices.

In 1991, Paul Ginsparg helped to develop what is now called the arXiv.org e-print archive while he was working for the Los Alamos National Laboratory. Since that time, he and Stevan Harnad, a cognitive scientist, have advocated for and written about the need for open-access electronic archives to subvert the time delays, access problems, and costs of scholarly publications. In a proposal, Harnad (1995) laid down the gauntlet for open-access archiving. He stated that if

> every esoteric [non-trade, no-market] author in the world this very day established a globally accessible local ftp archive for every piece of esoteric writing from this day forward, the long-heralded transition from paper publication to purely electronic publication (of esoteric research) would follow suit almost immediately.

His proposal spawned a series of online discussions among physicists, chemists, publishers, librarians, developers of the Web, and others. (A valuable archive of these exchanges is available, along with the original proposal, by the Association of Research Libraries.) More importantly, this conversation launched over a decade of advocacy, partnerships, experiments, research, dramatic growth of the e-print arXiv, emergence of thousands of open-access journals, and a host of self-archiving initiatives.

Soon after Harnad (1995) posted his proposal online, he helped to craft several important initiatives. He played an important role in galvanizing an international group of colleagues with funding from the Open Society Institute that led to the 2002 Budapest Open Access Initiative, which became a major turning point in the movement. Over 4,000 individuals signed the initiative; 380 organizations signed as well, including universities from all over the world, libraries, medical schools, non-profit organizations, journals, institutes, societies, councils, research centers, and other institutions (Chan, 2002).

Other declarations followed, including the 2003 Berlin Declaration on Open Access to Knowledge in the Sciences and Humanities and the 2003 Bethesda Statement on Open Access Publishing. The latter initiative established PubMed as a free digital archive of biomedical and life sciences journal literature at the U.S. National Institutes of Health (NIH). In July 2004, the U.S. House Appropriations Committee adopted a set of recommendations for the 2005 federal budget, which became the House Report 108-636. This bill expressed concern that insufficient public access was available for reports and data resulting from NIH-funded research. Citing the rising costs of scientific journal subscriptions, the report recommended that the NIH begin requiring a copy of any manuscript produced by or through NIH grant-funded work and that work be added to the National Library of Medicine's (NLM) PubMed directory. The report further stipulated that supplemental materials be "freely and continuously available six months after publication, or immediately in cases in which some or all of the publication costs are paid with NIH grant funds" (Wallace, 2004). In January 2008, the NIH announced a revision of its policy as a result of the Consolidated Appropriations Act, 2008. This law now stipulates that, when consistent with copyright law,

> all investigators funded by the NIH [shall] submit or have submitted for them to the National Library of Medicine's PubMed Central an electronic version of their final, peer-reviewed manuscripts upon acceptance for publication, to be made publicly available no later than 12 months after the official date of publication.

At the same time that the NIH pursued its public-access initiative, the RoMEO (Rights Metadata for Open Archiving) and SHERPA (Securing a Hybrid Environment for Research Preservation and Access, an institutional repository partnership of over 30 universities) projects were developing in the U.K. The former project studies "issues relating to the open-archiving of research papers by UK academics," while the latter lists publishers and their associated copyright agreements concerning self-archiving. SHERPA also runs a service called OpenDOAR, which lists a number of subject-based institutional repositories for self-archiving world-wide. Not surprisingly, PubMed sponsors a comparable list (the Open Access List) of publishers willing to participate in NIH's open-access archive.

Concurrently in the U.S., a similar initiative took root under the auspices of the Coalition for Networked Information (CNI). Clifford Lynch and Joan Lippincott (2005) described a CNI survey of its academic member institutions to examine the current state of institutional repositories in the U.S. Their survey went out to U.S. research institutions and colleges, with a return rate of about 80%. They found that about 40% of the responding universities and 43% of responding colleges had developed institutional repositories; 88% of the institutions that did not yet have repositories were planning to develop them or become part of multi-institutional repositories. Lynch and Lippincott concluded that IRs in the U.S. "are being positioned decisively as general-purpose infrastructure within the context of changing scholarly practice, within e-research and cyberinfrastructure, and in visions of the university in the digital age." The purposes of these repositories differ considerably, from dissertation or preprint archives to digitized music scores and campus blogs.

Based directly on the language of the open-access archive movement, the policies of the NIH, and the explosive growth of IR initiatives, the University of California system published white papers that directed faculty to participate in a mandatory state-wide archive. In December 2005 the University of California Academic Council's Special Committee on Scholarly Communication published a set of white papers in which they argued that:

> faculty shall routinely grant to The Regents of the University of California a limited, irrevocable, perpetual, worldwide, non-exclusive license to place the faculty member's scholarly work in a non-commercial open-access repository for purposes of online dissemination and preservation on behalf of the author and the public.

This proposal was bold and direct and was the biggest of its kind in the U.S. It met much more resistance from faculty than administrators anticipated; terms like "irrevocable," "perpetual," and "worldwide" are not humanities-friendly. Faculty expressed their concerns in a 2007 attitude survey. Perhaps the most telling response stated that "scholars are aware of alternative forms of dissemination but are concerned about preserving their current publishing outlets" (University of California, 2007). Furthermore, faculty asserted that "the current tenure and promotion system impedes changes in faculty behavior." As a result of faculty responses, the University of California Open Access Policy worked for 2 years to soften its mandate by qualifying which texts would be posted and by shifting its tone significantly. The 2007 revision sought to "increase authors' influence in scholarly publishing by establishing a collective practice of retaining a right to open access dissemination of certain scholarly works" (p. 2) and asserted that faculty would routinely grant the "Regents of the University of California a license to place in a non-commercial open-access online repository the faculty member's scholarly work published in a scholarly journal or conference proceedings." Although the tenor of the language shifted in useful ways from the initial white paper, the commitment from the universities dramatically increased. The new policy asserted that the Academic Senate, in collaboration with the President's office, would "contact scholarly publishers and establish support mechanisms for the policy and the use of scholarly work which it covers." The University would "support faculty in their efforts to retain open access dissemination rights, and to foster a broad spectrum of publication venues" and would not receive any money for doing so.

Faculty resistance outside of the sciences is disappointing, albeit not surprising; the economy of status that drives faculty work is fueled by tenure and promotion. As the work of Harnad (1995, 1997) and Ginsparg (1997) have demonstrated, faculty in the sciences have typically valued dissemination and first discovery in their scholarly work. Those of us in the humanities have typically valued scholarly achievement and production over immediacy and first ownership of ideas.

One might account for these differences in several ways: 1) scientific research often leads to time-sensitive medical or pharmaceutical developments; 2) scientific research may also lead to development of patents, licenses, or competitive grants; and 3) scientific culture is founded on a spirit of international cooperation and the desire for first recognition of discoveries. On the other hand, research in the humanities rarely leads to time-sensitive discoveries and does not foster a first-to-market ideology. Collaboration is typically based on personal relationships rather than teams of scholars striving to solve the same set of problems across international borders. Furthermore, although many humanities scholars lament the pace of production, few attempt to advocate for changes in the systems driving production practices. Perhaps most important of all, humanities faculty depend so much on peer-reviewed research for tenure and promotion that they are nervous about any changes that could jeopardize their chances for promotion. Ultimately, the sciences have proven that open access publication and institutional and professional association repositories have not negatively impacted tenure and promotion decisions. Physics, chemistry, and certain fields in math and computer science have been posting nearly all of their scholarly work as pre- and postprints since the 1980s in online archives. For humanities faculty to realize the benefits of disciplinary open-access archiving, the culture of publishing has to change, which involves shifting faculty attitudes and practices, participating in institutional promotion practices, garnering university support for open-access initiatives, and fomenting change in relationships with publishers. This is no small set of changes.

In 1998, Joan Latchaw and I called for open-access publishing of work in the field of computers and composition. Change in academic culture occurs slowly but is often marked by precipitating events. Assertive initiatives are necessary to stimulate the shift of culture needed in the humanities. The California open-access repository and the NIH mandate set the stage for what would become, according to Suber (2007a), the first U.S. open-access, faculty-initiated, university-wide mandate. On February 18, 2008, the Harvard University faculty of Arts and Letters unanimously voted for what has become the first open-access mandate "to be adopted by faculty rather than administrators, the first adopted policy to focus on permissions rather than deposits, and the first to catch the worldwide attention of the press and blogosphere" (Suber, 2008). Suber, an open-access activist with Public Knowledge, a nonprofit group in Washington, D.C., explained the permissions focus of this mandate as opposed to a deposit mandate: Rather than requiring faculty to deposit copies of their articles after they publish postprints in an institutional repository, the Harvard mandate merely requires faculty "to give the university permission (non-exclusive permission) to host the postprints in the IR." Harvard's mandate required all faculty in the College of Arts and Letters to participate in this open-access repository or write for permission to opt out. Further, the university takes responsibility for depositing the work itself. Such a model "reduces the demands on faculty and increases the certainty about permissions. As long as the university is willing to pay people, usually librarians, to make the actual deposits, it could be a faster and more frictionless way to move the deposit rate toward 100%." Suber cataloged the astounding range of reactions in the popular press, at universities worldwide, at open-access organizations, and on fair use advocacy sites.

Notwithstanding resistance to the California institutional repository, the California and Harvard initiatives mark an important turning point in IR and OA mandates, shifting the focus from the sciences to the humanities. Suber (2007a, 2007b, 2008), Harnad (1995), and Ginsparg (1997) continue to advocate strongly for the growth of the movement. Suber has consolidated recommendations from scholars into a comprehensive list of strategies that faculty can use to advocate for open-access publishing at all levels of our daily work. These recommendations include submitting research in the form of preprints, postprints, or simultaneous prints to open access journals; advocating for institutional repositories at our home institutions; asking publishers to release certain ownership rights so that scholars can post published work in an institutional repository; depositing research data with corresponding research in OA archives; accepting invitations to join peer-review boards of OA journals but not journals that are not open-access; and numerous additional possibilities (Suber, 2007b).

CONCLUSION

Composition scholars have typically been more open to change than others in the humanities. We were among the first to theorize assessment and make assessment part of our scholarly mission. We led the way in integrating all forms of computer technologies into the classroom and theorizing their many strengths and recognizing their liabilities. We have been the first to form an intellectual property caucus to educate our scholarly communities of the significance of copyright concerns in our classes and research. We are in a unique position as a discipline to extend the purpose, promise, and value of fair use by advocating open-access publishing in the humanities. In 2001, the emergence of CompPile, a comprehensive online composition bibliography of scholarship ranging from 1939 to the present, marked the most significant contribution to the spirit of free research and scholarship in the field. Even with this extraordinary resource, however, and several open-access initiatives in composition studies like the WAC Clearinghouse, the Computers and Composition Digital Press, and a few open-access text books (including Flat World Knowledge and Writing Spaces: Readings on Writing), compositionists as a whole have not invested in open-access publishing.

When Joan and I (1998) first proposed the development of a disciplinary preprint archive for the field of computers and composition, we were imagining something more than a bibliography—even more than an open-access archive. We explored the development of a community-based preprint archive that would serve as the hub of research, conversation, and professional development for a dynamic online community whose work was tied to such a home base resembling Michel Foucault's heterotopic spaces. Foucault used this term to define cultural spaces that have "precise and determined functions" that may shift over time. Among other traits, heterotopias function in relation to all spaces that exist outside of them. At the same time that they mark a culturally definable space that is unlike any other space, they also act as microcosms reflecting larger cultural patterns or social orders.

We wrote:

> If we developed a preprint archive system to which all members of the community contributed their pre-published texts,

> we could create the most complex heterotopic virtual archive available to date. And because this community is so diverse and crosses so many disciplinary boundaries, this site could eventually house most new knowledge that concerned intellectual property, copyright, fair use, cross disciplinary concerns of integrating technology into teaching, and more generally the impacts of computer technology on culture at large. (Galin & Latchaw, 1998)

At that time, we were imagining a living archive that would serve as a place to meet, do research, house and present scholarly work, and build community relationships beginning within the burgeoning community of computers and composition. We realized then that such a radical shift in academic culture would have to begin small within a community that was already innovative, accepting of cultural change, and ready or willing to make such a shift. We imagined that "not-for-profit academics, professional organizations, and electronic journal editorial boards could build in value added resources that would encourage regular and repeated use of this professional working space." In so doing, a crystallizing structure would emerge on which larger sectors of the discipline could build. We suggested that:

> Spin-off publications would surely emerge as the archives continued to grow exponentially. Students in undergraduate and graduate classes would likely develop real-world writing projects that contribute to the review and linking systems of the raw materials available online. Libraries would develop reference systems to manage the dynamic body of resources and materials online as professional organizations developed LASE-like disciplinary search engines and electronic agents developed more advanced on-the-fly annotated meta-hypertext engines. (Galin & Latchaw, 1998)

We offered this vision at the moment that the open-access movement had really just begun, building on Harnad's (1995) and Ginsparg's (1997) vision of preprint archives. The range of possibilities has grown exponentially since that time with the development of pre- and postprint open access archives, green and gold standard open-access journals, institutional repositories, open-access agreements and legislation, Creative Commons licensing, the emergence of advocacy organizations, and mandates for open-access publishing. All of these changes have made it possible to envision online disciplinary heterotopic spaces that challenge the ways in which we have done our work for over 100 years.

Just a decade ago, few could see the way forward to such a disciplinary culture. There were too many obstacles, too little attention to fair use and its impact on scholarly work, and too much habitual thinking. Still, substantial obstacles remain; as Bell explained (2007), "lobbying by special interests ... invariably ensure[s] that copyright and patent law favors private interests over public ones" (p. 7). In February 2009, the Fair Copyright in Research Works Act (H.R. 801) was introduced to the Judiciary Committee in the House of Representatives to reverse the NIH open-access mandate. The act seeks to amend the U.S. Copyright Code to prohibit "federal agencies from requiring as a condition of funding agreements public access to the products of the research they fund" (DigitalKoans, 2009). Such legislation and continued corporate pressure in high-profile lawsuits (like those of Napster, Grokster, and RDR Books) can only be overcome by organized efforts at all levels. While the faculty in the University of California system remind us that no such models can work that do not take into consideration tenure and promotion practices, the slow process of disciplinary change occurs with moderate steps forward.

Fair use practices lay at the heart of this vision. Faculty have to assert their rights to pursue their research despite corporate attempts to shut them down. Jane Caputi, Sut Jhally, Carol Shloss, Steven Vander Ark, and the advocacy groups that support them remind us how important it is to push back. Paul Ginsparg, Stephen Harnad, and Peter Suber offer strategies for us to push forward. The CompPile database, Joan Latchaw, and I offer a starting place to imagine future possibilities. The CCCC Caucus on Intellectual Property is keeping an eye on these larger concerns and making steps to educate National Council for Teachers of English (NCTE) members as a whole. The organization will continue to publish summaries of important cases affecting NCTE constituents and present on issues of fair use, open-access, open-source, and copyright in the classroom and our scholarly works, but we as faculty need to advocate at our own institutions, promote change on our campuses, and participate in institutional repositories and other open-access initiatives. It may take 10 more years before we realize the kind of heterotopic community that Joan and I were imagining in 1998. Certainly, it will take more work to articulate what that digital community will look like and to negotiate the changes necessary to arrive there; to get there, however, faculty must assume greater control over their scholarly works.

REFERENCES

Academic Council Special Committee on Scholarly Communication (AC-SCS). (2005). Responding to the challenges facing scholarly communication: Overview. http://www.universityofcalifornia.edu/senate/committees/scsc/copyrightproposal0506.pdf

Anderson, Nate. (2006). Is James Joyce's estate misusing its copyright? *ars Technica: The Art of Technology.* http://arstechnica.com/news.ars/post/20060613-7048.html

Bell, Tom W. (2007, November 2). Escape from copyright: Market success vs. statutory failure in the protection of expressive works. http://www.tomwbell.com/writings/(C)Esc.html

Bell, Tom W. (1998). Fair use v. fared use: The impact of automated rights management on copyright's fair use doctrine. *North Carolina Law Review, 76,* 557–619.

Bell, Tom W. (2002). Indelicate imbalancing in copyright and patent law. In Adam Thierer & Wayne Crews (Eds.), *Copy fights: The future of intellectual property in the information age* (pp. 1–16). Washington, DC: Cato Institute.

Caputi, Jane. (2004). *Goddesses and monsters: Women, myth, power, and popular culture.* Madison: University of Wisconsin Press.

Cavanaugh, Tim. (2007, June 5). Portrait of the old man as a copyright miser: How a lawsuit about some old books and letters sheds light on 21st century I.P. madness. *Los Angeles Times.* http://www.latimes.com/news/opinion/la-oew-cavanaugh5jun05,0,2402066.story

CCCC Caucus on Intellectual Property. (2000). Use your fair use: Strategies toward action. College Composition and Communication, 51 (3), 485–488.

Center for Social Media. (2008). Code of best practices in fair use for media literacy education. http://www.centerforsocialmedia.org/fair-use/related-materials/codes/code-best-practices-fair-use-media-literacy-education

Chan, Leslie. (2002, February 14). Budapest Open Access Initiative. Open Society Institute and Soros Foundations Network. http://www.soros.org/openaccess/read.shtml

CONFU: The Conference on Fair Use. (1997). What happened and what does it mean for fair use in the electronic environment? http://www.utsystem.edu/ogc/intellectualproperty/confu.htm

CONTU: National Commission on New Technology Uses of Copyrighted Works. (1976). Final report. http://digital-law-online.info/CONTU/contu1.html

Crews, Kenneth. (2000, May). Fair-use: Overview and meaning for higher education. http://www.copyright.iupui.edu/highered.htm

DigitalKoans. (2009, February 15). What is the sound of one e-print downloading? http://digital-scholarship.org/digitalkoans/2009/02/15/support-open-access-contact-house-judiciary-committee-members-to-save-the-nih-public-access-policy/

Electronic Frontier Foundation. (2002). Fair use frequently asked questions (and answers). http://w2.eff.org/IP/eff_fair_use_faq.php

Galin, Jeffrey. (2009). Own your rights: Know when your university can claim ownership of your work. In Steve Westbrook (Ed.), *Composition & copyright: Perspectives on teaching, text-making, and fair use* (pp. 190-216). Albany: State University of New York Press.

Galin, Jeffrey, & Latchaw, Joan. (1998). Heterotopic spaces online: A new paradigm for academic scholarship and publication. Kairos: Rhetoric, Pedagogy, Technology, 3 (1). http://english.ttu.edu/kairos/3.1/index.html

Ginsparg, Paul. (1997). The impact of electronic publishing on the academic community. Portland: Portland Press Limited. http://www.portlandpress.com/pp/books/online/tiepac/session1/ch7.htm

Harnad, Stevan. (1995). Universal FTP archives for esoteric science and scholarship: A subversive proposal. In Ann Okerson & James O'Donnell (Eds.), Scholarly journals at the crossroads: A subversive proposal for electronic publishing. Washington, D.C.: Association of Research Libraries. http://www.library.yale.edu/~okerson/subversive.html

Harnad, Stevan. (1997), March 14). Paper house of cards: (and why it's taking so long to collapse). http://www.ariadne.ac.uk/issue8/harnad

Jhally, Sut. (1990). Dreamworlds: Desire/sex/power in rock video. Northampton, MA: Media Education Foundation.

Jhally, Sut. (1992). MTV, cultural politics and the sex wars: The strange and illuminating case of Dreamworlds. Media Information Australia, 64, 48-59.

Jhally, Sut. (1995). Dreamworlds: Desire/sex/power in rock video. Northampton, MA: Media Education Foundation.

Jhally, Sut. (2007). Dreamworlds: Desire/sex/power in rock video. Northampton, MA: Media Education Foundation.

Lessig, Lawrence. (2004). Free culture: How big media uses technology and the law to lock down culture and control creativity. New York: Penguin Press.

Litman, Jessica. (2001). Digital copyright. Amherst, New York: Prometheus Books.

Lynch, Clifford A., & Lippincott, Joan K. (2005). Institutional repository deployment in the United States as of early 2005. D-Lib Magazine, 11 (9). http://cornyn.senate.gov/doc_archive/05-02-2006_FRPAAonepager.pdf

Max, D. T. (2006, June 19). The injustice collector: Is James Joyce's grandson suppressing scholarship? New Yorker. http://www.newyorker.com/archive/2006/06/19/060619fa_fact

McLeod, Kembrew. (2001). Owning culture: Authorship, ownership, and intellectual property law. New York: Peter Lang Publishing.

Modern Language Association. (2008). MLA style manual and guide to scholarly publishing (3rd ed.). New York: Modern Language Association of America.

Reidy, Chris. (2008, September 10). Potter court ruling gets Berkman Center's attention. Boston Globe. http://www.righttowrite.org

Silberberg, Carol M. (2001). Preserving educational fair use in the twenty-first century. Southern California Law Review, 74, 617–655.

Suber, Peter. (2007a). Open access overview: Focusing on open access to peer-reviewed research articles and their preprints. http://www.earlham.edu/~peters/fos/overview.htm.

Suber, Peter. (2007b). What you can do to promote open access. http://www.earlham.edu/~peters/fos/do.htm

Suber, Peter. (2008, March 2). SPARC open access newsletter http://www.earlham.edu/~peters/fos/newsletter/03-02-08.htm

University of California (2007, August). Faculty attitudes and behaviors regarding scholarly communication: Survey findings from the University of California. http://osc.universityofcalifornia.edu/responses/materials/OSC-survey-full-20070828.pdf

Wallace, Emily Lehr. (2004, October 26). Special update: Public access to federally funded scientific research. American Geological Institute. http://www.agiweb.org/gap/legis108/update_openaccess.html

Warner Bros. Entertainment Inc. and J. K. Rowling v. RDR Books et al. (2008). F.Supp.2d, 2008 WL 4126736, S.D.N.Y., (NO. 07 CIV. 9667 RPP).

2 PLAGIARISM AND PROMISCUITY, AUTHORS AND PLAGIARISMS

Russel Wiebe

When I was about 19 years old, a dissolute and desperate character, at least in my imagination of myself, a friend of mine was attending Everett Community College. He had been asked to produce a book report on Rollo May's *The Courage to Create* for a psychology class he was taking. He had determined that he did not have enough time to read the book and produce the requisite book report and asked me if I would do it in exchange for a case of beer. "Sure," I said. I read the book and produced a poor, but (barely) passing, report on the book's strengths and weaknesses. My friend passed the course. He didn't get caught. As an outsider to the entire enterprise of the academy, I didn't then, and maybe don't now, feel much in the way of guilt for my violation of academic codes of conduct. My friend never got a college degree; I doubt he ever reflects back upon this exchange. But I have occasion to think of it every time the subject of cheating comes up in one of my classes.

The classroom conversation about cheating, at least as I've observed it in classrooms over about 20 years, simply takes cheating of whatever stripe as a given. If I ask a question like "who has cheated in school?," it's the rare class in which there is more than one "no, I've never cheated" response. Far more common are the classes in which everyone admits that they've cheated. In the conversation that ensues, there is almost always both derision toward the claim that anyone might really assert that they are innocent and a pretty willing acknowledgment of shared guilt. In an abstract way, students seem to think that cheating is so much the norm that admitting it hardly needs cover. Of those unanimous or nearly unanimous in agreement, only a few are willing to say that anything at all is wrong with the practice. The airline pilot who cheated to get his pilot's license or the surgeon doing "your mother's surgery" who cheated his or her way through medical school usually elicits a response that differentiates those activities, which are real and therefore have consequences, from school tasks, which are largely "unreal" and therefore, outside the realm of ethical consideration.

At some point in that classroom conversation, some student will ask me if I have ever cheated. Just a little sheepishly, I tell the story of my foray into ghost-writing. Maybe like many of my students, I tell that story as a kind of rationalization. After all, I seem to claim, that is the worst of what I have done in the way of academic dishonesty. It was barely cheating. Despite more years of school than I like to count and more situations in which it might have been easy to cheat—to turn in someone else's paper, to look over the shoulder at someone else's calculus answer sheet, or to peek at the proper third-person possessive of some German verb or the dative case "Stan, Stane, Stanes" (which I'm sure even now is the wrong string of Anglo-Saxon words)—I only note this one single example of academic dishonesty. Excluded from that account are all of the lies of omission and commission that I have told and not told in order to wrangle an extension on a paper or postpone the date of a dreaded exam on rat psychology or the Franco-Prussian war. I guess that in the hierarchy of cheating these examples of dishonesty seem to fall into some other category of behavior than simple cheating, which points to a key problem with any consideration of plagiarism, which is just where it fits in the hierarchy of cheating, or what campus policies call "academic dishonesty" or, as Barclay Barrios' institution calls it, "academic irregularity" (see this volume). Because categories like "academic dishonesty" and academic honesty are so fraught with ambiguity, that definition (let alone action based on those definitional attempts) seems almost impossible.

As the Internet has inevitably entered our classrooms as well as student dorm rooms, cafes, bars, airport terminals, and many other places, the simplicity of cheating appears to have increased in some exponential way. It's no longer necessary to creep into the office after hours, sneak a folder out of a filing cabinet, and make copies to appropriate another's text. All you have to do is hack a password or find an obscure repository of textual information and claim it. It's easy to cheat on the Internet; multiple articles in the *Chronicle, Newsweek,* and daily newspapers notice and decry the increase in academic dishonesty of all kinds. In a study on Internet plagiarism among college students, Patrick Scanlon and David Neumann (2002) surveyed the recent public attention that student cheating has received. They noted that "a perception reflected in media accounts is that acts of academic dishonesty among students in college as well as high school have increased sharply" (p. 374). Rebecca Moore Howard (2001) wrote in *The Chronicle Review* that "if you are a professor in the United States and you have a pulse, you have heard about the problem of Internet plagiarism" (p. B 24). Several contemporary Web sites highlight both the apparent ubiquity of Internet cheating and the tone of some academic responses to the problem. The Web site Plagiarism Stoppers (2008) includes a statement that posits:

> ***Plagiarism*** is a rapidly growing problem in many venues today. Because it is so easy to locate information using the Internet, students have given in to the temptation to take materials and use them for their own. This needs to be addressed by all who are in the education field—by teaching the observance of proper citation and copyright compliance AND by making sure our students know that stealing someone else's work is wrong.

Another Web site, Plagiarized.com (2008) queries:

> Think plagiarism detection services are the answer? <u>Think again</u>! These services don't catch "custom essays", and they don't catch plagiarism when the original work isn't already in the digital domain. If you rely on detection, you are doing a disservice to your students. Do your research. Take a look at some of the custom essay services (they probably have ads on this page). If you are thinking of spending precious resources on these services, you should take on the role of a student to test their detection rates. Buy some custom essays, have them scanned by the services you are considering. The fact is detection services help to catch the cheaters who fall into the "not so bright" category. Smart cheaters can skate circles around these services. Well designed and original curriculum, attention to detail, and a true understanding of the plagiarism problem throughout your institution are the keys to dealing effectively with the issue.

I could multiply such complaints a thousand—maybe a hundred thousand—fold. Plagiarism, it seems, is everywhere. And perhaps we have even started to notice how common plagiarism is among at least some of the more high profile among us. As I drafted this chapter, Joe Biden, an admitted—

though perhaps accidental—plagiarist, had just become our vice president-elect and Doris Kearns Goodwin, yet another apparently inadvertent plagiarist, commented upon his election both through live online coverage and in static written text.

I begin with my story of "academic dishonesty" not to court academic embarrassment—though I've agonized about the confession—but to suggest that it is probably the rare academic who has not engaged in some form of "dishonesty" in school or in our professional lives. Perhaps any consideration of plagiarism—whatever we might think plagiarism is—would be well-served to consider and empathize with all of the simple and complex behaviors that "academic dishonesty" encompasses.

Michel Foucault (1984) wrote that

> The coming into being of the notion of "author" constitutes the privileged moment of *individualization* in the history of idea, knowledge, literature, philosophy, and the sciences. Even today, when we reconstruct the history of a concept, literary genre, or school of philosophy, such categories seem relatively weak, secondary, and superimposed scansions in comparison with the solid and fundamental unit of the author and the work. (p. 101)

In asking questions like "who is the author?" or "to whom does this work belong?," we are simply asking whether or not the work is plagiarized. Is it plagiarized? Is it a fraud? Is it "genuine?" We thus find ourselves in a definitional abyss.

In an attempt to define just what should be considered plagiarism and what should be seen to fall outside that definition, Moore Howard (1995) has suggested three categories that we might consider: cheating, non-attribution, and patchwriting. She continues:

> It is perhaps never the case that a writer composes "original" material, free of any influence. It might be more accurate to think of creativity, of fresh combinations made from existing sources, or fresh implications for existing materials. An important requirement of most academic writing is acknowledging one's sources. We all work from sources, even when we

are being creative. American academic culture demands that writers who use the exact words of a source supply quotation marks at the beginning and end of the quotation, so that the reader can know where the voice of the source begins and ends. In addition, the writer must use footnotes, parenthetical notes, or endnotes to cite the source, so that the reader can consult that source if he or she chooses. Writers must also acknowledge the sources not only of words but also of ideas, insofar as is possible, even when they are not quoting word for word. Moreover, in final-draft writing, academic writers may not paraphrase a source by using its phrases and sentences, with a few changes in grammar or word choice-even when the source is cited. Plagiarism is the representation of a source's words or ideas as one's own. Plagiarism occurs when a writer fails to supply quotation marks for exact quotations; fails to cite the sources of his or her ideas; or adopts the phrasing of his or her sources, with changes in grammar or word choice. (pp. 798-799)

As Moore Howard suggested, in academic writing, at least, there is no simple "originality," no such work that simply jumps from the student's mind to the page in some unmediated way.

Brian Martin (1994) offered two interesting lists of plagiarism types. The first might serve as a kind of taxonomy and the second raises what might seem to be some embarrassing questions about academic and social practice in the realm of "acceptable plagiarisms." Martin wrote that "the most obvious and provable plagiarism occurs when someone copies phrases or passages out of a published work without using quotation marks, without acknowledging the source, or both. This can be called word-for-word plagiarism. When some of the words are changed, but not enough, the result can be called paraphrasing plagiarism." This sort of "paraphrasing plagiarism" resembles Moore Howard's (1995) patchwriting. Martin continued: "A more subtle plagiarism occurs when a person gives references to [an] original source, and perhaps quotes them, but never looks them up, having obtained both from a secondary source—which is not quoted. This can be called plagiarism of secondary sources." A third and more elusive type of plagiarism that Martin described is the use of an argument's structure without acknowledgment. Related but more general is the case of plagiarism of ideas. And, finally, Martin described "the blunt case of putting one's name to someone else's work, which might be called plagiarism of authorship."

Having highlighted what he takes to be the primary forms of academic plagiarism among students, Martin generated a taxonomy of "institutionalized plagiarism"—a list of what we might think of as at least occasionally acceptable forms of authorial behavior. The list includes ghostwriting: "when a politician, famous sports figure, business executive, or movie star gives a speech or writes a book or newspaper column, frequently the actual writing is done by someone else." Martin noted also the phenomenon of "honorary authorship," such as political speech writing, some comedy writing, and much bureaucratic writing. As Martin's two lists demonstrate, the accusation of plagiarism is frequently the product of hierarchical relationships. When a student borrows a paper to turn in for a class, that's plagiarism. When an academic borrows another teacher's materials to produce a class lecture without citation, that's scholarship (however sloppy). When a supervisor takes credit for an underling's work, that's business. As Martin's taxonomy makes clear enough, the designation of plagiarism has at least as much to do with where you reside in a power structure as it does with whether you did or did not present someone else's text as your own. As Martin revealed, the practice of presenting someone else's text as one's own is widespread and unremarkable in a variety of corporate and academic contexts.

At the same time as the plague of plagiarism has come to seem a surpassing educational problem, plagiarism has also gained prominence in our contemporary shared culture. In addition to Vice President Biden and Doris Kearns Goodwin, historian Stephen Ambrose, presidential speech writer Timothy S. Goeglein, (Derringer, 2008), and the playwright Byrony Lavery have defended themselves against charges of plagiarism. But if a student who plagiarizes in a composition class can expect some actual punishment, most of these high-profile cases result in a lot of hand-wringing but no real consequences.

I began thinking of this chapter as a chance to articulate for myself the differences among "kinds" of plagiarism, or at least of creating a taxonomy that I could use to adjudicate—if for no one other than myself—the licit from the illicit forms plagiarism might take. But I find that my imagined taxonomy is blurred. As compelling as I find Moore Howard's consideration of patchwriting, I don't think we can solve the problem of plagiarism (if indeed there truly is a problem) by saying that the writer is multiple, written by as much as she writes her culture. I also doubt, likewise, that—a la Barthes and Foucault and Derrida—there is such a thing as origin. Almost all contemporary literary and artistic practice acknowledges this fact. And although this certainly complicates the adjudication of plagiarism, as Moore Howard and many others recognize, I don't think we can solve the problem by saying that an appeal to an author's intention can be a viable alternative when it is the category "author" as a single, originary unit that Moore Howard and others have acknowledged can never exist. More useful (at least for me) in providing some purchase on the question of plagiarism in the composition class are the pedagogies of Amy Robillard and Ron Fortune (2007) and Kelly Ritter (2006), who seek to bring the practices of forgery, impersonation, and the use of paper mills into the structure of our classes.

Robillard and Fortune (2007) articulated that "we believe that in order to expand our understanding of the work we do with texts, we must legitimate the work of both literary forgery and plagiarism as forms of writing" (p. 185). Of course, Robillard and Fortune don't mean that we should make forgery or plagiarism legitimate forms of student writing. Rather, they suggest that by moving the study of the forger and the plagiarist to the forefront of our pedagogy, we can more accurately and compellingly understand the kinds of questions the plagiarist and the forger force us to confront.

Robillard and Fortune (2007) offered one possible solution to plagiarism as problem—they urged us to move the study of plagiarism and forgery to the center of the composition classroom, to make of that study the new content of composition; through an examination of "legitimation strategies" in the creation of bogus texts, students can learn how to produce similar, though perhaps ultimately more honest, versions of such legitimation. They posited that "literary forgery and whole-text plagiarism as instances of writing dependent on the production of belief rather than as instances of anti-writing can help us understand the processes by which a text is authorized" (p. 185). By moving the conversation away from the notion of plagiarism as a legal question, Robillard and Fortune make an important contribution to our ability to rethink plagiarism as a strategy in our classes. If we study legitimation as they ask us to do, then perhaps we can also study the nature of the original as Sherrie Levine (discussed later in this chapter) and other appropriators have and continue to do. Robillard and Fortune argued that

> Composition's disciplinary attachment to the process paradigm together with a deep investment in our collective professional ability to differentiate between the "authentic" and the "fraudulent" have rendered the symbolic aspects of plagiarism unavailable for analysis. Just as English studies' dismissal of forgery as a species of writing has allowed us to avoid asking questions of it that we ask of legitimate writing, so too has our near dismissal of plagiarism as anything other than an

> academic crime allowed us to avoid confronting asking questions of it that we ask of legitimate writing. These questions we avoid have everything to do with belief. (p. 197)

Kelly Ritter (2006) argued that a better response to whole-text plagiarism than punishment is to attempt an understanding of the motives that drive a student to purchase an essay. She concluded by noting that students who purchase essays

> base their choices (of whether to purchase or produce) specifically on which site of authorship—that which resides within themselves or that which resides online—will provide the better product for gaining a college degree, which students believe is a proof-of-purchase certificate and faculty believe is in an intangible intellectual achievement.(p. 26)

Ritter suggested that students see the plagiarism question not as a question of morality but rather as a question of utility: "We cannot believe that simply bringing ethics into the classroom means that our students will either mimic what is 'right' or internalize what they should believe, reproducing those beliefs in their written work" (p. 31). Ritter posited that rather than treating plagiarism as a crime, we are better served to examine the paper mill and its rhetorical strategies in order to reveal the extent to which the purchase of a paper is a bad bargain.

The plagiarism question cannot be answered through better and better definitions of the term. As Moore Howard (1995) and others have shown, the term is tasked to define and organize too much at the level of the student, and, as Martin (1994) argued, too little at the level of the administrator or other high profile utilizer of text. As the search technologies of Google and plagiarism-detection programs and processes make it ever more possible to find the convergences—deliberate, inadvertent, and otherwise—of textual similarity, we can see that the problem of plagiarism is at least in part a product of the techniques of its discovery. In other words, what we didn't used to know might not have been hurting us as much we now think it must have been.

As a kid at the dinner table, I listened to my dad tell a lot of stories from his work. He was a medical malpractice insurance adjuster, with a perhaps twisted sense of humor. He'd tell these really gruesome stories of medical accidents—the man with gangrene in his right leg whose left was amputated and so on. For years he collected what he called "humorous incidents," and kept the documents and notes in a manila folder. One involved a naked man, a leaking kitchen sink pipe, and a playful cat—the inadvertent image of the ball being batted funny to all but the cat's victim. One year, my dad came home to tell us that his file had gone missing. It was sad but momentary—in its own perverse way just another humorous incident—until the day about 7 years later when my sister arrived at the house with a book called *Humorous Incidents*, made up of my dad's humorous incident file purportedly authored by a man my dad had worked with years earlier. Of course my dad was annoyed. I suppose this had ceased to be merely a humorous incident, but my dad wasn't sure what to do and ultimately did nothing.

 I guess I could say that this was an instance of plagiarism—though I confess I'm not sure that it really was. It seems to me that something wrong had happened, but my dad did not write the incidents; he was just the person who originally put them on the page and brought the documents together. If we think of the manila folder that was the humorous incident file we can think of the crime—if there was one—as the theft of property. But anyone who reads understands the limits of that idea of textual ownership. I could say that this "theft" was close to my friend's use of my work to pass his psychology class at Everett Community College, though there are some obvious differences. He had my consent; in fact, he paid for my consent. Whatever my friend was (plagiarist, slacker), he was also a consumer. He got exactly what he paid for. The guy who stole my father's file, whatever else he might have been, was a thief. Perhaps he was a plagiarist. He could probably be seen to have committed a fraud in presenting those incidents as his own experiences. But if we consider the totality of this process from my dad's collection of events, usually marked by their occurrence as descriptions in "incident reports" submitted to various insurance companies, through the stories he made of those events (and continues to tell to this day) to the placement of "copies" of those incident reports into a manila folder, through the removal of that file from my dad's possession through some clandestine means to an unknown set of events that led to their publication, we can see both plenty of room for dishonest behavior (though perhaps no more dishonest than my friend's and mine in the production of that book report) and room for change, transformation, and possibly even "genuine" authorship. The incidents about which or upon which my Dad built his stories were not themselves the stories.

 Those "incidents" as more or less discrete ontological events, were in fact available to anyone as the means of making a story. Any reading of the incident reports would include facts—for instance, the free-swinging genitalia of the naked plumber—but not the enabling context, the story, or the acts of compilation and authorship that made humor of those incidents. It is not clear to me that those incidents, collected in a folder and kept in a filing cabinet, constituted property that could really be stolen in the way that you could steal a hundred dollars. But, at the same time, I'm also pretty sure that there is a significant way in which my dad was the author of his humorous incident file. I'm certain that he is the author of the stories he makes of those incidents. I might even say that in some way he is made by those stories, or at least the guy I know as my dad is made of those and hundreds of other stories that he and I tell about him. But that guy—my dad—remains intact after the humorous incident file is stolen. Indeed, the theft of the file becomes yet another humorous incident in its own way. Perhaps there is no less postmodern guy than my dad, by which I mean no one who seems less like an amalgam of others. Yet, as my dad's own appropriation of other's reports to make his stories seems to suggest, his own authorship of the humorous incident file is at best dependent on the narratives of others; our ability to make of the stories solitary meanings attached to solitary authors comes to an end. As the actual insignificance of the theft of my dad's humorous incident file shows, my dad's ability to own, to tell, to compile, to publish, and to author all of those stories isn't stolen. They aren't taken from him when the file is. It might be argued that something else—credit, money, whatever—is, but my dad isn't truly diminished by that.

Malcolm Gladwell (2004) noticed the ways in which plagiarism can actually benefit its victim. In writing about the plagiarism case of Bryony Lavery and her play *Frozen*, Gladwell reported that when he read her play—which included lines taken directly from an essay he had written—and faxed her a letter objecting to her theft, he felt that

> Almost as soon as I'd sent the letter, though, I began to have second thoughts. The truth was that, although I said I'd been robbed, I didn't feel that way. Nor did I feel particularly angry. One of the first things I had said to a friend after hearing about echoes of my article in Frozen was that this was the only way I was ever going to get to Broadway—and I was only half joking. On some level, I considered Lavery's borrowing to be a compliment. A savvier writer would have changed all those references to Lewis, and rewritten the quotes from me, so that their origin was no longer recognizable. (p. 41)

Gladwell suggested that his own "aura" is actually enhanced by Lavery's "borrowings." He noticed, too, the ways in which Lavery's uncomplicated taking of his text might have been "complicated" by a savvier writer, which suggests exactly the difficulty of some of our students' plagiarisms. Example after example of plagiarisms that I have encountered in composition and literature classes display just the lack of sophistication that Gladwell noticed in Lavery's borrowings. Papers downloaded from the Internet and turned in with the URL still displayed on the corner of the page, papers submitted with the names of authors who are not students in the class, and papers with class names and numbers that are not those of the class for which the work is submitted are just the grossest of these examples, but so too are examples that come much closer to Moore Howard's (1995) patchwriting.

About two thirds of the way through her "Sexuality, Textuality, The Cultural Work of Plagiarism," Moore Howard (2000) admitted, "I don't like cheating. I'm mad when I discover that a paper has been ghostwritten. I don't think teachers should look the other way" (p. 487). These three sentences—offered almost in staccato, in a paragraph of their own—can be imagined by anyone who has encountered or engaged the academic discourse of the plagiarist. I can imagine Howard replying to a colleague as she makes her argument for the pedagogical utility of patchwriting or argues that the student who failed to provide adequate citation to his paper was not a cheater but misguided. I can imagine the anxiety of Moore Howard's response as she types into Google or some other search engine the suspicious sentences from some unnamed student's work only to find that work exists in a prehistory that is more than, or different from, the postmodern "death of the author." The line is not just the theoretical result of the student/author/non-author's situation or situatedness in a discourse, but also, and perhaps more (most?) importantly a line written by someone else.

Elaine Whitaker (2001), for example, responded to Moore Howard in *College English*, noting that, "for Howard, plagiarism is a purple cow—something you don't expect to see and don't wish to be. To me, nullifying the term is a form of erasure. I think we need a collective noun that will allow us to label all of the forms of textual appropriation that are likely to get our students in trouble with us or with others" (p. 374). Jonathan Malesic (2006) argued: "I believe in relentlessly exercising my students' critical abilities, but I also believe in punishing plagiarism. A student who plagiarizes refuses to be educated. There shouldn't be room in my classroom for that kind of student. Indeed, that person is not really a student at all" (p. C 3). Maybe we could say that Malesic and Whitaker represent one side of the contemporary debate over plagiarism. They are pretty much untroubled by the postmodern critique of the author, by any of the fancy semantical games that I or anyone might play in relation to the possibility of an origin from which to copy, and are pretty sure that they know plagiarism when they see it.

Moore Howard's reply—she doesn't like cheating and she is capable of anger—expresses both the ambiguity and the anxiety that any discussion of plagiarism generates. Despite my certainty that plagiarism is a complex issue that cannot be separated from other issues of academic (and even personal) honesty, I don't like plagiarism either. I too have had the vertiginous moment of realization—"I don't think this paper was written by this student." In a movie I admire called *The Year of Living Dangerously*, the character Billy Kwan asks "what then must we do?" He quotes his source as a text of Tolstoy's I don't know. If we don't like plagiarism but we aren't sure how to define it—what then must we do?

Since I began teaching composition as a graduate student I've been engaged in the job of ferreting out the plagiarist. For a long time that was a pretty clear mandate. The first "plagiarism" I dealt with was simple. I was teaching a freshman writing class and two students in the same class turned in the same paper—word for word. Like Moore Howard, I can get mad even now thinking about it. Neither student confessed—not even when confronted with the (was it truly?) shocking evidence of two identical papers, one with one name on it, and the other with another name. I suppose that I can infer that one or both of those students had framed a dishonest intent. Apparently one of them had copied the other and the copier would seem to have been the guilty party. But which one was it? Both students maintained their innocence.

In the late 1970s the artist Sherrie Levine began to engage in a form of postmodern art known variously as appropriation, plagiarism, or rephotography. In a well-known series of photographs, she reproduced nude photos of Edward Weston's son Neil. She displayed these works under the title "After Edward Weston." To examine the ways in which a consideration of Levine might speak to or about plagiarism in the comp class, I quote at length from Courtney Colbert (2005), a student who describes the "scene" of Levine's "crime" or intervention, or plagiarism, or forgery, or theft:

> In 1977, the Witkin Gallery in New York bought original Edward Weston photographic negatives from his son Neil Weston. They then commissioned artist/photographer George A. Tice to make new prints from some of those negatives for a collection that the gallery was going to show/publish. Tice was already a well-established artist at the time and had many pieces of his work in permanent collections throughout the

country. He went ahead and reprinted the negatives and had this to say about the process; "I'm not in business as a printer. I take an image and I make it an art object. I memorize it. It becomes mine." It is important to note that a lot goes into reprinting negatives beyond simply skill in photographic printing. A person reprinting photographs has the opportunity to embellish and interpret the negative in any way they please. In this way, Tice was able to do things in the printing process that might not have been done in the same fashion (or done at all for that matter) had Edward Weston done the printing himself. The Witkin Gallery had a series of large posters made to promote the publication and featured six of the reprinted negatives. An artist named Sherrie Levine rephotographed the prints featured in the poster and placed them in a show under the idea that they were her photographs… her art. The ideas inherent in most acts of appropriation in art fall along the lines of challenging originality within art. Levine made sure to emphasize this by giving the work the title, "After Edward Weston." This act of appropriation brought a lot of attention to Levine and her work. In fact, George Tice attacked Levine under the charges that he was a victim of copyright infringement and that Levine should be shunned for her "forgeries." The prints Levine made were not identical to the ones printed by Tice. Her reproductions of the photographs from the poster were changed subtlety in size and clarity (due to the fact that they were photographed from a mass produced poster).

Rosalind Krauss (1985) analyzed Levine's copies, and stated that Levine's work "seems most radically to question the concept of origin and with it the notion of originality. Levine's medium is the pirated print, as in the series of photographs she made by taking images by Edward Weston of his young son Neil, and simply rephotographing them, in violation of Weston's copyright" (p. 168). Krauss's point—that there can be no true original—is one made again and again in postmodern criticism: for instance, in Derrida's critique of origin and in Foucault's "death of the author." An original, whether in words, picture, or photographs, has never been and never will be seen has become a critical orthodoxy in both composition and literary studies.

Indeed, that critique of origin is one pole of Moore Howard's (1995) claim that we can no longer see patchwriting or other forms of collaborative writing as plagiarism because this view of plagiarism derives from a notion of the singular and original author. Although I find the critique of origin compelling, I'm concerned that Moore Howard's (2000) solution to this problem is to appeal to authorial intention: "The comprehensive term plagiarism asserts a unity among disparate textual practices; it often differentiates intentional and unintentional violations but derives these judgments from features of the text, not from actual author's intentions. It asserts a moral basis for textual phenomenon that are a function of reading comprehension and community membership, not ethics" (p. 474). I suggest that Moore Howard's claim that authorial intention can simply be known smuggles the unitary romantic author back into the discussion of plagiarism. If we could simply untangle authorial intention, then the issue of plagiarism, which is the problem of its definition, would already be solved. The author differentiated from all of his or her sources, either does—or perhaps more often does not—respect, acknowledge, and cite the necessary sources and is thus a plagiarist. But the problem of the author, as Foucault inquires, is precisely this problem of relation, priority, and so forth. It is one aspect of that problem that Levine foregrounded through her "interventions." Don Keefer (1991) described defenses of Levin's work, noting that Rosalind Krauss (1985)

> tells us that Levine's activity is no more parasitic than Weston's. He after all, Krauss concludes, was borrowing the classic forms of order and representation of the past. Moreover, Weston with his camera produced an image, or copy, of something that had been constructed. Levine, therefore, reveals to us, that her copy is no more than a copy of a copy.

As Levine's work makes clear, the appeal to "authorial intention" can't produce what Moore Howard and others seem to desire, which is a plagiarism policy grounded in what the author meant to do. To do so is simply to reinstitute the idea of a single unitary author, an original, if you will, who can frame the intent to deceive and produce a forgery. The most difficult aspect of identifying "intent" in the way Moore Howard (2000) suggested is that the "text" of that intent remains frustratingly unavailable. Although I often suspect that my students are not sophisticated plagiarists in the way of Sherrie Levine and others, that suspicion remains grounded in instincts that seem to defy definition.

In this description of Levine's "forgeries," her work, Weston's work, and Tice's work can be seen to illuminate the problems of the plagiarized essay encountered in almost any of our classes. Although Tice apparently called Levine's works "forgeries," I think this is one conclusion we can agree not to draw. Whether Levine's work is legitimate—that is, proper, moral, and acceptable—as art is either (or perhaps both) an aesthetic and a political question is not simply a question of her intentions, which are no doubt complex. I think it is clear that Levine's work calls into question the idea of a forgery just as it calls into question the idea of an original. By calling this and other works "After," Levine highlighted the relation her work has to a source; and, in doing so (and in other ways), it does not efface the source. At some level, her work actively depends upon that source. For Levine's work to be a "forgery," she would have to have endeavored to obstruct our recognition of the relation of her work to Weston's. By calling her work "After," she declines to do that. On the other hand, her relationship to Tice does seem somewhat problematic. She does not call her work "after Weston through Tice" or some other clumsy homage to both the photographer and the printer. Tice's claims to an artistic role in the production of the Weston photos are effaced by Levine's "intervention." But of course that effacement is licensed by our understanding of the nature of the photograph as something taken "in the field" and then "developed" by a technician. I doubt if many of us credit the woman who staffs the photo center down at the Rite Aid when we show our photos. And while Levine's failure (or omission) to credit Tice certainly erases his artistic role in the creation of the Weston prints, that erasure is licensed by practice.

My own first encounter with Levine's works resulted in my asking the question "what can be photographed?" And perhaps this question can help us think about what kinds of writing we can or will allow in our classes. What makes Levine's photo of another photo unacceptable? In general, I think most of us would say that almost anything can be photographed—our dog, coffee table, son or daughter, our parents, our houses, our friends, cars, books. The list is truly endless and the dissemination of these photos is ubiquitous with smart phones and Web 2.0 technologies.

On the wall of my office is the photograph of a picturesque lighthouse just outside the coast town of Bandon, Oregon. Although the photo is "original," my wife took it with her new digital camera and I printed a copy on my digital printer, bought a two dollar frame and hung the picture on the wall to remind me—all pathos and sentimentality—of the beautiful and borrowed summer that my family spent with my mother just months ago. In another way the photo is nothing but a cliché—absolutely conventional and unoriginal—all pathos and sentimentality. The lighthouse in the background of a conventional beach shot—the stuff of dollar post cards in beach shops up and down both coasts. To think about plagiarism and forgery at all, we have to engage the question or the differentiation of the enterprise of the writing class. What do we want to have happen? The "badness" of my wife's photo (or perhaps its goodness, when seen from the angle of my mother's recovery) cannot be separated or understood except in terms of its associations, which are not simply the intentions of the photographer or the viewer, but the unspeakable threshold upon which they meet.

In a *New Yorker* article, Gladwell (2004), himself the "victim" of a high-profile plagiarism, asked whether or not a charge of plagiarism should ruin one's life. His conclusion is a sort of qualified "no." His essay is an illuminating take on a plagiarism case that seems somehow more real than the plagiarisms we may be called on to deal with in our classes, if only because it happens outside the cloistered walls of the academy. Gladwell asked one of the central questions of any conversation on the subject of the plagiarist: "So is it true that words belong to the person who wrote them, just as other kinds of property belong to their owners? Actually no" (p. 44). This is merely the linguistic version of the question Levine seems to force upon us: To whom does the object photographed belong? To whom and under what circumstances can words be said to belong to someone? Can we really say that once a picture has been taken that picture becomes an object outside the realm of the photographable? This question becomes even more vexed when we think of the nature of language as a shared medium. If we do not all "own" the words, then the words themselves are worthless. In fact, to the almost exact extent that we "own" a single word, that word will become without value either to us or to anyone. The precondition of writing is the shared vocabulary, the fact that we are all in language together.

Perhaps inevitably, I, too, have become a collector of incidents however unhumorous—of appropriation, theft, plagiarism, art—whatever we can agree to call these textual "events." Although the convergence of Levine's photos and my students downloaded papers is apparent to me—I mean I can see that although my students might (or at least theoretically might not) lack Levine's self-consciousness—the accusation that Levine faced had its source in exactly the feelings that I had when my students turned in another's work as their own.

I got a paper last week that referred to a play by John Van Brugh that we had not read in my class. In fact, it was a play I had never read and the paper compared *The Country Wife* (which we had read) to this Van Brugh play. Right away I knew that the student had "copied" his paper, though I could not find its source. I know he did something wrong, even if I'm not sure what name to give it.

I am pretty sure that Levine is doing something different than my student who downloads a paper except when I am not sure at all. In addition to my collections of student plagiarisms, I've recently begun to work on another collection—texts that explore various contemporary plagiarisms. It would not be hard for me to delineate dozens, maybe more than dozens, of vexed examples of textual "borrowing." Jonathan Lethem's (2007) "The Ecstasy of Influence" is just such a catalog, meditation, collage, or plagiarism. Lethem's essay confronts, even transforms, the conversation about plagiarism. In the essay, subtitled, "A Plagiarism," Lethem appropriates and arranges, twists and transforms, the works of others to foreground the ways in which all writing is derived from, owes its origins, meanings, and significances to the ways in which it engages texts that belong *and* don't belong to each and all of us. Lethem ends the essay:

> Any text is woven entirely with citations, references, echoes, cultural languages, which cut across it through and through in a vast stereophony. The citations that go to make up a text are anonymous, untraceable, and yet *already read*; they are quotations without inverted commas. The kernel, the soul—let us go further and say the substance, the bulk, the actual and valuable material of all human utterances—is plagiarism. For substantially all ideas are secondhand, consciously and unconsciously drawn from a million outside sources, and daily used by the garnerer with a pride and satisfaction born of the superstition that he originated them; whereas there is not a rag of originality about them anywhere except the little discoloration they get from his mental and moral caliber and his temperament, and which is revealed in characteristics of phrasing. Old and new make the warp and woof of every moment. There is no thread that is not a twist of these two strands. By necessity, by proclivity, and by delight, we all quote. (p. 68)

On his Web site, Lethem has provided groups of his own texts as the basis for the texts of others. In essence, he has renounced his copyright/write and offered what he calls the "promiscuous materials" project. On the Web site, he writes "I recently explored some of these ideas in an essay for *Harper's Magazine*. As I researched that essay I came more and more to believe that artists should ideally find ways to make material free and available for reuse. This project is a (first) attempt to make my own art practice reflect that belief."

Lethem's promiscuous materials, Levine's rephotographs, Robillard and Fortune's (2007) examination of fraud and forgery, and Ritter's (2006) focus on the rhetoric of the paper mill begin to suggest some ways in which we might engage the question of plagiarism without simply viewing plagiarism as a crime with a catalog of possible punishments. Rather than simply submit to the impossibility or impermissibility of claiming some single, stable author of our students' papers and therefore abandoning the category of plagiarism as something against which, however tentatively we may choose to stand, we can choose rather to embrace a discourse which includes an awareness of plagiarism as a foundation or a beginning.

In conclusion, I'd like to suggest that as teachers we engage Lethem's promiscuity—that we highlight and foreground the extent to which all writing is "plagiarized." I confess that I do not know if we can do this and cope with students who refuse to engage the honor of this promiscuity. But I prefer that risk to the risk that we surrender our role as teachers to our role as policemen, gatekeepers, or keepers of the cultural heritage of the west or the United States. Perhaps all of our students will not be Lethem or Levine. But I suggest that if we engage the best of our students rather than using the Internet and plagiarism-detection programs to investigate our students in the mistaken belief that this somehow helps them, we will be far better able to impact the reality of our student's integrity than any honor code or plagiarism policy can make us.

REFERENCES

Colbert, Courtney. (2005). *Appropriation and reprinting: Separated at birth?* http://www.cfa.arizona.edu/are476/files/puzz05.htm

Derringer, Nancy N. (2008, March 3). *Gone in 60 seconds: How my blog started the avalanche that buried presidential aide Tim Goeglein. Slate.* http://www.slate.com/id/2185657

Foucault, Michel. (1984). What is an author? *Foucault: A reader* (pp. 101-120). (Paul Rabinow, Trans.) New York: Pantheon.

Gladwell, Malcolm. (2004, November 22). Something borrowed: Should a charge of plagiarism ruin your life? *New Yorker, 80(36)*, 40-48.

Keefer, Donald. (1991, March 16). The rebellion of art/the art of rebellion. http://students.risd.edu/faculty/dkeefer/web/rebel.htm

Krauss, Rosalind. (1985). *The originality of the avant garde and other modernist myths.* Cambridge: MIT Press.

Lethem, Jonathan. (2007, January 31). The ecstasy of influence: A plagiarism. *Harpers,* pp. 59-71.

Lethem, Jonathan. The ego is remarkably quiet in the glove compartment. http://www.jonathanlethem.com/promiscuous_materials.html

Malesic, Jonathan. (2006, December 11). How dumb do they think we are? *Chronicle of Higher Education*, 53(17), C 3.

Martin, Brian. (1994). Plagiarism: A misplaced emphasis. *Journal of Information Ethics, 3(2)*, 36-47.

Moore Howard, Rebecca. (2001, November 16). Forget about policing plagiarism: Just teach. *Chronicle of Higher Education,* p. B 24.

Moore Howard, Rebecca. (1995). Plagiarisms, authorship, and the academic death penalty. *College English, 57(7)*, 788-807.

Moore Howard, Rebecca. (2000). Sexuality, textuality: The cultural work of plagiarism. *College English, 62(4),* 473-491.

Plagiarism Stoppers. http://plagiarismstoppers.com

Plagiarized.com. http://www.plagiarized.com

Ritter, Kelly. (2006). Buying in, selling short: A pedagogy against the rhetoric of online paper mills. *Pedagogy: Critical Approaches to Teaching Literature, Language, Composition, and Culture, 6(1)* 25-51.

Robillard, Amy E., & Fortune, Ron. (2007). Toward a new content for writing courses: Literary forgery, plagiarism, and the production of belief. *Journal of Advanced Composition, 27(1-2)* 183-206.

Scanlon, Patrick & Neumann, David. (2002). Internet plagiarism among college students. *Journal of College Student Development, 43(3),* 374-385.

Whitaker, Elaine. (2001, January). A comment on "Sexuality, Textuality: The Cultural Work of Plagiarism." *College English, 63(3)* 373-375.

3 AUTHORING ACADEMIC AGENCY: CHARTING THE TENSIONS BETWEEN WORK-FOR-HIRE UNIVERSITY COPYRIGHT POLICIES

Timothy R. Amidon

> "Writing... occurs within a matrix of local and more global policies, standards, and practices. These variables often emerge as visible and at times invisible statements about what types of work are possible and valuable (encoded, often, in curricula, assessment guidelines, standards, and policies)."
>
> DeVoss, Cushman, & Grabill, 2005, p. 16

For the better part of two decades now, writing and technical communication specialists have engaged in a spirited discussion about, as Andrea Lunsford and Susan West (1996) described it, "the question of who owns language" (p. 383). Taking seriously Lunsford and West's call to action, writing and technical communication specialists have problematized the intersections of authorship, intellectual property, and copyright. The substantive body of research dedicated to topics such as plagiarism (DeVoss & Rosati, 2002; Johnson-Eilola &

Selber, 2007; Moore Howard, 2007; Valentine, 2006), the commodification of texts and authors (Lunsford, 1999; Ritter, 2005; Selfe & Selfe, 1994), the ethics of collaboration (DeVoss & Porter, 2006; Ede & Lunsford, 2001), and the ways in which federal law affects writing and communication (DeVoss, McKee, & Porter, 2008; Herrington, 199a, 199b, 2003; Reyman, 2006; Rife, 2008) illustrates that writing and technical communication specialists have not only concerned themselves with addressing *who* owns language, but also the *when, where, why, what,* and *how* of the matter.

This chapter, then, is situated within an already rich conversation. Adding to that conversation, I argue that academic authors—tenured and non-tenured faculty, instructional staff, research and teaching assistants, and graduate and undergraduate students—are positioned "within a matrix of local and global policies, standards, and practices" that seeks to determine their relationship to the ownership of scholarly products (DeVoss et al., 2005, p. 16). More specifically, I examine the ways that Title 17 of the United States Code and university policies associated with copyright affect the work possible within academic contexts.

Throughout the chapter, I offer a narrative account of the types of challenges I encountered when licensing a thesis for a Master of Arts under a Creative Commons License. At times, I weave in scholarship that either seeks to inform the types of specific challenges I faced or scholarship that provides an entry point into the more technical aspects of copyright and/or institutional IP policy. I also offer the findings and implications of a qualitative study that investigated how 14 academic institutions approach the ownership of copyrightable texts. In extending this research, I hope to demonstrate how various policies and agents coalesce, affecting how agency is constructed within the distributed forms of authorship unique to academic contexts. More simply, I seek to understand how tensions between copyright policy and copyright law can be approached as sites of fissure where academic authors might exert agency to redefine how universities construct and maintain relationships with academic authors through policy.

A NARRATIVE ON DISTRIBUTED AGENCY AND TEXTUAL GENERATION

The thesis I composed as a requirement for the Masters of Arts in English at Indiana University-Purdue University, Fort Wayne (IPFW), is unlike most other M.A. theses—well, at least those at IPFW. That thesis, *Institutional Authors, Institutional Texts? An Analysis of the Intellectual Property Polices Pro-*

mulgated at IPFW and Its Peer Institutions carries a Creative Commons (CC) Attribution 3.0 License. It—if one reads policy literally—shouldn't. The standard formatting requirements of "A Guide to the Preparation of Theses and Dissertations" (2007) explain that the copyright page should contain the symbol for copyright, "©", my name, the year of submission, and the language "All Rights Reserved." Mine doesn't; my copyright page is improperly formatted. If you were to cruise over to the English Department Office at IPFW, pick up my thesis, and turn to its copyright page, you would find that the page proudly displays the Creative Commons (CC) by attribution logo, my name, the year of submission, and the language "Licensed Under a Creative Commons Attribution 3.0 License ... Some Rights Reserved" (Amidon, 2007, p. iii). Those formatting deviations are deceptive little buggers; they won't reveal the intensive process that enabled them. I, however, will.

But before I get to the crux of that story, it is important that I stress what is offered is *one* story. Certainly, it is *an* account of how agency might be constructed in academic contexts. As such, I wish to make clear that I am not presenting grand claims about agency, but rather a story representative of a specific place in time and space—a story about the discursive flows of a deliberative process that involved members of a thesis committee, agents acting on behalf of IPFW, policies and texts local to that institution, copyright law, and myself. It is, as they say, a pretty mundane tale, and it of course involves two equally mundane arguments: standards and formats are not rigid, but flexible, and veering from standards and guidelines is often the result of a collaborative act, or as Stuart Blythe (2007) told us, "individuals seldom act autonomously" (p. 183). As the epigraph to this chapter holds, authorial decisions (in other words, agency)—and the textual artifacts that evidence them—often obscure the full complexity of processes, agents, and artifacts that lead to their production.

The vantage point and framework I employ within this chapter, especially as it relates to agency, is not my own. It derives largely from James E. Porter, Patricia Sullivan, Stuart Blythe, Jeffrey Grabill, and Libby Miles' (2000) "Institutional Critique: A Rhetorical Methodology for Change" and Blythe's (2007) "Agencies, Ecologies, and The Mundane Artifacts in Our Midst." Blythe expanded on the nuanced conceptualizations of institutional agency offered in "Institutional Critique," arguing that writing and agency "are best understood ... by identify[ing] and relat[ing]" variables (p. 183). Stuart Selber (2009) also offered his understanding of this perspective towards agency, describing a framework "not so much about defining but positioning. Researchers who employ its techniques are interested in relative weightings and interpretations" (p. 14). As Selber lucidly explained, the type of agency Porter et al. envisioned is one already implicated within a complex interplay of "contexts and constituent parts (including operating procedures and working conditions)" where actors "acknowledge their own involvements and commitments" (p. 13). Agency for all of these scholars, then, is about working rhetorically *within* the parameters of a system, instead of fighting for change from the outside.

This was the case as I worked toward deviating from the formatting standards set forth for theses at IPFW. Deviating from those standards—that is, utilizing a CC license, instead of copyrighting my thesis—meant working within a community that consisted of the members of my thesis committee. And, like other academic communities, we worked in contexts where local documents and institutional policies defined the parameters of our productive efforts. Yet, as I learned, local communities are also often subject to more global documents and policies (e.g., Title 17 of U.S.C.) that also set parameters for productive efforts.

As a graduate student of English operating within a graduate program at IPFW, "I" composed a thesis to which a number of institutional agents and institutional texts converged to give shape. Through completing institutional forms; garnering signatures; organizing committee members; authoring proposals; meeting formally and informally with agents of the university (e.g., the department chair, the director of graduate program, and the members of my committee); reading and creating memos, notes, and emails; conducting and synthesizing research; examining and understanding institutional policies; and, finally, by writing in the more traditional sense, "I" composed a thesis. This statement is indicative of the type of agency I sketched above.

Moreover, my case demonstrates what Blythe (2007) called "the paradox of agency" (p. 173)—a form of agency gained "not by being an autonomous individual, but by being part of something larger, by being a part of systems that constrain and enable simultaneously" (p. 173). There were many junctures where agency was exerted. I encountered the paradox of agency because, as the production of the thesis progressed, agency was distributed among numerous members who made up the local community I was situated within, and we commonly turned to local and global texts to guide our actions. Many texts and many people constrained and enabled our efforts, but ultimately they were all influential (in the positive sense) in helping me produce a thesis.

For the purposes of brevity, I touch upon four texts and four agents that, most notably, did the constraining and enabling: The texts include Title 17 of U.S.C., the *Purdue University Faculty and Staff Handbook: 2005-2006*, Indiana University's "A Guide to the Preparation of Theses and Dissertations" (2007), and TyAnna Herrington's (2003) *A Legal Primer for the Digital Age*. The human actors (in the Latourian sense) involved were the three members of my thesis committee and myself. In retrospect, I now find it somewhat profound that my name on the thesis cover suggests sole authorship.

Given that, I wonder whether or not agency—in terms of writing—is synonymous with or inextricable from solitary notions of authorship. If not, how do we reconcile how ownership does or should relate to the types of more distributed understandings of agency and authorship emerging in disciplinary scholarship? It is my hope that this chapter convinces readers that these are the types of questions we in writing and technical communication should be asking.

THE NEBULOUS ORIGINS OF A RESEARCH PROJECT

It is difficult for me to determine what precipitating moment sparked my interest in questions of authorship and ownership and the complex spaces in which they exist. In a certain respect, my thesis research began before I was aware of it. In a graduate class on multimodal composition, the professor gave a lecture on open-source and free-source code, licensing, and publishing. That lecture sold me on the fact that the principles upon which open-source and free-source software, licensing, and publishing are built—cooperation, freedom, sustainability, and sharing—were principles I was concerned about (see Galin, this volume). I knew that I wanted to contribute to those principles. And I knew I could: I was a graduate student, and I had to write a pretty labor-intensive document (that is, an M.A. thesis), so I wanted that text to mean something. I also wanted to share it with others. I wished to produce a text that would be of institutional value (i.e., meet the university's requirements for theses) so I could graduate, but I also wished to create something of use to others. What I wanted to do, ultimately, was put a Creative Commons License on a text, and if it happened to be a totally awesome thesis, well, that would be good too.

I wasn't sure if I had the agency to make the licensing choice, so I did what other people do in these types of circumstances: I sought the assistance of the appropriate institutional agent. Oddly enough, the person who knew the most about copyright was also the chair of my thesis committee and the interim chair of the department. I went to his office with a list of topics I was interested in exploring in the thesis and asked if I could put a CC license on my thesis. I have a sense that, on first impression, he thought the timing of the question was kind of funny. It was as if he was thinking, "what does it matter at this point? Write the thing first, and we'll worry about the formatting issues later."

Having reflected on that moment, I realize that I had thought of the question as a document-shaping decision: If my thesis could be shared more openly with others, I would care about it more. I mean, honestly, how compelling is writing a document that takes up so much time when only four or five people are likely to read it? I'm serious. As a student who struggled through my freshman year of college and now has a strong background in rhetoric and composition scholarship, I think it is obvious that students enabled to create viable audiences and strong writerly motivation produce better quality work. As Dànielle Nicole DeVoss and James Porter (2006) put it,

> people write because they want to interact, to share, to learn, to play and to help others. They engage others for connection, compatibility, love, sex, desire, self-fulfillment (or egomania), the thirst for justice, the thirst for freedom, out of boredom, out of need for interaction, to make their lives more comfortable, and yes, they engage others for money, which they need to survive. (p. 203)

After a bit of discussion, my professor's interest was sparked too. He did what other people do in these types of circumstances: He turned to his shelves, located the *Purdue University Faculty and Staff Handbook: 2005–2006*, opened the index to find "copyright," and then turned to the appropriate page.[1] He read the passage on copyright, looked quizzically at me, and passed the book to me. I read:

> The University shall own all domestic and foreign rights in and to any and all inventions and materials made or developed by University personnel either in the course of employment by the University or through the use of facilities or funds provided by or through the University. [...] Materials, whether written or recorded, shall be considered as having been developed in the course of employment in those cases where the individual was employed by the University for the specific purpose of preparing or producing the materials or was specifically directed to do so as a part of his or her duties. The rights owned by the University include all economic and property rights as well as the right to patent inventions and copyright materials. In accordance with custom established in institutions of higher education, copyright ownership of textbooks and manuscripts prepared at the author's initiative for classroom, educational, or professional purposes, including all royalties from publication or distribution of such materials, belong to the author except when the material is prepared as an assigned project and/or University

facilities or resources were used, in which case these materials shall be University property, as described above. (pp. 55-56)

In turn, we each discussed portions of the policy that seemed ambiguous and contradictory. The text had failed to clarify how the institution would approach this type of action. Rather than clamping down on the idea (the too common institutional approach to problem solving), my chair suggested that I contact two scholars from our field more versed in issues of copyright. I emailed the two professors a copy of Purdue's policy, and asked if they thought I had the agency to license my thesis under a CC license. One suggested that doing so may have consequences, such as having to write another thesis if the thesis was not accepted. The other suggested I pose the question at the 2007 Conference on College Composition and Communication Intellectual Property Caucus (CCCC- IP) meeting. Unfortunately, I had to wait to ask that question, but in the meantime I was accepted to attend the 2006 Digital Media and Composition Institute (DMAC) at Ohio State University.

At that institute, a multimodal presentation by DeVoss, McKee, and Porter (2006) expanded the underdeveloped notions of copyright and IP that I had at the time. I came to understand that IP, copyright, and work-for-hire are wickedly complex conceptual entities. Prior to that institute, I had little understanding about my rights as an author. Prior to that, though, I had not had any reason to want to know about those rights. I took an important lesson home with me from DMAC: If the chair of my committee did not know if I had the right to utilize a CC license, and if other students didn't know if I had that right, it was likely that others encountered the same difficulty. The curiosity stemming from that lack of knowledge led me to an appropriate research question for my thesis: How do IPFW and its peer institutions approach copyrightable IP created by university authors? I knew by the time I was finished conducting the research I would be closer to having an answer to my about licensing the thesis through Creative Commons.

RELATING TEXTS: SITUATING HOW TEXTS SHAPE TEXTS

Up to this point in the chapter, my aim has been to argue that a number of agents and texts influence the composition of a text in educational contexts, focusing on the discipline of writing. But what mundane texts influence textual generation in these contexts? As Blythe (2007) posited, they are "documents that set parameters for our labor and for the labor of those who work with us—including secretaries, students, editors, and so on" (p. 181). Think about the influence an assignment sheet has upon how a student approaches an assignment; think about institutional policies like the excerpt provided earlier from the *Purdue Faculty and Staff Handbook*; think about documents like IU's "A Guide to the Preparation of Theses and Dissertations"; and think about texts that have the power of law behind them, like Title 17. I now delve deeper into how those "mundane" texts influenced the production of my thesis. As I began my research into how IPFW and its peer institutions approach copyrightable IP created by university authors, I encountered a number of difficulties.

First, I had to determine which universities were IPFW's peer institutions, and although this should have been relatively easy, in practice it was not. The administrative assistant I was directed to ask was somewhat reluctant to hand over the document containing that information. The document was for faculty; I was a graduate student and may not have been authorized to ask for such a document. She acted, in my assessment, quite appropriately. So, I talked to the chair of my thesis committee who, in turn, procured a copy of *IPFW's Strategies for Excellence: The Strategic Plan 2001-2006*. The document detailed 13 institutions with similar missions and identities (see Table 1).

Table 1. IPFW's Peer Institutions and Identifying Acronyms.

Institution	Identifying acronym
Boise State University	BSU
Cleveland State University	CSU
CUNY—College of Staten Island	CSI
Northern Kentucky University	NKU
Oakland University	OU
Portland State University	PSU
University of Central Oklahoma	UCO
University of Nebraska–Omaha	UN
University of New Orleans	UNO
University of Texas–El Paso	UTEP
Wichita State University	WSU
Wright State University	WS
Youngstown State University	YSU

Second, while collecting the respective policies dealing with copyrightable IP (all but one were available publicly online, and links to each are included in the references at the end of this chapter), I found that like IPFW (which follows Purdue's policy mandates in most instances), UTEP, UNO, UN, and CSI are governed via policy through the larger institutional systems of which they are a part. This finding posed a difficulty, because it excluded the ability to make claims or trace patterns based on institutional similarities. For example, IPFW and Purdue—while part of the same system—are quite dissimilar in many respects.

Third, I was underprepared to understand aspects of the policy language useful to the study. TyAnna Herrington (1999a, 1999b, 2003) proved invaluable in preparing me to analyze the respective institution's IP policy language.[2] From Herrington's work, I came to understand that copyright law defines four types of circumstances in which texts are authored: independent authorship, work-for-hire, contractual or commissioned, and collaborative. Put simply, U.S. copyright code defines authorship as contingent upon a variety of contextual factors.

Understanding who owns independent, contractual or commissioned, and collaborative works is relatively simple: If an author has not signed a contract to produce work or been commissioned to produce work (which is contractual or commissioned authorship), if an author is not working with another author to produce the work (which is collaborative authorship), and if the work is not work for hire, then the author is creating the work independently.

Work for hire is much more complex. Herrington (1999a) described work for hire as "a legal fiction that makes the author of a work the employer or hiring party who contracted for the work" (p. 129). An author is working under work for hire when two factors are met:

> 1) An author must be found to have produced the work as an employee, determined by a 13-element agency law test, and
> 2) he or she must have produced the work within the scope of employment and have not specifically contracted rights to the work (Herrington, 2003, p. 97)

However, the difficulty with this test is that many scholars do work under the provisions of signed or unsigned contracts, and institutions can and do—as the data I provide later suggests—claim these contracts to be binding. Additionally, Herrington (2003) informed us that work-for-hire relationships are fixed, those involved may negotiate the ownership of copyrights. Moreover, because little case law dealing with work for hire and university authorship exists, courts could find university policies to be binding just because those policies are overly restrictive (in relation to Title 17).[3] Those who work in business contexts, for example, routinely sign over rights to the copyrightable works they create, and it is not unlikely that courts could turn to those cases in making a decision about how work for hire operates in university contexts. Martine Courant Rife (2008) wrote in an essay focused on fair use that

> if our institutions have restrictive guidelines that we disobey, you can bet that the courts will not listen to our pleas when we explain. Judges love to use 'official guidelines' as heuristics for evaluation. Our institutional guidelines will be used, and the courts will tell us that, if we do not approve of the guidelines, we should change them rather than engage in blatant civil disobedience. (p. 152)

Still, as Herrington (1999a) advised, universities "distribute detailed guidelines listing additional criteria to help clarify their own interpretations of the work for hire doctrine, but these guidelines do not peremptorily carry the force of law" (p. 3). Herrington provided Brinson and Radcliff's 13-element agency law test to use in deciding who and what constitutes legal definitions of ownership. It is important for faculty, staff, and students to use these factors to approach policy as judges do—that is, as heuristics for gauging how to determine work-for-hire authorship and not legally supported dicta. Because these factors are important, I include here the 13-element test as found in Herrington (1999b):

1. whether the hiring party had a right to control the manner and means by which the product is accomplished;

2. the level of skill required;

3. whether the instruments and tools used were provided by the hiring party or the hired party;

4. whether the hired party worked at the hiring party's place of business or the hired party's place of business;

5. the duration of the relationship between the two parties;

6. whether the hiring party had the right to assign additional projects to the hired party;

7. the extent of the hired party's discretion over when and how long to work;

8. the method of payment;

9. whether the hired party had a role in hiring and paying assistants;

10. whether the work was part of the regular business of the hiring party;

11. whether the hiring party was doing business;

12. whether employee benefits were provided by the hiring party for the hired party;

13. how the hiring party treated the hired party for tax purposes. (p. 406)

Equally important are two aspects of this test: first, that the Copyright Act of 1909 held the first factor to be the "sole determinant of employment status"; and, second, that the 1976 act holds that the "'totality' of each of these 'factors' is important" in making these types of determinations (Herrington, 1999b, p. 407). In other words, after the introduction of the 1976 act, courts began to approach agency, ownership, and authorship as in a highly situated, highly contextualized way.

The fourth difficulty of the study arose out of the contextual distinctions associated with authorship under work for hire. Before reading and understanding the nuances of Brinson and Radcliffe's 13-point test, I originally believed that authors were the people who created a work. Once I came to realize that work-for-hire authorship complicates traditional notions of authorship, I developed not only a better ability to approach the policies through a legal lens, but also to understand the ways that work for hire relates to the prior discussions of agency and location *apropos* Blythe (2007), Selber (2009), DeVoss et al. (2005), and Porter et al. (2000). Most simply, determining one's "employeeness," and resultantly a text's author, has as much to do with challenging traditional notions of what a worker/author is as it does with the conditions under which the work was created. This poses difficulties for the work performed in writing classrooms for, and with, academic intentions; the work-for-hire doctrine challenges traditional concepts of employees and institutional authors and texts produced in these working environments.

The work-for-hire doctrine seems to suggest that full professors, associate professors, assistant professors, adjunct professors, visiting professors, emeritus faculty, lecturers, fellows, graduate students, undergraduate students, administrative assistants, maintenance personnel, safety and police staff, and even visitors to academic institutions could be viewed as producing works for hire. Herrington (1999b) indicated the problems tied to authoring in nonacademic contexts:

> Work for hire status usually is clear when nonacademic employees create their projects at the employer's work site, using their employer's equipment and supplies, within an ongoing business relationship. But conflict arises when any one factor or any combination of factors is otherwise. Disagreement often arises over whether a work was created within or outside the creator's scope of employment when industry employees create their own work away from their place of employment and on their own time. (p. 130)

However, these disputes are further exacerbated by authoring in academic contexts, where various faculty, staff, and students "work under unique circumstances" (Herrington, 1999a, p. 135). This is due in large part to the fact that "employee status," under the 13-point test, is not easily discernible. Courts may truly be, then, the only decision-makers in how various readings of the test might apply to faculty, students, and staff. It still seems reasonable to warrant that as more of the test's permutations are met a text is more likely to be considered a work for hire and its author an employee.

This has significant implications for the individuals who create texts for and within academic contexts. For instance, the expertise required to produce a literacy narrative, a manuscript for a journal, or a chapter like this varies; moreover, the institutions we write for and within often supply us with access to libraries, computer labs, and writing centers, all of which could be viewed as types of academic instruments and tools. Even more confusing is the variance with which institutions control the manner and means by which the products are produced. If an undergraduate student and an assistant professor compose literacy narratives, the agency test will apply much differently. The agency test will also apply differently if, for example, the professor writes the narrative in his or her respective office on a computer provided by the university while the student writes his or hers at home on a personally owned computer.

Understanding the basics of work for hire seems a good start toward clarifying complexities. However, many of us are not fully versed in the legal complexities associated with U.S. copyright law. My experiences (then and since) suggest that, relatively speaking, few professors and fewer students are aware of how these laws exert a shaping power on how we produce texts. Again, knowing how copyright and work for hire function is important, but approximating how these laws correspond to institutional polices and documents is just as important if we wish to better clarify our ownership claims to texts we produce.

For instance, recall the excerpt from Purdue's IP policy concerning copyrightable texts. As I noted, portions of the policy seemed ambiguous and contradictory. The policy both claimed and disclaimed certain copyrightable works. Why is it that the policy first claimed ownership to "all rights in all materials made or developed by University personnel either in the course employment ... or through use of facilities and funds," but then later disclaimed "ownership of textbooks and manuscripts prepared at the author's initiative" (p. 55)? What this policy fails to account for, acknowledge, or forward to those authoring in and for the institution is that work for hire does make these types of renderings. Simply put, such policies may not necessarily carry the force of law, whereas Title 17 does. PU's policy is problematic in that it does not fully disclose the totality of factors that constitute legal authorship. Rather, the institution works from the position that it owns a controlling interest in all works, but releases control of some. This fails to mesh with the 13-point agency test. Academic institutions cannot determine work for hire status; only courts can do this *legally*. Why, then, does the policy work from this premise?

WHAT DO ACADEMIC COPYRIGHT POLICIES TELL US?

Generally speaking, the policies I collected[4] sought to delineate three aspects: First, who was and was not included within the policy parameters; second, which texts were included or excluded from institutional ownership and control; and, third, when or under what circumstances authors would be creating work that would be considered under university control (i.e., the policies defined how the institution interpreted work for hire). These are the reasons why I, initially, felt that the analyses were less useful: The policies were not in line with the scholarly definitions of work for hire, authorship, and textual ownership with which I was familiar. The policies did not resonate with what I knew about work for hire and copyright. However, this aspect is precisely what made the analyses useful. Simply put, while Herrington's explanations of authorship, textual ownership, and work for hire suggest that Title 17 takes an ecological view that synthesizes the interconnectivity of these concepts, some policies seem to do the opposite.

Policies Delineate Institutional Authors

The institutional policies evidenced six different approaches to defining the types of authors generating texts in academic contexts. The policies also evidenced one wild card group that resists classification into the six otherwise normative approaches:

1. The ambiguous language[5] approach: Institutions used only ambiguous language to define authors (e.g., "originators," "creators").

2. The mixed-language approach: Institutions used both ambiguous and precise language (e.g., "faculty," "adjunct faculty," "emeritus faculty," "undergraduate student").

3. The one-tiered approach: Institutions used precise language situating authors into one category (e.g., "employee").

4. The two-tiered approach: Institutions used precise language situating authors into one of two categories (e.g., either "student" or "staff").

5. The three-tiered approach: Institutions used precise language situating authors into one of three categories (e.g., either "student," "faculty," or "staff").

6. Collective bargaining agreement (CBA) approach: Institutions used precise language situating authors into one category (e.g., "members of the union");

7. Wild card: Institutions used mixed language that suggested others were also subject to the provisions of policies (e.g., "visitors," "users of facilities").

At a general level, these approaches suggest that the institutions make distinctions regarding authorship in two ways: 1) the policies' language evidences that institutions either make authorial distinctions between faculty, staff, student, and/or other types of authors (BSU, CSU, IPFW, UCO, UN, UNO,

UTEP, WSU, WS), or make no authorial distinctions (CSI, NKU, PSU, OU, YSU); 2) the authorial distinctions suggest that policies may vary in applicability based on which type of author is creating a text (BSU, CSU, IPFW, UCO, UN, UNO, UTEP, WSU, WS). That there were at least six types of approaches within 14 institutions demonstrates a wide variance in how institutions approach concepts of institutional authorship (see Table 2).

This variance may suggest that these institutions, more specifically the administrators vested with the responsibility of creating those IP policies, are uncertain as to whom the policies should and should not apply. For instance, whereas a number of policies did not expressly state that policies applied to "faculty" (they used ambiguous language such as "originator," "creator," or "staff"; YSU, WS, WSU, PSU, OU, NKU, IPFW), other institutions used precise language denoting nearly every conceivable type of "faculty" ("postdoctoral fellows," "instructors," "visiting faculty," "adjunct faculty," "emeritus faculty"; UCO, UNO).

Table 2. Approaches to Application of Policies.

Approach	Institutions
Ambiguous language approach	CSI, NKU
Mixed-language approach	IPFW
One-tiered approach	PSU
Two-tiered approach	WS, WSU
Three-tiered approach	BSU, CSU, UCO, UN, UNO, UTEP
Collective bargaining approach	OU, YSU
Wild card	IPFW, UCO, UN, UTEP, WS

Identifying these approaches is important because the 13-factor agency test provided by Herrington (1999a) posited that distinctions cannot be made based solely on who performs the work conducted. The differences associated with the roles and functions performed by the various types of authors creating work will be important in determining if a work is made for hire, but these policy distinctions seem to blur some of the other factors important to determining whether or not a work is made for hire. The most troubling approach is that of PSU; PSU's policy either seems to hold that all institutional authors are "employees" or that "employees" are much different authors than faculty and student authors, but the policy fails to clarify which view it may be taking. Ironically, the works that utilize the terms "creator," "author," or "originator" may be most useful because they insist on the more wholesale renderings homogeneous to work for hire's 13-factor agency test.

Policies Claim and Disclaim Texts

The policies evidenced six different institutional approaches towards claiming work and five approaches toward disclaiming work. Analysis of the policy language also yielded a trend in how the institutions codify types of works: Texts can be independent works (commonly referred to by policies as traditional works), texts can be works made for hire, texts can be contractual works, and works can be those works that make significant use of facilities and/or funds. The conflation of independent works and traditional works problematizes independent works, because traditional works could be approached as works made for hire. This conflation suggests that institutions may not be aware of the 13-point agency law of the work-for-hire doctrine that aids in making these types of distinctions between works produced independently and works produced for hire. The presence of distinctions between works made for hire and works that make significant use of facilities and/or funds suggests that some of these institutions may not understand that uses and significant uses of facilities and/or funds is just one part of the 13-point agency test associated with work for hire. If the policies had subsumed uses and significant uses within works made for hire, and if the policies had included language on collaborative works, the policies would have been closely aligned with the four types of circumstances in which authors generate texts as posited by U.S. copyright law.

Texts policies claim include:

1. All-inclusive approach: Policies claim all works.

2. Catch-and-release approach: Policies claim all works but disclaim others.

3. Claim three–disclaim one approach: Policies explicitly claim works that make use of facilities and/or funds, works made under contract, and works made for hire, but disclaim traditional works.

4. Claim two–disclaim two approach: Policies explicitly claim works that make use of facilities and/or funds and works made under contract but disclaim works made for hire and traditional works.

5. Claim contractual–ignore others approach: Policies claim works made under contract and do not discuss other types of works.

Claim works made for hire-ignore others approach: Policies claim works made for hire but do not discuss other types of works. (See Table 3 for corresponding institutional approaches.)

Table 3. Approaches toward Claiming Work.

Approach	Institutions
All-inclusive approach	PSU
Catch-and-release approach	BSU, CSI, IPFW, WS,UN, UNO UTEP
Claim three–disclaim one approach	CSU, UCO
Claim two–disclaim two approach	NKU
Claim contractual–disclaim others approach	OU
Claim works made for hire-ignore others approach	WSU, YSU

Texts policies disclaim include:

1. Disclaim none approach: Policies disclaim no works.

2. Traditional works approach: Policies disclaim all traditional works.

3. Some traditional works approach A: Policies disclaim traditional works, except those subject to work for hire, but do not discuss use of facilities and/or funds.

4. Some traditional works approach B: Policies disclaim traditional works, except those that make significant use of facilities and/or funds, but do not discuss works made for hire.

5. Some traditional works approach C: Policies disclaim traditional works, except those which are made for hire or that make use of facilities and/or funds. (See Table 4 for corresponding institutional approaches.)

Table 4. Approaches toward Disclaiming Work.

Approach	Institutions
Disclaim none approach	PSU
Traditional works approach	CSU, NKU, UN, OU, YSU
Some traditional works approach A	WS
Some traditional works approach B	BSU, UTEP
Some traditional works approach C	CSI, IPFW, UCO, UNO, WSU

At a general level, the approaches suggest that institutions make distinctions regarding texts to which they claim or disclaim a controlling interest. The most noteworthy aspects of these approaches is the great variance in which works the respective institutions claim and disclaim and great variance in how the policies define works that will fall into the respective categories (for instance, works made for hire are delineated quite differently across policies). The most unique approach toward claiming and disclaiming texts appeared in PSU's policy, which claimed all works and disclaimed none.

This is problematic for two reasons: First, it seems to suggest that authors at PSU are always creating works for hire.[6] This cannot be the case, as the 13-factor agency test associated with work for hire tells us. Other problematic issues exist; for instance, BSU, CSI, IPFW, WS, UN, UNO, and UTEP—in what could be labeled the majority approach—claim all works but then disclaim others. Why these universities employ this catch-and-release approach is uncertain. It could be that these institutions seek to build false ethos with faculty (i.e., through claiming all works and then disclaiming some of the works) wherein the institution appears to be giving the authors back their work. It could be that the institutions are creating a back door (i.e., through claiming all works and then disclaiming some of the works so the institution can later reclaim those works with little resistance). It could be that those who wrote these policies do not realize that even if an institution disclaims works, the work-for-hire doctrine still applies to those works and the institution may still exert a controlling stake in those works. Although the first two explanations are certainly quite disillusioning if applicable, I would suggest it is the last that is the most troubling, because the institutions may be trying to cede authorial rights to the individuals who create texts, but are in actuality making a terrible go at it.

To reiterate, approaches to the works policies claim suggest that institutions make distinctions regarding textuality that are not representative of all of the factors yielding legal distinctions as to whether or not works may be works made for hire. Simply, an institution may claim to have a controlling interest in certain texts, or may claim and then disclaim those interests, but in many cases those claims or disclaims may not be accurate—or, worse yet, they mislead those who operate as authors within and for university contexts.

These findings correspond to a study similar to this one, but much larger in scope and conducted almost 20 years ago, in which Laura Lape (1992) noted that "none of the policies collected in this study fails to claim at least some faculty works, which suggests the purpose of [policy] adoption was to…claim ownership of certain works for the university" (p. 253). Lape also observed that genre is the basis upon which some policies claim and disclaim work. And, like Herrington, Lape indicated that the ambiguity of policies may be territory for future contentions.

What appears most striking, in relation to this chapter, is that Lape's (1992) investigation revealed the following aspect: "It should be noted that under neither the 1909 Act nor the 1976 act can an agreement between employee and employer determine whether a work is a work made for hire within the terms of the statute" (p. 239). With that in mind, I now shift attention toward how the policies defined or otherwise interpreted work for hire.

Policies Seek to Self Define Work for Hire

The policies evidenced four approaches to outlining or otherwise defining when or within what contexts institutions would approach texts as work for hire. Institutionally described contexts creating work-for-hire circumstances include:

1. All contexts approach: In all contexts authors are creating works for hire.

2. Some, but not other contexts approach: Specifically assigned tasks are works made for hire; traditional works are not.

3. Contractual contexts approach: Works made by, or under, provisions of signed contracts is work for hire.

4. These contexts are ignored, or ambiguously defined: Contexts signaling work for hire are not discussed, or unclear. (See Table 5 for corresponding institutions.)

Table 5. Approaches toward Work-for-hire Contexts.

Approach	Institutions
All contexts approach	PSU
Some, but not other contexts approach	CSU, UN
Contractual works approach	UCO, UTEP, WS, YSU
Ignores or ambiguously defines contexts approach	BSU, CSI, IPFW, NKU, UNO, OU, WSU

Generally, the approaches suggest that institutions often attempt to self-define contextual conditions for work for hire. As with the approaches toward defining authors operating under institutional control and texts that will or will not be regarded institutionally controlled or owned, the policies evidenced variance in how the universities sought to define or delineate work-for-hire contexts. All of the approaches in this section are problematic in one way or other; for instance, the *all contexts approach* does not account for the 13 factors creating work-for-hire distinctions. Quite simply, this approach takes no notice that authors performing within institutions can, and may, be operating outside of work for hire.

The *some, but not other contexts approach* attempts to disclaim certain contexts, but these institutions do not exert the legal agency needed to render these types of decisions. The *contractual contexts approach* is problematic in that it conflates contractual authorship with work for hire authorship. This is a misrepresentation, as the discussion copyright law designated that these are two distinct forms of authorship. The last approach is both more and less problematic. In ignoring contexts that could create work-for-hire distinctions, the policies are less problematic because they do not misrepresent how work for hire operates. However, the policies also fail to disclose circumstances that signal work-for-hire distinctions, which vests the responsibility for understanding work for hire with institutional authors—authors who may be unaware of the conditions that signal if a text was made as work for hire. The ambiguous approach is problematic in that it fails to acknowledge the complexity and vastness of the 13 factors that signal that texts could be made as works for hire. Consequently, it is difficult to determine which policy is most or least problematic, but one could argue that it again is PSU's, as it approaches all contexts in which institutional authors could be operating as work for hire. PSU's approach seems to suggest that authors at this institution are always creating works for hire. Certainly, this cannot be the case, as the 13-factor agency test associated with work for hire tells us.

Other problematic issues exist regarding how the policies delineated contexts and conditions that would signal when institutions would approach work as made for hire. Institutions also sought to outline which uses of facilities, funds, and institutional time would create an institutional claim (see Table 6 for examples and associated institutions). Again, use is just one of the thirteen provisions that help courts determine if a work is or is not made for hire. Trends in the approaches to use show that policies more ambiguously defined contexts or uses constituting institutional claims, and more clearly defined contexts or uses not resulting in institutional claims. This finding demonstrates the types of territories rife for future contention—the type of contention Lape (1992) and Herrington (1999a, 1999b) forecasted.

Table 6. Uses Signaling Institutional Claim.

Type of use	May signal claim	May not signal claim
Use of office		BSU, CSI, UCO, UN, WS
Use of facilities	UCO, UN, WS, CSI	BSU, CSU, CSI, UCO, UN, WS
Provision of salary		CSU, CSI, UN
Use of administrative staff	UN, WS	CSU, UCO, UN, WS
Additional costs	BSU, UCO, WS	
Research grants		CSU, YSU
Leave/sabbatical		CSU, CSI, UCO, YSU
Reduced instruction or other assignments	UCO, WS	CSU, CSI, YSU
Use of computers	UCO	CSU, UCO, UN, WS
Use of phones		UCO
Use of equipment/tools	UCO	UCO, UN, WS
Ambiguous language	CSU, UCO, WSU	
Does not specify (either)	IPFW, NKU, OU, PSU, UNO, UTEP, YSU	

Policies that attempt to undo some of the work-for-hire provisions are problematic in that they could lull institutional authors into a false sense of security, leading authors to believe that they are not authoring under the conditions that may create a work made for hire, when in fact they could be. Further, policies stressing the use provision fail to acknowledge the twelve other factors that aid courts in making work-for-hire distinctions are problematic in that they could lead institutional authors into believing they may be creating a work made for hire, when in fact they are not.

Lape (1992) noted that these types of policy provisions could lead to contention between institutions and institutional authors:

> Aside from the possibility that the university may be found to have waived promises by faculty members to assign copyrights by nonenforcement of the policy, broad claims that are selectively enforced will lead to surprise on the part of professors and increased conflict between professors and the university. (p. 258)

Institutional authors may still utilize the 13-factor test to produce baseline action. Additionally, authors could sign contracts explicitly delimiting ownership rights for each copyrightable text they create. Institutional actors could also use areas of ambiguity to prompt discussion and perhaps prompt revision of policies that administration, faculty, and students find problematic.

What, then, do these policies tell us? They tell us we should not be shocked, as evidenced in Blythe (2007): "the possibility that policy must be interpreted, and will be interpreted differently by different people, should not be surprising" (p. 178). The presence of institutional variances toward work for hire, authorship, and ownership of texts seems to suggest that Blythe's insight could be extended to readings of copyright upon which institutions base policies.

RECONSTITUTING AGENCY IN ACADEMIC CONTEXTS: OPPORTUNITIES FOR CHANGING COPYRIGHT POLICIES

There are many lessons to be learned about utilizing agency as authors performing work within and for academic institutions. Here, I have attempted to demonstrate how agency worked in such one specific context. The analysis of institutional policies suggests that institutional policy related to copyright might misrepresent or muddle legal distinctions of work for hire, authorship, and/or textual ownership. It is imperative, then, to keep two points in mind as we move forward.

First, as Rife (2008) and Jeffrey Galin (2008) posited, institutional policies and governing documents are not law, but courts may and often do use them to assemble interpretations of cases related to copyrightable intellectual property. Second, these policies and their implementation are not rigid but flexible; they are, as Porter et al. (2000) explained, important elements that give consistency to institutions. Porter et al. posited that institutions "are rhetorically constructed human designs (whose power is reinforced by buildings, laws, traditions, and knowledge making practices) and so are changeable" (p. 611). As such, it is important to remember that *we*—people that work for and within these institutions—are endowed with situated and distributed agency.

If we are dissatisfied by policies or governing documents, we can work rhetorically to change those documents and policies. Recall Blythe's (2007) statement on the paradox of agency and Rife's (2008) statement on civil disobedience. As these scholars suggested, ignoring these policies is not only a counterproductive action, but an act not responsible to our roles within the institutions within which we work. Working through and within the institutions is not just a way to affect change, but a *deliberate* way to do so. As this applies to institutional documents and policies concerned with copyright, we need to ensure that people entering institutional contexts are alert to and cognizant of not only the implications of these documents and policies and how they give shape to institutional knowledge about copyright, but also how these policies derive from interpretations of larger governing texts and policies.

Perhaps the most important contextual factor is the impact emergent technologies have had with how information and knowledge is invented and delivered. These technologies have already affected how scholarship is performed for and within academic institutions. Physicist Gordon Kane (2008), for instance, noted that in his field, an open-access publishing venue called arXiv has largely replaced and altered the way research is performed. Open-access venues, as Kane warranted, have extremely small operating costs with respect to traditional forms of information delivery; Kane noted that arXiv functions at approximately 2% of the budget of the largest traditional print U.S. physics journal. Journals like *Computers and Composition Online* and *Kairos* have turned to Creative Commons licensed open-publishing and sharing, and this might be a clue that CC is becoming a popular alternative to traditional forms of copyright with scholars from within our field.

However, policies that require institutional authors to protect their work with copyright may discourage—or, worse, prohibit—authors from pursuing these types of publications. For instance, if an author creates a text borrowing from others using "share-alike" forms of CC licensing, but that author's institution claims ownership to all texts, it places that scholar in a difficult ethical and legal position. Are authors working in institutions with restrictive IP policies prohibited from working with "share-alike" texts? If yes, then we need to seriously consider how these policies affect our abilities to perform scholarship. Doing so will mean preparing institutional constituents—staff, faculty, administrators, and students—to communicate so that they may act purposefully with regard to these issues. Preparing these individuals to partake (institutionally and communally) in this debate is the work that we perform as teachers of rhetoric, communication, and writing. Locally, this means working with others to decide what is in our institutions' interests. But, it also means thinking reflectively and globally to ensure that we are making the types of ethical choices that enable our disciplines to proceed in a sustainable fashion. We must work on various contextual levels to affect social change. What we do at one contextual level has implications for other contexts. The choices we make about how to act within institutions and which journals and publishers we choose to submit articles to will affect the coherence and cohesion of how connected contexts relate and assume consistency.

We must participate in the full breadth of that process—not in a solitary fashion independent from the ways that policies, documents, and people interrelate. As to the way copyright functions within institutions, we have to acknowledge questions about who owns language (Lunsford & West, 1996). Enabling individuals to affect change in informed, responsible, ethical, and fair ways is primarily the work our field advocates and performs. As Selber (2004a, 2004b) noted, writing can be approached as a tool, an artifact, and a process, and each perspective affords vantage points that are vital to one another. If we do not take up the work of identifying and relating, we are left with impartial views.

As I see it, it is difficult to exercise rhetorical change without a multitude of views. Blythe (2007) offered one way to exercise rhetorical action based on how texts function in context. Blythe explained that texts "derive power in three ways ... the way they are written, presented, and received" (p. 182). Acting locally, then, requires rhetorical action that attends to these matters. If Blythe were to apply this reading of power to the case of institutional copyright policies and documents, I bet he would argue that this is rhetorical action that faculty, staff, and students can precipitate. For example, there will be institutional constituents with the agency to revise policies by serving on committees that address and revise policies. These individuals can work to ensure that policies are more sensibly written. Those without the authority to write, however, can still educate those who do about the implications these issues hold for scholars and the multiple communities they inhabit. This may take the form of addressing policies within faculty and student senate meetings. Others with the agency to control how these policies are disseminated could ensure that all members of universities get copies of the policies. Those with knowledge of these topics can utilize the opportunities common to classrooms, departmental and institutional meetings, and scholarly and non-scholarly publishing—as well as local, statewide, and/or national conferences—to help bring others up to speed about how important these issues are for writers and readers. Quite simply, there are a number of routes we can take to prepare members of our communities to participate within these conversations.

SOME FINAL THOUGHTS

I learned a great deal about how texts derive power when I wanted to license my thesis through Creative Commons. I learned how different institutional perspectives toward policy (such as PU's institutional policy on copyright) relate to the perspectives found in documents such as IU's formatting guide (2007). Part of this meant understanding how to navigate IPFW, a hybrid of two institutional systems. I came to learn that as an employee of IPFW, I worked under PU's policy, but as a graduate student of IPFW, I worked under IU's policies. The expertise and professionalism of the members of my thesis committee facilitated this understanding. By helping locate institutional documents and by explaining how those documents shaped the thesis-composing process, I learned what it means to work within a system.

When it came time to make a formal decision about how I was to format the copyright page of my thesis, I also had to demonstrate to my committee that the knowledge I had procured strengthened the claims I made for my CC licensing choice. To accomplish this, I used the thesis itself to communicate; for instance, I included explanations of CC licensing in the review of the literature section, outlining that CC licensing operates not against, but in conjunction with, copyright. This section also provided explanations of copyright, work for hire, and concepts of legal authorship. In some senses, the text became a performative space, where law, policies, and interpretations converged. I was responsible for ensuring that my committee felt comfortable signing off on a text that deviated from the normative route of copyright formatting for theses at IPFW. In my rendering, then, to say "I" authored the thesis is reductive; this one project suggests just how collaborative our scholarly processes are. Without *our* interactions (neither wholly my own understandings, nor wholly theirs), the thesis and this chapter would not be possible. I conclude by echoing Blythe (2007): "I hope that my arguments here may prompt some to begin redefining our sense of agency [authorship, ownership, writing, and possibility] as a highly situated, ecological construct" (p. 183).

NOTES

1. At this point, I assume there will be some confusion, as I noted that I attended IPFW, consulted a Purdue handbook for the copyright policy, and consulted an Indiana University guide for thesis-formatting requirements. This confusion is quite precisely my purpose. Navigating institutions is a complex activity, and the confusion a reader likely feels here should mimic the confusion I felt when trying to come to understand the contexts in which I would have to defer to IU policy or PU policy as a member of an institution demonstrating a confluence of both the IU and PU institutional systems. I clarify the confusion later in the chapter.

2. It is important to make the following delimitation regarding my thesis study and this chapter: IP constitutes works that can be protected through trademark, patent, and copyright protection. Generally speaking, most of the work that writing scholars and students produce falls under the protection of copyright, and thus the study only covers works that could be regarded as copyrightable. Computer programs are examples of works not addressed here, as they could protected by copyright and/or patent protection.

3. Galin (2007), writing on one of the most recent cases of faculty work for hire, *Bosch v. Ball-Kell*, told us that the court's summary may suggest that "unless, there are explicit statements in letters of appointment or other university policies ... faculty may typically own copyrights in their teaching materials" and scholarship (p. 45). Moreover, as Galin reported, a number of documents were employed by the court (including the American Association of University Professors statement on copyright and a report from the university senate) in making this decision. This demonstrates the importance of weighing in within professional organizations and local contexts and producing documentation that supports a constructive political approach to changing policies.

4. In gathering and analyzing the policies, I did not conduct interviews of policy writers. Nor did I conduct interviews with members of the respective institutional IP offices. Yet, this seems a fruitful area for future research, and certainly would improve our understandings of how and why policies come to appear as they do. Additionally, I gathered the policies in 2007; in some cases, the policies have probably been updated, revised, and/or changed. I gathered policies; however, it is common for universities to have a number of other institutional IP documents that could be requested by courts in forming determinations of legal authorship and ownership.

5. I can think of a number of explanations for the use of ambiguous language in the policies: 1) Title 17 itself utilizes ambiguous terminology; policy writers may have applied this strategy; 2) policy writers may be writing a flex-

ible, fail-safe policy that allows them to apply the policy to institutional authors who create texts that they would like to assert ownership for; and/or 3) the language may evidence "zones of ambiguity ... where change can take place because of the boundary instability they highlight" (Porter et al., 2000, p. 623).

6. There are a number of reasons why universities may take a restrictive approach: 1) universities may have signed contracts with institutional members allowing them to claim these works; 2) universities may be using policies to create binding standards that hold members to the policies; and/or 3) the universities may have adopted an approach allowing them to claim works when they deem appropriate. Moreover, that policy language is restrictive does not necessarily denote that these institutions enforce these policies. Interviews would be useful in determining how, why, when, and in which circumstances institutions enforce policies claiming ownership. Another issue that might be best addressed through interviews is if and when ownership disputes are settled in house, which may partially account for the lack of case law on academic work for hire.

REFERENCES

Amidon, Timothy. (2007). *Institutional authors, institutional texts? An analysis of the intellectual property policies promulgated at Indiana University–Purdue University, Fort Wayne, and its peer institutions.* Unpublished masters's thesis. Fort Wayne: Indiana University–Purdue University.

Blythe, Stuart. (2007). Agencies, ecologies, and the mundane artifacts in our midst In Pamela Takayoshi & Patricia Sullivan (Eds.), *Labor, writing technologies, and the shaping of composition in the academy* (pp. 167–186). Cresskill, NJ: Hampton Press.

Boise State University. Boise State University intellectual property policy. http://www.boisestate.edu/policy/index.asp?section=6policynum=6320

City University of New York. The CUNY intellectual property policy. http://www.law.cuny.edu/app/legal/detail.jsp?assetId=2593

Cleveland State University. CSU patent and copyright policy. http://www.csohio.edu/research/TTS/CSU%20Patent%20Policy.pdf

DeVoss, Dànielle Nicole; Cushman, Ellen; & Grabill, Jeffrey T. (2005). Infrastructure and composing: The *when* of new-media writing. *College Composition and Communication, 57*, 14–44.

DeVoss, Dànielle Nicole; McKee, Heidi; & Porter, James E. (2006, June 8). Ethics and intellectual property. Presentation at the Digital Media and Composition Institute. Columbus, OH: Ohio State University.

DeVoss, Dànielle Nicole, & Porter, James E. (2006). Why Napster matters to writing: Filesharing as a mew ethic of digital delivery. *Computers and Composition, 23*, 178–210.

DeVoss, Dànielle Nicole, & Rosati, Annette. (2002). "It wasn't me, was it?" Plagiarism and the Web. *Computers and Composition, 19*, 191-203.

Ede, Lisa, & Lunsford, Andrea A. (2001). Collaboration and concepts of authorship. *PMLA, 116* (2), 354-369.

Galin, Jeff. (2008). *Bosch v Ball-Kell*: Faculty may have lost control over their teaching materials. In *The CCCC-IP Annual: Top Intellectual Property Developments of 2007*. http://www.ncte.org/library/NCTEFiles/Groups/CCCC/Committees/TopIP2007Collection.pdf

Herrington, TyAnna K. (1999a) Who owns my work?: The state of work for hire for academics in technical communication. *Journal of Business and Technical Communication, 13* (2), 125-144.

Herrington, TyAnna K. (1999b). Work for hire for nonacademic creators. *Journal of Business and Technical Communication, 13* (4), 401-426.

Herrington, TyAnna K. (2003). *A legal primer for the digital age*. Boston: Pearson/Longman.

Indiana University. (2007). *A guide to the preparation of theses and dissertations*. http://www.indiana.edu/~grdschl/thesisGuide.php

Indiana University-Purdue University, Fort Wayne. (2001). *Strategies for excellence: The strategic plan 2001-2006*.

Johnson-Eilola, Johndan, & Selber, Stuart A. (2007). Plagiarism, originality, and assemblage. *Computers and Composition, 24*, 375-403.

Kane, Gordon. (2008). Internet and open-access publishing in physics research. In Caroline Eisner & Martha Vicinus (Eds.), *Originality, imitation, and plagiarism* (pp. 48-52). Ann Arbor: University of Michigan Press.

Lape, Laura G. (1992). Ownership of copyrightable works of university professors: The interplay between the copyright act and university policies. *Villanova Law Review, 37*, 223-269.

Louisiana State University. Bylaws and regulations: Chapter VII intellectual property. http//:appl003.lsu.edu/oip/oip.nsf/$Content/Chatper+VII?OpenDocument

Lunsford, Andrea A. (1999). Rhetoric, feminism, and the politics of textual ownership. *College English, 61*, 529-544.

Lunsford, Andrea A., & West, Susan. (1996). Intellectual property and composition studies. *College Composition and Communication, 47*, 383-411.

Moore Howard, Rebecca. (2007). Understanding Internet plagiarism. *Computers and Composition, 24*, 3-15.

Northern Kentucky University. Intellectual property policy of Northern Kentucky University. http://www.nku.edu/~senate/FacultySenateDocuments/intellect.pdf

Oakland University. (2006). Intellectual property 2006-2009 faculty agreement.
Portland State University. PSU policy on intellectual property. http://www.gsr.pdx.edu/tt_intellectual_property.php
Porter, James E.; Sullivan, Patricia; Blythe, Stuart; Grabill, Jeffrey T.; & Miles, Libby. (2000). Institutional critique: A rhetorical methodology for change. *College Composition and Communication, 51,* 610-642.
Purdue University. (2005). *Purdue University faculty and staff handbook 2005-2006.*
Reyman, Jessica. (2006). Copyright, education, and the TEACH Act: Implications for teaching writing author(s). *College Composition and Communication, 58,* 30-45.
Rife, Martine Courant. (2008). Fair use, copyright, and the composition teacher. In Caroline Eisner & Martha Vicinus (Eds.), *Originality, imitation, and plagiarism* (pp. 145-156). Ann Arbor: University of Michigan Press.
Ritter, Kelly. (2005). The economics of authorship: Online paper mills, student writers, and first-year composition." *College Composition and Communication, 56,* 601-631.
Selber, Stuart A. (2009). Institutional dimensions of academic computing. *College Composition and Communication, 61,* 10-34.
Selber, Stuart A. (2004a). *Multiliteracies for a digital age.* Carbondale: Southern Illinois University Press.
Selber, Stuart A. (2004b). Technological dramas: A meta-discourse heuristic for critical literacy. *Computers and Composition, 21,* 171-195.
Selfe, Cynthia L., & Selfe, Richard J., Jr. (1994). The politics of the interface: power and its exercise in electronic contact zones. *College Composition and Communication, 45,* 480-504.
University of Central Oklahoma. Intellectual property policy. http://www.busn.ucok.edu/academicaffairs/Other/Intellectual%20Policy%20Procedures.pdf
University of Nebraska. University of Nebraska Board of Regents policies. http://extended.unl.edu/faculty/policies/regentspolicies.pdf
University of Texas System. Rules for intellectual property: Purpose, scope, authority. http://www.utsystem.edu/bor/rules/90000Series/90101%202004%2012%2010%2001.pdf
Valentine, Kathryn. (2006). Plagiarism as literacy practice: Recognizing and rethinking ethical binaries. *College Composition and Communication, 58,* 89-109.
Wichita State University. Policies and procedures: Intellectual property. http://webs.wichita.edu/inaudit/ch9_10.htm

Wright State University. Wright State University policy and procedures for intellectual property. http://www.wright.edu/techtransfer/patent_pol.html

Youngstown State University. University guidebook: Intellectual property rights http://www.ysu.edu/vpadmin/VPGuidelines/1018.01%20rvsd112206.doc

4 SOUL REMEDY: TURNITIN AND THE VISUAL DESIGN OF END USER LICENSE AGREEMENTS

BARCLAY BARRIOS

I'd like to open by asking you to consider three questions:

1. Your students use an online peer revision tool provided by the publisher of your textbook. Can that publisher then take those student papers and make them available as sample work to other teachers at other schools?

2. You upload your assignments, handouts, and other class materials to your institution's course management system. Can your institution claim ownership of those materials? Can the company that produces the software?

3. Your students upload papers to a central Web site service, which checks them for originality. Can that service then increase its profits by adding those papers to its proprietary database?

The answer to each of these questions may seem instinctively obvious to us as educators, yet the actual answers reside not in our guts or in common sense, but in the legal document governing the software in each case: the EULA.

You may not be familiar with the term, but if you've ever installed a piece of computer software or used a service on the Web you've certainly encountered one. EULAs—short for End User License Agreements—are the legal contracts that specify the rights and responsibilities of both the company offering the service or software and you, the end user. However, few people (myself included) ever stop to read the terms of these licenses (Gomulkiewicz, 2004), which are often written in long and dense legalese. Instead, we distractedly, hurriedly—perhaps even merrily—click "I Agree" where indicated in order to proceed, an act which explains the term "clickwrap" used to describe these contracts.[1] Usually, failure to read the EULA in a clickwrap license causes no harm, yet these contracts can often contain chilling elements such as agreements to be monitored while using the product or prohibitions against criticizing it while simultaneously limiting a user's options for redress through forum-selection clauses and agreements to arbitrate (Davis, 2007; Newitz, 2005). Particularly troubling EULAs often make the news (Blass, 2006; Ricker, 2006), such as the one for Google's Chrome Web browser, which included a clause granting Google "a perpetual, irrevocable, worldwide, royalty-free, and non-exclusive license to reproduce, adapt, modify, translate, publish, publicly perform, publicly display and distribute any Content which you submit, post or display on or through, the Services" (Frucci, 2008).

EULAs undoubtedly feel far removed from our primary concerns in the writing classroom, as legal documents often do. Yet, as my opening questions might suggest, EULAs have serious implications for the intellectual property rights of instructors and students. Each time we use a Web service, each time we write or have students write in an online environment, EULAs are at play. Every EULA to which we assent is a contractual obligation and failure to pay attention to the terms of those contracts is akin to making a deal with the devil. Should problems arise, your sole/soul remedy is already proscribed by the contract.

For students in the writing classroom, the most troubling EULA may perhaps be the one used by Turnitin, the online plagiarism-detection service offered by the company iParadigms and used by schools around the world (see Ballentine, this volume). Students upload their papers to the Turnitin Web site, which then checks those papers against Web sources as well as a proprietary database of other student papers previously uploaded to the Turnitin Web site; in the process, each student paper uploaded is added to the database, a move that seems to violate student intellectual property rights to their own writing. However, before they can use the service, students must create an account, in the process agreeing to Turnitin's EULA, which states in part:

> You hereby grant iParadigms a non-exclusive, royalty-free, perpetual, world-wide, irrevocable license to reproduce, transmit, display, disclose, archive and otherwise use in connection with its Services any paper You submit to the Site whether or not originally submitted in connection with a specific class.

> This license shall survive the termination of the User Agreement. Any cessation of use of the Site shall not result in the termination of any license You grant herein to iParadigms. (iParadigms, 2008)

We would do well to keep in mind that, as instructors, we must also assent to a clickwrap to use the service, one granting similar rights to iParadigms for all communications we make to and through the site, such as our assignments. Turnitin's EULA thus represents a unique intersection of intellectual property rights for the writing classroom: student rights to their papers, iParadigms' rights in its service, and the rights of other authors who may have been plagiarized.

Although both Turnitin's EULA and EULAs in general define these rights without negotiation, they do not do so without challenge. Compositionists have frequently expressed their general unease with Turnitin; four high school students recently sued iParadigms for copyright infringement, claiming that the clickwrap agreement was void because the students were minors and agreed to the EULA under duress, specifically the threat of receiving a zero for an assignment if they did not use the service (Dames, 2008; Warnecke, 2008; Young, 2008). The court rejected the student claims of copyright infringement, claiming iParadigm's use of their work was highly transformative, and rejected as well the claims of infancy and duress (*A.V. v. iParadigms*, 2008).

I am not ultimately interested in the legality of clickwrap agreements like those used by Turnitin; courts have continually affirmed their validity (Casamiquela, 2002; Dames, 2008; Davis, 2007; Gomulkiewicz, 2004). Instead, I am interested in how we as literacy educators can sensitize students to the serious intellectual property issues contained in EULAs and how we can prompt them to pay attention to and perhaps read the next clickwrap before clicking "I Agree." Specifically, as a technorhetorician I am interested in the visual design of clickwrap agreements and the ways in which that design encourages or discourages users from reviewing the document. Though this analysis could be applied to any number of clickwraps, Turnitin's EULA provides an extremely relevant example for examination, one with three benefits for the writing classroom:

1. giving students practice in considering the relation between design and meaning;

2. encouraging students to read EULAs; and

3. exposing students to intellectual property issues through the intersection of their IP rights and the rights of iParadigms.

After reviewing the history of clickwrap agreements and the role of design in questions of their legality, I will turn to an examination of Turnitin's clickwrap EULA design. By unwrapping this design, I hope to suggest strategies we can use in the writing classroom to teach students an awareness of these issues and their implications.

SHRINKWRAP, CLICKWRAP, BROWSEWRAP

Initially, software makers controlled rights to their property by printing End User License Agreements on paper and enclosing them in shrinkwrap around the product; end users agreed to the terms of these contracts when they removed the shrinkwrap from the software. With the advent of the Web, shrinkwrap became clickwrap or browsewrap, the former indicating EULAs such as Turnitin's that require a user to click a button indicating assent before proceeding and the latter indicating those situations in which the EULA is located on another webpage, reached by clicking on a hyperlink (Casamiquela, 2002). The legality of clickwrap was first confirmed in the 1996 case of *ProCD, Inc. v. Zeidenberg* (Davis, 2007), in which ProCD's software presented the EULA onscreen, requiring the defendant to indicate assent with a click before installation. Two years later this decision was validated in online contexts in *Hotmail Corp. v. Van$ Money Pie* (1998). The defendant in that case created several Hotmail email accounts to help with its spam-sending business; the court granted a preliminary injunction based on the fact that Hotmail would prevail on its breach of contract claims grounded in the clickwrap EULA for its service.

Since those cases, courts have continually upheld online clickwrap EULAs as long as two essential elements are present: the EULA is automatically presented to users, and assent (through clicking or checking a box, for example) is required before the user can proceed (Casamiquela, 2002). The fact that both elements are rarely present in browsewrap agreements, in which a link (often at the bottom of a page) directs users to the EULA, means that those license agreements have been successfully challenged, beginning in 2001 with the case of *Specht v. Netscape Communications Corp.* (Davis, 2007). In this case, the plaintiffs sued Netscape claiming that Netscape's Smart Download software violated federal law because it monitored users' Internet use. Netscape attempted to compel arbitration based on its software EULA. But the link to that EULA was located at the bottom of the page and was only visible if a user scrolled all the way down; a simple "Download" button provided access to the software without compelling the user to read the license agreement. In rejecting Netscape's claims, the court ruled in part that the "'Download' button, as contrasted with a button labeled 'I assent,' did not put the user on notice or indicate that he was entering into a binding contact" (Davis, 2007, p. 586).

As the Specht case suggests, design is an important issue in determining the enforceability of these agreements, an issue that Robert Gomulkiewicz (2004) argued has been inherited in part from their shrinkwrap predecessors:

> Unfortunately, many EULAs come on a small paper card, on product packaging, or in a user manual. The EULA is printed in black and white using 10-point type or less. There is very little white space in and around the EULA, making the text very dense. Many EULAs today are presented in electronic form. These EULAs tend to look a lot like the paper version (or worse). (p. 697)

Looking worse than a print EULA impacts the validity of both clickwrap and browsewrap. Indeed, in his review of clickwrap and browsewrap enforceability, Ryan Casamiquela (2002) suggested that design may be crucial when the dual elements of automatic presentation and clear assent are not both present: "Courts may consider whether the vendor has the link underlined or in a distinguishable color, or if conditional language occupies the text of the link. A prominent, colorful link next to an 'I Accept' icon may prove sufficient for a finding of consumer assent" (pp. 486-487). Thus in *Pollstar v. Gigmania* (2000), for example, the court found the browsewrap EULA unenforceable because the link to it was "in small gray print on a gray background. In addition, the court noted that some blue colored links failed to function, perhaps causing consumers to assume that all colored links would also fail" (Casamiquela, 2002, p. 485). Conversely, in *Lawrence Feldman v. Google, Inc.* (2007), the court found the clickwrap in question fully valid because of its design, specifically mentioning the use of bold font, the size of the font, and the visibility of the EULA above the "fold" of the screen/page.

Design also specifically played a role in the recent suit against iParadigms. As part of their counterclaims, iParadigms claimed indemnification based on students' agreement to the site's Usage Policy. However, that policy was not available in the clickwrap; it existed on a separate page on the site. At the time of this writing, the link to that page is located below the fold in gray text (RGB code #999999) on a white background, while most of the other links on the page are blue. In dismissing this counterclaim, the court cited *Register.com v. Verio, Inc.* (2004), in which language pointing to the license was repeatedly and prominently displayed to the user, something that did not occur on the Turnitin site (Warnecke, 2008). Instead, Turnitin's presentation of its Usage

Policy is more similar to the case of *Specht v. Netscape Communications Corp* (2001). As with Turnitin, the EULA in that case was reached only by a link located below the fold of the site (Casamiquela, 2002). As Michael Warnecke (2008) noted on his blog, "Even though Turnitin.com lost on the browsewrap point, it's easy to see how a little more effort on Turnitin.com's part could have produced a favorable outcome." And part of that effort would have been in terms of design.

Although courts have primarily evaluated clickwrap and browsewrap licenses through considerations of factors such as unconscionability, public policy violation, and the preeminence of federal copyright protection (Davis, 2007), design remains a factor in determining the validity of these contracts. Although Robert Gomulkiewicz (2004) found that the "unfriendly format of the EULA strongly suggests that the format was not chosen with readability in mind," he also suggested that "software businesspeople and their legal counsel seldom cynically connive to create an impenetrable EULA. It just happens naturally" (p. 697, 694). Seldom or not, users often suspect conniving is involved; perhaps more so when it comes to Turnitin.

COMPOSITION, PLAGIARISM, AND VISUAL DESIGN

The business of Turnitin is, on some level, suspicion. And compositionists have continually critiqued Turnitin and other plagiarism-detection services specifically for the ways in which they base pedagogical relationships in suspicion. As Sean Zwagerman (2008) argued, "plagiarism detection treats writing as a product, grounds the student-teacher relationship in mistrust, and requires students to actively comply with a system that marks them as untrustworthy" (p. 692). Zwagerman examined the ideological load of plagiarism itself and the disciplining work of "integrity." In his analysis, tools such as Turnitin are "the inevitable end point of the integrity scare: an efficient, perhaps even foolproof, technology of surveillance, a 'panoptic schema' (Foucault 206)" (p. 691). Zwagerman's title, "The Scarlet P: Plagiarism, Panopticism, and the Rhetoric of Academic Integrity," points to the socially disciplining function of Turnitin's panoptic technology. In this context, it is salient to recall Turnitin's logo, which features a red "it" between gray colored "turn" and "in." The "it" being turned in, of course, is the student paper, already marked scarlet.

Bronwyn Williams (2007–2008) found many of the same issues in plagiarism and the Turnitin service. Focusing on the emotional reactions of teachers who discover plagiarism, Williams discovered that "the use of such a service for student writers begins from a presumption of guilt" (p. 352). Rather than rest in this construction of the student, with its attendant emotional reaction when teachers discover that guilt, Williams instead suggested that instances of plagiarism offer possibilities for teaching. In this analysis, Turnitin obscures that pedagogical moment. Echoing Zwagerman, Williams suggested that using Turnitin "creates a prison culture of guards and the guarded—a cat-and-mouse game of detection and mistrust" (p. 352).

Jennifer Jenson and Suzanne De Castell (2004) registered many of the same concerns; however, they situated those concerns as reflected in the design of Turnitin's Web site. Using a semiotic analysis, they find that what

> stands out in Turnitin's web site, both iconographically and textually, is a consistent nostalgic return to the past, to the fifties, for the most part, using old photographs whose source, incidentally, is unacknowledged—the crisp black and white characters are emblematic of the clarity with which intellectual integrity can be seen, can be scientifically and precisely "detected" (p. 318)

The visual design of the site, in other words, relies on retro images to suggest "better, simpler and presumably more *honest* times" (Jenson & De Castell, p. 317), reflecting plagiarism's evolving function in a knowledge system in which autonomy and originality are called into question. Bill Marsh (2004) also analyzed Turnitin's Web site, reading the sample originality reports on the Web site as referential symbols that construct plagiarists as "pathological, deceitful, diseased, and/or violent" while the site's use of "photos of predominantly White, short-haired men and boys betray[s] an obvious appeal to a foregone age (mid-50s perhaps) of educational order and congeniality" (p. 430, 434). Although (perhaps consciously) the Turnitin site no longer uses such retro images in its design, one might still continue analyses such as these, focusing, for example, on the logo of Turnitin's related Web site, Plagiarism.org, which features a magnifying glass over a fingerprint with digital ones and zeroes scrolling through, reinforcing the links between identity, authenticity, deviance, and panoptic detection suggested by these critics.

Such analyses reinforce the ways in which design produces meaning, an axiomatic tenet in technorhetoric. Yet, as Anne Wysocki (1998) observed, design *does more* than create meaning; it also produces order. Wysocki argued that the design of webpages, framed with metaphors inherited from print literacy and art, produces a certain kind of order in users, akin to the disciplining functions observed by critics of Turnitin. At the same time, these metaphors of design efface themselves in order to become invisible and hence beyond discussion; visual designs function as "expressions of and means for reproducing cultural and political structures," simultaneously becoming invisible through their repeated and constant use. Wysocki's analysis begs us to unravel designs in order to unpack the order they impose. Her argument also suggests one of the problems with EULAs in general: They have become so ubiquitous as to be automatically accepted and assented to.

Clickwraps themselves borrow from the kinds of print literacy forms Wysocki (1998) explored. More specifically, they remediate shrinkwrap EULAs. Jay David Bolter and Richard Grusin (1996) explained the process of remediation and the desire for transparency: "Since the electronic version justifies itself by granting ... access to the older media, it wants to be transparent. The digital medium wants to erase itself, so that the viewer stands in the same relationship to the content as she would if she were confronting the original medium" (p. 45). In remediating shrinkwap, clickwrap tries "to absorb the older medium entirely, so that the discontinuities between the two are minimized. The very act of remediation, however, ensures that the older medium cannot be entirely effaced" (Bolter & Grusin, p. 46). That remediation is an imperfect process means that the design in clickwrap cannot be made fully invisible. Bearing traces of its shrinkwrap predecessor, clickwrap—no matter how ubiquitous—opens itself to an unwrapping analysis that can reveal the strategies used to promote or inhibit reading. In turning to such an analysis, I am guided by Wysocki's (1998) pointed question: "What order is reinforced by a design, and what designs give us chances to re-order?"

2005, 2006, 2008

Basing any analysis on a Web site's design is a risky venture. For one thing, designs change. More problematically, when it comes to the Web, design and appearance are not necessarily the same, given the vagaries of browsers, platforms, and screen resolutions. To mitigate these problems, I'd like to examine the clickwrap for the Turnitin EULA at three different moments in time, in three different browsers, at three different screen resolutions, and on two different platforms. Although the look of the clickwrap changes across all of these moments, certain design features remain consistent, features that discourage users from reviewing the terms of the EULA.

Figure 1 shows a screen shot of the Turnitin clickwrap from October 11, 2005, as viewed in Mozilla Firefox on a computer running the Windows XP operating system at a screen resolution of 1280 x 1024. At that time, the site still used the retro images noted by Jenson and DeCastell (2004) and Marsh

(2004). Two striking features of the clickwrap design—its size and color—reinforce the disciplining effects noted by those critics and suggested by Wysocki (1998). Those design aspects also actively discourage reading the EULA. Although the clickwrap has prominence on the page by being located above the fold—and, indeed, by being the only thing on the page—it is given relatively little space, both deemphasizing its importance and making the text it contains difficult to read. Judging from calculations made from the screen shot in image-editing software, this box takes up about 5% of the available space on the screen. Just over eight lines of the EULA are initially visible but when the text of the full EULA is copied out of the box and into word-processing software, it takes up just over *five pages* in Times New Roman 12 point font. Thus, the first way in which users are discouraged from reading the EULA is through a strict control of readable space. Note as well that the EULA is in white text on a gray background (the RGB code for the background is #B0B0B0), two colors with minimal contrast—which makes *any* reading difficult. Color thus becomes a second strategy to discourage readability. No common HTML elements are used to make the text more readable—no bold or italics or headings. Rather than make use of these visual cues, the text uses ALL CAPS for certain sec-

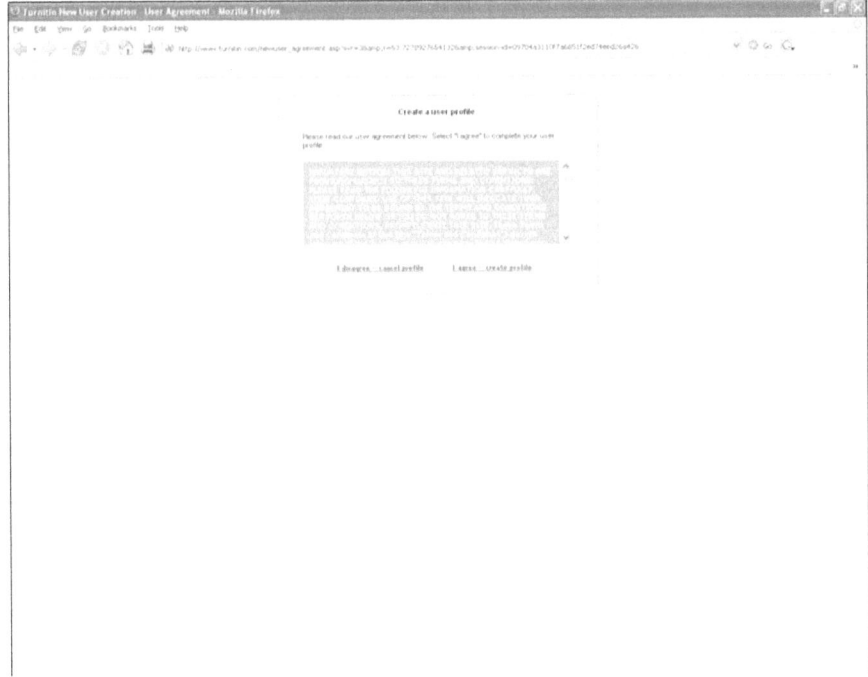

Figure 1: Turnitin EULA, October 11, 2005.

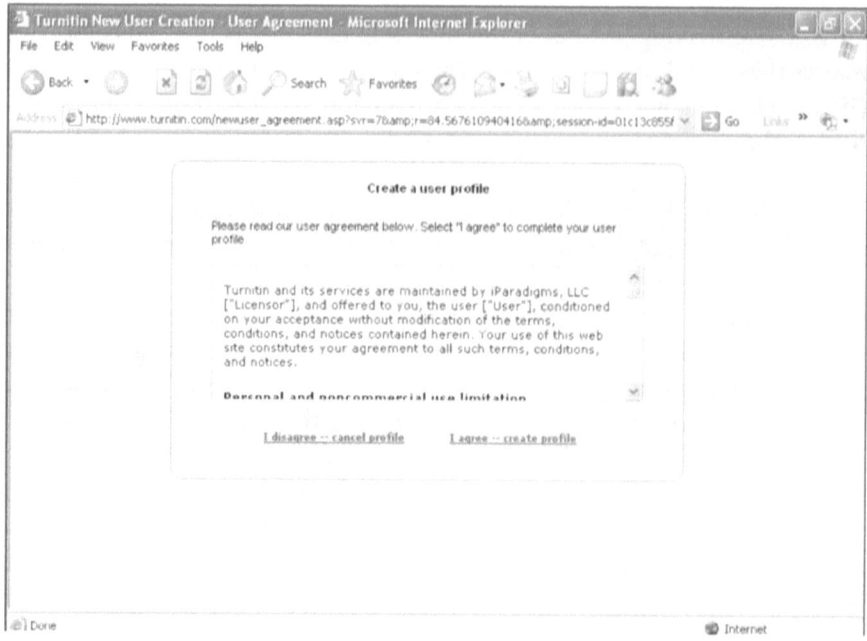

Figure 2: Turnitin EULA, March 20, 2006.

tions which, while perhaps common in some legal documents and thus pointing back to the remediation of shrinkwrap, is considered shouting in the online world; it is, too, more difficult to read.

I don't want to claim that iParadigms intentionally obscured this EULA from users in the clickwrap, though certainly that temptation is there. And perhaps Gomulkiewicz (2004) is right in claiming that the impenetrability of EULAs happens "naturally." But this particular EULA, the design of which is nearly impenetrable, contains particularly objectionable terms. The October 2005 version of the EULA includes not only license to all content uploaded to the site, both papers and any other communications, but also clauses to limit liability, indemnification, warranty, arbitration, and jurisdiction.

By March 20, 2006, the clickwrap for Turnitin had changed to one offering better readability. Figure 2 shows the site as viewed in Microsoft Internet Explorer in Windows XP on a monitor with 800 x 600 screen resolution. Even with this much smaller screen resolution (which consequently makes everything larger on the screen), the text box is allowed about 15% of available space on the page. While this does increase readability, users can still only read six to ten lines of text at a time, even though the revised EULA still takes up four pages in a word-processing file. The use of a white background with black text

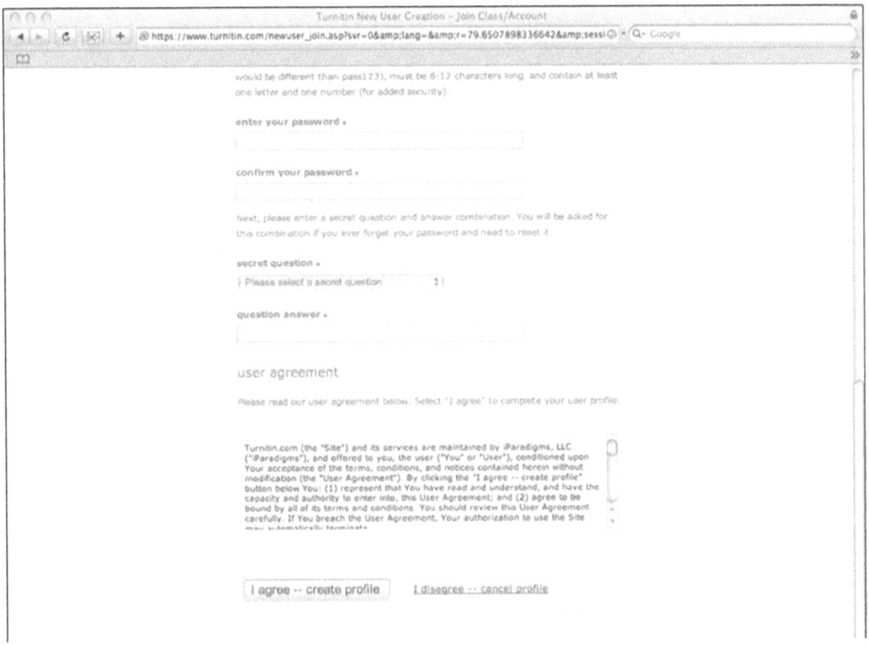

Figure 3: Turnitin EULA, October 23, 2008.

is, however, a significant improvement as is the use of bold headings to separate sections of the text.

This "liberalization" of the design is also reflected in a "liberalization" of the EULA itself. In agreeing to the 2005 EULA, users grant iParadigms "a non-exclusive, royalty-free, perpetual, world-wide, irrevocable license to reproduce, transmit, display, disclose, and otherwise use your Communications on the Site or elsewhere for [their] business purposes" (iParadigms, 2005). iParadigms is free, moreover, "to use any ideas, concepts, techniques, know-how in your Communications for any purpose, including, but not limited to, the development and use of products and services based on the Communications." The EULA does, at least, exclude personally identifiable information from students and actual student papers from its definition of "Communications"; instructor assignments, however, are offered no such protection. The revised EULA (2006), the more readable one, has no such objectionable provision. As the EULA has become less predatory of IP rights, it has been presented in ways that make it easier to read, or, conversely, the more unpalatable EULA is the one users are most discouraged from reading.

The third screen shot, Figure 3, is from October 23, 2008, and shows the EULA as viewed in Safari on a Macintosh computer running the operating system OS X with a 1680 x 1050 screen resolution. The EULA no longer exists on a separate page of the site, but is now incorporated into the user account creation screen. It is, however, located below the fold on that page, meaning that it is not immediately visible to users. And it continues to be allocated minimal space on screen—a mere 6% of the available screen space. Although the black text against the white background is more readable, the EULA occupies eight text-only pages of Times New Roman 12 point text. Bold headings are again used and, additionally, bold text is used within sections to highlight particular clauses. Visually, users are encouraged to agree to the clickwrap with a large button indicating that agreement (located next to a small link for disagreeing).

The longest EULA continues to receive precious little screen space, but its increased length is not in itself a sign of increased infringement of IP rights. In part, the increased length reflects legal developments in a post-9/11 world; there is now a specific clause prohibiting download or export of the service "to any person or entity on the U.S. Treasury Department's list of Specially Designated Nationals or the U.S. Commerce Department's Table of Denial Orders or otherwise prohibited by United States export control laws" (iParadigms, 2008). The EULA has also grown in length to accommodate specific classes of users. The "sole remedy" of students and instructors dissatisfied with the service is to stop using it; the sole remedy for educational institutions is specified separately and is limited to what they have paid iParadigms. Most interestingly, though, the license granted to iParadigms by users now has a specific disclaimer, visually highlighted through the use of bold text: "**This license does not include any right to use ideas set forth in papers submitted to the site.** Please note that papers submitted to the Site are not read or reviewed by any individuals, but rather are only analyzed using the Licensed Programs" (iParadigms, 2008).

Turnitin's EULA itself, then, has continued to evolve in response to both legal challenges and the general political climate. Despite these changes, though, the design of the clickwrap continues to discourage readers from reading the text of the license. In all three instances, the clickwrap is given minimal screen space. Each time, it is also presented through an inline frame, HTML tag <iframe>. Inline frames create windows within a page and, in doing so, activate a kind of hypermediacy in the process of remediating shrinkwrap. According to Bolter and Grusin (1996),

> hypermediacy offers a heterogeneous space, in which representation is conceived of not as a window onto the world, but rather as 'windowed' itself—with windows that open onto other representations or other media. The logic of hyperme-

diacy calls for representations of the real that in fact multiply
... the signs of mediation. (p. 329)

In making a window within the window of the browser, inline frames both suggest transparent access to the text through that window while simultaneously calling attention to the window itself, in this instance through a scroll bar and a thin 1-pixel border. They produce order—a limiting order based on relative size—yet they cannot do so without also calling attention to that production. Because the order produced cannot be made invisible, we are especially welcome to imagine a re-ordering.

After all, though many clickwraps use inline frames, many also provide frames large enough to show significant amounts of text, thereby allowing (if not encouraging) users to read the license. Turnitin's EULA is not the only configuration possible, and is, indeed, one of the worst. Apart from these issues of design, Gomulkiewicz (2004) explored many options for creating more readable EULAs and clickwraps, including better training of law students and "plain language" legislation. He most strongly advocated, however, a Web-based EULA non-governmental organization, suggesting that "an NGO could be a powerful vehicle for making licensing more user-friendly" through education, forums, feedback, and best practices (p. 715). Although not mentioned by Gomulkiewicz, Creative Commons points in just such a direction. In creating a simplified licensing process that allows content creators to specify rights for users, Creative Commons has transformed what a EULA might be—and it has done so not just legally but visually as well. Figure 4 shows a sample Creative Commons license. The text is short and readable, and visual icons are used to emphasize the terms of the license; design and content both promote readability. Although it is difficult to imagine such a streamlined EULA being adopted by companies such as iParadigms, the existence of Creative Commons options nevertheless allow us to imagine a different order for clickwraps.

TEACHERS, STUDENTS, ADMINISTRATORS

EULAs in the Writing Classroom

In incorporating an analysis of the visual designs of EULAs in the classroom, we might consider three pedagogical goals. First, such an exercise might be consistent with local programmatic goals concerning critical thinking and close textual analysis; asking students to decode the EULA and its implications involves sustained attention to a complicated text while considering the

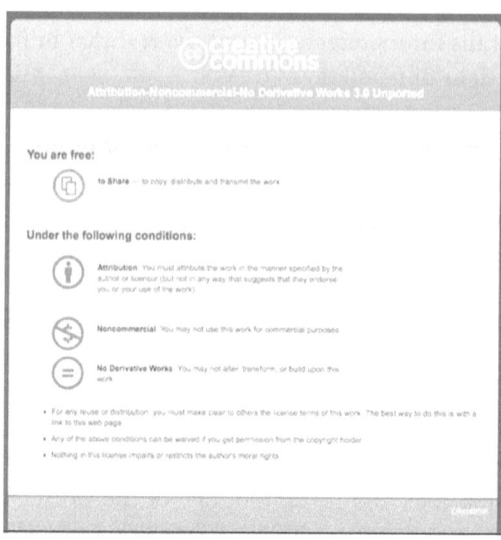

Figure 4: Creative Commons license.

visual design of clickwraps expands student experience with electronic rhetorical forms. Second, such a pedagogical practice is consistent with Cynthia Selfe's (1999) call for a critical technological literacy, which moves beyond instruction in merely how to use technology and towards an ability to "carefully analyze, to pay attention to, the technology–literacy link at both fundamental levels of conception and social practice" (p. 148). Rather than empowering students with a functional literacy in relation to electronic writing tools—the ability to use those tools—such a literacy asks students to consider the conditions and implications of these tools themselves, for themselves and for the social relationships in which they participate. Finally, working on EULAs in the classroom can also help meet the Council of Writing Program Administrators' (2009) recommended outcomes for first-year composition by understanding how genres (in this case clickwrap) shape meaning by promoting inquiry, and by exposing students to the relationships between language, knowledge, and power. In specifically using the clickwrap designs from Turnitin, these classroom activities are also consistent with the Council's recommendations regarding plagiarism.

To meet such goals, we can invite students themselves to imagine a different order for clickwrap agreements. Such an exercise might start by asking them to perform the kind of visual analysis offered here, locating clickwraps and considering their design in relation to the text of the agreement. Students who spend any amount of time online will be able to find many different clickwraps and browsewraps at sites such as World of Warcraft, Facebook, or Flickr.

Interestingly, many of these sites use a hybrid of the clickwrap and browsewrap forms, requiring assent by clicking a button to create an account as in a clickwrap, but containing the terms of the license on a separate page as in a browsewrap. Twitter, a site that allows for a kind of condensed, text-message-like blogging, serves as a particularly interesting example, since its EULA is clearly presented in simple terms. Its section on copyright, for example, labeled "Copyright (What's Yours is Yours)," not only maintains user IP rights but also encourages "users to contribute their creations to the public domain or consider progressive licensing terms" (Twitter, 2008). In analyzing the design of these pages, students can note the visual and rhetorical placement of the clickwrap/browsewrap, its size, the choice of colors and fonts, as well as the use of HTML elements that promote readability, such as bold text to delineate sections.

Asking students to locate and unwrap EULAs also gives them practice in decoding the linkages between design and meaning. Such exercises also prompt students to read the terms of these licenses. As part of this exercise, students might use the License Analyzer provided by SpywareGuide (http://www.spywareguide.com/analyze/index.php). After pasting in the text of any EULA, students can obtain information not only on questionable clauses in the license (flagged by the analyzer) but also the overall readability of the text, noted by the number of words and sentences, the average words per sentence, and ratings on several different readability scales. Students can also use readability analysis tools, one of which claims that the Turnitin EULA requires a post-graduate education for comprehension; Twitter's EULA, in contrast, requires at most a 10th grade education.

Beyond these activities, teachers can invite students individually or in groups to design better clickwraps. Working within the same spatial constraints for webpages as corporate Web designers, students can consider the tradeoffs required to encourage readability while economizing design and screen space. In making these models, students can locate and compare a spectrum of EULA designs, such as the ones provided by Creative Commons. In Web design classes, students can consider whether or not to use inline frames as well as other HTML elements that can enhance readability. Even outside of classes explicitly covering webpage construction, students can design static mockups of more successful clickwrap designs.

Congruent with these practices, we as teachers should pay more attention to EULAs, an act consistent with Selfe's (1999) goal to "pay attention" to questions of technology and its linkages to literacy. After all, students are not the only ones whose IP rights are at stake in clickwrap agreements; most, such as Turnitin's, do not distinguish between classes of users. Although there are separate links for students, instructors, and teaching assistants to create accounts on the Turnitin site, the EULA is the same for all three. In creating an account, instructors agree that

> any communications or material of any kind that You e-mail, post, or transmit through the Site (excluding personally identifiable Registration Data of Students, any papers submitted to the Site, and grades and assessment related information), including, questions, comments, suggestions, and other data and information (Your 'Communications') will be treated as non-confidential and non-proprietary

and thus any class materials you post become the property of iParadigms, which claims a

> non-exclusive, royalty-free, perpetual, world-wide, irrevocable license to reproduce, transmit, display, disclose, archive and otherwise use Your Communications on the Site or elsewhere for our business purposes. (iParadigms, 2008)

What's more, the EULA for Turnitin places the responsibility for determining plagiarism squarely on the instructor's shoulders:

> You further agree to exercise Your independent professional judgment in, and to assume sole and exclusive responsibility for, determining the actual existence of plagiarism in a submitted paper with the acknowledgement and understanding that the Originality Reports are only tools for detecting textual similarities between compared works and do not determine conclusively the existence of plagiarism, which determination is a matter of professional judgment of the Instructor and Institution. (iParadigms, 2008)

These terms should certainly give us pause, but of course Turnitin is not the only EULA we will encounter. Many publishers now offer a variety of electronic resources in connection with their textbooks; we should consider the EULAs for those services carefully as well, along with the EULAs of online and local software.

EULAs and Writing Program Administrators

For me, the greatest challenge with the Turnitin clickwrap in particular comes from my role as the writing program administrator (WPA) at my institution. As the WPA, I see all suspected cases of "academic irregularity" (as plagiarism is termed at my school) and am forced to negotiate between my concerns about IP rights and my responsibility to uphold my institution's Honor Code which, as a state university policy, is also state law. From this institutional position, I am able to witness all of the concerns voiced by composition scholars about the general enterprise of plagiarism. In particular, I regularly encounter the kinds of emotional responses from instructors with cases of plagiarism that Williams (2007–2008) described. Teachers with such concerns in their classrooms often react, I find, like those who have found their lovers cheating on them. There are similar feelings of betrayal, anger, and vindictiveness. As a first response to any possible academic irregularity, then, I ask all teachers in my program to consult with me or another experienced instructor before even speaking to the student. Often having a second opinion can provide a rational perspective that can diffuse the emotional content of the situation.

More generally, however, though I can guide our program's policy, I do not control those who teach within it; indeed, to do so would be to invert the disciplining systems surrounding plagiarism onto instructors themselves. As a program, we advocate against using Turnitin precisely because of the IP concerns related to the service. In that way, we try to limit its use. Those teachers who wish to pursue charges of academic irregularity against a student using Turnitin are invited to send me the student's paper. I use my account on Turnitin and upload only parts of the student paper to generate an originality report, limiting the risk to the IP rights of both the instructor and the student, and offering my own soul to the EULA. In conjunction with this limited use, we as a program work hard to provide students an understanding of plagiarism and its subtleties. Our program Web site, for example, contains an extensive set of Frequently Asked Questions about plagiarism, which is also presented in the supplemental text that we use with our writing courses.

However, WPAs might be uniquely empowered to create greater change in response to this situation. Although licenses for Turnitin are usually negotiated by institutions, and while we as faculty may participate in systems of institutional governance that can influence those negotiations, the truth is that there is little we can do once an institution has subscribed to a service like Turnitin. However, there may be action we can take based on the economic power of writing programs and by the sheer number of students who move through the core writing courses offered by such program. While serving as a WPA at my previous institution, just such a possibility emerged. At the time, we were considering a new handbook that included Turnitin in its support technology. After reading the terms of the EULA and the objectionable language concerning the IP of both teachers and students, I immediately emailed our local sales representative to indicate we had no interest in this handbook. However, with a possible 11,000 handbooks at stake, a reply quickly followed. My concern was transmitted up through the corporate structure and soon the publisher was working with iParadigms to revise the language of the EULA. Because we did not end up adopting that handbook (for reasons unconnected to its inclusion of Turnitin), I am unable to say whether or not the license ultimately would have been revised. However, that experience offers a glimpse of the possibilities enabled by the economic leverage of writing programs.

CONCLUSION

All of these strategies are, at best, partial. As long as courts broadly support EULAs and as long as users rely upon software and digital services, the issues explored here will continue to be at play. Thus EULAs in general, and clickwraps specifically, should continue to be a point of advocacy for anyone interested in protecting IP rights in the digital age. In pursuing this agenda, we should keep in mind Wysocki's (1998) observations about the ways in which the repetition of design makes the order it imposes invisible. For Wysocki, that which is not seen is not questioned. Given the designs of clickwrap agreements, we might extend her point: That which is not read is not questioned, either. By unwrapping the designs of EULAs, we can pay attention to their terms and through that attention we can question those terms.

Without such attention, our sole remedies to infringement of IP rights in the electronic spaces of the writing classroom will continue to be specified by clickwrap or browsewrap EULAs. In taking the time to read EULAs and to consider their effects on our teaching and our students, we may instead be able to forge a soul remedy of our own in these deals with potential devils.

NOTE

1. Online licenses are termed either "clickwrap" or "browsewrap," both of which are named after "shrinkwrap," which was used to describe licenses printed on paper and shrink wrapped in plastic with the physical media for installing software. Removal of the plastic wrap indicated assent to the terms

of that license. For clickwrap, clicking a button such as "I Agree" indicates that assent; for "browsewrap," the user is pointed to the license (usually on another webpage), but is not required to indicate acceptance of the license before proceeding.

REFERENCES

A.V. v. iParadigms, F. Supp. (E.D. Virginia, 2008).

Blass, Evan. (2006, Nov 2). *Microsoft changes Vista EULA to appease modders; pirates still screwed.* http://www.engadget.com/2006/11/02/microsoft-changes-vista-eula-to-appease-modders-pirates-still-s/

Bolter, Jay David, & Grusin, Richard. (1996). Remediation. *Configurations.* http://muse.jhu.edu.ezproxy.fau.edu/journals/configurations/v004/4.3bolter.html

Casamiquela, Ryan J. (2002). Contractual assent and enforceability in cyberspace. *Berkeley Technology Law Journal, 17*(475), 475-495.

Council of Writing Program Administrators. (2009). Defining and avoiding plagiarism: The WPA statement on best practices. http://www.wpacouncil.org/positions/WPAplagiarism.pdf

Council of Writing Program Administrators. (2009). WPA outcomes statement for first-year composition. http://www.wpacouncil.org/positions/outcomes.html

Dames, K. Matthew. (2008, June). Turn you in: Scholarly ethics in a culture of suspicion. *Information Today*, 23-25.

Davis, Nathan. (2007). Presumed assent: The judicial acceptance of clickwrap. *Berkeley Technology Law Journal, 22*(577), 577-598.

Frucci, Adam. (2008, September 3). Google Chrome EULA claims ownership of everything you create on Chrome, from blog posts to emails. *Gizmodo.* http://gizmodo.com/5044871/google-chrome-eula-claims-ownership-of-everything-you-create-on-chrome-from-blog-posts-to-emails

Gomulkiewicz, Robert W. (2004). Getting serious about user-friendly mass marketing licensing for software. *George Mason Law Review, 12*(3), 687-718.

Hotmail Corp. v. Van Money Pie, Inc. (1998). U.S. Dist. LEXIS 10729,. 47 U.S.P.Q.2d (BNA) 1020 (N.D. Cal. 1998).

iParadigms. (2005). *Turnitin new user creation–user agreement.* http://www.turnitin.com/newuser_agreement.asp?svr=3&r=53.7278927654132&session-id=09704a3110f7a6851f2ed74eed26a426

iParadigms. (2008). *Turnitin new user creation-join class/account.* https://turnitin.com/newuser_join.asp?svr=6&session-id=01afc39518726a87de5d5c182ce224af&lang=&r=74.7315523537459

Jenson, Jennifer, & De Castell, Suzanne. (2004). "Turn it in": Technological challenges to academic ethics. *Education, Communication, and Information, 4*(2), 311-330.

Lawrence Feldman v. Google, F. Supp. (E.D. Pennsylvania, 2007).

Marsh, Bill. (2004). Turnitin.com and the scriptural enterprise of plagiarism detection. *Computers and Composition, 21*, 427-438.

Newitz, Annalee. (2005, February). Dangerous terms: A user's guide to EULAs. http://www.eff.org/wp/dangerous-terms-users-guide-eulas

Register.com v. Verio Inc., 126 F. Supp. 2d 238, 245 (S.D.N.Y. 2000).

Ricker, Thomas. (2006, June 7). Norway reads iTunes Music Store EULA, hires angry lawyers. *Engadget.* http://www.engadget.com/2006/06/07/norway-reads-itunes-music-store-eula-hires-angry-lawyers/

Selfe, Cynthia L. (1999). *Technology and literacy in the twenty-first century: The importance of paying attention.* Carbondale, IL: Southern Illinois University Press.

Specht v. Netscape Communications Corp., 150 F. Supp. 2d 585 (S.D.N.Y. 2001).

Twitter. (2008). Twitter terms of service. https://twitter.com/terms

Warnecke, Michael. (2008, March 18). Turnitin.com lawsuit yields rulings on browsewrap contracts, fair use of copyrighted expression. http://pblog.bna.com/techlaw/2008/03/turnitin-lawsui.html

Williams, Bronwyn T. (2007–2008). Trust, betrayal, and authorship: Plagiarism and how we perceive students. *Journal of Adolescent and Adult Literacy, 51*(4), 350-354.

Wysocki, Anne. (1998). Monitoring order: Visual desire, the organization of web pages, and teaching the rules of design. *Kairos, 3*(2). http://kairos.technorhetoric.net/3.2/binder.html?features/wysocki/mOrder0.html

Young, Jeffrey R. (2008, April 4). Judge rules plagiarism-detection tool falls under "fair use." *The Chronicle of Higher Education, 54*(30), 13.

Zwagerman, Sean. (2008). The scarlet P: Plagiarism, panopticism, and the rhetoric of academic integrity. *College Composition and Communication, 59*(4), 676-710.

5 IMAGES, THE COMMONPLACE BOOK, AND DIGITAL SELF-FASHIONING

Bob Whipple

The way we use, collect, and acquire digital images can be guided to some extent by an understanding of the late medieval and renaissance-through-mid-19th-century concept of the commonplace book. As these earlier texts provided their collectors ways of constructing, altering, and mediating identity, so the ways that we collect visual images in digital–visual "commonplace books" may provide ways of self-definition and self-construction.

COMMONPLACE BOOKS AND SELF-CONSTRUCION

We know of the commonplace book as a handwritten artifact, popular among the literate in the late middle ages through parts of the 19th century, consisting of a bound blank book wherein a reader would hand-copy information that struck him or her as interesting, useful, necessary for future use, or that simply sounded memorable. "In the strictest sense," according to Earle Havens (2002), "the term commonplace book refers to a collection of well-known or personally-meaningful textual excerpts organized under individual thematic headings" (p. 8). Literacy historian Kenneth Lockridge (2001) extends and focuses this definition, asserting that "commonplace books are blank books in which genteel men and eventually women wrote down, and in some instances transformed, selections from their reading that they thought particularly interesting or significant" (p. 337).

While these descriptions are useful, perhaps more revelatory is another assertion from Havens (2001) about manuscript commonplace books (as opposed to printed ones):

> These more undisciplined and disorganized commonplace books appeared in every permutation and degree of sophistication, and included nearly every imaginable type of text: lines of epic poetry, lofty quotations, and, just as often, medicinal and culinary recipes, ribald couplets, hermetical numerical tables, cartoons, monumental inscriptions, magical spells, bad jokes; in short, all the literary flotsam and jetsam of the more vigorous sort of reader. (pp. 9-10)

Thus the actual commonplace book as assembled by the compiler (and not cleaned up for printing, as were many commonplace books intended to serve as "examples" of what a commonplace book should be) are an unruly space, a space wherein the compiler can both record and try out. They are places wherein the compiler sets down material for future use and reference, and catchalls for the miscellany of one's determined knowledge. They are, in essence, places wherein the compiler begins a kind of making, a kind of building of intellect, of storing material that one keeps not for the simple sake of keeping but for the purpose of making the material part of one's intellect and therefore constructing part of one's self. Why else, indeed, would one collect a miscellany of material if not to improve oneself, to provide oneself with ready building material?

"Manuscript commonplace books," Havens (2002) wrote, "were essentially practical, written expressions of the larger enterprise of reading itself, in the *legere* sense of gathering selecting, and collecting."[1] They are, in effect, places of private self-fashioning. Commonplace books, as Lockridge (2000) stated, "often function as [arenas] for the shaping and consolation of a self" (p. 338)— sites for individual identity formation, reinforcement, and negotiation.

VISUAL COMMONPLACES

We can see this identity formation at work, but in a primarily non-textual way, in a mid-20th-century scrapbook collected and collated in the late 1930s. (see figures 1 and 2).[2] This text shows a passion—one common in the 1930s, especially to boys[3]—for airplanes and their pilots, an exciting, relatively new, and contemporary technology, and the heroes who operated that technology. In this way, this portion of the book seems to identify a segment of what that compiler might want to be at some later point. Does the compiler have distinct plans to become a pilot? Join the Army Air Corps? We don't know. Do airplanes make up a significant part of the compiler's interest and focus? We can probably say a fairly strong "yes" to this. Through the use of deliberately

Figures 1 and 2: Images from a 1930s commonplace book.

selected visual texts (often accompanied by alphabetic text in the form of captions), the collector has expressed a focus of importance, that, in its own way, is equally as indicative (if not more so) of the compiler's *ethos* (in the word's meaning of essential or habitual element of character) as, for example, the copied text of an apothegm or pithy argument.

THE DIGITAL COMMONPLACE BOOK

The commonplace book is no longer a construct only of ink and paper. Jen Almjeld (2006), drawing on Kenneth Lockridge, crafted a persuasive connection between the commonplace book tradition on the one hand and blogs on the other. Blogs, to Almjeld, can be knowledge storehouses, keeping-places for information and knowledge, in much the same way textual commonplace books served as repositories of information for future use.[4]

Almjeld (2006) also noted the use of blogs as commonplace book-like storage spaces, as does Lucia Dacome (2004), who argued that "throughout the early modern period commonplace books provided repositories for arranging notes, excerpts, *drawings, and objects*" (p. 603; emphasis added). Thus the 1930s airplane scrapbook is noteworthy because it is largely a collection—a set of commonplaces, if you will—of some text, but mostly, almost entirely, photos of airplanes and some pilots cut from the pages of contemporary magazines. It is a visual commonplace book of its compiler's passion.

I've written elsewhere about what I believe might be a new kind of writing process—or, perhaps more accurately, a production process—for multimedia composing. I've noted that, in my multimedia composing process, I rely on a process of collection. In an earlier article (Whipple, 2008), I noted that

> I find myself collecting media in a kind of semi-serendipitous "gleaning" process as I go through my days, collecting digital images and clips... that I may not need right then for the project under construction, but might need later, or which seems, for lack of a better word, "useworthy." I take more advantage of visual opportunities. Indeed, I find that I am keeping a commonplace... of... digital images.... as a medieval or renaissance scholar would keep a commonplace book in which to keep aphorisms, quotations, exercises, and ideas... I find myself keeping a video/still image commonplace book with the camera on my cell phone.

Almjeld (2006) reminds us that digital "storehouses" may be found not only in blogs, but also in "hard drives, memory sticks, and other storage devices." We can add to these storage places others such as built-in digital camera memories, and cell phone cards, as well as Flickr, Photobucket, Google's Picasa, MSN Photo spaces, and other Web 2.0 storage entities. Indeed, my own digital commonplace book is scattered in several locations: the iPhoto archive on my MacBook, on a collection of flash drives in a pocket in my briefcase, on a card in my digital camera, and in the internal memory of my camera-equipped smartphone. While Kenneth Lockridge (2000) told us that individuals such as John Locke advocated complex and exhaustive systems of organizing commonplace books into personal knowledge systems (we might call them 17th- to 18th-century content management systems), this just doesn't work—at least for me, and perhaps for others. "People", said Lockridge (2000), "simply do not use commonplace books the way Descartes or Locke want them to" (p. 338).

Not all of the pictures in my digital commonplace-book are ones I've generated myself; the right-click/copy afforded by most browsers offers an effortless way to collect pictures—to appropriate them from someone else to make them, even if only for purposes of reference and storage, one's own. Consider, for example, the pictures below.

What is the importance of these pictures, each of which lives in my aforementioned storage spaces? To analyze each one in isolation is to lose sight of the context; an effective reading of my digital/visual commonplace book would involve the viewing of hundreds of pictures. The picture of the cat on the keyboard is a "taken for the moment" picture showing one of my cats in a favorite posture. Does this say something about me, how I wish to be perceived—or, since this is a private volume, how I perceive myself, beyond the fact that I like cute pictures of cats? Figure 4 is an "acquired" image, though I've had it for at least 10 years now, since I first began to construct webpages, and I have no idea

Digital Self-Fashioning

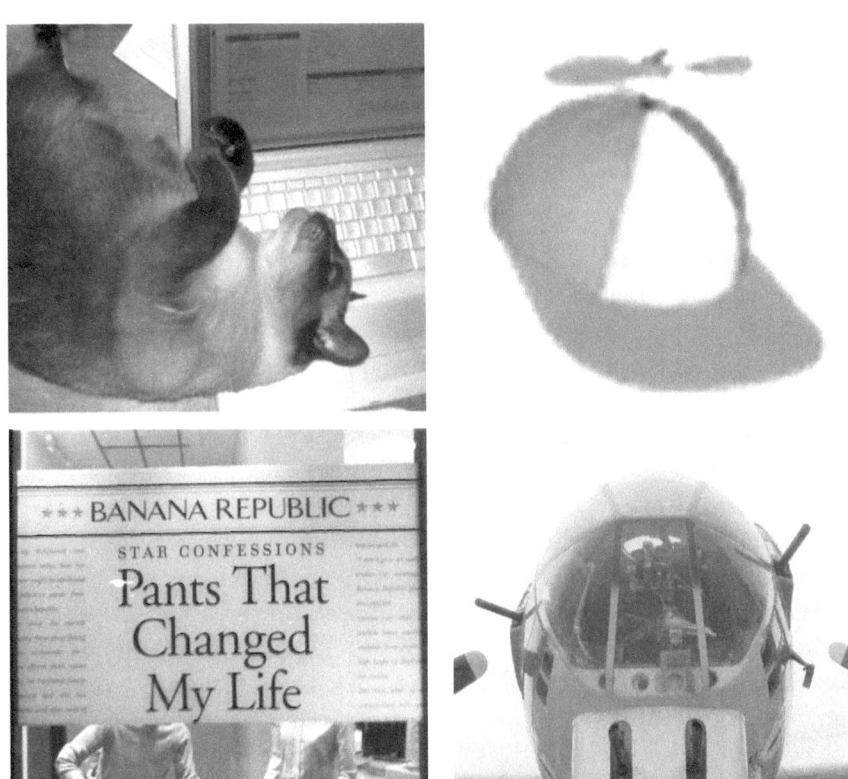

Figures 3, 4, 5, and 6: Photos I have taken or collected.

of its provenance. The last two are self-taken, one at an air show and the other in front of the window of a local clothing store. What can these say about me beyond the facile guess that I am a cat-loving airplane fancier with an appreciation for the silly and the incongruous?

Lockridge (2000) asserted that "if you know well the life of the keeper of a commonplace book, you soon find that the seemingly routine selections from his or her readings incorporated there, are startlingly revealing of that person's crises or issues of identity" (p. 338). I'd hazard, then, that we collect visual images for some of the reasons we collect text in more traditional commonplace instantiations: because *they are connected with our sense of what we are, or what we wish to become, or both.* We may know what we will do with the pictures we take, keep, and acquire; we may not. We may acquire them for specific present or future projects, or because they seem interesting. What about the things that we acquire on impulse, feeling some inchoate need that we cannot easily express? What about the acquisition, collection, and preservation of visual knowledge akin to the 18th-century reader's writing down of the pithy *apothegmata* of his time? Lockridge would call this the "trying-on of bits and pieces" (p. 339) of the intellectual fashions of the time. Are not these digital commonplace books, then, private places "in which to construct and console the self?"

For answers here, we may need to look at a common item found in commonplace books—*sententiae*, or the particularly memorable, well-stated line or passage. I suspect strongly that there is a bit of *sententiae*-collecting going on in my digital commonplace. If a phrase or sentence were collected because it is particularly well-put, then wouldn't a visual image or object be selected for a similar reason? As not all items in a traditional commonplace book were necessarily selected for immediate or near-immediate use in a text, why must digivisual items be collected only for immediate use? What, then, is the difference between a striking image that we collect or take simply because it is striking, and the sentence we write down because it is just as cool? In each case, there is an unspoken, and perhaps difficult-to-articulate, need to *have* the image.

Lockridge (2000) told us that commonplace books tell modern historians of literacy "what various forms of literacy did to the mentality of persons who acquired, possessed, and used" them (p. 337). Our visual, digital commonplace books inevitably perform the same function. They will turn out to be, as an anonymous 17th-century writer said, in penning yet another manual on organizing commonplace books, "a treasury (like that of an honest heart) where are good things stored up, both old and new, and a fair garment may be made of the shreds that are in such a repository" (Havens, 2002, p. 137).

NOTES

1. Havens (2001) earlier expressively defined *legere* as not only "the act of reading" but also to single out, select, extract, gather, collect, even to plunder and purloin. One did not merely encounter a text; one harvested it, separating the wheat from the tares in order to glean the pith and marrow. The term also signified a kind of rapine, even the violent confiscation of the fruits of another man's tree. (p. 8)

2. Almjeld (2006) also provided photographic images of similar commonplace-book scrapbooks.

3. Although, much as we would like to guess, we do not know the gender of the compiler of the book, as there are no gender-indicative cues, such as a name, on it.

4. By the same token, we can add social bookmarking systems such as Digg, cite.u.like, and del.icio.us to the list of commonplace-like digital systems, in

that they allow us to save information in a "place" whence they may be retrieved.

REFERENCES

Almjeld, Jen. (2006). Making blogs produce: Using academic storehouses and factories. *Computers and Composition Online.* http://www.bgsu.edu/cconline/almjeld/gradblogs.htm

Dacome, Lucia. (2004). Noting the mind: Commonplace books and the pursuit of the self in eighteenth-century Britain. *Journal of the History of Ideas,* 65(4), 603-625.

Havens, Earle. (2001). *Commonplace books: A history of manuscripts and printed books from antiquity to the twentieth century.* New Haven, CT: Beinecke Library and the University Press of New England.

Havens, Earle. (2002). "Of common places, or memorial books": An anonymous manuscript on commonplace books and the art of memory in seventeenth-century England. *Yale University Library Gazette,* 76(3/4), 136-153.

Lockridge, Kenneth. (2000). Individual literacy in commonplace books. *Interchange,* 2/3, 337-340.

Whipple, Bob. (2008). Notes on a new writing process: Multimediation as personal change agent. *Computers and Composition Online.* http://www.bgsu.edu/cconline/WhippleC&COnline/start.html

6 INTELLECTUAL PROPERTIES IN MULTIMODAL 21st-CENTURY COMPOSITION CLASSROOMS

Tharon W. Howard

In "Who 'Owns' Electronic Texts," first published in 1996 (and for which I wrote a reflection in 2004), I described the commonplace view in the United States that the ownership of writing, images, music, animations, or videos is a "natural right" of the person who created them. Although this natural right view is far less pervasive among educators and students in other countries such as China or even the United Kingdom, here in the U.S., students and teachers alike hold an unshakable, unimpeachable, and unexamined view that their creative works are, in actual fact, their "private property." Because of popular metaphors like "giving birth" to an idea in their writing, many in the U.S. have been socialized to believe that they're like the hero of an Ayn Rand novel, giving birth to works fathered by some kind of mysterious intercourse with their own inner genius. As a result, they don't perceive that they owe anything in their creative process to the society that educated and nurtured them. So when the editors of the current collection asked me to reprise the often-anthologized "Who Owns Electronic Texts," I was thrilled to do so, because I continue to find both students and colleagues laboring under some disabling ideas about who owns and, perhaps more importantly, who can make claims on the rights to copy and to use a created work. They lack an understanding of the history of copyright law; they lack an awareness of the intended purpose of the law; and—because they've only been exposed to metaphors about copyright—they lack the ability to distinguish between metaphor and actuality. As a result, they are ill-prepared to deal with intellectual property issues confronting them far more frequently than in the past because of the demands for multimodal composing in the 21st-century classroom.

Today, as Pat Sullivan (1991) also observed, writers can no longer afford the luxury of just being a "good wordsmith" able to focus solely on the words on the page. The convergence of media in contemporary texts, particularly those of professional communicators in the workplace, requires that we teach students to integrate visual arguments, video demonstrations, and even audio illustrations into their verbal texts. The combination of media, our multimodal understanding of text, and students' merely metaphorical understanding of copyrights has created an educational environment where students are dangerously vulnerable. Consider the following five scenarios—all of which are based on actual intellectual property questions my students have faced in the last 6 months:

> Scenario 1: Imagine you're a student in a technical writing class, and you've been assigned to write a manual on Web design for other students at your school. You're using icons, screen captures, and other visual elements from Adobe Dreamweaver, Adobe Photoshop, and Microsoft Word. You know your university has severe penalties for students who steal other people's intellectual property and plagiarize in a class, but you're not sure if you're in that situation here. Can you legally use the visual elements you copied from these interfaces?

> Scenario 2: Assume you've posted email messages to a public email discussion group for a couple of years. You discover that a graduate student is using the messages posted to the email group as part of her dissertation research on political correctness in email; however, you've never been contacted about whether your messages could be used as part of the research. You're not sure you want your messages used in what might be a potentially embarrassing way, but aren't sure of your rights.

> Scenario 3: You've given a conference presentation on user-support systems, and it catches the attention of a software manufacturing company looking to revamp its documentation systems. They offer to pay you for the time it would

take you to expand on the work you've already done and to conduct a more extensive review of current approaches to documentation and delivery systems. You'd like to do the review for them, but you also want to publish a journal article on the same subject; can you legally do both?

Scenario 4: You work for a Web design/consulting company, but on the side, you also maintain a personal blog where you publish tips and thoughts about the latest in Web design techniques. Your manager finds the blog and tells you to take the blog down or threatens to fire you.

Scenario 5: You're taking a class called "Creative 21st-Century Digital Publishing," and one of the assignments in the class is to create a "cyberpoem" in Adobe Flash that takes a poem like Robert Frost's "The Road Not Taken" and uses sound and animation to change its meaning. You want to use photos you found on Flickr.com and music from Nickelback to change the meaning, but you're not sure using these are legal.

As these scenarios hopefully illustrate, writers need a much richer and more complete understanding of copyright laws than the "natural right" metaphor provides, and because professional communicators are dealing with a much wider range of media in their texts, they need to be able to apply that understanding to more than alphabetic texts. As these scenarios from my technical writing classes and professional communication seminars reveal, I can no longer afford to depend solely on a grammar handbook explanation of plagiarism and on discussions of when to quote someone's work in an essay and when to summarize and cite it. Social media and other vast digital networks have complicated the intellectual property landscape in contemporary classrooms; writers must often have to differentiate plagiarism and copyright. As we know, the academically ethical citation of a source a student may have used doesn't protect him or her from being sent a cease and desist letter from the Recording Industry Association of America (RIAA) for violating a copyright. In the rest of this chapter, I describe some of the basic principles from the history of U.S. copyright laws I typically address in my classroom and then address how students and I use those principles to negotiate each of the scenarios introduced above.

Tharon W. Howard

UNBALANCING THE NATURAL RIGHTS METAPHOR

Back to Medieval Publishing

To get any traction with modern U.S. copyright and intellectual property law and the problems with the natural rights metaphor, it's best to begin with an examination of the origins of copyright law in the 16th century and the publishing revolution created by the introduction of the printing press. Many people are shocked to learn that modern copyright law didn't start from a desire to recognize and protect the natural rights of their authorial genius; instead, its origins lie in the "ignoble desire for censorship" and in the greedy lust to "protect profit by prohibiting unlicensed competition" (Beard, 1974, p. 383). Indeed, it took another 200 years after the first copyrights were granted to publishers before an author's rights were really even considered. As Martha Woodmansee (1984) pointed out, it wasn't until the 18th century that authors like Alexander Pope were able to begin to make claims on the right to profit from their work. In the 16th century, the purposes for granting copyrights were far more sordid and Machiavellian in nature than the protection of creative genius.

Prior to the introduction of the printing press, the technologies of medieval publishing were such that copyright laws really weren't needed. The cost of creating copies of what books were available virtually ensured that only the rich and powerful could afford to make copies. Peter Yu (2006) pointed out that "when Bishop Leofric took over Exeter Cathedral in 1050, he found only 5 books in its library" and in 1424, "the Library of Cambridge University had a remarkable collection of 122 books" (p. 7). The physical materials alone of medieval publishing were cost-prohibitive. Because vellum was a favorite choice for books of the highest quality, and because vellum is made from animal skins, a single volume could easily require harvesting 200 farm animals— or the equivalent of the entire annual output of a feudal lord's estate. And this is merely what's required to produce the raw material for the book. Extensive tanning and other labor-intensive processing was required to prepare the vellum for use in a book. As a result, ownership of a book of any sort was an extraordinary status symbol and a testimony to the wealth and power of the owner.

Yet, beyond the extraordinary costs of the raw material needed to produce a copy of a book, the literacies needed to physically copy a text also helped ensure that capricious copying of "unimportant" texts did not occur. Literacy was essentially controlled by the medieval church, and the scribes who did the laborious and painstaking work of hand-copying words on the page underwent an ideologically saturated disciplining process as an essential part of the education necessary for their work. Indeed, so thorough was the disciplining of the acolyte that the penknife, nib, and other tools of the scriber's craft all carried metaphorical significance so that, when the scribe used his penknife, he believed that he was providing a service to the Church by cutting through the ignorance of heresy. It should come as no great surprise then that few texts challenging the authority of either the Church or the State were copied. Only those with sufficient wealth could afford to produce copies, and their wealth almost certainly came from the support of the State; it's thus unlikely the wealthy would wish to undermine the State by copying and disseminating "dangerous" ideas. Even if the wealthy were willing to do so, the disciplined copiers of the day would have censored the work (see Putnam, 1897, for a more thorough discussion of the education and role of medieval scribes in knowledge production).

The Publishing Revolution and the Stationers' Charter

Just as Internet technologies are revolutionizing and reshaping our modern world, the technologies of paper and the printing press changed the 16th century. Even though books remained extraordinarily expensive by modern standards, the printing press did make book ownership possible for more than just the über-wealthy. The printing press made books affordable to new classes of people—people who wanted what had been status symbols for the super-rich and powerful. A new industry grew around the need for books. Enterprising publishers of the 16th century, called the "Stationers," used new technologies to rapidly produce books for this new class of consumers. However, unlike the monk-scribes, the limners (or illustrators), book binders, and editors who made up the Stationers Company had undergone a different disciplining process and were motivated by profit before religion. They were happy to satisfy the new consumer demand for books dealing with secular rather than religious topics (Putnam, 1897), books for consumers who were not indebted to the State and thus were far less concerned with supporting the State than their predecessors.

The convergence of these forces meant that books began to be produced that were no longer restricted by the interests of the State or the Church, and books that Mary Tudor and Phillip of Spain believed to be subversive appeared on the markets. So in 1556, Mary and Phillip granted the Stationers Company a royal charter that stated in its preamble that the charter was issued "to satisfy the desire of the Crown for an effective remedy against the publishing of seditious and heretical books" (Beard, 1974, p. 384). The Stationers' royal charter co-opted publishers by playing on their desire to "protect profit by prohibiting unlicensed competition" (Beard, p. 383). The charter "limited most printing to members of that company and empowered the stationers to search out and destroy unlawful books" (Patterson & Lindberg, 1991, p. 23). In so doing, the Stationers' Charter effectively reestablished the State's control over what books could be published. It gave the Stationers exclusive rights to copy and to profit from sanctioned texts in exchange for policing the publishing industry in much the same way that scribes had previously done. It turned the Stationers into agents of the State, and, more importantly, it did nothing to recognize or establish the rights of authors.

COPYRIGHT AND THE U.S. CONSTITUTION

Of course, when I teach students this history, they are rarely surprised to learn that 16th-century monarchs engaged in censorship or that the monarchs exploited the greed of the merchants around them to advance their interests. That's an old story we all have heard repeatedly in history classes. However, they are often stunned to learn that the U.S. Constitution is equally manipulative when it comes to copyright and that, just as Mary and Phillip used copyrights to exploit the greedy profit motive of individuals to advance the interests of the State, the first article of the U.S. Constitution does essentially the same thing. Article 1, Section 8 of the Constitution states that

> The Congress shall have the power ... to Promote the Progress of Science and useful Arts, by securing for limited Times to Authors and Inventors the exclusive Right to their respective Writings and Discoveries.

Just as the Stationers' Charter made clear that the purpose of government giving copyright privileges to the Stationers was to prevent the publication of seditious and heretical books, the Constitution makes clear that it is giving the legislative branch of the government authority to grant copyright privileges in order to improve the science and technology in the State. It does not say that "Authors and Inventors" have a natural right to "their respective Writings and Discoveries;" instead, it says that *Congress* has the authority to secure copyrights for authors. Furthermore, it also makes that authority conditional upon promoting scientific and technological discoveries and inventions that will improve living and economic conditions in society. In other words, Congress doesn't have authority to grant copyrights or to create copyright legislation *unless the purpose of that legislation improves society.* Article 1, Section 8 doesn't say anything about protecting authors' rights for the sake of individual authors. Instead, it recognizes that, without a profit motive, authors and inventors will not have a reason to pursue new knowledge and new discoveries and thus publish the sorts of books that the Founders wanted to see published. Consequently, just as the Stationers' Charter gave the Stationers exclusive rights to profit from books the Crown thought were in the best interests of the State, the U.S. Constitution gives Congress the authority to make the same deal with "Authors and Inventors."

REPLACING NATURAL RIGHTS WITH THE LICENSE METAPHOR

Ownership of copyrights, as this brief history hopefully makes clear, is not a natural right. Copyrights are, instead, temporary privileges granted by the State to persons or organizations the State chooses, for purposes intended to benefit the people the government is supposed to serve. As members of a participatory democracy, we can argue about whether modern copyright legislation has, in fact, benefited the people of the U.S. and whether modern congresses have failed to promote creativity and discovery to benefit our whole society (as the Constitution originally charged them). However, it's important to observe here that U.S. copyright laws don't protect the natural rights of authors or the corporations who employ them; instead, they actually limit the rights of copyright holders to profit by imposing time restrictions on the copyrights and by creating other conditions under which it is possible for members of a society to copy texts without having to pay for the privilege. It could be argued, in other words, that copyright legislation exists to protect society from greedy speculation by copyright holders. As Pierre Leval (1990) stated, "fair use is not a grudgingly tolerated exception to the copyright owner's rights of private property, but a fundamental policy of copyright law" (p. 1107).

However, once educators teach students that the U.S. Constitution doesn't recognize the absolute, natural property rights of authors, they need to fill the vacuum this creates, or we run the risk of allowing future citizens to fallaciously conclude that, because the Constitution doesn't recognize their natural rights, authors have no rights. The metaphor I have successfully used with college students is that of a driver's license. In a society where the ability to operate a motor vehicle is almost universally expected, the analogy works particularly well. People who own vehicles and who consider their cars to be their private property tend to believe that they ought to have the right to operate and use their property in pretty much the same way that copyright owners tend to feel they ought to have the right to use their copyrights. However, as we all know, even though it's conceivable that someone could own a car without a driver's license, it is not legal to operate a vehicle without having obtained a license from the state in which you live. Operating a vehicle on public roads isn't a natural right of private property owners; rather, it is a limited privilege granted by the State for a temporary period and only under conditions established by the State. As citizens, we accept these licensing conditions and the limits imposed on our individual freedoms because they protect the public from abuse and because, in the long run, they ensure that society as a whole will benefit from the increased commerce and quality of life made possible by public roads (although, as I discuss later, many believe changes in copyright legislation since 1990 have broken faith with this principle).

Although U.S. Code doesn't require that authors take a test and obtain a license before they can benefit from copyright, many of the same rules of the road still apply so that copyright holders don't crash into each other. For example, copyrights do not give the creator of a text ownership of ideas in the text; it only protects the tangible expression of those ideas. This is critical—without it, someone could claim to own universal truths. Imagine the impact it would have on the pharmaceutical industry if, for example, every time during the course of a drug study, lab technicians had to calculate the value of 2+3, they had to pay a royalty to some copyright holder who claimed to own the rights to the idea that 2+3=5. The effect on our economy would be just as chaotic and debilitating as it would be if cars were no longer required to drive on the right side of the road and it was left up to individual drivers to decide where to take their half of the road. The effect of having to pay copyright owners for ideas rather than expressions would be analogous to the impact that increasing costs of energy has on an economy. As we saw when Hurricane Katrina shut down oil refineries on the gulf coast, sky-rocketing fuel prices threatened to plunge our economy into a catastrophic recession. And while energy costs are certainly pervasive in an economy, imagine the impact of having to pay for ideas like the effects of gravity every time you used gravity. Consequently, copyright laws don't give Sir Isaac Newton or his estate the right to profit from the discovery of gravity beyond initially protecting his expression of the idea. Copyright laws allow him to recover and profit from the sales of books in which he described the discovery of gravity; they also protect our society and economy from the predatory and debilitating practice of attempting to charge for ideas. Indeed, in this pay-per-use scenario, it could be argued that Newton would never have discovered gravity in the first place because doing so would have required that he use mathematical equations that might have been "owned" by other mathematicians whom Newton could not have afforded to pay.

Copyright laws also both work against and protect society from abuses of the natural right metaphor. It recognizes that inventors and creators owe a debt to the society that nurtured and educated them and thereby enabled the creation, discovery, or production of a new idea from which the creator seeks to profit. The fair use clause is another speed limit and rule of the road that the State uses to ensure public safety and to force copyright holders to recognize the debt which they owe to society. As discussed by other authors in this collection, Statute 17, Section 107 of the U.S. Code grants the public the right to copy a work "for purposes such as criticism, comment, news reporting, teaching (including multiple copies for classroom use), scholarship, or research" without having to pay for the privilege. However, composition students need to understand that just because they are students in an educational environment and fair use does grant the right to copy works for educational purposes, that does not give them the right to copy everything. Statute 17 states that the four factors have to be taken into consideration when attempting to copy under the Doctrine of Fair Use:

- the purpose and character of the use, including whether such use is of a commercial nature or is for nonprofit educational purposes;
- the nature of the copyrighted work;
- the amount and substantiality of the portion used in relation to the copyrighted work as a whole; and
- the effect of the use upon the potential market for or value of the copyrighted work.

I have had writers create instructional videos in my technical writing classes and invariably several will attempt to use popular, copyrighted music as background audio with their digital videos to improve the quality of the production and to add interest to what would otherwise by a dry and uninteresting video clip. They mistakenly believe that because they are producing the video for a writing class, the fair use education clause gives them the right to copy all or most of, say, "Let It Be" by the Beatles. However, even though it meets the purpose and character test because it's being used for a non-commercial, educational purpose, copying the whole song into the video clip fails to meet the other three tests because "Let It Be" is copyrighted and sold for entertainment purposes, because the entire song is used rather than just a portion, and because making the song available through a digital video that might be published on YouTube means that potential consumers of the song wouldn't have to buy it from the publisher. In conclusion, fair use is very much like imposing speed limits on drivers: It seeks to achieve a balance between allowing copyright holders to use their property in an expeditious fashion in the same way that one can use a car to go to work or transport goods to market. The speed limit lets them drive fast enough so that they arrive at their destination in a timely manner, but it also protects other drivers on the road from people who want to drive too fast and operate their vehicle in a dangerous way. Fair use seeks to protect the rights of the property of an individual and the reasonable expectation that the creator of a work should be able to profit from the labor expended, while at the same time protecting the rights of society and the good of the whole. It is important to replace the natural right metaphor many bring into our classrooms with the more balanced metaphor of a driver's license.

COMPLEX COPYRIGHT SCENARIOS

Scenario 1: Screen Captures

For teachers in technical writing classes, this scenario is probably familiar, because many of us ask students to produce instruction manuals from readily available products such as popular software packages. However, what many of my colleagues find surprising and disturbing is that they might be encouraging students to violate copyright laws when they ask them to use screen captures from software and Web applications to produce their manuals. The practice of making screen captures and using them in training and documentation materials is so commonplace and so easy to accomplish that many people never stop to consider whether it's legal or not. Most people don't realize that, from a legal perspective, screen captures are considered "derivative works." According to the U.S. Copyright Act of 1976, Section 101:

> A derivative work is a work based upon one or more preexisting works, such as a translation, musical arrangement, dramatization, fictionalization, motion picture version, sound recording, art reproduction, abridgment, condensation, or any other form in which a work may be recast, transformed, or adapted. A work consisting of editorial revisions, annotations, elaborations, or other modifications which, as a whole, represent an original work of authorship, is a "derivative work."

In this case, capturing a screen from a copyrighted piece of software is the same as taking a photograph of a famous work of art in a museum. It's essentially copying a protected work to produce a derivative. As such, copying an interface by making a screen capture would be a copyright infringement unless the production and use of the derivative work can be defended by fair use or some other legal precedent or defense. The idea of *defense* here is worth discussing before moving on to consider the possible legality of making and using screen captures. Copying a piece of copyright-protected work always exposes the copyist to potential litigation. Fair use is a legal defense, but it doesn't mean that the copyright owner doesn't still have the right to sue in a civil case. In other words, it's important to understand that using a derivative work, like a screen capture, even if it's probably covered by fair use, doesn't protect you from being contacted by a copyright owner and eventually from being sued if the copyright owner isn't satisfied with your response once you've been contacted.

Copyright owners have the right to challenge copying of their property, so short of securing documented permission from the copyright holder before creating a derivative work, there's no absolute guarantee that you won't get sued and then have to defend your use of copyrighted material in court. An example of a copyright holder attempting to protect their property in the case of screen captures can be seen by Apple Corporation's attempt to protect its iPhone interface. In 1999, Apple sent cease and desist letters to webmasters who posted screen captures of Apple's iPhone interface on their Web sites ("Apple Uses Copyright to Silence"). According to Chilling Effects (a joint project of the Electronic Frontier Foundation and Harvard, Stanford, Berkeley, and other universities), Apple attempted to protect the look and feel of their interface and the iPhone experience by preventing other software companies from using their icons and interface design. As a result, they contacted any Web site that posted screen captures of the interface regardless of whether they had positive things to say about the interface or were offering critiques of it. The question here is whether the iPhone screen captures were being used for non-commercial criticism, comment, or news reporting, because these uses would likely be defensible under fair use. Similarly, to return to our original scenario, if a student were to produce an instructional manual on how to use the iPhone interface to complete some task and if they were to post their instruction manual on an electronic portfolio or on their Web site, it's entirely possible that the student would be contacted by Apple and informed that they must stop using the screen captures in their work. In this case, the fact that Apple contacted the students does not, however, mean that students can't legally use the screen captures. What it does mean is that the webmasters who posted the screen captures and the students could potentially go to court and defend their use of the material or alternatively, they could comply with Apple's potentially inappropriate request that they remove the material. Even though copyright holders have a right to sue, the costs of doing so make it unlikely that they would unless they were reasonably sure that they would win and realize a profit for doing so. Consequently, even though there's never a guarantee that you won't be sued, having a strong defense makes it extremely unlikely that the average person will be sued unless the copyright holder can show that they suffered sufficient damages to warrant bringing the case to court and sees a financial gain by bringing the suit.

Because there are no guarantees and it's important to be able to be able to weigh the strengths of your defense for copying a piece, it's important for students to be able to understand if they do have a strong defense. There are a number of defenses students can provide. One of the these is that many software companies actually do automatically grant their customers the right to use screen captures and visual elements in documentation. Apple Corporation, obviously, does not; however, Microsoft Corporation does allow the use of screen captures (but they do have requirements about the way their copyrighted visuals can be used). The following excerpt from Microsoft's Terms of Use Web site describes how screen captures may be used:

> You may use screen shots in advertising, in documentation (including educational brochures), in tutorial books, in videotapes, or on Web sites, provided you adhere to the following guidelines:
>
> 1. Your use may not be obscene or pornographic, and you may not be disparaging, defamatory, or libelous to Microsoft, any of its products, or any other person or entity.
>
> 2. Your use may not directly or indirectly imply Microsoft sponsorship, affiliation, or endorsement of your product or service.
>
> 3. You may not use the screen shot in a comparative advertisement.
>
> 4. You may not alter the screen shot in any way except to resize the screen shot. You may not use portions of the screen shots, and you may not include portions of a screen shot in your product user interface.
>
> 5. You may not use screen shots from Microsoft beta products or other products that have not been commercially released by Microsoft.
>
> 6. You may not use screen shots that contain third-party content.

7. You must include the following copyright attribution statement: "Microsoft product screen shot(s) reprinted with permission from Microsoft Corporation."

8. If your use includes references to a Microsoft product, you must use the full name of the product.

9. When referencing any Microsoft trademarks, follow the General Microsoft Trademark Guidelines.

10. You may not use a screen shot that contains an image of an identifiable individual.

11. For screen shots of Xbox and Games For Windows games, please visit our Game Content Usage Rules.

As item four above makes clear, students who wish to comply with Microsoft's guidelines need to use the entire screen rather than a portion, and, as item seven makes clear, they need to give credit using the language provided. Other software vendors also provide similar permissions. And, naturally, students and educators who wish to avoid potential legal conflicts can choose to comply with the vendor's guidelines.

Not following a software vendor's screen capture guidelines to the letter still, however, doesn't mean that using screen captures is necessarily illegal or inappropriate. It's safer and would probably be the recommended course of action, but there are legal defenses that allow students to use screen captures in an instructional manual, or other works, produced for a course. Is the student making a profit? In this case, they're not; they're making it for a class. They're not providing a copy of the entire software package; they're only illustrating a portion of the software to help users complete tasks with it. In terms of the effect of the instruction manual on the software's use or marketability, the manual is actually likely to increase the sales of the software, because an instruction manual that makes it easier to use is likely to encourage more people to purchase it. The use is potentially also defensible thanks to a precedent set by the U.S. Court of Appeals for the Second Circuit in the case of *Bill Graham Archives v. Dorling Kindersley Ltd.* In this case, as Martine Courant Rife (2009) observed, the court ruled that if the use of an entire image, not just a part of the image, is transformative, then its use is permissible. In this particular case, Dorling Kindersley was producing a history of the Grateful Dead and wished to use posters of Grateful Dead concerts in the book. The publisher contacted Bill Graham Archives (which held the copyright on the posters) and requested permission to reproduce the posters in the book. The Archives requested what the publishers perceived as "an unreasonable licensing fee" and, consequently, "permission agreements were never reached" (Rife). When the history was published, the Archives sued the publisher for copyright infringement. The court ruled the publisher's use of the visuals was fair use, even though they used the entire visual, and that "the use of the Grateful Dead images was transformative since the images were used in a time line and for historical purposes rather than for the poster's original purposes of concert promotion" (Rife). In our scenario it could be argued that, even though screen captures are considered derivative works and, therefore, are covered under copyright, a student using them in an instructional manual is a transformative, non-commercial use of the works for educational purposes that do not negatively impact the commercial viability of the product and is likely to be covered under fair use. Yet there's no guarantee that a software company wouldn't contact the student in spite of this defense, and thus it's always best to check the software vendor's Web sites to see if they give permission for screen captures and other uses.

Scenario 2: Public Email

This scenario asks you to imagine that you have posted email messages to a public email discussion group and you discover that your messages are being used by a graduate student as part of her dissertation research without having contacted you. It's tempting to think that this is a copyright issue, because U.S. Code does grant an author copyrights as soon as a work is created. Thus, as the author of the email messages, you might assume that you have rights to control the use of those messages. If we were dealing with hard-copy letters and print personal correspondence, the issue would be far more clear; the courts have determined that the person who receives a letter owns the physical property (i.e., the letter itself), but the author continues to own the tangible expression of ideas in the letters and thus can still make claims on its use.

Nevertheless, the lack of physical property and the situation of electronic messages on a system owned by another entity also complicates this scenario, as the 2005 case of Marine Lance Cpl. Justin Ellsworth illustrates. Ellsworth had a personal email account on Yahoo where copies of both his sent messages and received messages were stored. Ellsworth died attempting to defuse a bomb in Iraq, and his parents claimed that as next of kin they had right to his personal effects and thus sued Yahoo for access to Ellsworth's account in a Michigan probate court. The terms of Yahoo's service agreement, however, made clear that individual accounts are non-transferable and are deleted if the account holder dies (Hsieh, 2006). The case was settled when the court ordered Yahoo to provide copies of Ellsworth's messages to the parents (Olsen, 2005). Although the Ellsworth case is not considered definitive and it is still Yahoo's corporate policy that they are obligated to protect the privacy of both the deceased and of those individuals who may have sent email to the deceased account holder, the case certainly suggests that an author or an author's estate can still assert some ownership claim over the expression of their texts.

In this scenario, however, as soon as the messages were posted to a public discussion group, the issue changes, because the information in the posts may be considered in the public domain and because the posting of the messages is somewhat analogous to surrendering copyright when you publish a book. Typically, and especially in academic publishing, once an author of a book signs a publishing contract with a book publisher, the author transfers the copyrights to that publisher and usually can no longer make claims on the copyright. This scenario is similar *if* the discussion group or forum where the messages were posted also treats the messages as publications and, to participate in the forum, the author has entered into a terms of use agreement granting the owners of the forum specific usage rights to the messages. An example of this would be, for example, messages posted to one of the online forums hosted by Adobe Corporation. By posting a message on one of these groups:

> you grant Adobe a worldwide, royalty-free, nonexclusive, perpetual, irrevocable, and fully sublicensable license to use, distribute, reproduce, modify, adapt, publish, translate, publicly perform and publicly display Your Content (in whole or in part) and to incorporate Your Content into other Materials or works in any format or medium now known or later developed. (Adobe Systems Incorporated, 2008)

Consequently, even though Adobe doesn't claim ownership of messages posted to their forums, if the messages in the scenario were published elsewhere, the licensing agreement above would make it difficult for an author to complain about Adobe's uses of messages posted there.

In our scenarios, if a graduate student is merely using material deliberately posted to a public site, if the email discussion group makes clear that the postings are "publications," and if the student is not selling or profiting from the use of the material, then her use is probably defensible, and this question is probably not resolvable as a copyright issue. However, her use of the material might still be considered inappropriate (but most likely not) because of the federal guidelines governing empirical research conducted with human subjects. Before any research project can be undertaken at a college or university, it must be approved by the school's institutional review board (IRB) to ensure that the research complies with federal guidelines regarding the use of human subjects in research studies. One critical component of empirical research IRBs take into consideration is the principle of "informed consent" that requires that researchers obtain the voluntary consent of people to participant in the study before collecting data from them. Because the graduate student had not contacted posters to the list and obtained consent and voluntary agreement to participate in the study, you would be within your rights to contact the IRB at the student's school to discover if the research study had been approved and to learn what (if any) precautions were being taken to protect your privacy and other rights (see Frankel & Siang, 2009).

Scenario 3: Work for Hire

This scenario asks you to assume that you're a faculty member at a college and that you've been contacted by a company wishing to sponsor research you will conduct on their behalf to help them better understand the future of documentation. In other words, you're entering into a contract to write a report for the company in exchange for remuneration from the company. This is known as a work-for-hire agreement, and, typically, even though you may be the sole author of the report you are producing for the company, the agreement stipulates that you must surrender any claim you might make on the copyright to the company sponsoring the research. This means that you're transferring your rights to tangible expression of the ideas to the company and giving up the right to publish significant portions of the report in a trade magazine or journal. Even though you wrote the research report, you couldn't use the same expressions used in the research report in a future article because the company would own "your words" and those expressions at that point (see Amidon, this volume, for an extended discussion of work for hire).

Of course, because academics live in a publish-or-peril world, this arrangement usually isn't in our best interests. The long-term benefits obtained from the impact publication has on tenure and promotion are usually worth far more than the short-term remuneration a company might offer in a work-for-hire agreement. Consequently it's useful for academics to know that it's not necessary to accept the traditional work-for-hire agreement and to surrender all copyright privileges to a company. One can, for instance, stipulate in the contract the right to publish some or all of the material developed in a research report. Often companies will agree to this stipulation if you'll also compromise by further stipulating that you won't publish the material in a peer-reviewed journal or other publication for 6 months or a year or some other period of time sufficient to allow them to develop a competitive advantage using the information you provide. Companies are also usually sensitive to revealing information about trade secrets, manufacturing processes, or other confidential and proprietary information its competitors might be able to use. Therefore, you may also have to negotiate a compromise that allows the company the right to review the article before it is submitted for publication to ensure that it doesn't reveal information the company feels is confidential or of a proprietary nature. If you have graduate students collaborating with you on the project, you also need to make sure that the work-for-hire agreement doesn't in any way prevent you or the graduate students from publishing in the future. Some work-for-hire agreements can be so rigid and exclusive that they can put entire subject areas off limits. This was the case for me when I was working on usability testing research on three-dimensional interfaces sponsored by a technology company I can't name in this article. Because I didn't specify a time limit in the contract that would allow me to publish on the topic, both the graduate students who worked on the project and I are still legally obligated not to publish or reveal information to which we were privy as part of that project without the expressed written consent of the company's legal department.

The point to be made here is that work-for-hire agreements don't necessarily preclude publication and don't necessarily mean the surrender of all copyright claims. If you're careful, and are able to successfully negotiate with the funder, it may be possible to publish sponsored research in public venues. That said, it's also your responsibility to make sure that when you do publish sponsored research in a public venue that you notify the editors, publishers, and peer reviewers of the fact that the work had been produced with sponsorship.

Scenario 4: Non-disclosure Agreements

In this scenario, the question is whether or not an employer has the right to terminate employment for maintaining a blog. Although it's repugnant and potentially scary to many, in fact, it may be the case that an employer does have the right to impose limits on the information you can make publicly accessible. Employment in a Web consulting company typically involves a work-for-hire agreement, and an employer probably required a signed contract outlining the scope of information you have the authority to reveal. As a condition of your employment, you probably also signed a non-disclosure agreement (commonly known as an NDA) that prevents you from publishing information the company considers proprietary in nature. Consequently, if we assume that you are operating under this NDA, and if we assume that you revealed proprietary information about the processes or business practices of the consulting firm for which you work, then your employer does have the right to require that you remove that information from the blog. The information is copyrighted and proprietary, and you are only privy to it because of your employment; hence, your employers are perfectly within their rights to ask you to remove it. If you refuse to do so, they may terminate your employment and even bring suit against you.

However, your employer probably does not have the right to require that you completely take down your blog and cannot order you not to maintain a blog on your own time using your own computer equipment and network access. The company can prevent you from using equipment and Internet access they provide, but they don't have a right to tell you what to do with your own resources on your own time as long as you aren't violating your NDA or some other aspect of your contract with them. They have copyrights you need to respect, but you also have free speech rights they are also legally obligated to respect. As was the case with the work-for-hire agreements in the previous scenario, what is and is not permissible and copy-protected by an NDA depends largely on the nature of the agreement, and it's important that teachers help students understand that they have rights and that they need to carefully review and potentially even negotiate the limitations a potential employer may attempt to impose on them.

Scenario 5: Remixes

In this scenario, a student is asked to change the meaning of Robert Frost's poem "A Road Not Taken" through the use of Flash animations and audio clips. The first question that needs to be addressed is whether or not the student can use Frost's poem without having to pay royalty to the copyright holder of Frost's poem. Because the assignment asks for the creation of a parody of and thus a transformation of the meaning of the poem, the student is actually creating a new work. Because the student's use of Frost's poem is deliberately transformative and because it is being used as an educational, not-for-profit exercise intended to teach the power of animation, this transformative use is defensible. Creating a parody or remix of the poem might cover the student's use of Frost's poem, but in this case the student is creating a multimodal composition and also wishes to use photos from Flickr and a song by Nickelback.

A key factor in determining use would depend, for example, on how much of the photograph the student was using and how much was being changed. In the case of the poem, because the meaning is deliberately being changed for parodic purposes, its use is covered (see Hall, Gossett, & Vincelette, this volume, for an extended discussion of parody). However, the student is probably using the images without significant transformation, so the copyrights for the photographs are still the property of the photographer—even though they were taken from Flickr, which is a social-networking site that encourages people to share their photos with other Flickr users. Unless the photographer gave permission for Flickr users to use the images royalty free, then the student should probably be advised to contact the photographer and request permission to use the photographs for the course assignment. Of course, even when they obtain permission to use the images, students should give credit to the photographers whose images they used (see the licensing structure of Flickr) by citing the works in the credits. As has been stated previously, citing sources isn't a condition of fair use, but it is the ethical thing to do and is nearly always required by an educational institution's anti-plagiarism policies.

Regarding the Nickelback songs, once again, the question is how much of the song is being used and for what purpose. It is typically the case when students complete this assignment in my class that the student uses all or a significant portion of the song without any audio editing (such as changing the tempo, adding reverb, or creating distortion of any kind), and the student is typically using the lyrics to convey the meaning as the artist intended. The use is often an attempt to give the audience the same experience of the music that they would hear on the radio; it's not transformative and may not be defensible under fair use. What's more, if the student is putting the unmediated music on the Web, where the audio can be copied by others in a way that might allow them not to have to purchase the song from the music publisher, and because the music industry has been aggressively and vociferously defending its copyrights, the student would be advised to find royalty-free music clips or to record music rather than ripping audio from a commercial CD. On the other hand, if the student is only using a short excerpt from the song and using it in a way that would be considered transformative and somehow changes the meaning of the work in the same ways that a parody would change the work, then its use would be covered by fair use.

CONCLUSION

Obviously, as these scenarios show, the issues here are very complex and require a fairly sophisticated understanding of copyright laws and potential defenses for the acceptable uses of copyrighted works. We need to provide this understanding to students, because the consequences of copyright infringement are far more damaging than has ever been the case in the history of U.S.

copyright legislation. Unfortunately, since the 1990s, modern copyright law has changed more dramatically and more in favor of natural rights than it has since the Statutes of Queen Anne. Today, both educators and students are at greater risk of suffering from copyright infringement, litigation, and capital expenditure than ever in our history. The five scenarios are all based on actual situations encountered in a mere 6-month period, and what I hope they illustrate is that 21st-century composition students live in a far more dangerous world than they did in 1996. Today, teachers must prepare them for a world:

- where they can be attacked by Apple Corporation for using a screen capture in a manual intended to help other students use their iPhones;
- where they may not be able to conduct basic research on ethical email communication practices in public forums without prior permission from a federal oversight board;
- where they can be fired or be prosecuted for posting messages to their blogs or for publishing an article about an idea they learned while working as lab assistant in a university research lab; and
- where they may face criminal prosecution for using a song to enhance the meaning of a poem in a multimodal composition.

Writers of the future can't afford to learn about copyright by trial and error in the corporate world. The lesson that world teaches is that it is the natural right of Walt Disney's inheritors to continue to make us pay for pictures he drew over 75 years ago; the lesson is that the society that educated and nurtured Walt Disney and the economy that supported and enabled his company to grow and to become successful don't deserve some rights to use the cultural icons we helped create. The lesson this world wants to teach today's students is that using pictures of cultural icons like Mickey Mouse and King Kong without paying Disney and Paramount makes them criminals who deserve to have records of their federal offenses follow them for the rest of their lives. In 1996, a student violating a copyright in a class project like that in scenario 5 meant that her copyright infringements were limited to civil courts. Pretty much the worst that could happen was that the copyright owner could sue for damages. The risk to students and educators of infringing on a copyright was relatively small compared to today. But the introduction in 1997 of the No Electronic Theft (NET) Act changed all of that by making copyright infringement a criminal offense even for non-commercial infringement. Thus, the student in Scenario 5 who knowingly and "willfully" used a Nickelback song and who makes it available for copy "by the reproduction or distribution, including by electronic means, during any 180-day period" (17 USC Section 506a) can now be imprisoned for up to 5 years for the first offense and 10 years for a second (18 USC Section 2319b).

Those of us who teach composition owe it to students to make them aware of the copyright infringement risks they will encounter when they produce works for class and for future employers. We need to prepare them to work in a world where the incredible reproduction and distribution power of the Internet magnifies the impact of their actions in ways that may have significant financial consequences for them personally or for the companies employing them if they lack a sophisticated understanding of copyright laws and principles.

However, I would also argue that teachers and writers have a responsibility to do more than merely become aware of the risks and consequences of copyright infringements. Writers need to be more than good self-governing employees who won't get themselves or their companies in trouble. They also need to function as informed citizens in a participatory democracy. We need citizens who do not suffer from the foundationalist mythology that tells them truths are discovered by geniuses rather than socially constructed by a society—a mythology that tells them that copyrights are "natural rights" belonging to authors or inventors and their estates forever and for all time.

Citizens of a participatory democracy need to know that the original length of time a creator could benefit from a copyright was 7 years. The Statute of Queen Anne increased it to 14 years, and it has steadily increased in length. Thanks to the activities of corporate lobbyists in Congress throughout the 1990s, in the United States today, works created on or after January 1, 1978, have copyright protection for the life of the author plus 70 or 95 years from the date of publication for works produced under work-for-hire agreements. We need citizens who realize that congressional legislation of this sort runs counter to the purposes for copyright authorized by the U.S. Constitution. The Constitution gave legislators the authority to create copyright laws that stimulate creativity in the arts and that encourage originality in scientific investigation and technological inventions. We need educated citizens who can ask their legislators if allowing an artist and the inheritors of the author's estate to profit from a work for the entire life of the author plus 70 years is consistent with the kind of creativity the Constitution sought to stimulate. We need writers who question whether or not laws like the NET Act encourage creativity and protect society's right to use works for non-commercial purposes. We need students who, once they graduate and become future legislators and corporate executives, have had the kind of educational experiences that allow them to ask if it is really in the best interests of "Promoting the Progress of Science and useful Arts" in society to threaten students who create Web-based multimodal compositions or employees who maintain blogs with criminal prosecution.

REFERENCES

Adobe Systems Incorporated. (2008, October 15). Terms of use. http://www.adobe.com/misc/copyright.html

Apple uses copyright to silence both fans and critics. (2009). Chilling Effects Clearinghouse. http://www.chillingeffects.org/copyright/notice.cgi?NoticeID=6222#QID809

Beard, Joseph. (1974). The copyright issue. *Annual Review of Information Science and Technology, 9,* 381–411.

Bill Graham Archives v. Dorling Kindersley Limited. (2006). 448 F.3d 605

Frankel, Mark S., & Siang, Sanyin. (1999). *Ethical and legal aspects of human subjects research on the Internet.* American Association for the Advancement of Science. http://www.aaas.org/spp/sfrl/projects/intres/report.pdf

Howard, Tharon. (1996). Who "owns" electronic texts? In Jennie Dauterman & Patricia Sullivan (Eds.), *Electronic literacies in the workplace: technologies of writing* (pp. 177–198). Urbana, IL: National Council of Teachers of English.

Howard, Tharon. (2004). Reflection on "Who 'owns' electronic texts?" In Johndan Johnson-Eilola & Stuart Selber (Eds.), *Central works in technical communication* (pp. 397–408). New York: Oxford University Press.

Hsieh, Sylvia. (2006). Who owns your e-mail after you die? *Business Resources, Advice and Forms for Large and Small Businesses.* http://www.allbusiness.com/services/legal-services/4102944-1.html.

Leval, Pierre. (1990, March). Toward a fair use standard. *Harvard Law Review,* 1105–1136.

Microsoft Corporation. Use of Microsoft copyrighted content." http://www.microsoft.com/about/legal/permissions/default.mspx#E3C

NET Act: 17 U.S.C. and 18 U.S.C. as amended. (1998). United States Department of Justice. http://www.usdoj.gov/criminal/cybercrime/17-18red.htm

Olsen, Stefanie. (2005). L/Cpl Justin Ellsworth. CNET News.com. http://www.justinellsworth.net/email/cnet-apr21-05.htm

Patterson, L. Ray, & Lindberg, Stanley W. (1991). *The nature of copyright: A law of users' rights.* Athens: University of Georgia Press.

Putnam, George Haven. (1897). *Books and their makers during the middle ages; A study of the conditions of the production and distribution of literature from the fall of the Roman empire to the close of the seventeenth century.* New York: G.P Putnam's Sons.

Rife, Martine Courant. (2009). Remix as "Fair Use": Grateful Dead posters' republication held to be a transformative, fair use. National Council of Teachers of English. http://www.ncte.org/cccc/committees/ip/2006developments/remix

Sullivan, Patricia. (1991). Taking control of the page: Electronic writing and word publishing. In Gail E. Hawisher & Cynthia L. Selfe (Eds.), *Evolving perspectives on computers and composition studies: Questions for the 1990s* (pp. 43–64). Urbana, IL: National Council of Teachers of English.

Woodmansee, Martha. (1984). The genius and the copyright: Economic and legal conditions of the emergence of the "author." *Eighteenth-Century Studies, 17*(4), 425–448.

Yu, Peter. (2006). Of monks, medieval scribes, and middlemen. *Michigan State Law Review*, 1–31.

7 IS DIGITAL THE NEW DIGITAL? PEDAGOGICAL FRAMES OF REFERENCE AND THEIR IMPLICATIONS IN THEORY AND PRACTICE

Robert Dornsife

The very concept of "the copy" comes into play first in all that relates the digital to the analog, and second in all that defines the digital, *per se*. As composition teachers, we have been generous to our inherited analog forms—such as "the paper." We have allowed—even required—that the analog form ("the paper") continue to exist digitally. To the same extent, we have allowed our analog aesthetic and its concerns with plagiarism and the like to be "copied" into the digital realm. That we should "do more" is an old argument. What is not so old is that perhaps we as teachers should see that analog content—even "mediated" digitally from the beginning—doesn't work and doesn't fit as well as forms that are impossible to imagine, create, or experience in forms other than digital.

Thus far in the thinking of our discipline, the question of computer composition has proceeded in the following direction: Shouldn't we allow the digital text its place, too? Drawing on my personal experience with popular technologies, in part one of this chapter I explore whether the question should not now be asked from the other direction; that is, we might ask whether or not it is okay to allow or require (or whatever we do as teachers) the analog form to exist at all. The process of moving our classrooms to a place where digitalness begins no longer as a complement to or copy of the analog but instead as its own whole and unapologetic frame of reference carries with it the obligation to revise analog definitions of the copy. In part two, I discuss the central obstacle to the full embrace of the digital as its own frame, arguing that analog definitions and implications of the copy do not hold or apply within a digital frame, and I engage the implications that extend from such a new frame. I conclude by offering some practical pedagogy as regards inhabiting the digital paradigm via a discussion of "artistic license."

IS DIGITAL THE NEW DIGITAL?

My undergraduate poetry professor, John Taggart, invited me over to listen to some records. His stereo had Magneplanar speakers the size of doors—about as tall and as wide and as thick. His turntable's cartridge had its own amplifier, and the turntable itself offered a vacuum that ensured the flatness of the vinyl. A few months before, I had heard my first compact disc—the emerging notes of Rush's "Red Barchetta" coming out of the silence—from a CD player that had a futuristic font on its front panel announcing the player was "digital." When I asked Dr. Taggart about CDs, he responded that they didn't sound good and that vinyl was superior. I had recently heard that a digitally outputted signal was a digitally outputted signal. As it was described to me by the salesman, "there is not a whole lot of difference between the least expensive CD player and the most expensive." So—believing that—as naïve as digitalness was new, I concluded that maybe my mentor was a little concerned about his investment. That, perhaps, his vinyl and its system were in danger of becoming less exclusive or even extinct, and that such fears motivated his discrediting of this background-noiseless sound I had heard via my friend's digital CD player. I even adopted my own smug counter-attitude, something like "if you prefer the clips and pops of vinyl, that is your choice."

Six years earlier, I saw *Star Wars* at the local dollar movie theater, as an analog, celluloid, film. The film was badly scratched and worn. My own Super 8mm copy—titled, also, *Star Wars*—was 12 minutes of silent excerpts in black and white. Still, though, the neighborhood kids paid their quarters to watch it again and again, as it was "Star Wars" in my basement after all. My attempts to freeze frame the most fantastic moments resulted in my projector bulb burning the film in many key places.

The first time I saw high-definition television was in a large chain store. It was a basketball game being piped clearly into those televisions via some sort of high-end signal. For the first time, I could read the t-shirts of the people in the crowd and see the holes in the mesh of the players' jerseys. A high-definition DVD format holds about 25 gigs of data. To capture every nuance of the "film" would require exponentially more capacity than that. But the grain of the film is random and so film's apparent clarity is therefore compromised.

Is Digital the New Digital?

I remember Stevie Nicks talking about hearing Fleetwood Mac's album *Rumours* in high-resolution 5.1 surround channel audio for the first time. She reported that the experience so closely replicated what she heard while making the album decades earlier that she broke into tears. So Stevie Nicks moved me. A friend had assembled a 5.1 channel audio system in his living room. We listened to *Rumours*. Six speakers do something that two cannot. Vinyl doesn't offer six channels; this higher-resolution disc did. Then I saw the "oldest" Star Wars movie (episode IV) on his high-definition television. It was the best version of the film I had ever seen—I exclaimed that I was, in fact, seeing it for the first time.

At that point, having heard *Rumours* in the way that made Nicks cry over its moving accuracy and having seen *Star Wars* with a clarity previously unavailable to me, I began to wonder about vinyl and film. Both were and were not nostalgic. I was engaging texts from my youth, after all—but not the same texts. These were better, except for the fact that, for example, my dad might have popped his head in back in 1977 in a way that would not happen in 2009. So I missed that version of the experience of the text. But, now, *Rumours* had six channels and I was closer to where Stevie and the band had been. There were parts of the arrangement that I could not hear in stereo, but which I now heard—I was now in the midst of them, with detail and space and moments not possible in analog. I value nostalgia as much as the next person—maybe more. But *Rumours* sounded better and *Star Wars* looked better; since my experience with this version of the movie and this version of the album, digital moved past being the new analog. It was, then, free to move beyond copying the analog. New digital became the new digital.

But the potential to be free of the copy had another step—a step that at once furthers and undermines just how good *Star Wars* looks, remastered. My friend's high-definition television is still forced to deal with non-high definition, so called "standard definition," material. And if you ever saw that, you would have noticed how the image of, for example, the newscasters does not look as good as the logos and so forth that introduce and share the screen with them. The logos and all such apparatus are digitally made. And, as good as *Star Wars* looks, visually—in the technical sense—*300* looks better; *300* looks almost three-dimensional, with clarity and detail the likes of which I had not seen previously. I watched *300* as a result of a student's insistence; it is among, for the moment, a small number of films to employ a digital backlot. A digital or virtual backlot describes sets that do not have genuine locations on sound stages. They are, to some extent, simulacra constructed on a blank background or green screen. An artificial environment—a computer-created "location"—is added in post-production. Similarly, Sting's *Brand New Day*, which, unlike

Rumours, was mastered originally in the digital and exists in a high-resolution surround format, sounds in a way very similar to the way *300* looks: pristine, detailed, deliberate.

I submit that digitally captured content that has always been digital content—in other words, that has not been remastered from the analog—is "better" (that is, more faithful) when mediated via a digital medium. It is better still than remastered content that is now digital but was once analog. The act of having to copy the original condition is a fraught act of translation that announces itself as presenting the primary space in which to observe degradation: As the analog is converted to the digital, there is risk. The risk is less pronounced, and at once ideally and possibly negated, as analog mediates analog and digital digital. Going from two channels to six channels from an analog master at once faces some of the same challenges, but offers something new—not primarily a copy but an extension of the analog into a new, digitally possible text. In sum, then: originally digital content is more faithfully mediated when mediated digitally than originally analog content remastered into digital is. The 5.1 high-resolution surround format of *Rumours*—necessarily mediated digitally—might be seen as more faithful than the two-channel vinyl version via even its native analog mediation because it is not a copy as regards the stereo master. The obligation is one of faithfully serving the master, be it the master tape, the voices at play within the studio space, or the analog or digital metaphor that underlies the aesthetic.

Jay David Bolter (2001) articulated how the digital writing space is limited by the way culture understands it as a place for writing that remains subservient to the analog:

> The space of electronic writing is both the computer screen, where text is displayed, and the electronic memory, in which text is stored. Our culture has chosen to fashion these technologies into a writing space that is animated, visually complex, and malleable in the hands of both writer and reader. In this late age of print, however, writers and readers still often conceive of text as located in the space of a printed book, and they conceive of the electronic writing space as a refashioning of the older space of print. (p. 13)

This chapter calls for an examination of this seemingly inherent connection between the digital and the analog in an attempt to realize the resulting implications if they are understood distinctly, allowing each to manifest within its own framework and according to its own rules. The analog, remediated digitally, may strive to preserve the analog aesthetic—including its rules—but does so at the risk of remaining less faithful to its own possibilities. Bolter argued that "the very fact that electronic writing must confront the tradition of print makes electronic writing different from print; it means that our culture will have at least some different uses for electronic texts" (p. 45). We must identify these differences so that the analog and the digital can be distinguished and utilized knowingly, emphasizing the benefit of each within its respective framework.

When the widescreen 16:9 format first appeared on televisions in stores and in a few early-adopting homes, service centers were bombarded with calls about "the bars on the screen." These bars, or dead spaces, resulted from 16:9 texts being played on the then-standard 4:3 screens. Conversely, those who purchased 16:9 screens were forced to deal with the translation of 4:3 content.

Many viewers elected to squash the 4:3 picture down so that it filled the widescreen—even though the image was flattened and distorted in a striking way. Had an analog television suddenly started to squash the image in a way that it is now *chosen* to be squashed by 16:9 screen owners, many of these same viewers may very well have looked to correct the problem. In one sense we are maximizing the provided digital screen space—and in that sense the image does fit, but it is squashed and in that sense it does not fit or is a bad fit.

Composition teachers and scholars who continue to work with (or against) digitalness by attempting to house the digital within an analog frame may, too, be pursuing a bad fit. Seeing new digital not as new digital but as obliged to "copy" the analog is not allowing the digital, in practice and in theory, its due potential. (I address the implications of this bad fit specifically as regards plagiarism and the copy later in this chapter.) Generally, a bad fit may result if we do not consider how students' daily interactions with rapidly changing technologies compose their working, public, and personal lives, an impact explored by the New London Group (2000), which argued that "pedagogy now must account for the burgeoning variety of text forms associated with information and multimedia technologies" (p. 9). For example, I wonder if I am doing the best I can when I so much as allow a paper to be written on the computer.

The question has to this point proceeded in the direction of asking whether or not we should allow the digital text its place. Of course students can still compose and print papers, but let's also allow and explore *this*. Let's allow for a certain amount of this other, digital thing. We even talk of composing an analog paper, via computer, as though it were a meaningfully digital act. But, as I mentioned earlier, I wonder whether the question should not now be asked from the other direction: Should we allow or require the analog form to exist at all? Should we not abandon any obligation to the analog copy? After all, our obligation is to students, as articulated by the WIDE Research Collective (2009) in their "Why Teach Digital Writing?": "If we want to teach writing or help students learn how to write more effectively, then we have to be with them where they write. Networks are classrooms." I felt a strange discomfort as I watched *Star Wars*. I felt I was behind.

Once, in a first-year composition course, each group chose an art form (sculpture, poetry, dance, etc.) and the goal was to push on these forms until we could get at the essential compositional processes of each. As we concluded on the second day, we found that the compositional mechanisms were themselves all the same: contour, rhythm, emphasis, organization and so forth. So these compositional concerns as such may carry across media and space. But I think I might do better to change the direction—at least, for example, to include writing prose words in the longer list of compositional ends. As soon as I think this, though, I immediately fear that I am including a "dead" form—a form that I am preserving for reasons that may not hold up to much scrutiny. Should we not allow students to engage writing prose words as such? Progress—even in the examined, deliberate sense—might tempt us in this direction, but, instead, I think our question might be: What do prose words do better and under what circumstances than competing, digital, mediations? To what meaning is prose a better channel than music? Toward what texture is prose at least the equal option and ideally the only option? I think in engaging such questions we may finally shift the direction of our consideration. Such a shift requires that we engage our analog frameworks with an eye toward revision.

COMING TO TERMS WITH DIGITAL AS THE NEW DIGITAL: THE COPY AS OBSTACLE

To the extent that *Rumours*, *Star Wars*, and high-definition and high-resolution formats have prompted composition to consider a starting point that is not analog *per se*, there has been one obstacle with which we are still coming to terms. A December 2008 article offers this representative report:

> A long time ago in a galaxy far, far away, when people wanted to see a film, they went to a movie theater. They never entertained the idea of copying a movie, mainly because of all the industrial chemistry involved. Then videotape came along—followed by attorneys. Now we have the latest dust up in the long battle of the technical ability to copy movies vs. a little thing called copyright.

The article then outlines this latest manifestation of the argument, this time as regards a certain DVD-copying software and the large legal battles it faces. Nowhere is there a greater difference between the analog and the digital than as regards the copy.

First, as regards the vinyl album, there was no technology commercially available to reproduce its contents on another vinyl album; to copy, while remaining within the same vinyl medium, was not possible. The album announced itself as the standard in part because the listener needed to acquire the actual album to have access to the album as album. Thus, the trip to the record store was a one-sided trip—a trip to a place where one could only consume, once removed, at least, from the medium being engaged. Although plenty of listeners may have dreamed of making it to the other side of this one-way mediation, few had the capacity to do so, as home-recording studios able to produce a product on vinyl were rare or non-existent. The act itself of "making it" onto vinyl marked a step toward legitimacy, in part because access to this medium was a rare access.

The copy introduced itself primarily via magnetic tape. Anyone who owned one of the once-ubiquitous portable audio cassette tape players/recorders that offered two decks or anyone who has copied from, for example, the television to VHS tape or from VHS tape to VHS tape will probably have experienced the nature of the analog copy. It is marked as copy by its degradation in contrast to the original. Other analog systems of value make manifest this degradation and the resulting determination of worth. For example, bootlegged tapes, both VHS and audio cassette, were valued by how far removed from the master they were. This concept of generation determined the value of the tape. For example, a second-generation tape, which usually referred to a copy from the copy that had been made from the master, would be worth more than a fifth-generation tape. Later generation tapes, priced far less, were often listed with the warning "collectors only" or some other notice signaling that the tape was so many generations from the master that it was hard to make out the content, and was thus only of any value to the completist collector. The extent of the generational degradation depended, but only relatively, on the quality of the equipment used to facilitate the reproduction. The nature of the analog tape is such that even a fully analog signal chain will result in loss and distortion with each successive generation.

Similarly, analog reproductive technologies resulted in wear with each engagement. The claim that "I listened to that vinyl album so many times that I wore it out" was, in fact, the truth, as the contact between the (usually) diamond stylus and the vinyl was a microscopically violent one, resulting in the paring away of the vinyl itself with each engagement. Again, the extent of such reduction depended, but only relatively, on the quality of the equipment used—a heavier, commercial tone arm did more damage than a finely balanced one. But the nature of the friction between diamond and plastic, or between analog magnetic tape and the metal tape head, resulted in loss. In cases where vinyl albums were repeatedly subjected to heavy tone arms, the album could even visibly change its appearance from glossy to matted and could wear out. Even in less severe cases, the state of wear of the analog medium was visibly or sonically apparent and contributed to the devaluing of the analog object.

Generational degradation and wear defined analog media so that the most valuable analog medium was the one that was unplayed. For example, the still sealed vinyl album—sealed against wear, and most likely not to be generationally compromised—commanded and still commands the highest price. Still sealed vinyl (especially unrecycled so-called virgin vinyl) remains a gold standard. Regarding analog, virgin and otherwise: the less play, the more value.

Similarly, consider the quality of the photographs of great-grandparents or their own great-grandparents. Those that existed and survived will be marked not only as different from more recent photography, but seen as degraded compared to the photograph when first produced. A picture of my own grandfather that is cherished because he is a young man in his twenties is at once a valuable artifact and a badly decayed artifact. The image—about 2" by 4"—is badly cracked. To discern its original shading of whatever sort is impossible, as it has faded. It is washed out and its only hues are of a brown that does not appear to be a native part of the summer baseball field on which is playing. In short, the photograph began its existence as wholly marked by the capacities of its own mediation and declined markedly from that point. Were I not to have known its subject, he would be unrecognizable. As the decades pass, this photo continues to degrade.

Digital is different. By way of focusing this analogy I offer the following two scenarios. Imagine first a series of analog tape player/recorders. The second in the series records the first, the third records the second, and so on down the line, always remaining in the analog domain. The degeneration would be successive, and, eventually, reach a point where there may be little if any resemblance between the first generation and, say, the thousandth. In the second scenario, the first in the series is digital, as are the rest in the series. The second records the first, the third records the second, and so on down the line, always remaining in the digital domain. There exists a state of such technology that the thousandth such digital rendition would not be a lot like the first; it would *be* the first, just as the second would be the first, the first the second, and the twentieth the fourth. The implications here extend into all aspects of digital as the new digital.

I submit, then, that the very concept of the copy is an analog concept, borne from the material conditions of analog technology. The concept of the original is simultaneously constructed and marked. The differences between the analog and the digital as regards copy and original can be illustrated by way of an engagement of the central values at play.

Within an analog metaphor, the value of the original is attained as a result of the fact that the copy is by definition a degraded rendition. The person seeking to hear the content of a vinyl album with as little distortion as possible as regards the recorded content of the album will be best served by obtaining the album, preferably still sealed. The magnetic tape recorded from the album may or may not, depending on the equipment used, be a relatively excellent, faithful copy, as copy. But, again, of and through analog circumstances, the term copy itself marks the rendition as once removed, while the technology is prone to manifest itself into a taped rendition that represents some loss as regards its "original" source. The greater value of the undegraded version is not without cause; again, remember that the goal is to get as close to the content of the album as possible, which necessitates an absence of loss as regards said content as content, including the loss that accompanies the introduction of distortion. The VHS tape would offer another such example: The copy of the VHS tape would be marked as copy as a result of being defined and announced as once removed, and all subsequent generational copies would exhibit that much more such degradational distance. Therefore, to the person seeking the uncorrupted content of the analog tape, the still-sealed, non-copied, non-played version of the tape offers the best such opportunity. Such a version may be reasonably seen as of greater value and worth, such are its material conditions.

Digitalness does not offer the same conditions and as a result does not provide for the value system of the analog. Bit-by-bit copying exists. Thus, the person seeking to hear the content of a compact disc with as little distortion as possible as regards the recorded content of the compact disc will have limitless options. Theoretically and, depending on whom is asked, practically, the original is available from many quarters. Rarity is not at play digitally, and thus the values attendant to rarity do not apply. There is no digital text that is necessarily rare, as it can be reproduced in a way that does not mark it as in any way different as such. An analog painting, such an oil on canvas, cannot be reproduced faithfully and is thus valued for its being rare, indeed unique: It may be housed so that we might view it, with all proper security at play, and any attempt to cross the velvet rope and revise the text may very well be a criminal act. Similar consequences may result from the engagement of the counterfeit or forgery. The image constructed digitally can be reproduced faithfully, *ad infinitum*. To the extent that its value might depend on its singular existence, it has no such value.

This is not to say that there are not degraded digital copies. In fact, many elect to degrade the digital text via "lossy" compression schemes, exposure to digital-to-analog conversion and perhaps back, inferior equipment of various sorts, and the like. The reasons for such degradation may be ignorance, or, for example, convenience-motivated choice. But the technology exists so that the digital rendition need not be degraded. And, where it does not yet exist, it is the realizable goal. For example, newer high-definition DVD soundtrack data is to be not *like* the theatrical version, but is to *be* the theatrical version. The mediation that results in the presentation of this data is a variable. One may not elect to have the same sort of playback technology within a home as is encountered in the theater, but the same data is there and available for processing. Similarly, one may not have the same sort of processor or screen on which to view the digital image, but the same data is available, thus allowing the same data to be engaged, and, when the mediating technologies are the same as those engaged by the person from whom the image was created and sent, both the original data and the reproduction artifact are indiscernible, generationally.

COMPOSING THE DIGITAL TEXT: DIGITAL VALUE(S)

I argued above that digitally captured content that has always been digital content—in other words, that has not been remastered from the analog—is more faithful when mediated via a digital medium. I also suggested earlier that an analog painting, such an oil on canvas, cannot be reproduced faithfully. In terms of composition, then, the digital text is only fairly engaged via digital rules. Given that the digital text can be replicated without degradation, the attendant values are best digital values, fundamentally different from analog values. Jay David Bolter (1992) conveyed this point by emphasizing that we must acknowledge the opportunity that exists within digitalizing text:

> Wherever and however we use computers, we are turning the world into a digital text, we are textualizing the world. All the computer can ever do is to read and write text, if we take the word *text* to mean in the largest sense all systems of discrete symbols. I find this an exciting prospect because it places our work with computers and writing at the center of the computer revolution. We as humanists know and care about reading and writing, and it is therefore our responsibility to help make sense and to make good use of this new technology of literacy. (p. 42)

As with other texts, the analog text copyright exists most comfortably within its native analog terms. When considered against all the values and mechanisms thus far outlined here, copyright must come to new terms or be abandoned altogether. The value of the original oil on canvas extends in part from the impossibility of exactly reproducing the given oil and canvas onto another oil and canvas. Thus, such a text is in a specific sense unique and, even when considered along with those in its family or genre, rare or limited. Rarity contributes to value. (I often use the example in my courses that if limestone were as rare as diamond, we might marvel at the engagement ring using a fundamentally different set of qualifications: "Oh—the stone is so *opaque*—look at how it *absorbs* the light" and so forth.) Extending from such dynamics, copyright is further expressly concerned with authorial credit. This credit itself may not be unrelated to rarity. But it is also motivated by fair remuneration for the creator. The "original author" of the "original text" expects, via copyright, to receive recognition, expressed via attribution and, in many cases, via monetary payment. Any attempts to claim the text without such attribution is an act of theft.

The nature of digitalness argues against such a value system. Without an (analog) original, the concept of the originator becomes slippery. One such argument notes how "additional concerns develop when composing with multiple media that are borrowed, reformed, and recast into compositions. Considerable work has been done and continues to develop in the realms of intellectual property and copyright" (WIDE Research Collective, 2009). As the nature of the copy and the original are changed digitally, so are the natures of originator, creator, author, and the like. One way to measure the tensions associated with these fundamental shifts is to observe the volume of attention paid to the analog notions of plagiarism. Such concerns are often expressed in terms of what digital mediation seems to provide for. Such potential, however, is, instead of being seen as new and with its own positive and creative potential, often seen as a threat to the old. That fundamental shifts in commercial dynamics happen slowly and are marked by transitional compromises is nothing new. At a certain point, anyone whose livelihood depends on a set of soon-to-be extinct conditions has a set of choices. For example, as the kerosene lantern was being replaced by the electric light bulb, the lantern makers may very well have faced a genuine dilemma. One can imagine they could argue against the new technology and for the superiority of the kerosene lantern, they could re-tool their shops so as to make electric filament, they could elect to sell their wares to a smaller cult of users, or they could cease their businesses as such. These or some transitional combinations of these might well be the primary choices presented to many industries faced with fundamental paradigm shifts in their business modes and models. Further, such strategic options and responses would also no doubt be informed by the political clout of those involved. It is not hard to imagine attempts to make the "new threat" itself into an illegality, thus allowing for the status quo to be preserved. Such an act of criminalization would be one example of how those dependent on the threatened technology might seek to indict producers, users, or anyone else involved with the "crime."

Ours is an age of CDs, DVDs, the Web, digitally mediated satellite communication, digital cameras, iPods, iPads, email, computers in our homes and on our laps. As a result of the (mandated) switch to digital broadcasting regulations, local television stations run public service announcements as to how to discard analog televisions in an environmentally sound way. In practical terms, the digital paradigm is already engaged. These shifts have already occurred and continue to grow and expand. But allowing digital to be the new digital obliges us to allow the attendant theoretical frameworks to catch up to the ubiquitous practical engagement. These theoretical frameworks may be legal, compositional, pedagogical, or other. The analog rules regarding copyright, plagiarism, and the like are one such site for a necessary reconsideration. Defined by concepts no longer at play in the same ways, new definitions that respond to digital as the new digital should find a better fit if and when they are permitted to exist in on and through their own native terms. I offer ownership, stewardship, and artistic license as ways to begin to engage digital as the new digital.

First, I suggest that, within our digital paradigm, the concept of ownership be replaced by something we might call stewardship. Stewardship suggests much of what ownership suggests, except that the steward recognizes that her relation to the artifact is not permanent—that she is in a line of stewards who will at one point or another in the artifact's existence be responsible for the artifact. Jay David Bolter (1989) explained the dynamic interaction that occurs among this line of stewards:

> As a technology for writing, the computer promises to redefine the relationship between author, reader and writing space ... Unlike printing, which lends fixity and monumentality to the text, electronic writing is a radically unstable and impermanent form, in which the text exists only from moment to moment and in which the reader joins with the writer in constituting the text. (p. 129)

When transferred to the digital paradigm, the steward does well to recognize that many will own—and thereby none will own—and that her work with the text is not necessarily part of a linear sequence but is instead a part of a collage already engaged with the text.

Digital stewardship is at once—especially as regards its analog tradition—a two-way street and, ultimately, a whole community of roads and paths and dead-ends and cul-de-sacs. In the short term, the digital composer might learn to compose with the idea of his work being open to such stewardship. Whether or not this consideration changes the way he composes will of course be up to him, within that moment. In the same way, stewards have a set of obligations as well, although they are not traditional. Stewards might see their engagement of the text as transitory, as they become the steward of their engagement with an appreciation of the dynamics that will subsequently engage their compositions. An awareness of the analog implications of copy may help spur this shift in understanding on the parts of readers, composers, and ultimately reader–composers. Such a shift is necessary to engage the digital on its own, non-copying, terms.

There may be within this web—a web with no beginning or end—a place for the recognition of the steward from whom there appears to be an influence. Such recognition, however, will be defined digitally—that is, it will recognize the absence of the original, the copy, the copyright, and will instead proceed more from what we might think of as artistic license. Composition teachers may very well already recognize composition as art or as *an* art. But the circumstances in which we teach often seem to work against us as we make any claims toward art—toward us teaching art and students producing art. We can speculate as to why such challenges arise. For instance, since elementary school, writing and art have been separate. We go *to* art, to the art room. We have an arts and crafts area or at least a time of the day that we devote to art. Seldom in such spaces were we expected to primarily engage just the written word, unless as part of a more colorful art project.

Later, art is arguably in popular and even curricular terms most commonly attached to (analog) painting. Although sculpture, music, dance, and poetry could lay a relatively easy claim to being art, composition papers would, I think, have a harder time making any such claim. As teachers in the digital age, we know that so-called multimedia compositions by definition replace any such disciplinary lines. And, yet, as of today, even the teacher whose course is titled "Multimedia Composition" or "Computer Composition" or any such variant would encounter strangeness if, upon being asked what she teaches, she were to respond "art."

I am not sure what term best explains any such tension. But whatever that term is, I think it applies to our administrators and more importantly to our students as well, since such deeply entrenched analog traditions are slow to evolve; that is our challenge. Seldom do students come into my digital composition class with an understanding that different rules apply—that the better or more useful parts of artistic license might be at play, both in my expectations and in their latitude toward responding to the course. For example, even my repeated insistence as regards their compositions that form must follow from meaning—which I exemplify by saying that if you want to *mean* a high C played on a flute it may be at least *harder* to convey that meaning via a drum—is as of mid-2010 met by at best a quick re-orientation and at worse by a feeling of my somehow having betrayed the agreement that the student and I allegedly undertook when she signed up for my composition course. This is not to say that students are not computer literate, of course. Only that, at least as regards my students, most still enter, for example, "Freshman Composition" apparently expecting something mostly analog-based. It seems as though most have engaged "computer composition," but have not fully engaged the digital rules that should accompany such composition. The idea that the flute sound, digitally sampled itself, better or at least differently conveys the meaning of the flute sound than, say, a prose description of the sound seems to fall beyond student understanding of the "fair parameters" of digital composition. Thus, as contributing stewards, we and our students might look to the notion of artistic license as a way to expand these parameters.

Here, as representative of what Wikipedia might offer by way of definition, is the (current) Wikipedia entry on "artistic license:"

> **Artistic license or license** (also known as **dramatic license, poetic license, narrative license, licentia poetica,** or simply **license**) is a colloquial term used to denote the distortion or complete ignorance of fact, or the changing of an established work that an artist may undertake in the name of art—for example, if an artist decided it was more artistically "correct" to portray St. Paul's Cathedral next to the Houses of Parliament in a scene of London, even though in reality they are not close together, that would be artistic license....
>
> In summary, artistic license is:
> - Entirely at the artist's discretion
> - Intended to be tolerated by the viewer (cf. "willing suspension of disbelief")
> - Neither "good" nor "bad"
> - Useful for filling in gaps, whether they be factual, compositional, historical or other gaps
> - Used consciously or unconsciously, intentionally or unintentionally or in tandem

Artistic license often provokes controversy by offending those who resent the reinterpretation of cherished beliefs or previous works. Artists often respond to these criticisms by pointing out that their work was not intended to be a verbatim portrayal of something previous and should be judged only on artistic merit. Artistic license is a generally accepted practice, particularly when the result is widely acclaimed. William Shakespeare's historical plays, for example, are gross distortions of historical fact but are nevertheless lauded as outstanding literary works.

If the first step toward making art is building the art museum, then we as digital composition teachers might do well to start to do that, it seems to me. There will of course be challenges as we move toward teaching and evaluating art. Such challenges extend from the Wikipedia definitions, as enacted, and are already well known by, among others, our creative writing colleagues. Such an argument might be: "Well, if you are requiring me to produce 'art' and we are invoking my 'artistic license' to do so, then by default your evaluation must be *accepting*, since to evaluate otherwise would endanger the manifestations of my prerogatives as an artist." In other words, as we may have heard, "my poem is good because I say it is and by definition as an art you are not qualified to suggest otherwise."

The best definition of coddling that I can craft is that coddling refers to the "reinforcement of the sentiment that no change need occur on the part (of the coddled)." And it seems that we might be at some risk of introducing—simultaneously—art and coddling. At least there may be some *tension* between students' felt claims toward artistic license and our roles as evaluators, even as art critics. So if we are interested in taking advantage of digital options under the name of art—and if we are aware that doing so may be accompanied by some tensions in our classrooms—how might we begin to address such tensions? I suggest three things we may want to think about as we continue to inhabit the digital paradigm.

INHABITING THE DIGITAL PARADIGM

To begin to address some of the tensions described above, first, we must make our aesthetics—in part at least as requirements or expectations—as transparent as is productively possible but with the realization that they will not be wholly transparent. I think a good introduction to a course—via syllabus or spoken—strives to be an honest and forthright reflection of what the student might expect in the course. But "honest and forthright" need not mean mathematically defensible, and it need not appeal to any sort of objectivity. Imagine, instead, something like this to describe an A: "An A composition is marked as excellent in part by its being different in positive ways from more typical coursework. An A project is exceptional. It allows form to follow from meaning and engages its meanings with deliberateness. It shows evidence of an awareness of stewardship both in response and in contribution." To imagine a student saying "I read your description of an A—it doesn't say anything" is easy and, in certain quantifiable senses, all but fair. But what such a description does say, I think, is that less of this sort of math or formula is at play—that in this course we move into the perilous waters of art and that the student–reader will need to *look elsewhere* toward producing excellent work.

Second, and closely related, is our obligation to establish trust with students, which will work to reinforce the fact that our aesthetic expectations, though never able to be represented in formulaic and/or wholly transparent terms, are not being applied arbitrarily. In other words, while our expectations may be expressly "mysterious" they will not be applied in an *ad hominem* way. Establishing such trust is hard and gets at broader issues of our classroom ethos. But, specifically, one such site may be in our responses to drafts of the projects—responses that may invoke the need for the engagement of a higher-powered microscope or for more of a push, but to some extent allow almost all of the choices therein—or certain sorts of choices—to be made by the student. To me, our endnotes to student work are where we first make the case. Prior to these endnotes, in many cases, our expectations could be read as hypothetical. So our endnotes offer proof that we mean it. In short, then, if we follow through on our stated expectations, we can build trust through reliability (especially in comparison to those who, for example, talk of risk only to deduct x points for some petty structural concern).

Third, and finally, I think we need to trust our instincts. We need to be comfortable within the part of the expectations that we cannot make transparent—we need to inhabit that uncertain, even wordless digital space with the certainty that it is a space that does right by our students and their arts, and that values our roles as stewards engaging stewards, free from an obligation to copy our analog inheritance, and to move toward our own new digital spaces.

ACKNOWLEDGEMENT

I wish to acknowledge the invaluable assistance of Graduate Research Assistant Erin Herrmann in the revision of this chapter.

DEDICATION

This chapter is dedicated with all my love to the ongoing presence of my truest friend and collaborator, the late Russ Wiebe.

REFERENCES

Bolter, Jay David. (1989). Beyond word processing: The computer as a new writing space. *Language and Communication: An Interdisciplinary Journal,* 9(2-3), 129-142.

Bolter, Jay David. (1992). Literature in the electronic writing space. In Myron C. Tuman (Ed.), *Literacy online: The promise (and peril) of reading and writing with computers* (pp. 19-42). Pittsburgh: University of Pittsburgh Press.

Bolter, Jay David. (2001). *Writing space: Computers, hypertext, and the remediation of print* (2nd ed.). Mahwah, NJ: Lawrence Erlbaum Associates.

New London Group. (2000). A pedagogy of multiliteracies: Designing social futures. In Bill Cope & Mary Kalantzis (Eds.), *Multiliteracies: Literacy learning and the design of social futures* (pp. 9-38). London: Routledge.

WIDE Research Collective. (2009). Why teach digital writing? *Kairos, 10* (1). http://english.ttu.edu/kairos/10.1/coverweb/wide/index.html

8 RESPONSE TO PART I—"AN ACT FOR THE ENCOURAGEMENT OF LEARNING" VS. COPYRIGHT 2.0

John Logie

COPYRIGHT 1.0

On May 31, 1790, President George Washington signed into law an act passed by the first United States Congress in its second session. The title of the act reads as follows:

> An ACT for the ENCOURAGEMENT of LEARNING by securing the Copies of Maps, Charts, and Books, to the Authors and Proprietors of such Copies during the Times therein mentioned. (p. xx)

This is, of course, the United States' first copyright law. Although the title's language, which describes the Act as "for the encouragement of learning," is taken directly from the title of the United Kingdom's 1710 copyright law, the Statute of Anne, the two laws are markedly different. The Statute of Anne addresses learning only briefly, within a larger discussion of the problems caused by unauthorized copying. Such copying was—according to the Statute—occurring "without the Consent of the Authors or Proprietors of such Books and Writings, to their very great Detriment, and too often to the Ruin of them and their Families" (p. xx). Against this backdrop, the Statute of Anne announced itself as a means "for the Encouragement of Learned Men to Compose and

Write useful Books" (p. xx). By so doing, the Statute conflated "encouraging learning" with the protection of (and compensation for) copyrighted works.

But United States law does *not*.

The 1790 Copyright Act does not contain a rationale; it does not decry the depredations of unauthorized copying. Rather, it moves directly to the technical details of the law, specifying the rights of the author and outlining the penalties for violations of those rights. Because the Act itself does not articulate the motivating factors that led to its existence, we now understand it in tandem with the Constitutional clause stating that *Congress* shall have the power "to promote the Progress of Science and useful Arts, by securing for limited Times to Authors and Inventors the exclusive Right to their respective Writings and Discoveries" (Art. I, sec. 8). Against this backdrop, the description of copyright as "an act for the encouragement of learning" takes on new meaning.

Unlike the Statute of Anne, the United States' first copyright law was directed at promoting *progress* in science. The specification of *limited* times for the copyright term strongly implied that this encouragement was directed not only at encouraging authors to avail themselves of this limited monopoly right, but also at those who could—at the end of the then-14-year copyright term—make fuller use of texts as they moved into the public domain. If we assume—as is the current fashion—that our founding fathers were both wise and serious-minded, this assumption necessarily implies that they were serious about hardwiring the promotion of *learning* into the first United States copyright law.

And, yet, this collection is filled with accounts of committed educators struggling to manage the complexities and apparent contradictions of copyright laws in the 21st century. In the preceding pages, Timothy Amidon recounts his experience of being vaulted down the rabbit hole when he asks, simply, whether he might employ a Creative Commons license (rather than the traditional, restrictive copyright notice) for his master's thesis. Rob Dornsife illuminates the degree to which the concept of the copy itself is a functional obstacle to student pursuit of the full range of possibilities within digital composing spaces. Barclay Barrios examines end user license agreements and concludes that "every EULA to which we assent is a contractual obligation and failure to pay attention to the terms of those contracts is akin to making a deal with the devil." As readers of this volume know all too well, those deals are made hundreds of thousands of times each day in our institutions of higher learning. Barrios is not exaggerating when he suggests that the souls of educators are at stake when we are placed in circumstances where language—like the impenetrable legalese of most "clickthrough" licenses—is deployed as a functional obstacle to clarity and understanding.

In perhaps the saddest of these engagements with current law, Tharon Howard surveys the copyright landscape with a particular eye toward the implications of copyright for educators and concludes (rightly) that:

> The consequences of copyright infringement are far more damaging than has ever been the case in the history of U.S. copyright legislation. Unfortunately, since the 1990s, modern copyright law has changed more dramatically and more in favor of "natural rights" than it has since the Statutes of Queen Anne. Today, both educators and students are at greater risk of suffering from copyright infringement, litigation, and capital expenditure than ever in our history.

Which leads us to an important question ... Just what the hell happened?

Our forefathers, 220 years or so ago, spoke with clarity about the way copyright should work in our then-newborn nation. While directly considering the language of the Statute of Anne as a model, they rejected those sections that were situated as a response to the apparently pitiable circumstances of authors and publishers in the United Kingdom at the dawn of the 18th century. The first Congress wrote an act for the encouragement of education grounded not in a presumed "natural right" of authors to their words, but in a public grant (via elected representatives) of a limited monopoly right. Where the Statute of Anne presented authorial (or publisher) ownership as the default circumstance for any given text, the Copyright Act of 1790—when paired with the Constitution's language—points toward the public domain as the default status for texts. The limited monopoly granted by the law was an exception to the more general (and preferred) circumstance in which no monopoly right would inhere.

U.S. Copyright Law's bias toward learning was maintained for at least the nation's first two centuries. The 1976 Copyright Act—a comprehensive revision of copyright law *in toto*—codified the common law principle of fair use. The four-factor fair use "test" imposed by this Act begins with a determination as to whether the use is "of a commercial nature or is for nonprofit educational purposes," with non-profit educational uses pointing strongly toward a determination that the use in question is fair. Additionally, the initial paragraph describing fair use states "the fair use of a copyrighted work ... for purposes such as criticism, comment, news reporting, teaching (including multiple copies for classroom use), scholarship, or research, is not an infringement of copyright" (p. xx). Thus, for most of our nation's history, the United States adhered to the principle that the use of copyrighted material *for educational purposes* was likely not an infringement of copyright.

But that time is gone.

COPYRIGHT 2.0

Between 1997 and 2002, the United States Congress passed four acts that—taken together—effectively revised copyright law in ways that constituted a decisive break with the founders' "act to encourage education." Not *all* of the elements of these laws were problematic. Indeed, given the rise of the public Internet (in the form or the World Wide Web) in the early 1990s, the legislators were wise to revisit and reexamine copyright. But each of these four laws *did* contain egregious violations of the spirit and principles of laws prior to that point. Here are some of the lowlights:

- **The No Electronic Theft (NET) Act, November 1997**—After passage of this act, for the first time in U.S. history, copyright infringements could prompt criminal (rather than civil) penalties. Even non-commercial infringements could trigger criminal penalties of up to 5 years in prison and $250,000 in fines. The NET Act detached the calculus for mitigating infringements from the demonstrable or potential financial harm experienced by the copyright holder.
- **The Sonny Bono Copyright Term Extension Act, October 1998**—The CTEA added 20 years of additional copyright protection to existing terms (moving, for example, the base term for single-authored texts from the life of the author plus 50 years to the life of the author plus 70 years). Notably, the law was constructed to apply not just prospectively but retroactively. This had the effect of "freezing" the cut-off point for works entering the public domain at 1922, where it will remain until 2018, barring no further term extensions. As a result, research on materials from 1923 forward, which would have been freely available, has been delayed owing to the possibility of copyright entanglements.
- **The Digital Millennium Copyright Act, October 1998**—The DMCA criminalized circumvention of digital rights management (DRM) systems without significant attention to whether the use prompting that circumvention should qualify as a fair use of the underlying text. Putting the DMCA to test, Wendy Seltzer, lawyer, teacher, and founder of Chilling Effects, snipped the NFL copyright notice during the 2007 Super Bowl and posted it on YouTube. The television notice includes a voiceover: "This telecast is copyrighted by the NFL

for the private use of our audience. Any other use of this telecast or of any pictures, descriptions, or accounts of the game without the NFL's consent, is prohibited." Within 5 days, Seltzer received a YouTube notice that the copyright notice clip had, ironically, been removed due to a DMCA copyright violation reported by the NFL. Seltzer sent a counter-notice and argued that the clip was being fairly used for teaching purposes. The clip was re-posted, but then removed again after the NFL sent YouTube a second takedown notice (see Cheng, 2007; Seltzer, 2007).

- **The Technology, Education, and Copyright Harmonization (TEACH) Act, November 2002**—While purportedly directed at expanding opportunities for use of copyrighted materials in distance learning environments, the TEACH Act offers a cumbersome and restrictive set of rules that place both instructors and their home institutions at considerable risk for practices once considered unremarkable in classroom settings. If, for example, an instructor in a face-to-face classroom chooses to screen the University library's copy of Charlie Chaplin's 1923 short *The Pilgrim* to prompt a discussion of Chaplin's depiction of the Mexican border at that time, that use is widely understood as acceptable, reasonable, and fair. Under the TEACH Act, screening the same film in a distance-learning classroom would be curtailed, as only "reasonable and limited portions" of dramatic, literary, or audiovisual works are allowed (p. xx).

The aggregate effect of these laws is the replacement of our founders' approach to copyright with a more restrictive copyright regime—a regime that might fairly be described as "Copyright 2.0" were it not for the implicit suggestion that version 2.0 of any given concept is an improvement upon what is retroactively thought of as version 1.0.

In 1994, in the early days of public access to the World Wide Web, John Perry Barlow famously wrote, "intellectual property law cannot be patched, retrofitted, or expanded to contain digitized expression any more than real estate law might be revised to cover the allocation of broadcasting spectrum." But Copyright 2.0 *is* a regime of patching and retrofitting. Copyright 2.0 stubbornly clings to print practices as the model for how we are to interact with and understand digital media. Meanwhile, in his classrooms, Rob Dornsife is working to help his students unthink the printed page and all of the baggage associated with it before they commence writing. Dornsife embraces the notion that in the 21st century, ideas are "born digital" and need not map onto the conventions and demands of print. Copyright 2.0 stubbornly demands print-based patterns of "ownership," where Dornsife calls for digital "stewardship."

John Logie

COPYRIGHT 3.0?

Ironically, Copyright 2.0's restrictive and criminalizing policies were solidified and stabilized just prior to the recognition of a generational shift in the social use and functionality of the Internet's core applications, commonly referred to as "Web 2.0." While the Web was filled with people leveraging its potential for networking and publishing, the United States Congress was busy drafting laws that sharply curtailed the use, appropriation, and even critique of copyrighted materials in Internet spaces. In his article for this volume, Jeffrey Galin argues that "corporate interests have achieved a decided advantage" in a running debate over the limits of fair use. Galin also cites Carol Silberberg's assessment that restrictive trends now in place "will eventually eliminate fair use for schools, colleges, and universities" altogether. On a bad day, I might be persuaded that Silberberg is right.

I have long argued that academics are the canaries in the coal mine of copyright jurisprudence. In particular, teachers of writing and composition—given the nature of their work—develop a particularly keen sense of both the opportunities and obligations facing composers when they wish to build upon others' ideas. Like Russel Wiebe, many compositionists have had to struggle with the apparent tension between their endorsement of works like Sherrie Levine's allegedly "plagiaristic" appropriations of Edward Weston's photographs and institutional demands for the policing of plagiarism. And many of us have felt the air grow by turns thin and foul when we have engaged with the practical realities of 21st-century copyright laws.

But I have tired of the "canary in the coal mine" analogy, and here's why: My colleagues are *not* helpless little birdies in tiny cages, singing their little lungs out, blissfully unaware of the fact that their singing serves only to protect those who are carrying them into danger.

Although much of the work in this volume is diagnostic, much of it is also directed at action. Some of this action can be as personal as Bob Whipple's revisitation of the function and meaning of the commonplace book as the genre is ported to digital spaces. But some of it is overtly political, including many of the efforts of the Intellectual Property Caucus of the Conference on College Composition and Communication (CCCC-IP) and the work of Creative Commons to stabilize functional alternatives to copyright's business-as-usual approaches. These efforts are staving off the most egregious excesses of Copyright 2.0 and educating a generation of students to the range of possibilities inherent in the circulation, use, and appropriation of scholarly and creative work.

In the process of letting go of my analogy, I briefly considered (and quickly rejected) reinventing that metaphoric canary as a bird tough enough to contend with the challenges of the current Copyright 2.0 landscape. My search for a "tough" canary eventually led me (perhaps inevitably) to the webpage for a Seattle band calling itself "Killer Canary" (http://www.killercanary.net). The band's site features an array of MP3 files freely distributed by the band for downloading if the visitor to the site so chooses. Among five tracks from a recent show, I recognized the title of one, "Aneurysm," and clicked on the band's cover of a well-known song from Nirvana. While Copyright 2.0 would demand that Killer Canary seek permissions and licensing from Nirvana, the practical realities of Web 2.0 have prompted Killer Canary to put the song online and to assume the risk of what will—at worst—probably be a cease-and-desist letter from legal counsel .

But is that what *should* happen in such a case? Here, a Seattle band posts a considerable amount of original music online, for free. Then, as a showcase of the band's skills, the band includes a cover of a song by perhaps the best-known Seattle band ever. This is, in addition to appropriation of Nirvana's song, a form of tribute. And Killer Canary, by making this song available via the Internet for free, will not receive any compensation for this use of Nirvana's composition. Do we, as a culture, want Killer Canary treated—even momentarily—as criminal? And if I, for my own purposes, take this unauthorized cover song and place it in my own digital commonplace book, what is the worst that should happen to me?

I wish the answers were clear and obvious, but in each of these cases Copyright 2.0 leaves a tiny measure of possible legal threat hovering over these banal acts of use and appropriation.

We don't yet know what "Web 3.0" will look and feel like, though it is a good bet that it will be faster and depend on greatly increased storage space. However Web 3.0 unfolds, I am confident that the use and circulation of appropriated works will be a big part of how the next generation of the Web is structured. And I worry (as do some of my colleagues herein) about the increasingly panoptic levels of surveillance that might be cheap and easy in the coming years.

So what ought we do?

Clearly, the Killer Canary approach is at odds with our various obligations. But we *do* have a special understanding of what it means to compose texts and of ways to plan for how those texts might circulate and in turn be used and appropriated to make new texts. So it falls to us, in part, to help craft the practices and policies that will ideally form the backbone of "Copyright 3.0." This volume's measured and insightful accounts of where we are, where we could be, and where we should be will help to point the way forward.

REFERENCES

Barlow, John Perry. (1994, March). The economy of ideas: A framework for patents and copyrights in the digital age. Wired Magazine, 2 (3). http://www.wired.com/wired/archive/2.03/economy.ideas.html

Cheng, Jacqui. (2007, March 20). NFL fumbles DMCA takedown battle, could face sanctions. *ars technica*. http://arstechnica.com/business/news/2007/03/nfl-fumbles-dmca-takedown-battle-could-face-sanctions.ars

Seltzer, Wendy. (2007, February 8). My first YouTube: Super Bowl highlights and lowlights. http://wendy.seltzer.org/blog/archives/2007/02/08/my_first_youtube_super_bowl_highlights_or_lowlights.html

Statute of Anne. (1790). http://avalon.law.yale.edu/18th_century/anne_1710.asp

Vineyard, Jennifer. (2006, April 13). Courtney Love sells substantial share of Nirvana publishing rights. http://www.mtv.com/news/articles/1528625/20060413/love_courtney.jhtml

PART II: THE TOOLS

9 WHAT WE TALK ABOUT WHEN WE TALK ABOUT FAIR USE: CONVERSATIONS ON WRITING PEDAGOGY, NEW MEDIA, AND COPYRIGHT LAW

STEVE WESTBROOK

I have not even completed the opening sentence of this chapter and I may have already committed an act of theft. T.S. Eliot (1920) said that "mature poets steal" (p. 5); Roland Barthes (1977) suggested that all writers—mature or immature—cannot help but steal, because every text is inevitably unoriginal, a "tissue of quotations" (p. 146) drawn from the ready-made dictionary of a culture's common language. By fashioning the title of this chapter after the title of a famous short story by Raymond Carver, I may have taken something that, perhaps, was not my property, or I may have simply and innocently harnessed the technique available to me, according to Barthes, "to mix writings" (p. 146). In either case, I have done what all writers ultimately do: appropriate and transform material. Theoretically, because we rely on a shared system of language with (at any particular moment in history) a finite number of words, we would be unable to write or talk without "stealing" words from one another, whether off of the page or out of one another's mouths. In less accusatory language, I might say we "share" words in order to communicate. But there is sharing and then there is *sharing*—borrowing a number of words necessarily versus borrowing exact syntaxes for entire pages. Luckily, my little act of appropriation does not make me guilty of any crime, as far as I know, except perhaps the writerly crime of making a rather dull change to a perfectly good title. In my defense, although the subject of fair use might not be as grandiose or romantic as love, it appears to be at least as complicated, especially at this particular moment in history when copyright law—an idea designed largely to protect entire books from being pirated in the print culture of early 18th-century England—is being applied to bits of language, sounds, and pixels from contemporary electronic texts and the multimedia, hypertextual cultures of the Internet.

In Carver's short story, four characters sit around a table drinking gin. As they drink, they struggle to define love—what it is, how it affects their thinking and their lives—often in relation to what love is not, according to conventional thought: namely, abuse. Mel and Terry argue over whether and how it might be possible to discern if seemingly abusive behavior contains evidence of something called love, and as the characters talk and drink, it becomes clear that Carver's story will not offer a resolution to the debate, nor will it concern itself with any particular outcome to any particular plot or sequence of events. The story is simply about a conversation taking place. In a sense, then, it is purely academic.

This chapter is about an academic conversation taking place, albeit a quite different one. Usually, we are far too sober when we gather around a table or linger in our department's hallways, talking about intellectual property in composition studies and trying to understand just what separates, or should separate, fair use from infringement and, further, how the distinction between these terms affects us and the writers we teach. The subject of our conversation may not be as ephemeral or exalted a subject as love; nevertheless, the substance of our talk is vital to our daily practices. It is usually motivated by a genuine love for freedom of speech and an accompanying desire to understand and protect fair use for ourselves and for students. It is in this spirit that I turn to the characters' speech within our own story and examine the rhetoric of our conversation—what exactly we are saying about fair use and how we are saying it.

THE STORY WE'VE BEGUN

Our conversation has been taking place for some time now, at least since the founding of the Conference on College Composition and Communication's Intellectual Property Caucus in 1994. Since then, as Lisa Dush (2009) suggested, this conversation might be characterized by three movements or "waves." The scholarship of the first wave tends to focus on how legal policy concerning the World Wide Web reflects the commercial interests of the content industries and, in doing so, often subscribes to antiquated, Romantic notions of solitary authorship that do not support cultural and compositional norms of collaborative practice. The second wave tends to provide a deeper inquiry into "theories of the public domain, fair use, and the rhetorical systems surrounding text ownership" (p. 114). Dush likened the tone of the conversations taking place in first- and second-wave scholarship to a "wake-up call," as compositionists tend to issue alarms or warnings of what might happen to both the field and practice of composition if those of us teaching writing do not keep abreast of legal changes, understand how proprietary biases might stifle writers' freedoms, and protect our own and our students' right to fair use. Dush suggested that within the current third wave of scholarship, compositionists have just begun moving beyond the wake-up call and turning toward the subject of pedagogy. It is this pedagogical turn in our conversation—"the question of *how* we talk with students about copyright and IP issues" (p. 115, Dush's emphasis)—that deserves further address.

The turn Dush described has come about for a number of reasons, all of which have to do with the changing nature of student texts and the contexts of their distribution; to some degree, the turn is a result of practical necessity. Today, students often compose new media texts by appropriating sounds, images, and hypertext from the work of others, and they often distribute these texts in both academic and public spheres. Students in my classes, for instance, have brought their new media compositions into the classroom for purposes of evaluation and also posted them on Web sites or blogs for purposes of public communication. As a discipline, we have not been entirely correct in assuming that we and students may appropriate material fairly within academic environments; we have, however, worked rather successfully under this assumption. Also, we have been able to remain largely immune to the problem of infringement when we confine the circulation of texts to the classroom. In this case, texts simply do not reach a wider audience and do not participate in external economic markets: In short, because virtually no one sees them, virtually no one is aware of whether they might infringe on copyright. However, when texts traverse academic and public arenas, they radically complicate the question of fair use; this is especially true for non-print genres that rely on appropriated images or audio clips. For instance, while I might be able to appropriate eight words from Raymond Carver's short story within the context of this print essay, I might not be able to appropriate the same number of words within the context of a song or a multimedia text published on the Internet.

In fact, the economic value of sampled language within the entertainment industry has made it seemingly difficult to appropriate even a small number of words without facing threats of litigation. In the landmark case *Grand Upright v. Warner* (1991), Gilbert O'Sullivan sued rapper Biz Markie for appropriating three words ("alone again naturally") and a small portion of music from one of his songs. Although Markie's song "Alone Again" repeats only these three words—all of the other lyrics are original—and samples only a portion of O'Sullivan's melody, this instance was found to be one of copyright infringement. Without recognizing any sense of irony, the judge who heard the case, Kevin Thomas Duffy, began his opinion by appropriating four words from Exodus 20:15—"Thou shalt not steal"—and proceeded to claim that Biz Markie was not using material fairly; Markie was, in fact, guilty of theft. Although I do not have the time or space here to address what exactly makes Biz Markie's use of appropriated language "theft" and Judge Duffy's appropriated language "quotation," I find it important to note, for the moment, the complications and confusions in determining fair use and the particular legacy of this case. Since the ruling, which led to the development of the clearance industry within the music business, the process of sampling language—whether melodic or verbal—has become increasingly expensive. According to attorney Alan Korn (2007), major record companies now seek a flat fee of $100–5000 per sample or $.01–.07 in royalties per sale. Lucky for me, I am not singing the title of this chapter.

Although not as expensive as music samples, appropriations from visual images can carry a significant price tag and, when not officially permitted, can lead to accusations of infringement. Martine Courant Rife (2009) cited four recent trials concerned with the use of copyrighted visual images: *Mattel Inc. v. Walking Mountain Productions aka Tom Forsythe* (2003); *Kelly v. Arriba Soft Corp.* (2003); *Video Pipeline, Inc. v. Buena Vista Home Entertainment, Inc.* (2003); and *Bill Graham Archives v. Dorling Kindersley* (2006). The subjects of these cases range from the display of Barbie dolls in fine art photography to the reproduction of Grateful Dead posters in a coffee table book. The outcomes of the trials vary. Regardless, all of them point to the unique problem of visual images within copyright law. While the music business has its clearance industry, the fields of art, art history, and publishing have permissions clauses and *chases*. For instance, while art publishers rarely require authors to obtain permission to quote from other writers in their texts (except in the case of whole works or very lengthy quotations), they have defaulted to the practice requiring authors to obtain permissions for reproducing artworks they comment upon. Seeking and paying for rights to visual reproduction have become enormous problems. The College Art Association's Committee on Intellectual Property (2004) has described these processes as overly "complex, painstaking, and financially onerous" (p. 4), and publishers have actually begun suggesting that art historians avoid using images altogether because they have become "impossibly expensive" (Bielstein, 2006, p. 101). Relying on an animated icon from popular culture, Jonathan Lethem described the general problem of attempting to use visual images instead of words this way:

> the truth is I could write a whole book ... describing [Homer Simpson's] yellow skin and protuberant eyes, and no one

would ever be able to block my choice as an artist there, or make it too expensive for me to do it. But if a visual artist or a filmmaker or a digital montage maker tried to capture that image, which is just part of a visual language that is floating around, they wouldn't have my freedom. (Benfer, 2007)

By citing these examples, I don't mean to suggest that students are in a position equivalent to that of established musicians and artists within the publishing and entertainment industries (although some of them, in fact, are), but I do mean to suggest that when their work enters a public forum, it is subject to the same laws and perceptions of law, which largely favor the content industries. Given this complication, let me return to Dush's question: How are we talking with students about copyright and IP issues? More specifically, what are we saying about fair use to 21st-century writers who have already moved beyond the confines of traditional print technology to appropriate images, sounds, or electronic text in Web writing and new media projects?

WHAT OUR TEXTBOOKS TELL US

Although textbooks and handbooks may not offer the most accurate reflections of how individual teachers discuss fair use in their classrooms, they remain the most widely available pedagogical materials for study and, as such, offer insight to our discipline's larger conversation with students. To an extent, they reveal our field's assumptions about what students do and do not need to know about fair use in an era of new media.

One of the most common assumptions found in our pedagogical materials—one that I think most of us subscribe to and support—is that students' experience of writing instruction should be relevant to their public lives; moreover, the texts they produce should be designed for use inside and outside of the classroom. In *Seeing and Writing 3*, a visual rhetoric textbook that offers some opportunity for new media production, Donald McQuade and Christine McQuade (2006) articulated one of their goals as cultivating "skills identified with both verbal and visual literacy" that will "enable [students] to learn, recognize, understand, and create compelling and convincing messages for audiences within and beyond the halls of higher education" (p. 4). This is a fine goal. Of course, if this is our goal, and if students are already producing texts that circulate in academic and public spheres, then their work is subject to the problems associated with copyright law that I have described above. It is somewhat surprising, then, that McQuade and McQuade's textbook, which concerns the appropriation and integration of visual images, does not mention issues of infringement or fair use, and perhaps even more surprising that this absence is not particular to their textbook. Rather, it is indicative of our conversation as a whole: If we talk about fair use at all, we don't talk much.

Citing Sources

Our pedagogical materials reveal three approaches to discussing the subject with students, the first two of which address fair use only tacitly. In the first approach, textbook authors do not mention fair use or permissions explicitly, but rely on the incorrect assumption that source materials—mainly visual images—are being used fairly if they are cited according to prevailing academic conventions. For instance, in *Writing in a Visual Age*, Lee Odell and Susan Katz (2006) tell students that "all visuals copied from another source should be cited, either in the caption or in the text, according to the documentation style you are using" (p. 623). Although Odell and Katz position students to write brochures and newsletters for public consumption, they do not introduce the subject of permissions or reveal to students that the conditions for determining fair use are independent of documentation: That is, in public contexts, new media writers might cite a source with utmost accuracy but might still infringe on copyright if they have not acquired permissions, depending upon the purpose, nature, amount, and effect of their appropriative compositions. Biz Markie cited his source; he was found guilty of infringement.

A number of visual rhetoric textbooks rely on the misconception that students need only be concerned with accurate documentation of visual images, including *Design, Compose, Advocate* (Wysocki & Lynch, 2007) and *Beyond Words* (Ruszkiewicz, Anderson, & Friend, 2006). In the latter text, Ruskiewicz et al. exaggerate writers' liberties. When offering students advice for beginning a visual collage of images downloaded from the Web, they state that "you can find images for your collage just about anywhere ... Use Google or another online search engine ... and remember to save citation information" (2006, p. 145). They do not suggest to students that they may need not only to cite their sources but also to acquire permissions for the images they download. Although the authors' underlying assumption might be that the use of appropriated images for this project is so radically transformative (within the context of a collage) that it clearly qualifies as fair use, this logic remains tacit, and the entire subject of fair use and permissions goes unmentioned. Further, while assuming that citing appropriated images is enough, the authors misdirect students by suggesting they use images from "just about anywhere"—a step toward potential copyright infringement—rather than leading them toward freely available resources like Creative Commons, where they might find images that are designated as clearly appropriable under specified conditions. While encouraging students to engage in public, multimedia composition, these textbook authors revert to the discipline's default-treatment of student writing as if it were isolated to the classroom; they misapply academic standards to public writing. I suspect this is the case because they are mired in the ideology of our field: They don't readily consider the prospect that student writing—which, historically within composition and rhetoric, has served mostly as disposable evidence for evaluation—might have consequences in the public sphere.

Silencing Potential Conversations

If the first approach to our conversation with students errs on the side of attributing writers too much freedom, the second errs on allowing too little. Rather than present the question of fair use as contextual and subject to debate, textbook authors subscribing to this second approach inform students that seeking permissions for appropriated material is mandatory. This assumption can be found in a number of our pedagogical materials, including *Picturing Texts* (Faigley, George, Palchik, & Selfe, 2004), *Everything's an Argument* (Lunsford & Ruszkiewicz, 2004), *The McGraw-Hill Guide* (Roen, Glau, & Maid, 2009), and *Designing Documents and Understanding Visuals* (Munger, 2008). In this last text—a handbook for students engaged in visual production—Roger Munger (2008) presents the problem of appropriation this way: "If you include copyrighted visuals in a document you intend to publish (in print or on the Web), you must credit your source and obtain written permission from the copyright holder" (p. v-31). The language of this imperative is echoed elsewhere: "if you are going to disseminate your work beyond your classroom—especially by publishing it online—you must ask permission for any material you borrow from an Internet source" (Lunsford & Ruskiewicz, p. 408); "if your writing will be made available to an audience beyond your classroom ... you will need to ask permission to use any visual from a source that you include" (Roen et al., p. 822); "if you use someone else's images, including those you find on the Web, you need to obtain permission from the owner" (Faigley et al., p. 455). Although this rhetoric acknowledges the very real problem of permissions in the public sphere, it oversimplifies the complexity of this problem by reverting to the language of mandates; here, students "must" and "need to" seek permissions, even though—according to the law—this may not be the case. The very concept of fair use is designed to provide writers and artists the liberty *not to* seek permissions in cases where they are, for example, working toward the cultural and intellectual advancement of society, using material for educational or journalistic purposes, or asserting their protected right to free speech. Practically speaking, Heartfield, Duchamp, Picasso, Warhol, Rauschenberg, and many more modern artists would not have been able to produce art if they had always sought to obtain permissions. More recently, pictures of Abu Ghraib would not have been seen by the American public if reporters had heeded the mandates for permission seeking listed above.

The problem I see in this approach to discussing the appropriation of copyrighted materials is that its permission-seeking imperative obfuscates or even erases the concept of fair use, which disappears from the conversation before a productive dialogue can even get started. When permission seeking is treated as mandatory, the authority for determining whether appropriated materials may be used is placed entirely outside of the borrowing writer's purview; the writer is thus stripped of her agency and ability to participate in a complex process of decision-making. Instead, the permission granter is free to say "no" to a request for reproduction, and the permission seeker is beholden to this decision. Recognizing this problem, fair use advocates have begun waging a campaign against unnecessary permission chases. In her scholarship on the issue, Rife (2009) suggested to teachers and students quite plainly that "we should not ask permissions every time" we seek to use copyrighted material (p. 148). When discussing the reproduction of visual images in his recent book, *Peers, Pirates, and Persuasion*, John Logie (2006) stated that: "while I have done my best to identify and acknowledge the copyright holders for these images, I have determined not to seek permissions for these obviously fair uses" (p. 149). The logic of this determination works to deny ultimate power to holders of derivative rights, to recover a sense of agency and authority for the writer who relies on appropriative practices, and to counter abuses of copyright law that scholar-activists like Logie feel are too proprietary in nature. In short, Logie has made the decision to assert his right to fair use to protect this very right from disappearing; the motive underlying Rife's advice fulfills a similar purpose. Of course, both Logie and Rife make their assertions from positions of expertise: they are obviously familiar with the four factors used to determine fair use according to U.S. Code and they have been exposed to four-factor analyses (the decision-making process that the law relies upon to distinguish fair use from infringement). It is this very step—exposure to definitions of fair use and four-factor analysis—that has been left out of the textbooks surveyed above and the majority of those produced with our discipline.

Engaging Fair Use

The third approach to discussing fair use is the rarest; it is also the most important, for it exposes students to the four factors of fair use and attributes to them the agency to decide whether permission-seeking is necessary. This approach takes two forms. The first, as exemplified by *Designing Writing* (Palmquist, 2005), does not reproduce the four factors but asks students to consider "copyright and fair use regarding the use of digital illustrations, such as photographs and other images, audio clips, video clips, and animations" (p. 28) and refers them to the law itself by way of a URL that contains the actual text of the fair use provision as articulated in Title 17. In the second form, textbook authors reproduce and discuss the four factors by way of questions students may ask themselves about the use of copyrighted materials. Somewhat paradoxically—and I have no good explanation for this—the handbook that includes the most robust discussion of fair use is one designed largely for print culture and contains only limited discussions of new media composition. In *A Writer's Resource*, Elaine Maimon, Janice Peritz, and Kathleen Yancey (2008) offer students exposure to four-factor analysis during one of their brief discussions of new media and Internet technology. I reproduce their advice in full:

> The popularity of the World Wide Web has led to increased concerns about the fair use of copyrighted material. Before you post your paper on the Web or produce a multimedia presentation that includes audio, video, and graphic elements coped from a Web site, make sure that you have used copyrighted material fairly. The following four criteria are used to determine if copyrighted material has been used fairly:
>
> - **What is the purpose of the use?** Educational, nonprofit, and personal use are more likely to be considered fair than is commercial use.
> - **What is the nature of the work being used?** In most cases, imaginative and unpublished materials can be used only if you have the permission of the copyright holder.
> - **How much of the copyrighted work is being used?** If a writer uses a small portion of a text for academic purposes, this use is more likely to be considered fair than if he or she uses a whole work for commercial purposes.
> - **What effect would the use have on the market for the original?** The use of a work is usually considered unfair if it would hurt sales of the original. (p. 269)

The language here echoes the fair use provision in Section 107 of Title 17, and mimics the kind of analysis practiced regularly by professional artists, librarians, writers, and legal experts alike. It approximates the sort of analytical questioning judges engage in when making decisions on copyright cases.

Here, as well as in *Designing Writing*, textbook authors move away from the language of imperative. Maimon and colleagues (2008) do not suggest that students "must seek permissions" but that they should "make sure" they have "used copyrighted materials fairly," and Palmquist (2005) states that students "*might* need to request permission" (p. 28, my emphasis). While the difference between "must" and "might" may seem negligible, it represents a dramatic change in constructions of student identities and understandings of copyright law. The more nuanced language of ambiguity invites students to participate in larger processes of analysis and negotiation, to which they should be exposed if they are being treated professionally as writers in a new media culture and as citizens in a democracy. Rather than hide the complications of determining fair use in a strangely paternal fashion, it exposes them to these complications and, in doing so, positions them to be agents responsible both for their decisions as critical thinkers and for the consequences of these decisions within public culture.

WHAT MIGHT WE SAY? A CASE IN POINT

The introduction of four-factor analysis within the pedagogical materials of our field is, of course, only a preliminary stage in engendering a larger conversation about writing and fair use. In the remainder of this chapter, I build upon the discussion of fair use initiated by Palmquist (2005) and by Maimon et al. (2008). More specifically, I draw from one case study to suggest how and why we might further pursue this conversation in our classrooms so that we better prepare students to conduct fair use analysis within the contexts of their own textual production and its online dissemination.

In 2003, thousands of internal emails from Diebold, the largest manufacturer of electronic voting machines, were leaked and spread across the Internet. Because these emails revealed serious flaws in the reliability of Diebold's voting machines—which had been used in national elections—and exposed their vulnerability to hacking, Diebold sought to immediately contain their dissemination. The company did so by invoking copyright law, specifically a provision from the Digital Millennium Copyright Act. They sent a flurry of cease and desist letters not simply to Internet users who were displaying this material on their Web sites but to Internet Service Providers (ISPs) who were hosting these Web sites. In one instance, when Diebold discovered that Nelson Pavlosky and Luke Smith, Internet users and students at Swarthmore College, were displaying contents from the email archive on their Web site, they sent cease and desist letters to three parties associated with the allegedly infringing Web site: Swarthmore College, the students' ISP; Online Policy Group, the ISP for an IndyMedia Web site that contained a hyperlink to Pavlosky and Smith's site; and Hurricane Electric, Online Policy Group's upstream provider. In their letter to Swarthmore, attorneys for Diebold stated the following:

> The website you are hosting infringes Diebold's copyrights because Diebold Property was placed on this website without Diebold's consent. The purpose of this letter is to advise you of our clients' rights and to seek your agreement to the following: (1) to remove and destroy the Diebold Property contained at the web site identified in the attached chart and (2) to destroy any backup copies of the Diebold Property in your possession or under your control. (Cohn & Seltzer, 2004, p. 6)

Faced with the threat of litigation, most individuals and ISPs who received cease and desist letters from Diebold removed the allegedly infringing material and/or hyperlinks to this material immediately. Swarthmore College was no exception. The institution succumbed to pressure from Diebold and stopped hosting Pavlosky and Smith's site even though it was related to an academic study of electronic voting authored in preparation for an academic conference, "Choosing Clarity: A Symposium on Voting Transparency."

Although their site was removed by Swarthmore, Pavlosky and Smith refused to accept Diebold's claim of infringement, for they considered the use of the appropriated material journalistic, fair, and protected under their constitutional rights. In the words of Pavlosky, Diebold's tactic of invoking copyright law effectively to censor access to materials of public interest represented "a perfect example of how copyright law can be and is abused by corporations" to prevent freedom of speech (Schwartz, 2003, p. 1). The students joined forces with Online Policy Group, which had refuted Diebold's cease and desist letter through claims of fair use and, further, had refused to stop hosting IndyMedia's Web site or remove its hyperlink to the email archive in question. Together, Pavlosky, Smith, and Online Policy group sued Diebold, asserting the company's accusation of infringement "was based on knowing material misrepresentation," an actionable claim under a provision of the DMCA (17 U.S.C. 512(f)) and, furthermore, "interfered with [the] contractual relations" between the students and their Internet service providers (*Online*, 2004, p. 2). As is now widely known, they were successful in court; the judge hearing the case found that Online Policy Group, Pavlosky, and Smith had all used material fairly and that Diebold had, indeed, abused the tenets of copyright law for its own self-interest, essentially as a public relations effort to remove material damaging to its reputation.

Luckily, when faced with a censorial copyright claim, Pavlosky and Smith did not acquiesce to Diebold's or Swarthmore's decisions or heed the advice of composition textbooks that suggest writers *must* have permission to use copyrighted material; if they had not asserted their agency to publish their appropriated material, the Diebold scandal may have been effectively covered up through the misuse of copyright law as a censoring mechanism. The problems of electronic voting and questionable election results may not have been exposed to public scrutiny, and the California legislation that banned the use of Diebold's faulty voting machines may not have been developed. In short, these students' ability to conscientiously resist seeking permissions mattered; it had economic, political, cultural, and legal consequences in the public sphere. Of course, in this story, the students were not the ideal, docile subjects constructed by most composition textbooks.

The story of their case, *Online Policy Group v. Diebold, Inc.,* is important here for two reasons. First, it suggests the need to develop our conversations with students in ways that better acknowledge how contested appropriations of new media can be in the public sphere, what sort of censorial pressures contemporary writers can face, and what sort of issues are at stake when rights to fair use are determined or asserted. In this example, two writers reproduced appropriated material and created a hyperlink to this material, which led to a significant contestation of authorial agency, control, and power. Further, this contestation was characterized by the sort of hegemonic and counter hegemonic positioning that, according to Rosemary Coombe (1998), "is operative when threats of legal action are made as well as when they are acted upon" (p. 9). In light of this reality, it becomes clear that willful ignorance of fair use or simple acquiescence to copyright holders' demands—the trends of our textbooks— are not sufficient for students, and our conversation needs to move well beyond these norms. Second, the case reveals how we might develop conversations with students by examining the very process of fair use analysis.

In his decision in favor of the Online Policy Group, Pavlosky, and Smith, Judge Fogel claimed that "Diebold knowingly materially misrepresented that Plaintiffs infringed Diebold's copyright interest, at least with respect to the portions of the email archive clearly subject to the fair use exception" (*Online*, 2004, p. 7). Pivotal to the overall decision on material misrepresentation was the right to fair use, which Fogel concluded was applicable to the students' appropriative composing practices. In his determination of whether their use of material was indeed fair, Fogel quoted Section 107 of Title 17 (the fair use provision) in its entirety and engaged in the sort of four-factor analysis that Maimon et al. (2008) approximated (on a much smaller scale) in *A Writer's Resource*. In his summary judgment, he analyzed each of the four factors: (1) the purpose and character of the use, (2) the nature of the copyrighted work, (3) the amount and substantiality of the portion used, and (4) the effect of the use upon the potential market for or value of the copyrighted work.

When discussing the first of the four factors, legal experts often address the key questions of whether appropriations of copyrighted material are used for commercial, nonprofit, or educational purposes, and whether the function of the use is transformative (i.e., beyond mere reproduction). In his discussion of this factor, Judge Fogel concluded that the primary purpose of the use in question was to inform the public through a form of journalistic criticism. In this sense, the use was both noncommercial and transformative. None of the parties involved sought to profit from the publication of the email archive (it was not being sold) and the archive itself was transformed within its new publication context. Fogel stated, "Plaintiff's and IndyMedia's use was transformative: they used the email archive to support criticism that is in the public interest, not to develop electronic voting technology" (*Online*, 2004, p. 6). In other words, the content of the emails was no longer being used to communicate problems with voting machines (for the purpose of improving the machines and making them a more saleable product); rather, it had been "reframed," as the plaintiff's attorneys had suggested, "as part of a political discussion about the mechanics of democratic elections" (Cohn & Seltzer, 2004, p. 10). For these reasons—and emphatically because the appropriated material was used "in the public interest," a phrase Fogel deployed several times in his judgment—factor 1 was found to weigh in favor of fair use.

Decisions on factor 2 tend to hinge on questions of whether copyrighted material is creative or factual in nature and whether it is published or unpublished at the time of appropriation. When analyzing the second factor, Judge Fogel argued that because the material under question was, indeed, factual and not creative, the plaintiff's use of it was not infringing. In his summary judgment, he claimed, "copyright law protects only creative works, not facts" (*Online*, 2004, p. 3). Although it is arguable whether emails might be considered "creative" (akin to "imaginative" genres like fiction or poetry), it appears that in this instance, the emails under examination—which consisted of "questions and answers from Diebold support staff, feature reports, bug reports, update notes" (Cohn and Seltzer, 2004, p. 11)—were used to communicate factual information within a business setting, and, further, were not defined by the kind of marketable potential that "imaginative" literature possesses. Although fair use determinations tend to favor published over unpublished works, Fogel asserted that the unpublished status of Diebold's archive was "not dispositive." In this particular case, he claimed, "the fact that the email archive was unpublished does not obviate application of the fair use doctrine," largely because Diebold never intended to publish (and thereby seek profit from) the archive. (*Online*, p. 6). For these reasons, Fogel determined that analysis of factor 2 supported fair use.

The third factor is concerned with how large a portion of a copyrighted work is used and how crucial or central the appropriated portion is to the original work. Under Fogel's analysis, the third factor revealed particular complications. The plaintiffs appropriated or linked to an entire archive of Diebold employee email; however, as the plaintiff's attorneys argued in their request for summary judgment, this archive represented only a small fraction of Diebold's total email correspondence. Furthermore, according to Pavlosky and Smith, they were required to post the whole archive for reasons of journalistic integrity after Diebold accused them in news reports of "taking individual emails out of context" (*Online*, 2004, p. 6). Recognizing these issues, Fogel turned to the question of whether crucial information was reproduced. Diebold's attorneys had argued that the emails contained proprietary information "as well as Diebold trade secret information, and even employees' personal information" (Mittelstaedt, 2004, p. 9). While Justice Fogel suggested that the reproduction of emails that contain proprietary code might be infringing—as contended by attorneys for Diebold—he noted the defendants' failure to "identify which of the more than thirteen thousand emails support its argument," that is, to prove that certain emails did, in fact, contain "trade secrets" or strictly private, proprietary information (*Online*, p. 6). Given this failure, Judge Fogel suggested that factor 3 tended to weigh in favor of fair use.

When discussing the fourth factor, Fogel contended that Pavlosky and Smith's use of Diebold's copyrighted materials had no effect on the market for or value of these materials. According to Fogel, the defendants could not prove that the appropriated email archive had any particular marketability or economic value in the first place:

> Diebold has identified no specific commercial purpose or interest affected by the publication of the email archive ... Publishing or hyperlinking to the email archive did not prevent Diebold from making a profit from the content of the archive because there is no evidence that Diebold itself intended to or could profit from such content. (*Online*, p. 6)

Fogel then moved beyond the issue of the emails' potential profitability to briefly acknowledge the overall economic effect of the archive's publication on the company as a whole. Although he consented that Pavlosky and Smith's use of materials could have a negative economic impact on Diebold—because it raised consumer awareness of serious flaws in their products—he found this to be a moot point. He stated that the use of material might have "reduced Diebold's profits because it helped inform potential customers of problems with the machines" but concluded that "copyright law is not designed to prevent such an outcome" (*Online*, p. 6). In his judgment, then, Fogel drew a clear line between the potential profitability of the appropriated material itself (the emails) and the result of the plaintiff's journalistic critique (negative publicity for Diebold). He clearly asserted that although copyright law might apply to the former, it should not be applied to the latter: That is, the law should not be misused or abused, as it was by Diebold, to suppress the sort of informed critical commentary characteristic of investigative reporting.

TALKING OUTSIDE OF COURT TRANSCRIPTS AND COMPOSITION TEXTBOOKS

I have described Judge Fogel's decision-making process at length here because I believe it represents exactly the sort of analytical practice we should expose students to and also ask them to perform. As Brian Ballentine (2009), Rife (2009), and others have already suggested, we would do students a great service by moving the four-factor analysis out of the courtroom and into the classroom. We should provide opportunities, particularly for those composing for the Internet or in new media, to understand how four-factor analysis might apply to existing texts (by examining cases such as the one described above) and to their own in-process works so that they can be in better command of the work they produce for both academic and pubic audiences. As Rife (2009) recommended, developing a fair use heuristic or *techne* based on judges' fair use determinations would enable us and our students to create "probable knowledge when determining whether a use ... is likely a fair use" (p. 135). As Ballentine (2009) suggested, examining four-factor analysis within the rulings of foundational cases such as *Sony Corporation of America v. Universal City Studios* and *MGM v. Grokster* might be used for assignments and class discussion or debate so that they become a definitive part of the curriculum.

The purpose of the sort of inclusion Rife (2009) and Ballentine (2009) recommended is not by any means to create a canon of cases or to produce lawyers-in-training, but, as I see it, to fulfill three goals. First, the process of familiarizing students with four-factor analysis works to protect the right to fair use in an increasingly proprietary culture. The more people who understand their right to fair use, the more people who may assert this right and thereby influence culture and law (as Pavlosky and Smith did in the example above). In short, raising student awareness of the relationship between fair use and freedom of speech has the potential to influence policy on a broad scale. As Rife (2009) suggested, we are currently working within a crucial timeframe, in which "we still have a space to shape law by practice" (p. 150). Second, reviewing four factors in legal cases may help foster an understanding of the ethics of appropriation and the struggles for power involved in this process. By examining cases, students might better understand how writing is situated within the public, legal, and cultural contexts that define the terms of its reception. With student work brought out of isolation, they may be better prepared to negotiate these contexts successfully. Third, and most importantly, familiarity with four-factor analysis might help increase student agency as writers in at least two particular ways.

First, it may influence their capacity for rhetorical decision-making and sharpen their critical thinking skills. Four-factor analysis is, by nature, rhetorical; for instead of relying on any sort of transcendent rules, it utilizes criteria that are radically contingent upon context. As suggested above, each decision about fair use is made on a case-by-case basis, and each factor used to determine this decision is weighed within a specific context of use. In other words, one cannot make the kind of overarching determination that would insist, for example, that works reproducing 60% of copyrighted material are infringing while works reproducing 59% are not. Instead, one would have to analyze the third factor—the amount of material copied—by examining situational phenomena: how text is produced and reproduced within sets of particular circumstances. In *Online Policy Group v. Diebold, Inc.*, the reproduction of an entire email archive was found fair; in *Grand Upright v. Warner* the reproduction of three words and several notes was found infringing. This sort of analysis, then, situates decisions and decision-making as always within the realm of argument; it requires students not to offer ultimately correct answers, but to participate critically and actively in cultural and textual debate while asking questions related to context, genre, and power.

Second, four-factor analysis might increase student agency by making them more cognizant of their rights as writers. As Rife (2007) suggested, students are often uninformed about fair use and misunderstand its relevance to their work. Rife cited the example of a student who unnecessarily "purchased *every* image she used when creating new media class assignments" to insure the avoidance of infringement (p. 156). Teaching four-factor analysis, Rife argued, encourages students to make more informed composing choices and improves their information literacy. Applying the factors to their own work, students may better determine when, why, and how to appropriate and integrate material from sources and whether to seek permissions; they may be better armed to make their own informed decisions about whether to risk accusations of infringement; and they may more thoroughly understand what Rife called the economic, social, and legal "infrastructure" that affects composing practices. Ultimately, Rife insisted that students "need to know what their options are in order to act responsibly and within their own political, social, spiritual, and personal beliefs" and she suggested that teaching the four factors provides them "a high level of knowledge coupled with a high level of agency" (p. 172).

I find the issue of agency—the radical notion of allowing students responsibility for their decisions—perhaps the most compelling reason for talking more substantially about fair use and introducing four-factor analysis. As writing teachers, we are responsible for helping students make informed compositional choices;, ultimately we are not in charge of deciding whether they can or cannot appropriate and reproduce images, sounds, or portions of hypertext in work that crosses academic and public boundaries. It is not our job to offer them imperatives about whether they *must* seek permissions when they borrow material or whether they *must* remove allegedly infringing material from their compositions upon receipt of a cease and desist letter. It is high time we move beyond such mandates, and, as Ballentine (2009) suggested, facilitate classroom discussion that is "informative without being prescriptive" (p. 86), that is, discussion that provides students knowledge of concepts and consequences by exposing them to the factors at play. I recommend we talk with students about fair use in a way that enables them, as Rife (2009) suggested, to "insert themselves into larger conversations" about writing, culture, power, and law, and, within these conversations, to develop their own theories about their work. In short, discussing four-factor analysis in its rhetorical complexity is a complicated task, but students should be exposed to—not protected from—this complication.

It may seem difficult to sacrifice precious class time to discussing fair use analysis, but it is imperative to do so. In fact, it is not a sacrifice at all. As the case of the two Swarthmore students demonstrates, in an era in which the technology of writing is changing rapidly and private and public audiences are collapsing, the consequences of understanding the fair use provision affect our basic practices as writers, our right to free expression, and—I am not being hyperbolic here—the very foundations of our democracy. Although conversations about fair use may take up class time, they may also help writers make some of the most significant decisions facing them today, particularly as composers of new media. Frankly, I cannot think of any subject more worth talking about with contemporary writers—except, perhaps, love.

REFERENCES

Ballentine, Brian. (2009). In defense of obfuscation: Questioning open source and a new perspective on teaching digital literacy in the writing classroom. In Steve Westbrook (Ed.), *Composition and copyright: Perspectives on teaching, text-making, and fair use* (pp. 68-92). Albany: State University of New York Press.

Barthes, Roland. (1977). *Image, music, text*. New York: Hill and Wang.

Benfer, Amy. (2007, March 25). Writing in a free world: Interview with Jonathan Lethem. salon.com. http://www.salon.com/books/jonathan_lethem/index.html

Bielstein, Susan M. (2006). *Permissions, a survival guide: Blunt talk about art as intellectual property*. Chicago: University of Chicago Press.

Cohn, Cindy A., & Seltzer, Wendy. (2004). Plaintiff's notice of motion and motion for summary judgment. *Online Policy Group v. Diebold, Inc.* http://www.eff.org/files/filenode/OPG_v_Diebold/OPG_MSJ.pdf

College Art Association Committee on Intellectual Property. (2004). Q & A. *CAA News: Newsletter of the College Art Association, 29*(1). http://www.collegeart.org/pdf/caa-news-01-04.pdf

Coombe, Rosemary. (1998). *The cultural life of intellectual properties: Authorship, appropriation, and the law*. Durham, NC: Duke University Press.

Dush, Lisa. (2009). Beyond the wakeup call: Learning what students know about copyright. In Steve Westbrook (Ed.), *Composition and copyright: Perspectives on teaching, text-making, and fair use* (pp. 114-132). Albany: State University of New York Press.

Eliot, Thomas Stearns. (1920). *The sacred wood*. http://www.bartleby.com/200/sw11.html

Faigley, Lester; George, Diana; Palchik, Anna; & Selfe, Cynthia. (2004). *Picturing texts*. New York: W. W. Norton & Company.

Grand Upright v. Warner: 780 F. Supp. 182 (S.D.N.Y. 1991). Copyright Infringement Project. Retrieved November 20, 2008, from http://cip.law.ucla.edu/cases/case_grandwarner.html

Korn, Allen. (2007). Digital sampling. *Articles on Music Law*. http://www.alankorn.com/articles/sampling.html

Logie, John. (2006). *Peers, pirates, and persuasion: Rhetoric in the peer-to-peer debates*. West Lafayette, IN: Parlor Press.

Lunsford, Andrea A., & Ruszkiewicz, John J. (2004). *Everything's an argument* (3rd ed.). Boston: Bedford/St. Martin's.

Maimon, Elaine P.; Peritz, Janice H.; & Yancey, Kathleen Blake. (2008). *A writer's resource: A handbook for writing and research*. Boston: McGraw-Hill.

McQuade, Donald, & McQuade, Christine. (2006). *Seeing and writing 3*. Boston: Bedford/St. Martin's.

Mittelstaedt, Robert A. (2004). Memorandum in support of defendants' motion for summary judgment. *Online Policy Group v. Diebold, Inc.* http://www.eff.org/files/filenode/OPG_v_Diebold/Diebold_MSJ_Memo.pdf

Munger, Roger. (2008). *Designing documents and understanding visuals*. Boston: Bedford/St. Martin's.

Odell, Lee, & Katz, Susan M. (2006). *Writing in a visual age*. Boston: Bedford/St. Martin's.

Online Policy Group v. Diebold, Inc: 337 F.Supp.2d 1195 (2004). http://www.eff.org/files/filenode/OPG_v_Diebold/OPG%20v.%20Diebold%20ruling.pdf

Palmquist, Mike. (2005). *Designing writing: A practical guide*. Boston: Bedford/St. Martin's.

Rife, Martine Courant. (2007). The fair use doctrine: History, application, and implications for (new media) writing teachers. *Computers and Composition, 24*, 154-178.

Rife, Martine Courant. (2009). Ideas toward a fair use heuristic: Visual rhetoric and composition. In Steve Westbrook (Ed.), *Composition and copyright: Perspectives on teaching, text-making, and fair use* (pp. 133-153). Albany: State University of New York Press.

Roen, Duane; Glau, Gregory R.; & Maid, Barry M. (2009). *The McGraw-Hill guide: Writing for college, writing for life*. Boston: McGraw-Hill.

Ruszkiewicz, John; Anderson, Daniel; & Friend, Christy. (2006). *Beyond words: Reading and writing in a visual age*. New York: Pearson Longman.

Schwartz, John. (2003, November 3). File sharing pits copyright against free speech. *The New York Times*. http://query.nytimes.com/gst/fullpage.html?res=9E07E4D81130F930A35752C1A9659C8B63

Wysocki, Anne Frances, & Lynch, Dennis A. (2007). *Compose design advocate*. New York: Pearson/Longman.

10 PARODY, PENALTY, AND PEDAGOGY

E. Ashley Hall, Kathie Gossett, and Elizabeth Vincelette

INTRODUCTION

Plagiarism has long been a central concern for the field of English and particularly for those of us specializing in rhetoric and composition. In some ways, this conversation can be traced back to traditional concerns in the field over authorship, invention, and the value placed on a writer's original contributions in a new text. But a central problem with starting a conversation about copyright from this point is that it foregrounds a reliance on the printed text and academic citation conventions in the equation of plagiarism with theft or copyright violation. With the turn to the visual in our field, and a large body of work emerging around multimedia and multimodal text, this frame is no longer appropriate in all instances. Recently, there has been a swell in the research and scholarship within the field arguing that copyright matters to literacy and to our work as compositionists (Logie, 1998, 2006; Rife, 2006, 2007; Westbrook, 2006, 2009). Like many of the scholars working in the field, we recognize that the way in which copyright matters is varied and contextual. The emergent focus on intellectual property represents a shift from research predominantly on plagiarism to a more expansive conception including the nexus of issues that arise with multimedia and multimodal composing. These contributions echo some possibilities and concerns from other fields such as legal studies, media studies, Web design, and information architecture, helping us push our thinking beyond the linear connection between copyright and plagiarism in our scholarship (DeVoss & Webb, 2008; Johnson-Eilola & Selber, 2007).

There seems to be a growing consensus that copyright matters ever more in this late age of print and the new media that comes with it. We agree, and we accept this position as a starting point for this chapter. But, we also acknowledge that the ways in which copyright matters exist on a continuum representing the interests of diverse and often opposing parties in intricate and complex ways. By focusing on non-alphabetic text, we hope to illuminate one of the ways in which the context, materiality, and modes of composition all matter a great deal when our agenda is to explore copyright in meaningful ways that move beyond reductive oversimplifications, ones which assume that any time another person's work is used without proper academic citation or prior copyright clearance, it *must* be morally wrong, is likely legally inappropriate, or is at least academically prohibited. We think this is particularly true in the context of a multiliteracies pedagogy that accepts non-traditional texts circulating in Web 2.0 spaces as legitimate and valuable workspaces for analysis and production. Although we agree that copyright is important, we do not intend for this chapter to lament the immoral and unconscionable actions of students. Doing this would simply bolster the agenda and interests of certain powerful parties in the larger debate over copyright in a variety of legal and commercial contexts. It would also reinforce the very position we want to push against: that which insists on equating plagiarism in print with other modes of intertextual borrowing and sampling online without regard for the change in materialities and purpose. Moreover, simply lamenting the dangers involved with this type of composing would devalue some student work by implicitly deeming them illegitimate or outside the scope of our interest or inquiry, and perhaps even by implying that these texts are illegal.

Instead, we envision this chapter as one way of pushing the conversation forward by arguing that we should augment the scope of inquiry into copyright across our field by addressing online video in the context of YouTube. Doing this is a way of responding to the belief that "it is time for more of us in rhetoric and composition, and computers and writing specifically, to have a louder voice and a more persuasive say in the intellectual property debates going on in our culture and in our world" (DigiRhet, 2008). Yet, while this chapter is a response to this position, it is not simply an echo. We believe this is important because we see online video—especially on YouTube, as it is an increasing area of textual consumption and production by and for students—as remaining largely on the periphery of our field. Grounded in the widely held belief that writing is inherently social, this decision to focus specifically and exclusively on YouTube's content is sensitive to the ways students are engaging with and responding to their peers, their culture, and even corporate America in what is seen predominantly as a social or leisure activity. To accomplish this goal, we examine the interface of YouTube, a particular Web 2.0 site that provides the context through which we open the conversation about how copyright matters to online video texts. Using the design of the interface to begin the conversation, we address online parody videos. We have chosen to focus on parody videos in particular because they foreground practices of sampling, remixing, and appropriation in the composing process. The meaning-making processes involved in understanding and constructing parody videos naturally rub against our traditional print-based notions of authorship and originality, thus inviting discussions related to copyright.

To help distinguish how context is critical to this endeavor, we define what we mean when we employ the term "Web 2.0"and why we believe YouTube qualifies as a Web 2.0 site. We explore how this context changes the conversation about copyright infringement—moving beyond theft and simple file sharing to a more nuanced understanding, revealing the complicated motives and decisions made in these spaces. We use the case study of "Condi Rice Raps," a particular parody video, to examine parody as a genre of online video dependent on this nuance and complication to demonstrate the distinction between earlier appropriation practices that are highly publicized and criticized for being illicit. We also use this case study to illustrate what we see as a growing form of expression that intentionally relies on appropriation to recompose new meaning in online video.

Finally, we tie this phenomenon back to the central mission of producing powerful communicators capable of critically consuming a range of texts and producing texts in which the communicators move out of defensive postures concerning copyright and into roles in which they actively recognize the significance of their practices and thoughtfully engage in discourses that promote and promulgate the value of these practices. This ultimately allows us to respond to the call issued by DigiRhet (2008) to support technological literacies in our classes and help cultivate students who realize, understand, and value a wide range of digital composing strategies, who are sensitive to the ways in which copyright connects with these strategies, and who can articulate and communicate why these strategies are important, meaningful, and legal.

WEB 2.0: FROM TEXT TO CONTEXT

Materiality and Variegated Composing Practices

Materiality matters, and in a range of ways (DeVoss & Porter, 2006; Hayles, 2000; Reid, 2007; Wysocki, 2004). It matters to writing in general, but it takes an even more central position of importance when our writing/composing bumps against copyright issues (DeVoss & Webb, 2008). Stealing is wrong;

there are few who would disagree with the moral, ethical, or legal validity of this claim, save for the minority who choose to defy our existing conventions and codes out of deliberate choice, basic necessity, or ignorance. Yet, despite our willingness to accept the importance of materiality to a host of composition questions, we tend to forget about it when it comes to copyright and new media, where we heavy-handedly equate many of the appropriation practices used in new media composition with outright plagiarism in a printed document. In other words, as we move beyond alphabetic text into the realm of sound, visual, and especially online video-composing practices in Web 2.0 spaces, we move from text to context. As rhetoricians comfortable and familiar with the importance of context, materiality (and, increasingly, immateriality) of new media compositions changes the nature of the debate we are engaged in concerning copyright.

We hold a basic assumption that one of our primary goals as rhetoric and composition specialists is to expand the literacies students bring to the classroom and to help develop new literacies in critical, analytical ways. Indeed, this tenet is central to a multiliteracies pedagogy that places value on the composing practices our students engage in outside of the standard curriculum, inviting them to bring these practices into the classroom as a way of expanding their existing literacies and giving them valuable strategies to return to their everyday discourse communities (Cope & Kalantzis, 2000; Selber, 2004). However, when some of these practices seem to cross the line between legal and illegal by involving copyrighted content in multimodal compositions distributed to large public audiences, we are presented with a set of unique challenges that force us to heighten our development of media literacy and technological literacy so we can respond appropriately and guide students responsibly. To cultivate a classroom of technoliterates, mere alphabetic literacy on our part is no longer sufficient. Instead, we need to be keenly aware of the nuances and subtleties involved in the variegated composing practices that we now encompass and facilitate in the composition classroom—ranging from the savvy and critical analysis of the texts circulating in popular online spaces to the production of multimodal texts that students can (and often will) circulate and make public in Web 2.0 settings.

The Digital Copyright War becomes Guerrilla Warfare

When we use Web 2.0 to describe YouTube, we do so with the awareness that this term is both new and disputed. Critics of using the term claim that the technologies and functionalities used on sites described as 2.0 have been around since the earliest days of the World Wide Web and, therefore, implies a false sense of revision or versioning characteristic of software applications that use numerical naming conventions to distinguish more recent releases from earlier ones. The counter argument to this claim is that, although technically true that the functionality is not new, the uses of the spaces and sites are. Advocates of the term explain that there are two clearly different philosophies to architecting Web sites today; the philosophy described as Web 2.0 is fundamentally different from the one commonly found on Web sites in the late 1990s and early 2000s. What makes 2.0 sites different is that the site creators build the architecture and the interface but do not produce the content; instead, user-generated-content populates the sites. YouTube fits this model, as do many popular social-networking sites such as Facebook, and other types of media-sharing sites, such as Flickr and Delicious. This places Web 2.0 sites in square opposition to a traditional media Web site (think of msn.com or cnn.com) in which the company that owns and builds the site is also the primary producer of content for the site. In other words, the owners of a Web 2.0 site produce little-to-no original content, and instead depend entirely on users to upload and share files to produce content and aggregate an audience. This clear distinction between professional, corporate authorship of content on a traditional media Web site and the de-professionalized prosumer authorship of content on a user-generated site (Anderson, 2003; Jenkins, 2006) is the basis for our decision to adopt the term.

It is important to understand that when students engage in the diverse set of composing practices used to generate content for these sites, they often do so with a disregard for the fact that what they are doing is a contested form of composition. Certainly they don't call it this or discuss it in these terms. But more importantly, they don't conceive of it in the same ways that other interested parties do—namely the copyright holders and corporate entities interested in controlling the flows and uses of the material they own rights to. Perhaps this is the legacy we are left with in what Dànielle Nicole DeVoss and Jim Porter (2006) called the post-Napster era, a period recognizing the lasting effects of the values embodied in the file-sharing practices characteristic to Napster and other similar network spaces. It is possible that this logic was so quickly adopted that it became invisible in the same ways that the interface of Microsoft Word (and the social, economic, political, and cultural baggage that come with it) became invisible to us with constant use. After all, the original Napster application was only distributed to a mere 30 people by Shawn Fanning in 1999, but had been downloaded by 15,000 people within a week, culminating with an estimated 60–80 million users at the pinnacle and decisive period in 2001 when the site was shut down after being challenged for willful and knowing abetment of copyright infringement (DeVoss & Porter, 2006). The Napster interface gave users the opportunity to "share" files across vast, open networks. The question remains: How many of the original 15,000 users really understood that they were violating copyright laws, and how many of them simply took advantage of the affordances of the interface?

Interestingly, though, it seems to be students who are the most implicitly aware of how the (im)materiality of the texts circulating in online spaces disconnects from our traditional conceptions of intellectual property and even authorship or invention. The materiality of earlier forms of artistic and intellectual labor—from bound manuscripts to painted portraits to sculpted stone statues—were largely one-of-a-kind objects and therefore existed as rivalrous goods as Lawrence Lessig (2001) used the term: *If I own the original, no one else can own it and I can easily control access to it*. This materiality helps to justify traditional copyright regulations that privilege the original work of a single creator and recognize the intentionality and effort related to manufacturing replicas of the artifact in question. The physical qualities of analog productions help maintain the battle lines between sides jousting over copyright and intellectual property in offline settings.

Yet, copyright is not synonymous with control; in fact, quite the opposite is true. One of the important purposes of copyright, as interpreted by Sandra Day O'Connor in the 1991 decision of *Feist Publications, Inc. v. Rural Telephone Service Co.*, is to spur progress in the arts and sciences by making possible new works based on another's "original expression." Her decision explained that ideally copyright "encourages others to build freely upon the ideas and information conveyed by a work." This notion of freely using others' content to create new works can be found readily in many Web 2.0 spaces where users can quickly and easily see, hear, experience, and then save, edit, and reuse digital texts. The inherent immateriality of digital texts and their concomitant affordances change a traditional text-based dynamic; physical manufacturing is no longer required, and the distribution of one copy or one thousand copies requires the same degree of skill and exertion, often without any loss of quality in comparison to the original (see Dornsife in this volume). The appropriation and remixing practices we see flourishing on Web 2.0 sites underscore both the difference in materiality and in context between these and other forms of composing that present copyright questions.

In the case of online video, then, as one form of new media that intersects the copyright debate, the ways composers go about building freely upon other people's work complicate our existing understandings and applications of copyright. Lev Manovich's (2002) definition of new media includes texts that are necessarily digital, existing as numeric representations that can be reproduced and manipulated freely and easily using the appropriate hardware and software to interact with the files.[1] The infinite reproduction and manipulation of digital text, Manovich argued, forces us beyond the conception of the single-author-genius and into a new context in which the author participates inter/actively with the audience in meaning-making processes. This ultimately led him to propose that the logic of new media is in direct opposition to the logic of art in the romantic sense. This is a logic that seems instinctual, if albeit implicit, to the digital natives (Prensky, 2001; if we accept the term *natives*) of the post-Napster era and to the work they produce and circulate on Web 2.0 sites. Yet, despite the soundness of this bifurcated logic grounded in the materiality of the text, frequently the (attempted) application of copyright disavows this important distinction—insisting instead on the romantic conceptualization of the primacy of the original author (and thus often serving the agenda of powerful media elites). This is problematic when we recognize that copyright is not only important to us as educators because it is rhetorical; it is also important because it is highly contested in legal disputes that extend into the lives and spaces our students inhabit. Using the metaphor of war, DeVoss and Porter (2006) explained that the "cultural and ethical battles lines have been clearly drawn" (p. 185), situating the copyright "skirmishes" in this complicated and ongoing war as not just confined to courtrooms and boardrooms, but also on university campuses. This realization makes the case for exploring the relevance of YouTube videos to the copyright debate even more exigent for us. One important consideration that emerges is whether or not students realize their campus is a war zone, or that they are the perceived aggressors in this war—or even that they are participants in the war to begin with.

In the past (even the recent past), many appropriations of intellectual content, including those forms distributed over networks, required a cognizant and deliberate set of actions including the physical modification of pre-existing hardware and network connections typically configured by professional installers. Stealing cable is an example of this process. The tools required for this type of illicit activity are not sophisticated, but the sheer fact that one must explicitly choose to employ this set of tools to accomplish the task helps foreground the act of theft. It would be difficult to suggest that someone could get caught up in this type of theft without realizing it. But, as more and more Web sites such as YouTube remediate earlier media forms by creating hybrid spaces that combine the structure of a webpage, a message board, a blog, and television into a single integrated platform, user access to illegally posted copyrighted content increases. At the same moment, the steps a user must go through to access, appropriate, and reuse this content diminish. Further, casually browsing or searching YouTube can often and easily lead to the consumption of illegally posted copyrighted content. This concept of the (im)materiality of digital works that can be easily and flawlessly reproduced and then distributed to large audiences is in part what leads DeVoss and Porter (2006) to describe the particular historical and cultural post-Napster moment as a "paradigm shift" (p. 188). In this transitional moment, we find that students' ability to create, produce and distribute sophisticated new media texts in the form of YouTube videos incorporating other people's original work is surpassing their awareness of the debate they are entering.

While this entire scope of activity invites a discussion concerning copyright and the violations and complications that arise as we witness the dominance of Web 2.0 sites, which increasingly rely on user-generated content, we composition instructors are particularly concerned with the instances when students engage in the illegal consumption and production of copyrighted content without a critical awareness of their actions. Therefore, it is this aspect of the larger conversation that we take up in the remainder of this chapter: Exploring the appropriation of copyrighted content in Web 2.0 spaces to re/compose and respond to both specific texts, and responding to larger discourses circulating in the popular sphere. We begin by interrogating the nature of the interface as it connects directly to both the consumption and production of texts in these spaces, in many ways structuring the very nature of the discourse that transpires on such sites.

THE INTERFACE

If YouTube's users aren't primarily trying to beat the system by watching videos for free that they should have to pay for, then what are they doing? How is this different from simply downloading music? And why does it matter to writing? Examining the interface of YouTube can help us answer these questions.

In 1994, long before YouTube was conceived, Cynthia Selfe and Richard Selfe argued that the interfaces we invite into the classroom are often politically motivated whether we realize and accept it or not.[2] Therefore, if we choose to invite online video into the classroom as part of a multiliteracies pedagogy, we must examine how the interface can be used to reveal seemingly seamless embedded political or legal assumptions related to copyright. Selfe and Selfe's work urges rigorous reflection on our uses of interfaces in composition classrooms and how these uses can produce a range of outcomes spanning from reification of existing power distributions to renegotiation of such structures. Selfe and Selfe suggest that considering the role of the Web 2.0 interface and related metaphors might offer us a more critical and reflective understanding of how informed decisions about selection and use of particular interfaces can help us enact and articulate the forms of social change required to engage with copyright issues. To employ the interface in this manner, we must make visible some of the dominant features of the interface itself that have become so familiar to many Web users who see certain icons and buttons repeated so ubiquitously that they have become invisible.[3] Then, once we have made these elements visible, we must develop technoliterate strategies to translate awareness into action that promotes and protects the values that support our copyright agenda by making informed choices about the features embodied in the interface.

Although YouTube isn't exactly a social-networking site in the same way as Facebook or MySpace, it does borrow from the conventions of this genre and situating it as such helps to foreground the social nature of the practices the site fosters. Users create accounts, entering personal information into form fields to represent themselves to the public and to connect with other users. Users don't simply post, share, and consume files on YouTube for personal use; they circulate these texts in social practices, interacting with them in multiple ways presented within (and authorized by) the interface. These social practices are an important facet of the site that helps to distinguish it from other file-sharing sites such as Napster or LimeWire. Moreover, the idea that the texts circulating on YouTube are social in nature helps us link the composing practices users are engaged in back to our widely held belief in the field of rhetoric and composition that all writing—even user-generated videos posted and shared on YouTube—is inherently social.

YouTube could be used for the illegal file-sharing activities that have captivated corporate attention and media coverage and that situated Napster users as villains who pirated copyrighted music and threatened the massive enterprises of the recording industries with their illicit behavior. But, importantly, that is not what happens most of the time on YouTube. Yes, YouTube has been challenged for acting as a facilitator of widespread copyright infringement from national and international corporations claiming damages. As we mentioned earlier, one need not look too long or hard to find copyrighted content illegally posted to the site. However, the motivations, practices, and uses of this copyrighted content is often distinctly different from other forms of appropriation in other spaces, which have typically formed the basis of concerns over pirating and plagiarism. As Johndan Johnson-Eilola and Stuart Selber (2007) persuasively argued, not all forms of appropriation are equal, nor are they all illicit; Johnson-Eilola and Selber cite as a primary example our academic peer-to-peer file-sharing of syllabi and plagiarism policies. Asserting that some forms of appropriation and reuse are consensual and understood practices in certain discourse communities such as Web design and architecture, Johnson-Eilola and Selber's claims can help us identify the agenda behind certain aspects of YouTube's interface.

It would be logical to assume that the same threats Napster (supposedly) presented to the music recording industry by allowing users to download copyrighted music for free would be repeated with television shows and perhaps even full-length movies on a file-sharing site devoted to video. And some of the copyright suits brought against YouTube certainly rely on the extension of this line of reasoning. Yet examining key elements of the interface reveal that this is not the primary agenda of the site; the maximum length of a video uploaded to YouTube is 10 minutes, significantly shorter than either a movie or television show. If YouTube's intention was to facilitate distribution of entire television shows, the minimum time limit on a video would have to be at least 20 minutes (the typical length of a half-hour television show, minus commercials). YouTube's interface also reveals a logic informed by the cultural values of the post-Napster era; every video plays on a page that presents the user with various ways to redistribute the content, with sharing features such as emailing a link, sharing via Facebook and Twitter, and embed code so that the video can be separated from the original context of YouTube itself and be integrated into a blog post or other web page. If we accept that the design of an interface can and often does contain metaphors that embody cultural values and, therefore, can be seen as advancing particular agendas, relying on Selfe and Selfe's (1994) observation that, "in general, computer interfaces present reality as framed in the perspective of modern capitalism, thus, orienting technology along an existing axis of class privilege" (p. 486), then we can understand these affordances as communicating a willing consent to share and circulate *freely* the content appearing on YouTube. This would seem to be in line with the logic Justice Sandra Day O'Connor articulated in her important 1991 decision, and also with the tendencies of the post-Napster generation of digital natives, liking interaction with texts of all sorts, including online videos they watch and make.

INTERFACING THE SOCIAL AND CONTEXTUAL

These interface characteristics can help us establish a clear connection between the interface of YouTube and issues related to copyright. Users who post videos to YouTube are inserting their content into a setting that allows others to quickly and easily circulate the content in a variety of ways and contexts. The very decision to post video content to YouTube reveals a new cultural logic, one that says "go ahead, take my video and post it to your blog, put it on your Facebook wall."

Turning to the broader organization and arrangement of the interface, several key features reveal that each video is at once social and contextual. The video player is certainly the dominant feature on the page, attracting the viewer's attention with the sound and motion that begin to play as soon as the page loads. But all around the player are design elements that put the video into context. The box to the right of the video indicates the date the video was posted and provides the username of the author along with a textual description of the video. Below are two containers that put the video into context by displaying the thumbnail image, title, and number of views in two categories: 1) "other videos posted by this user" and 2) "related videos" or videos posted by other users identified algorithmically by YouTube as similar. These features of the interface are also important to authorship and the establishment of ethos on a site where a user's identity can be (and often is) concealed and where peer review of material is informal. As such, the number of times a video is played, its appearance on YouTube's "featured" list, and the frequency and content of responses from other users become a measure of credibility. This underlying logic is in stark contrast to print-based academic traditions where an author uses a bibliography to build credibility, or when a writer uses citation conventions to "showcase the author's knowledge of related texts and to allow the author to speak to those texts he or she embraces or rejects" (Hess, 2006, p. 284). Therefore, when average users load Michael Wesch's video "A Vision of Students Today," for example, even if they don't know who "mwesch" is, they can see that he has nine other videos that appear in the "more from: mwesch" container on the page. In addition, they can easily see that the top video has received over 10.9 million plays (as of June 2010). This gives viewers a good idea—even if they don't know that Wesch is a well-known professor at Kansas State University—that mwesch is an active participant on the site and that he creates very popular videos, thereby giving him higher credibility than other less active or less popular users. The viewer can also discern that mwesch's videos are very effective at sparking conversation. This observation highlights a number of other key interface elements and returns us to the issue of copyright.

INTERFACING COPYRIGHT

The commentary section below the video is the space where conversation transpires in the form of alphabetic text posted as comments and video responses. The video mentioned above, for example, has received 8,859 text comments and 75 video responses to date (June 2010). The 500 maximum character limit imposed on the text comments can, arguably, limit complications related to copyright matters. The video responses, however, are a different matter; instead of using a bibliography to account for an awareness of the ongoing conversation to which a composer is responding, the video functionality affords users the opportunity to respond in a high-context fashion, reliant on the ability of other users to understand the site and the connection between the source video and the response. This aspect of the interface design, then, reinforces the notion that a new and different cultural logic is at play throughout the site, one that, in many ways, opposes the systems and conventions we are comfortable and familiar with when working with print sources.

One particular scenario in which complications related to copyright come to the forefront is when the response video takes the form of parody; parody provides a lens for us to look at the connections between authorship and copyright because parody demands the use of someone else's original content in the creation of new meaning. Using this lens affords a way to engage students in the serious treatment of these concepts. Moving these issues to the center of our pedagogy pushes us into a new and sometimes uncomfortable space, especially when it comes to teaching argumentation strategies, but it is precisely this move where we see the most opportunity.

PARODY, AUTHORSHIP, AND PEDAGOGY

Definitions of parody and authorship inform our stance on copyright and parody video. Student inclinations to seek out and consume parodic content provides an ideal gateway for delving into working with source texts to understand how authors and composers of parody alter an original work when they create a new, and often subversive, message. Parody "both legitimizes and subverts that which it parodies" (Hutcheon, 1989, p. 117) because it requires the deconstruction of existing texts and (re)construction of new ones. This inherent duality of purpose is exactly why parody is so valuable. It requires us to acknowledge texts as separate and distinct, while at the same time it requires us to understand that the existence of an intertextual relationship; the parody is an offspring of the original, but it is still intrinsically tied to it. This inseparable relationship between the two texts situates parody squarely in the center of the ongoing debate surrounding intellectual property when remixed and repurposed content is used to create a new work. Parody videos manifest a form of multimodal pastiche, reflecting infinite possibilities of reflexivity and reproduction—the same qualities that cause parodies in general to conflict with notions of copyright and ownership, especially when we are uncertain about how much copying is "too much."

Using parody helps us reframe the conversation by moving away from traditional and simplistic treatments of copyright that equate it solely with plagiarism; the classroom can become a transformative space where students can be "social critics" (Selber, 2004, p. 95). Instead of being passively engaged with the texts picked for them by instructors or publishers, in which they may have little-to-no interest, students bring their experiences with popular video into the classroom, positioning themselves as stakeholders in the selection of course content. Ultimately, this leads to a higher level of engagement with copyright and its relevance to students' everyday lives. Rather than simply laughing at a funny parody video, students can begin to uncover how the composer made it funny and then use this newfound understanding to create complex arguments that take the form of parodic social criticism. This moves us into the realm of an activist pedagogy concerned with copyright.

Invoking Awareness Rather than Inciting Fear

Instead of being taught that copyright is a cut-and-dry issue that positions copyright holders as the interested and powerful parties in the debate, students can take a more informed and active role by questioning their positions in relation to the copyright holders, their multimodal composing practices mediating this encounter. All too often, we feel, copyright is understated or oversimplified in most of our existing pedagogical texts and approaches (see Westbrook in this volume, for an analysis of copyright-related textbook content). There is certainly a tremendous amount of effort and capital expended by corporate entities interested in perpetuating or advancing this tone concerning copyright. And our campuses are not immune to the influence of corporate giants who would rather terrify students about what might happen to them if they are caught using copyrighted material inappropriately than educate them on how to use content effectively and legally. On our campus, for example, there are mouse pads in most of the computer labs with reminders about illegal downloading and appropriation of copyrighted content. The intent of these reminders is to invoke awareness and even fear in students. Fear is not a productive pedagogical approach when dealing with issues as complicated and nuanced as copyright and fair use, especially in this particular historical moment, when many of the rules about how these practices and policies relate to multimodal composing remain largely undecided in both legal and academic realms.

Reticence to action regarding copyright pedagogy certainly exists; this reticence became starkly apparent in a course discussion focusing on intellectual property, copyright, and fair use in a spring 2009 graduate pedagogy seminar at Old Dominion University. During the discussion, the students, all of whom had experience teaching composition at the secondary or postsecondary level, willingly acknowledged that when copyright does come up in their classrooms, they either shy away from the conversation with a sense that copyright and fair use issues are too complex and legalistic for them to delve into, or they treat them in a prescriptive manner by issuing a set of rules and consequences (usually related to grade penalties if the rules are broken). Unfortunately, these prescriptions were based on little more than hearsay and word-of-mouth guidelines (e.g., students could sample up to 30 seconds of video or audio material and still be "legal"). This is a critical moment—one in which our professional responsibilities, as scholars, preclude us from simply ignoring the gravity of these issues or assuming that our classrooms are insulated from their reach. Students will encounter more and more of these remixed texts; we must equip students with the literacy and agency to manipulate the technologically saturated landscape they will continue to encounter on a perpetual and daily basis.

Composing as Technoliterates

Moving from a broad and theoretically based inquiry about new media authorship to a more specific investigation focused on a particular author's choices when composing a video affords a prime opportunity for using parody videos as a scaffold for student learning. The requisite assemblage of original and borrowed or imitated content inherent to the parody genre allows for a rich exploration of concepts related to fair use and copyright. When we move into the area of using a new genre and a new medium, such as parody videos on YouTube, matters become complicated; this complication, however, is a positive outcome. If our end goal is to invest students with the agency to participate in copyright debates and to produce media for digital spaces, the fact that matters remain unsettled might compel them even further, especially if they embrace their position as interested stakeholders with the potential to help shape the outcome of popular composing practices and the legal acceptance of these practices. This is what we envision as the embodiment of technoliteracy—composers who make choices intentionally and grounded in purposeful decisions about the rhetorical efficacy of those choices to (re)use copyrighted content parodically, as social criticism, and who have the capacity to respond to challenges about the legality of their choices. But even for those rhetoric and composition instructors who accept this as an ideal position for students, the jump from discussing use and citation conventions of traditional print texts to online parody videos may at first seem like a chasm too wide to span. This is a challenge, certainly, but not one that is impossible to accomplish.

ANNE FRANCES WYSOCKI, MEET CONDI RAPS

Using existing and effective pedagogical approaches can help us in creating this bridge. The turn to the visual and acceptance of new media, multimedia, and multimodal compositions as legitimate artifacts for study in our field has laid the foundation for our work with parody videos on YouTube. This recent, but rich, tradition has offered us many possibilities and points of departure. We find that using Anne Frances Wysocki's (2004) rhetorical approach for working with new media texts is particularly effective. Writing in 2004, before YouTube even existed, Wysocki anticipated many of the potentials realized on the site including "more, larger and smoother video to watch and analyze on screen" (p. 136). And while her approach—intended to cover a wide range of new media texts ranging from webpages to computer games—does not address YouTube directly as the focal site for analysis, we find that many of Wysocki's techniques support our work. We envision our application of her approach as a model that can be adapted for use with other videos, other Web 2.0 platforms, or for other purposes related to working with online video. As such, we offer a case study of a particular parody video, "Condi Rice Raps" (volgkarate, 2007), illustrating how the approach might be effectively applied in an analysis of a parody video.

EXAMINING VIDEO AND AUDIO

For an effective close reading of multimodal texts, Wysocki suggested that we break the text into parts. She provides a framework for how to do this in a series of steps, beginning with the visual:

1. Name the visual elements in the text. (This might include static images, video clips, or moving textual titles or static frames of text).

2. Name the designed relationships among those elements.

3. Consider how the elements and relations connect with different audiences, contexts, and arguments. (p. 137)

These steps can then be repeated with the audio parts of the video:

1. Name the auditory elements in the text. (This might include distinct sounds, a music track, vocals that are sung, spoken or rapped, or any combination of these elements).

2. Name the designed relationships among those elements.

3. Consider how the elements and relations connect with different audiences, contexts, and arguments.

Wysocki underscored the importance of including sound in the analysis process by suggesting we watch "MTV without the music to hone your sense of what sound and visual strategies bring to texts together and separately" (p. 137). The "Condi Rice Raps" video, which draws from the MTV tradition by using Fergi's song "Fergalicious" as the basis for the parody, is a prime example of this concept in action. Watching the video with muted sound changes the viewing experience entirely and significantly impacts viewers' ability to recognize the video as a parody. For example, while watching the video on mute, viewers can detect that the visual part of the video contains multiple layers, some sampled and some original, but because viewers can't hear the dialogue or the music, there is little else to help them figure out that what they are seeing is the intro to a parody video using C-SPAN footage and a popular song/music video as social criticism of a political leader. Turning the sound back on, just nine seconds into the video, drum beats are audible, layered over the audio tracks that mash C-SPAN audio with original audio spoken or rapped by actors.

When all three audio elements work in unison with the visual elements, it is clear that the whole composition is an entertaining critique of former Secretary of State Condoleezza Rice. Without the sound, viewers must watch 24 seconds of material that combines sampled and original video footage until the first indicator of the music video genre appears in the form of actors dancing in front of a marquee reading "Condoleezza." Viewers familiar with the "Fergalicious" video would finally be able to recognize the parody, but not until much later than is possible when the audio and visual parts are played simultaneously.

Going through this process makes apparent the deliberate and rhetorical changes the author employed when composing the parody. Using Wysocki's

Parody, Penalty, and Pedagogy

Figure 1: "Condi Rice Raps" video begins with CSPAN footage depicting Senator Barbara Boxer.

Figure 2: Senator Barbara Boxer is quickly replaced with the Condoleeza parody figure.

Figure 3: "Condoleeza" marquee.

(2004) framework helps viewers move from passive roles of consumers to active roles as investigators. Instead of simply smiling or laughing at the unusual depiction of a serious political figure who assumes the role of a highly sexualized rap artist in the video, viewers may be prompted to ask more specific questions about the author's choices when selecting specific elements and arranging them in a particular fashion. For example, when analyzing the audio elements of "Condi Rice Raps," the music is easily recognized as "Fergalicious" because the underlying audio track has been sampled from the song, but, importantly, it is not taken wholesale. Listening closely reveals that small fragments of the original music are cut, and then looped in a way that resembles the original so that it can be recognized, but is still different from the original in both its arrangement and composition. Once again, issues of copyright demand questions about the legality of these appropriation practices. Without remixing the audio in this way, the parody might still be funny, but it would not be able to rely on the "Fergalicious" video as strongly for the basis of the parody and it may be less effective as a result. Therefore, it is possible to conclude that the decisions made by the author in this instance were rhetorically sound and strategic towards the creation of a specific parodic argument.

ANALYZING COMPLEX LAYERS

Ordinarily, if our only purpose was to be entertained by a particular video such as the one we have chosen to study, we might notice the layers occasionally, but our focus would be on the complete whole—the different parts blended together working as a unified text. This is precisely the author's intention. The audience must be able to recognize the video as a parody and therefore be able to pick up on the references to the original. Yet, to be effective, the audience must also be able to easily identify the differences, the elements that have been modified to create a new meaning in the act of social critique. These modifications might exist in any or all of the layers and they might occur in sequence or simultaneously. Therefore, using Wysocki's (2004) approach—which requires viewers to slow down or pause the video during analysis and examine each layer independently—can help shed light on the myriad choices the author made to construct each of the layers and better understand how each of the layers plays an essential role in the formation of a larger argument that says something new, funny, and critical. This approach can also help viewers classify the elements found in each layer into one of two very important categories: original and borrowed/remixed.[4] We see tremendous value in completing a rhetorical reading/viewing when analyzing parody videos because of their complexity and intentional blending of elements, layers, and modes. Using a series of worksheets or rubrics during this analytic process can be helpful; we have included several in the appendix. This type of analysis can help students gain a deeper understanding of parody and copyright by rhetorically analyzing the decisions authors make when composing parody videos and the implications these decisions have for copyright matters.

Composing as Technoliterates

Once the analytical foundation has been established, students will have a strong basis upon which they can build when moving from analytic work into production. As students participate with increasing frequency in Web 2.0 publishing outside of the classroom, they insert themselves into spaces that may appear harmless and safe. However, as the "peers" or "friends" comprising social networks grow to include politicians, artists, and corporations, students may quickly find themselves in adversarial encounters *vis-à-vis* these copyright holders, who may feel their rights have been infringed. In such instances, the battlefield, to borrow a metaphor often applied to the copyright debate by legal scholars such as Jessica Litman (2001), is extremely uneven. However, students who can draw from the theoretical understanding they have developed when studying other composers and use it to articulate why their choices are rhetorically effective, strategic, and, most importantly, *legal* will find themselves in a much better position than others who lack this ability.

To achieve this, activities that build upon the analysis techniques adapted from Wysocki (2004) can be used to help students as they begin to plan, organize and produce their own parody videos. One approach would be to ask students to find a video they feel invites a strong response based on the elements they can now easily identify and track when critically viewing online videos. Allowing students to chose their own videos rather than prescribing a single video for the entire class encourages further investment in the student-as-stakeholder role. Starting from this motivated position, students can begin to work with their source, making decisions about what to sample and what to leave out with a new-found emphasis on the rhetorical nature of these decisions. Then, students might be required to decide how much of the original needs to be altered and what other visual and audio elements they need to complete these alterations. As they search for and collect these elements, they can re-use the rubrics (included in the appendix of this chapter) to help them keep track of their sources and their decision-making process about why each source was chosen and how it is rhetorically effective in the larger composition. This process of moving back and forth between analysis and production and writing and video breaks down the often assumed bifurcation between these two activities. As Maria Lovett, James Purdy, Kathie Gossett, Carrie Lamanna, and Joseph Squier (2010) argued, "writing and video can serve to reinforce and strengthen an overarching intellectual journey whose end result is video, but whose process is writing-intensive. The goal [here] is to present video production and writing as a creative and intellectually rigorous symbiotic process" (p. 288). Armed with scholarly analytic methods and grounded in rigorous investigation and purposeful production, students become composers with agency to navigate a broad range of composing contexts while making informed decisions during their research and composing processes.

CONCLUSION

If students have a sound understanding of how parody works, and that the choices made in remixing content to produce a parody are deliberate and rhetorical, they will be better positioned to intelligently engage with a copyright holder who might challenge their composing practices, whether they are created for an academic assignment or for sheer entertainment as part of their leisure activities in a peer-to-peer online environment, such as YouTube.

We encourage using this approach even when working with a wider range of new media compositions—whether understanding parody and copyright in the context of online video are central learning goals or not. Neither social criticism itself nor parody as a form of social criticism is new—but the shapes, forms, and practices of parody as social criticism found on YouTube powerfully demonstrate the expansion of multimodal composing practices in popular culture. Integrating online video into the composition curriculum under a multiliteracies framework allows a deeper understanding of the author–text–audience relationship. It also fulfils an appeal issued by Johnson-Eilola (2004), who observed that "despite the realization that our culture increasingly values texts that are broken down, rearranged, recombined, we rarely teach forms of writing that support such production" (p. 209). We view the analysis and production of parody videos like those found on YouTube as a ripe opportunity for this endeavor—an ambitious process involving risk and care. We believe such work is valuable and even necessary as a means of expanding literacy in ways that are relevant to the lived experiences of students. At the moment, when many of our familiar print-based conventions are beginning to fail us, we must be prepared to negotiate murky boundaries carefully, often with little or no legal or academic framework delineating the rules of engagement. We believe that the field can no longer abdicate this responsibility; doing so would be a disservice to students that could lead to the devaluation of their work with unnecessary restrictions and penalties hampering their creative and intellectual expressions of social criticism.

NOTES

1. We recognize that Manovich's definition of new media has been criticized as being too narrow, with Wysocki as one of his primary challengers contending that new media does not have to be digital. We accept that this is an ongoing debate, but choose to incorporate Manovich's definition to help draw the contrast between copyright applied to unique material artifacts and copyright applied to digital compositions.

2. Within the virtual space represented by these interfaces, and elsewhere within computer systems, the values of our culture—ideological, political, economic, educational—are mapped both implicitly and explicitly, constituting a complex set of material relations among culture, technology, and technology users. In effect, interfaces are cultural maps of computer systems, and as Denis Wood (1992) pointed out, such maps are never ideologically innocent or inert.

3. See Selfe and Selfe (1994) for a discussion of how the borders represented in interfaces have become so familiar that they have become invisible; also see Manovich (2002) for a discussion of how particular interfaces and the metaphors they use have become so familiar that they have also become invisible.

4. Wysocki did not include this classification step in her initial approach because her focus was much broader and not concerned specifically with parody or copyright. Because ours is, we propose this addition that illustrates how an existing rhetorical approach can easily be scaffolded and applied to working with online parody videos.

REFERENCES

Anderson, Daniel. (2003). Prosumer approaches to new media composition: Production and consumption in continuum. *Kairos: A Journal of Rhetoric, Technology, and Pedagogy, 8*(1). http://english.ttu.edu/kairos/8.1/

Cope, Bill, & Kalantzis, Mary. (2000). *Multiliteracies: Literacy learning and the design of social futures.* New York: Routledge.

DigiRhet. (2008). Old+old+old=new: A copyright manifesto for the digital world. *Kairos: A Journal of Rhetoric, Technology, and Pedagogy, 12*(3). http://kairos.technorhetoric.net/12.3/topoi/digirhet/index.html

DeVoss, Dànielle Nicole, & Porter, James E. (2006). Why Napster matters to writing: Filesharing as a new ethic of digital delivery. *Computers and Composition, 23*(2), 178-210.

DeVoss, Dànielle Nicole, & Rosati, Annette C. (2001). "It wasn't me was it?" Plagiarism and the Web. *Computers and Composition, 19*(2), 375-403.

DeVoss, Dànielle Nicole, & Webb, Suzanne. (2008). Media convergence: Grand theft audio: Negotiating copyright as composers. *Computers and Composition, 25*(1) 79-103.

Feist Publications, Inc., v. Rural Telephone Service Co. (1991). 499 U.S. 340

Hayles, N. Katherine. (2002). *Writing machines.* Cambridge, MA: MIT Press.

Hess, Mickey. (2006). Was Foucault a plagiarist? Hip-hop sampling and academic citation. *Computers and Composition, 23*(3), 280-295.

Jenkins, Henry. (2006). *Fans, bloggers, and gamers: Media consumers in a digital age.* New York: New York University Press.

Johnson-Eilola, Johndan. (2004). The database and the essay. In Anne Frances Wysocki, Johndan Johnson-Eilola, Cynthia L. Selfe, & Geoffrey Sirc (Eds.), *Writing new media: Theory and applications for expanding the teaching of composition* (pp. 199-235). Logan: Utah State University Press.

Johnson-Eilola, Johndan, & Selber, Stuart A. (2007). Plagiarism, originality, assemblage. *Computers and Composition, 24*(4), 375-403.

Lessig, Lawrence. (2001). *The future of ideas: The fate of the commons in a connected world*. New York: Random House.

Litman, Jessica. (2001). *Digital copyright*. Amherst, NY: Prometheus Books.

Logie, John. (1998). Champing at the bits: Computers, copyright, and the composition classroom. *Computers and Composition, 15*(3), 201-214.

Logie, John. (2006). *Peers, pirates, and persuasion: Rhetoric in the peer-to-peer debates*. West Lafayette, IN: Parlor Press.

Lovett, Maria; Purdy, James; Gossett, Kathie; Lamanna, Carrie; & Squier, Joseph. (2010). Writing with video: What happens when composition comes off the page? In Cheryl Ball & James Kalmbach (Eds.), *Reading (and writing) new media* (pp. 287-304). Cresskill, NJ: Hampton Press.

Manovich, Lev. (2002). *The language of new media*. Cambridge, MA: MIT Press.

Prensky, Marc. (2001). Digital natives, digital immigrants. *On the Horizon, 9*(5), 1-6.

Reid, Alexander. (2007). *The two virtuals: New media and composition*. West Lafayette, IN: Parlor Press.

Rife, Martine Courant. (2006). Why kairos matters to writing: A reflection on its intellectual property conversations and developing law during the last ten years. *Kairos 11*(1). http://kairos.technorhetoric.net/11.1/binder.html?topoi/rife/index.html

Rife, Martine Courant. (2007). The fair use doctrine: History, application, and implications for (new media) writing teachers. *Computers and Composition, 24*(2), 154-178.

Selber, Stuart A. (2004). *Multiliteracies for a digital age*. Carbondale: Southern Illinois University Press.

Selfe, Cynthia, & Selfe, Richard. (1994). The politics of the interface: Power and its exercise in electronic contact zones. *College Composition and Communication, 45*(4), 480-503.

volgkarate. (2007, February 6). Condi Rice Raps. *YouTube*. http://www.youtube.com/watch?v=C0f2dHJ6A18

Westbrook, Steve. (2006). Visual rhetoric in a culture of fear: Impediments to multimedia production. *College English, 68*(5), 457-480.

Westbrook, Steve. (Ed.). (2009). *Composition & copyright: Perspectives on teaching, text-making, and fair use*. Albany: State University of New York Press.

Woods, Denis. (1992). *The power of maps*. New York: The Guilford Press.

Wysocki, Anne Frances. (2004).The multiple media of texts. In Charles Bazerman & Paul Prior (Eds.), *What writing does and how it does it: An intro-*

duction to analyzing texts and textual practices (pp. 123-163). Mahwah, NJ: Lawrence Erlbaum Associates.

APPENDIX

Rubric for Video Analysis

Video Title: _____

User/Author Name: _____

Visual Elements, Relationships among Elements, and Audience		
Name each visual element that you see and classify each one as original or borrowed.	*Classification*	
	Original	Borrowed
Element 1:		
Element 2:		
Element 3:		
Element 4:		
Element 5:		
Review the classifications you made above. For each item you marked as borrowed, explain why you think the author would make that change to form a parodic argument.		
Element 1:		
Element 2:		
Element 3:		
Element 4:		
Element 5:		

Audio Elements, Relationships among Elements, and Audience			
Name each audio element that you hear and classify each one as original or borrowed.	Classification		
		Original	Borrowed
Element 1:			
Element 2:			
Element 3:			
Element 4:			
Element 5:			
Review the classifications you made above. For each item you marked as borrowed, explain why you think the author would make that change to form a parodic argument.			
Element 1:			
Element 2:			
Element 3:			
Element 4:			
Element 5:			

Relationships between Audio, Visual, and Peripheral Elements and Audience	
Descriptors	
Title	What implications does the title have? What expectation does it create? How do the visual elements conform to or disrupt the expectations set by the title?
Rationale	Does the video offer a rationale for its content or design, either in the video or in an introduction or other information on the web page?
Genre	Do the design elements of the video suggest a particular genre? Does it copy a certain genre, like a music video or comedy skit? Which of the YouTube categories has the author chosen to use to categorize the video? How do the tags the author has added relate to the chosen category?

Authorship	
Institutional, individual, etc.	Is there one author or multiple authors? Was the video directed by a university, company, or other organization? Does the author identify him/herself? If so, how?
Contact information	Does the author provide an email address and/or other contact information?
Ethos	How does the author establish credibility? What else gives this author credibility (e.g., number of views for the video, number of times video has been "favorited," number of sites linking to this video, etc.)?
Content	
Emphasis	Is the emphasis on one text or many? Is the emphasis on the context or content of documents, or on both?
Theoretical approach	Is there an overt theoretical point of view, such as feminist, Marxist, or postcolonial? How can you tell? Does the video directly state its theoretical stance?
Audience	
Intended audience	Can you determine who the intended audience is? How?
Intertextuality	What source texts would the audience have to be familiar with to understand the parody? Why is this important?
Interactivity	Is this video a response to another video? Does the author invite a response from viewers? Has the video generated any textual or video responses?

Adapted from Anne Frances Wysocki (2004).

11 COPY-RIGHTS AND COPY-WRONG: INTELLECTUAL PROPERTY IN THE CLASSROOM REVISITED

Janice R. Walker

THAT WAS THEN

Sometime in the mid-1990s, part of my graduate assistantship entailed providing support for teaching assistants introducing the Internet, including Web authoring, into their courses. I walked into class prepared to help an instructor teach students to right-click on images they found online so they could include them in their Web publications. My graduate research at this time had been centering on citation of electronic sources, which led me directly to considerations of authorship—and hence to concerns about intellectual property. Yet, it had never occurred to me that these images *belonged* to someone. After all, they were just *there*. The new technologies that allowed such easy access to information, images, and so much more, also made it very easy to save this information and re-use it. Suddenly, however, I realized I was standing in front of a class of 24 undergraduate students preparing to teach them to... *steal*.

In 1998, *Computers and Composition* published a special issue on intellectual property. Guest editors Laura Gurak and Johndan Johnson-Eilola (1998) saw a distinct need for this focus, arguing that "few of us truly understand copyright, fair use, or the implications that new technologies and new legislation will have on future legal decisions in our classrooms, our Universities, and the World at large" (p. 121). John Logie (1998) agreed: "Whenever composition instructors use computer technology within their classrooms, they raise exponentially the likelihood that the work completed within their classes will run afoul of current intellectual property laws" (p. 201). *Kairos: A Journal of Rhetoric, Technology, and Pedagogy* also published a special issue on IP issues during the same year, with articles addressing citation and plagiarism, legal issues, and issues surrounding the effect of IP legislation on scholarly publishing. In the special issue, Tyanna K. Herrington (1998) debunked some popular myths about the reach of IP laws and argued that "current law **does** apply to digital communication" (emphasis in original). Thus, she concluded, "the public is granted both constitutional and explicit statutory rights to use copyrighted intellectual property, despite common blanket claims from owners that it is illegal to do so."

However, based on my experiences in the classroom, I argued then—and now—that without some clear-cut guidelines for students (and for scholars) as to what constitutes educational use and without teaching students to carefully consider the issues raised for both online and print sources, we may find ourselves more and more limited as to what material we are allowed to cite as legislators debate how to protect the economic value of intellectual property.

These two special issues and the conversation on the topic in such venues as the Conference on College Composition and Communication's (CCCC) Caucus on Intellectual Property, as well as the many questions raised by students, teachers, authors, editors, publishers, and others in those closing years of the last century were, of course, an important point for the 21st-century classroom, as more and more of our work is now at least mediated online and shared prolifically via blogs and wikis, RSS feeds, Facebook, Twitter, or any number of a multitude of other digital means.

The More Things Change...

Much has changed since those days, of course. More and more courses have moved online, often into course-management systems, both commercial and home-grown. Many publishers have developed proprietary content for these spaces or software of their own. Even traditional composition handbooks often incorporate at least some information on conducting online research, producing multimedia projects, or writing for the Web. Students in brick-and-mortar, hybrid, and online classrooms are not only encouraged to include graphics in their print assignments or to write hypertextual documents for Web publication, they are now sometimes tasked with creating mash-ups and "rip-mix-burn" multimedia offerings, with music, video, graphics, and text borrowed or adapted from multiple sources as well. It seems blogs and social-networking sites have sprung up overnight and entered our classrooms in a myriad of ways. Yet, I am struck by how much has remained the same.

...the More They Remain the Same

In 1998, I noted that although "students often use graphics, as well as text, *borrowed* from published sources in their written reports for the classroom" (p. 245; emphasis in original), few textbooks and style guides included "any prescriptions to students regarding the need for acquiring permission" (p. 245) to do so (see Westbrook in this volume for an extended discussion and specific examples). Nearly a decade later, Alexander Reid (2007) noted that "copyright and plagiarism may seem tangential to the issues of new media rhetoric... but their centrality in public discourses regarding composition and technology requires that they be addressed." That is, he said, because "copyright and plagiarism are the primary cultural domains where new media compositional practices are being defined, they are issues that cannot be ignored" (p. 127). It is still true, however, that few of our textbooks and style guides provide adequate guidelines or discussion of the ramifications of intellectual property legislation on new media compositions we are teaching students to produce beyond discussions of avoiding plagiarism. Even while lawyers and legislators are debating issues that directly affect the work of new media compositionists and the lives of many students—both in and out of the classroom—few of our textbooks offer much in the way of guidance.

The *MLA Style Manual* (2008) does a good job presenting the history of intellectual property law and the intricacies of some of the issues involved, devoting approximately 24 pages to legal issues: a brief history of copyright, an overview of the subject matter it covers, ownership issues (including work-for-hire), and the difference between owning a material object and owning the rights to the content of that object. Also briefly covered are issues of copyright registration, notice and transfer or termination of rights, fair use, permission requests, damages for infringement, and international copyright issues. Although the manual does err on the side of caution, recommending that "authors who plan to use another's work but doubt whether they have the right to do so should refer the question to copyright counsel" (p. 38), given its intended audience as a "guide to scholarly publishing," such caution might make sense.

Contrast the extended presentation of copyright issues in the *MLA Style Manual*, however, with that of the *MLA Handbook* (2009), which is much more widely used by teachers and students in composition classrooms (or at least is more widely referenced by authors of textbooks used in such classes). The handbook summarizes all of these issues in one lonely paragraph, basically stipulating only that even if a source is acknowledged, using entire documents or significant portions thereof "is an infringement of copyright law and a legal offense" (p. 60). Most of our handbooks do even less, with some notable exceptions. For example, *The Brief McGraw-Hill Guide* includes a section on "Using Visuals Responsibly" (Roen, Glau, & Maid, 2008, pp. 822–824). Mike Palmquist's (2009) *The Bedford Researcher* discusses fair use and permissions and includes a sample letter that students can modify to request permission to use copyrighted material (pp. 92–93). Jim Lester (2010) includes a section on "Seeking Permission to Publish Materials on your Web Site" in the most recent edition of *Writing Research Papers*. However, none of the handbooks and rhetorics I have perused provide sufficient context for students (or teachers) to understand the often complicated conversations about fair use of copyrighted work in the classroom, nor do they explain how to cite multimedia elements not included in a works cited or references list.

SHIFT HAPPENS

According to Tom Reedy (1998), "some of the most successful paradigm shifts have occurred by building on previous knowledge." Indeed, as noted elsewhere in this volume, the stated purpose of copyright legislation is to allow for just this kind of knowledge building. Unfortunately, as TyAnna Herrington (1998) argued, "misperceptions and inaccuracies regarding intellectual property law are both extreme and ubiquitous in this age of digital communication, when ease of access, copying, and dissemination of copyrighted materials has created a backlash of fear against public access to information." Nowhere was this more apparent than in the brouhaha surrounding Napster and its ilk, when the RIAA thought it desirable to sue even grandparents and 12-year-olds. Unfortunately, many students still seem to believe that material must be formally registered with the U.S. Copyright Office to be protected, something that has not been required for more than 30 years now. Moreover, many of my students believe that sans the once-required visual notification of copyright—the symbol © or the word or abbreviation for copyright (*copy.*, *copyr.*, *copr.*, or even just *c.*)—a work is not protected, which is, of course, just plain wrong. Thus, students tell me, they believe that most material on the Internet is not copyrighted, since most of the material they encounter is not "marked." And, of course, music, they argue, *should* be free (their justification for this is that performers, they believe, make their money from concerts and not CD sales). YouTube has now made it exceptionally easy to embed videos, with single-click links to post to social-networking sites, a "share" link for emailing videos, and source code to copy and paste into blogs or webpages. Because most people do not understand—or indeed care—that the videos are in fact linked, not downloaded and re-published, it's no wonder they are confused.

In the midst of this confusion, it is requisite that we consider the ramifications of intellectual property law and its effects on new media composing beyond issues of access, citation, and plagiarism. Beyond the confusion (or perhaps at least partly as a result of it) are threats to the very principles that copyright was designed to protect in the first place, as included in the U.S. Constitution: "To promote the progress of science and useful arts, by securing for limited times to authors and inventors the exclusive right to their respective writings and discoveries" (U.S. Const., art. 1, sec. 8., cl. 8). That is, not merely access to information (threatened by the ever-lengthening term of copyright protection and the subsequent dwindling of the public domain), but also use in other works (derivative or otherwise) is now being threatened. How does one "quote" from a picture or musical score, for example? If we teach students to re-purpose a copyrighted musical work as a soundtrack for a YouTube video or mash-up, will students be at risk of being sued for copyright violation? Existing fair use policies just do not adequately address new media configurations, and most books and Web sites discussing these issues are addressed to teachers and their use of materials in the classroom.

TEACH

Teach: The Movie?

The Technology, Education, and Copyright Harmonization Act of 2001 (S. 487), fondly known as the TEACH Act, was signed into law in 2002. It provides a set of guidelines for educational use of certain copyrighted material, specifically "performances or displays for educational uses" (S. 487 ES). Conditions for use required under the TEACH Act include the following:

- Use is limited to works that are *performed* (such as reading a play or showing a video) or *displayed* (such as a digital version of a map or a painting) during class activities. The TEACH Act does not apply to materials for students' independent use and retention, such as textbooks or articles from journals.
- The materials to be used cannot include those primarily marketed for the purposes of distance education (i.e., an electronic textbook or a multimedia tutorial).
- Use of materials must occur "under the actual supervision of an instructor".
- Materials must be used "as an integral part of a class session."
- Use must occur as a "regular part of the systematic mediated instructional activities."

- Students must be informed that the materials they access are protected by copyright. (Reyman, 2006, pp. 33-34)

Further, it remains incumbent on faculty and/or administrators to ensure that the following restrictions are adhered to:

- limiting access to material to only those students enrolled in the class;
- ensuring that digital versions are created from analog works only if a digital version of the work is not already available;
- employing technological measures to "reasonably prevent" retention of the work "for longer than the class session";
- developing copyright policies on the educational use of materials; and
- providing informational resources for faculty, students, and staff that "accurately describe, and promote compliance with, the laws of the United States relating to copyright." (Reyman, 2006, p. 35)

Much of this use is already allowed under fair use guidelines, and this Act in no way is meant to limit such use. However, although the TEACH Act may make some educators and administrators feel a bit more comfortable including copyrighted work in their online or face-to-face classes, it might also serve to stifle uses that many would argue fall under the doctrine of fair use even if they are not stipulated therein. The Emerging Technology Center at Georgia Southern University, for example, helps faculty digitize and stream media for the classroom (face-to-face or online), specifically excludes "fented, purchased, or borrowed media with copyright or DRM protection," and warns that "all media to be streamed must meet with the GSU Campus Attorney's approval for copyright restrictions" (Georgia Southern University).

However, these guidelines are not sufficient to help teach students what is proper for *them* to use in our classrooms. That is, as "The Code of Best Practices in Fair Use for Media Literacy Education" (Center for Social Media, 2008) noted, we need to

> explore with students the distinction between material that should be licensed, material that is in the public domain or otherwise openly available, and copyrighted material that is subject to fair use. The ethical obligation to provide proper attribution also should be examined. And students should be encouraged to understand how their distribution of a work raises other ethical and social issues, including the privacy of the subjects involved in the media production. (p. 14)

Teach: The Verb?

In 1998, I called for clear-cut guidelines for the classroom. Although this may seem to fly in the face of my (and others') understanding of fair use, I still contend that such guidelines can be a way of helping students enter the conversation, especially because students' digital lives are so intimately involved in the outcomes of these conversations.

The distinctions between educational use of material for teaching and student use of copyrighted media are not inconsequential ones, but thus far, there is little direction for students. And, of course, students need to be taught not only what and how they can use information in the classroom, but how such work may (or may not) play out in their lives beyond it. Students really *do* want to know, but many faculty themselves do not understand copyright and fair use, complicating the teaching environment still further (see Nguyen in this volume for research findings on teacher and student perspectives). This fact was recently brought home during the 2008 Georgia Conference on Information Literacy. Carol Simpson's keynote address presented some fairly basic information about copyright and fair use. Even so, much of the information she presented was new to her audience, consisting of librarians, media specialists, and instructors from kindergarten through college levels. A lawsuit filed on behalf of Oxford University Press, Cambridge University Press, and Sage Publications speaks to this lack of knowledge: The suit alleged that Georgia State University "systematically facilitated access to a significant volume of copyrighted works online without paying the proper licensing fees or even seeking to do so" (Guess, 2008). It is likely that faculty believed they were well within the confines of educational fair use, even though we are now in an era when the very definition of "classroom" is up for grabs. Truthfully, I have heard numerous (and often fallacious) arguments from otherwise intelligent faculty who believe that almost anything goes in the name of "educational" use— from re-recording movies to show in the classroom to including musical sound tracks in YouTube videos to capturing screen shots from webpages to include in conference presentation slideshows or in published articles. And, of course, many of the editors of our learned journals are just as confused as the rest of us. Notably, commercial publishers—those responsible for our textbooks—are much more knowledgeable in this realm; however, because textbook authors are responsible for any unlawful use of copyrighted material, sometimes even these works allow a few questionable bits or bytes to slip through.

Our university attorneys are sometimes hesitant to address these issues as well, often preferring to counsel faculty to seek permission (and pay royalties) for use of copyrighted material that would seem to clearly fall within the realm of fair use. And, of course, in this post-Napster era, it is difficult for any of us to understand what we can and cannot use without culpability. Nonetheless, as I argued previously,

> suggestions that authors request permission to quote portions of online sources that, in print, would fall within fair-use guidelines (such as portions of logs published online, publically disseminated e-mail messages, and public meetings in synchronous communication sites) can only lend force to those who would eliminate the doctrine of fair use altogether and make it difficult or impossible to carry on the work of scholars—inside or outside the classroom. (Walker, 1998, p. 246)

Heidi McKee (2008) agreed, stating that "if as instructors and researchers, we adhere to a strict acceptance of copyright maximalists' expectations for copyright, we could be contributing to the erosion of the Fair Use *Doctrine*" (p. 118; italics in original). As Lawrence Lessig (2004) argued in *Free Culture*, "for the first time in our tradition, the ordinary ways in which individuals create and share culture fall within the reach of the regulation of the law, which has expanded to draw within its control a vast amount of culture and creativity that it never reached before" (p. 8). Unfortunately, relying solely on Creative Commons licensing, CopyLeft arguments, or whatever other options we may turn to, or arguing taking the stance that "information wants to be free"[1] is also playing into this same dichotomy.

Although it is important to protect our right to fair use of material, at the same time we must ensure that we protect students as they go out into the workplace. That is, if we believe the use is fair, then we *should* go ahead and use it, regardless of what the legal pundits argue. On the other hand, we also need to be careful that, in so doing, we are not modeling behavior that puts students at risk of legal retribution. By failing to teach students about adherence to the law—even though I agree we also need to teach them why the law may need to change in light of changing technologies and cultures—we may be placing ourselves as well as students in an untenable position. As McKee (2008) argued, her own "failure to discuss copyright with students was inappropriate as a teacher because it was not helping to prepare students for considering the complicated issues of copyright" (p. 118). Furthermore, these same students may soon be in positions to affect these laws (for good or ill), so we should make sure they are privy to these important conversations.

WHERE DO WE GO FROM HERE?

As educators in a digital age, we have a responsibility to students, to our field, to our institutions, and to the public at large to continually upgrade our knowledge and skills in the areas in which we teach. Today, for composition teachers, that may require a considerable investment of time in learning how to use new technologies or at least in learning about the impact of new technologies on what it means to compose. And, of course, we need to be aware of the conversations taking place regarding issues of copyright and intellectual property law as these conversations impact our use as well as student uses within (or without) the classroom. Those of you reading this collection are in the forefront, then, as, admittedly, many of our institutions do not adequately support and reward such professional development efforts—neither by awarding sufficient time and money, nor by adequate recognition of such work at tenure-and-promotion time. However, we can no longer pretend that classrooms are a "safe space"—a haven into which these issues do not reach. We can no longer continue to teach as we always have.

Teach All Students the Basics of Copyright

Beginning with first-year students and, indeed, in all of our classes, we need to teach students the basics of copyright and intellectual property law. In 1998, I presented the following guidelines for the classroom. Primarily targeting use of online resources, I developed this page in response to the dearth of materials available to help introduce students in the composition classroom to this complex topic. Revised in 2007, this list is still far from complete, but it is nonetheless a useful starting point for conversations with students (or others) on the intricacies of intellectual property laws and the use of multimedia in student compositions. On the webpage on which this material is published, I include a brief history of copyright and an admittedly all-too-brief explanation of what copyright was designed to protect, (mostly as a way of introducing students to the conversation), before offering students the following guidelines to consider for their use of the intellectual property of others:

1. *Follow guidelines already established for published (i.e., print) sources, if possible.* For print, generally the polite convention has been that use of 10% or less of a work constitutes fair use.[2] For online sources, we should continue to abide by this same guideline. We should also give as much information as possible to allow readers to access the original source. For projects that will be used only in the classroom,

you may not need to actually obtain permissions for use, however, you should be aware of the steps necessary to do so and should try to locate the information necessary. For work to be distributed outside the classroom (for instance, to be published on the World Wide Web), it is imperative you at least make an attempt to acquire permission.

2. *Point to (i.e., link to) images, audio, and video files rather than downloading them, if possible.* Some sites offer graphic images or other multimedia files to users at no charge and may specifically request that users download them; requests such as these should be honored. However, graphics, audio, or video files should not be downloaded without permission. Users may instead point to images and other types of files rather than downloading them. Of course, courtesy may require that users request permission even to link to an image or file, because this may entail additional traffic on the file server where the file is stored. Additionally, pointing to such files may cause problems as files may move or change without notice or routes between sites may become jammed. However, without specific permission to download files and publish them on the user's file server, doing so constitutes a clear violation of copyright law.

3. *Always cite sources carefully, giving as much information as possible to allow the user to relocate the source.* In addition to citing the source of text, any graphics, audio, or video files included should include proper citation as well. The elements of citation for electronic sources should include the name of the person responsible (i.e., the author, creator, or maintainer of the site); the title of the individual work and the title of any larger body of work of which it may be a part; the date of publication or creation; the protocol and address[3] along with any directories or commands necessary to access the work; and the date of access. It may often take a bit of detective work to locate important elements of citation for Web files, but it is important to try and find as much information as possible. Where some of the information is missing, include as much information as possible.

4. *If in doubt, ask.* If it is unclear whether or not a given use is permitted, ask the owner or author of the site, if possible, explaining the nature of the intended use and noting the portion or portions of the work to be included. If unable to locate information, include as much information as possible along with, perhaps, a note explaining that the work is being

used without permission of the owner. If asked by a copyright owner to remove material, be prepared to do so promptly. (Walker, 2007)

Of course, as Dànielle Nicole DeVoss and Suzanne Webb (2008) argued,

> if we teach students to ask for permission to fairly use media work in their educational endeavors, we risk pushing them into a wall—a wall that they likely will not be able to climb and conquer within the 15-week semesters in which we typically teach. It is phenomenally difficult—and deliberately so—to find out who actually holds the copyright to a work. (p. 95)

Susan M. Bielstein (2006) agreed, noting that "it is becoming harder and harder and impossibly expensive to include illustrations in books" (p. 9). Thus, Bielstein eventually concluded, "if you don't need illustrations to make a point, don't use them" (p. 101). I provide students with information about how to request permission, as well as links from my webpage to an *eHow* article, "How to Get Permission to Use Copyrighted Material" and links to sample copyright permission letters, but most students prefer to avoid the issue, either by creating images, searching the commons for free media, or by circumventing the problem entirely and simply including "stolen from" or "used without permission" in citations. Once again, I am teaching students to steal.

Unfortunately, too, many of the uses students make of multimedia in their compositions are not adequately addressed by our style manuals. Although they do present guidelines for a variety of multimedia cited in a "paper," style manuals do not usually address how to cite such files when they are included in a work without being referenced in the text. In *The Columbia Guide to Online Style* (2006), an alternative to MLA and APA and other documentation styles for citation of electronic and electronically accessed work, Todd Taylor and I (2006) argued that "it is usually not necessary to include multimedia files in the list of works cited unless you are referring to them in your text. That is, if graphics or other types of multimedia files are used merely for decorative purposes, then the source information in the label or credits is sufficient" (pp. 72-73). Students need to know how to include such a source line or credits page for images or other multimedia files they include in their papers, their mash-ups, or whatever form their compositions may take. Jim Kalmbach's (2003) "Giving Credit for Use of Images or Other Material" is still one of the best sites I have found for quick examples. I have also created a tutorial for students on "Citing Sources in Presentations," which demonstrates uses of material in non-traditional projects. Of course, citing the source of a graphic image in a paper or webpage project or even in an electronic presentation may be quite straightforward, but demonstrating how to credit audio or video files in other types of multimedia work may be a bit more complex. Nonetheless, here, too, we need to do much more than we do currently. Most of our style manuals and textbooks are focused on helping students avoid plagiarism. Thus, although these resources may stipulate that authors include the source of information in a label for tables, images, and graphics, they provide little if any information that addresses the uses many students are now making of multimedia files in their work.

Teach Other Faculty about Copyright

I believe it is incumbent on those actively involved in considering these issues to help other faculty understand them so that they, in turn, can help students. We need to start discussions or participate in ones already underway about the issues. We need to provide lists of resources, attend conference presentations, and invite people from other departments to participate in the discussions. As "The Code of Best Practices in Fair Use for Media Literacy Education" (Center for Social Media, 2008) argued,

> this is an area in which educators themselves should be leaders rather than followers .... More generally, educators should share their knowledge of fair use rights with library and media specialists, technology specialists, and other school leaders to assure that their fair use rights are put into institutional practice. (p. 8)

We need to do what we can to present opportunities for discussion about copyright to faculty and administrators at our institutions. We can recommend bringing people to our campuses or conferences to speak on these topics; we can share readings; and we can raise questions. For example, my institution, like so many, is encouraging faculty to teach more courses online (in our case, that usually means through a course-management system). Our Emerging Technology Center (ETC) works with faculty to develop course material, but, as I mentioned earlier, specifically excludes streaming copyrighted movies, even though the TEACH Act would seem to allow this use. When I mentioned this to ETC staff, however, they were not impressed; they have a rule, and they are sticking to it. But we can (and should) broach this with our university counsel to get that rule changed. Faculty might also want to question how intellectual property laws might affect ownership of their teaching materials when they use university resources to develop them and make them available in their online courses (see Amidon in this volume for an extended discussion of work-for-hire).

Graduate student work is also at stake. The College of Graduate Studies at Georgia Southern University, for example, no longer accepts paper theses and dissertations; instead, we have moved to electronic theses and dissertations. In the instructions, students are warned:

> It is the student's responsibility to ensure that the copyrights of documents used in the preparation of the thesis or dissertation are protected and adequately cited, and that all necessary permissions and/or copyright releases are obtained from copyright holders. (Georgia Southern University, 2008, p. 3)

Students must include signed copyright permission forms for any copyrighted materials they may include. But few of our courses actually instruct students in how to do any of this; therefore, it often falls on the staff in the College of Graduate Studies to instruct students and answer their questions, usually after the thesis or dissertation has been accepted and approved by the student's committee. And of course, as my university, like so many others, moves toward developing an e-portfolio mandate for both faculty and students, we need to make sure that we understand the possible consequences of including copyrighted material—our own or that of others.

Keep Abreast of the Conversations

Finally, it is incumbent upon all of us to continue following the conversations that affect our professional (and perhaps personal) lives in so many ways. We need to be aware of the ramifications of the continued attacks on fair use and the public domain; of asking for permission where, perhaps, we should not; and of allowing those with a vested interest in protecting intellectual property *qua* property to make the decisions for us. That is, do we really want the Recording Industry Association of America (which insists on filing suits for theft of property that may or may not be "real"), Disney (which refuses to allow Mickey Mouse to age gracefully and retire to the public domain), and McDonald's Corporation (for which the "Golden Arches" are sacrosanct) to determine what we can use and how we can use it?

Of course, it is equally important that, as scholars and educators, we ensure the ethical and fair use of the work of others by employing adequate citations and credits, and that we respect the moral and ethical values that we purport to hold dear. And, of course, we need to remember that

> the World Wide Web is an international publishing space. As such, many of the images, texts, and other files may fall under the copyright laws of other nations, whose attitude toward ownership of intellectual property may be far different from our own. Thus, a key word in our own consideration of intellectual property should be *respect*, including respect for the moral and ethical as well as economic rights of authors, creators, and publishers. (Walker, 2007)

Admittedly, in some countries, those "moral and ethical" rights sometimes work against criticisms of the work of others, but, then, the United States' focus on economic rights may soon mitigate any and all use of copyrighted materials—to the point that the Constitutional objective of promoting progress becomes, if not an anachronism, at least an idyllic dream. Indeed, followed to its apogee, we may find ourselves fulfilling Theodor Nelson's 1960 vision of the "docuverse" (see Nelson, 2003), wherein "'published' materials are available to anyone, yielding a royalty to the owners" (p. 460), creating, in effect, the Internet as a "vending machine" of information.

THIS IS NOW

Now it is nearing the end of the first decade of the 21st century, and I am in a tenured faculty position, chairing my department's Teaching, Technology, and Writing Committee. As such, I am often asked by other faculty to help them with "techie" stuff. So when a colleague showed me her public wiki page with articles she had printed, scanned, and posted for student access, proud of her newly acquired digital skills, I took a deep breath. The articles were all freely available on the Internet, she said; like the images I had taught students how to "steal" almost 15 years ago, they were just *there*.

I could have gone into my rant about how some sites that make information available for free sell advertising on their sites and charge based on the number of page hits. So when she posts the information to her site, that means traffic might be directed to her site to read the information rather than to the original site, hence potentially costing the copyright holder and/or publisher money.

I could have gone into my rant about copyright being the right to make copies. By making copies herself, and "publishing" those copies (i.e., by making them available to the public on her webpage), without asking permission of the copyright owner and barring any possibly transformative or "value-added" use, she is breaking the law.

Or I could have gone into my rant about fair use, Creative Commons licensing, copyleft, digital civil disobedience, or any of the other standard "rants" I have on hand (or can come up with).

By now, of course, my colleague's eyes would have glazed over. She just wants to know what to *do*—and she wants it to be easy, as it was in the days only a few years ago when she would have photocopied these articles and handed them out to her students in class without a second thought.

In this case, there are two "easy" answers: 1) simply link to the articles, or 2) ask our library staff to make the information available through their online course reserve service—and let *them* worry about copyright issues. Because access to the online course reserve materials is limited to patrons, such copying will often fall under fair use.[4]

But as I walked away, I realized I *wanted* to rant. I *needed* to rant. I wanted my colleague to understand the issues, and, in turn, I wanted her to help students understand. Later, I slip a copy of the "The Code of Best Practices in Fair Use for Media Literacy Education" onto the mail room counter, hoping someone might pick it up. I continue to offer workshops and brown bag discussions for faculty in my department, and I am preparing to teach a course on intellectual property issues for undergraduate writing majors as well as for students from a variety of programs who might be interested. And, of course, I continue to try to keep up with and understand the proliferating conversations in this area myself, admittedly a daunting task. In the meantime, students will continue to make use of "stolen" work if they so choose, so long as they make it clear to me they understand that what they are doing is defined by many as stealing. That way, I am at least protecting myself (the students' citations "prove" that I have taught them that what they are doing might be in violation of copyright law), even if I allow students to take these risks.

In other words, the more things have changed, the more they remain the same. Thus, although I do provide students with guidelines to follow, I hope that I provide students with an entry into the conversations about the legal and ethical ramifications of their choices as well—both their choices to adhere to the guidelines as well as their choices not to. At the end of the 20th century, I taught students to steal, without realizing it. So, now, at the end of the first decade of the 21st century, I am teaching students that, as long as they cite their source, "stealing" might sometimes be the ethical thing to do.

NOTES

1. According to Wikipedia, "the expression is first recorded as pronounced by Stewart Brand at the first Hackers' Conference in 1984." Although probably not Brand's original intent, the expression has come to be used to argue for the "right" to download (music, software, text) without regard to copyright or ownership. As Wikipedia notes: "Under this line of thinking, hackers, crackers, and phreakers are liberators of information which is being held hostage by agents demanding money for its release. Other participants in this network include Cypherpunks who educate people to use public-key cryptography to protect the privacy of their messages from corporate or governmental snooping and programmers who write free software and open source code."

2. Fair use guidelines do *not* actually stipulate a 10% rule, although many people seem to think this is a safe amount; instead, fair use is predicated upon a four-factor consideration (see Galin and Westbrook, this volume, for a detailed discussion of such analysis).

3. Unfortunately, the third edition of the *MLA Style Manual and Guide to Scholarly Publishing* (2008) now recommends omitting the URL for online sources: "Inclusion of URLs has proved to have limited value," they argued. Instead, they contended, that "readers are now more likely to find resources on the Web by searching for titles and authors' names than by typing URLs" (p. 212). Although I believe this "google-ization" of research documentation is a dangerous practice (see my "MLA Rant" at http://mywabbit.blogspot.com/2008/09/mla-rant.html), the seventh edition of the *MLA Handbook* (and thus most of our composition handbooks) now follows suit.

4. As I am putting the finishing touches to this article, the University System of Georgia has announced a new copyright policy, putting the onus of determining fair use on individual faculty members for electronic reserves or online course materials. Faculty are asked to complete a "checklist for each 'fair use' of a copyrighted work" to be submitted along with the material, with a copy to be retained by the faculty member "to establish a 'reasonable and good faith' attempt at applying fair use, should any dispute regarding such use arise" (University of Southern Georgia Copyright Policy).

REFERENCES

Bielstein, Susan M. (2006). *Permissions, A survival guide: Blunt talk about art as intellectual property.* Chicago: University of Chicago Press.

Center for Social Media. (2008). The code of best practices in fair use for media literacy education. http://www.centerforsocialmedia.org/files/pdf/Media_literacy_txt.pdf

DeVoss, Dànielle Nicole, & Webb, Suzanne. (2008). Media convergence: Grand theft audio: Negotiating copyright as composers. *Computers and Composition, 25* (1), 79–103.

eHow. How to get permission to use copyrighted material. *eHow: How to do just about everything.* http://www.ehow.com/how_18035_permission-copyrighted-material.html

Georgia Southern University. Streaming media. http://academics.georgiasouthern.edu/etc/services/streaming.php

Georgia Southern University. (2008). Electronic thesis and dissertation (ETD): Student guide to preparation and processing. http://academics.georgiasouthern.edu/etd/ETDManual.pdf

Guess, Andy. (2008, April 17). A press revolt against e-packet practices. *Inside Higher Education.* http://insidehighered.com/news/2008/04/17/gsu

Gurak, Laura J., & Johnson-Eilola, Johndan. (1998). Letter from the guest editors. *Computers and Composition, 15* (2), 121–123.

Herrington, Tyanna K. (1998). The unseen "other" of intellectual property law. *Kairos: A Journal of Rhetoric, Technology, and Pedagogy, 3* (1). http://kairos.technorhetoric.net/3.1/index.html

Kalmbach, Jim. (2003). Giving credit for use of images or other material. http://www.english.ilstu.edu/351/fall2003/imagecredit.html

Lessig, Lawrence. (2004). *Free culture: How big media uses technology and the law to lock down culture and control creativity.* New York: Penguin.

Lester, Jim D. (2010). *Writing research papers* (13th ed.). New York: Pearson/Longman.

Logie, John. (1998). Chomping at the bits: Computers, copyright, and the composition classroom. *Computers and Composition, 15* (2), 201–214.

McKee, Heidi A. (2008). Ethical and legal issues for writing researchers in an age of media convergence. *Computers and Composition, 25* (1), 104–122.

Modern Language Association. (2008). *MLA style manual and guide to scholarly publishing* (3rd ed.). New York: Modern Language Association.

Modern Language Association. (2009). *MLA handbook for writers of research papers* (7th ed.). New York: Modern Language Association.

Nelson, Theodor H. (2003). Proposal for a universal electronic publishing system and archive. Reprinted in Noah Wardrip-Fruin & Nick Montfort (Eds.), *The new media reader* (pp. 443–461). Cambridge: MIT Press.

Palmquist, Mike. (2009). *The Bedford researcher* (3rd ed.). Boston: Bedford/St. Martin's.

Reedy, Tom. (1998, Spring). *Ethos* and the use of citation as revision. *Kairos: A Journal of Rhetoric, Technology, and Pedagogy, 3* (1). http://kairos.technorhetoric.net/3.1/index.html

Reid, Alexander. (2007). *The two virtuals: New media and composition.* West Lafayette, IN: Parlor Press.

Reyman, Jessica. (2006). Copyright, distance education, and the TEACH Act: Implications for teaching writing. *College Composition and Communication, 58* (1), 30-45.

Roen, Duane; Glau, Gregory R.; &, Maid, Barry M. (2008). *The brief McGraw-Hill guide: Writing for college, writing for life.* Boston: McGraw-Hill.

Simpson, Carol. (2008, October 4). *Can you? Should you?* Keynote address at the Georgia Conference on Information Literacy, Savannah, GA.

U.S. Const. art. I, sec. 8, cl. 8.

Walker, Janice R. (1998). Copyrights and conversations: Intellectual property in the classroom. *Computers and Composition, 15* (2), 243-251.

Walker, Janice R. (2007). Intellectual property in the information age: A classroom guide to copyright. http://personal.georgiasouthern.edu/~jwalker/ip/ipdummie.html

Walker, Janice R., & Taylor, Todd. (2006). *The Columbia guide to online style.* New York: Columbia University Press.

Wikipedia. (2008, November 9). Information wants to be free. Retrieved November 12, 2008, from http://en.wikipedia.org/

12 RHETORICAL VELOCITY AND COPYRIGHT: A CASE STUDY ON STRATEGIES OF RHETORICAL DELIVERY

Jim Ridolfo and Martine Courant Rife

In this chapter, we examine a case concerning a Michigan State University student (Maggie) whose image, taken in 2005 on university grounds during a student protest for fair trade apparel, was unknowingly appropriated and remixed by the university in 2006, 2007, 2008, and 2009. We argue that the appropriation of her image raises serious questions for rhetorical strategies of delivery, as well as emerging issues of intellectual property and copyright. Maggie's case poses a question to legal studies and to rhetoric and composition; in this case, there are no immediate or easy answers, but we argue that the case example itself may serve as a useful pedagogical tool. First, we describe Maggie's case, provide an overview of rhetorical velocity and remix, and then address intersections between copyright, rhetorical velocity, and the commons. Next, we overview legal issues arising from Maggie's case—issues of free speech, privacy, orphan works, the role of the institution as parent, publicity/contractual rights, and fair use. We conclude with a discussion of how composing for re-composition relates to the legal concept of the commons, as well as a discussion of pedagogical implications.

THE MAGGIE CASE

As part of a national effort by United Students Against Sweatshops (USAS), Movimiento Estudiantil Xicano de Aztlan (MEXA), and Students for Economic Justice (SEJ, a local affiliate of USAS), student activists at Michigan

State University (MSU) participated in a social justice campaign from fall 2000 to spring 2005. During this period, they tried to convince the MSU administration to join the Worker Rights Consortium (WRC), a fair labor monitoring body that investigates and certifies college apparel as sweatshop free.

In spring 2005, the SEJ and MEXA anti-sweatshop campaign at MSU underwent a major shift in tactics and strategy due to a change in university leadership. From fall 2000 to spring 2005, the students were unsuccessful in their efforts to convince the MSU administration, led by then-president Peter McPherson, into joining the WRC, and by 2004 the campaign was in a complete deadlock. As a result, from 2004 to 2005, the campaign tactics shifted to event disruption and other forms of direct action that included actions such as dressing up as waiters to surreptitiously attend alumni events and hand out "sweatshop menus" to hungry university donors.

Once President Peter McPherson resigned in spring 2005 and a more responsive and progressive leader, Lou Anna K. Simon, assumed the presidential position, however, the SEJ and MEXA student activists changed their strategy and tactics to better address the new rhetorical situation. On March 3, 2005, the first of approximately half a dozen large, media-centered protests took place. These actions were designed to be what scholar Kevin DeLuca (1999) described as an "image event"—a particular action designed to achieve media coverage through visual display. In this case, the SEJ and MEXA activists' primary strategic objective for the protest was to obtain broadcast coverage and to continue their strategy of maintaining a consistent presence in the local news. Consequently, they attempted to use the media to continue to exert public pressure on the MSU administration.[1]

Maggie Ryan, one of the activists involved in planning the protest, recalls that the action, which took place in front of the MSU Administration Building (a prominent space on central campus), moved the campaign in a new, more creative direction. She explains:

> we were .... trying to integrate new ideas because just having a bunch of people gather with signs was getting a little boring and the media wasn't really paying very much attention when there was like fifteen students with a sign—[but] the media started paying more attention when there was like fifteen students doing something way different.

The March 3 actions included a far more creative and visual rhetorical appeal, one that moved beyond the simple stand-with-signs protest. In the group's attempt to involve more activists as well as more media, they took a new ap-

Rhetorical Velocity and Copyright

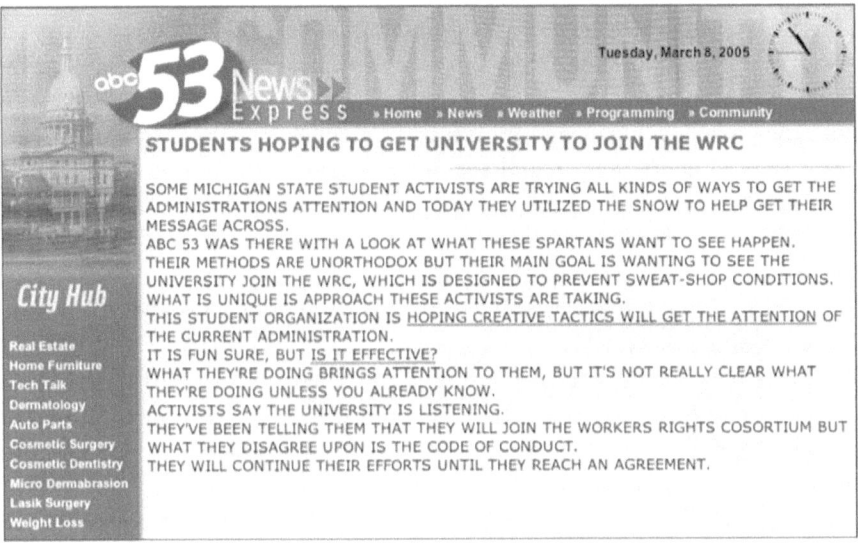

Figure 1: Corresponding broadcast and Web news coverage (March 8, 2005).

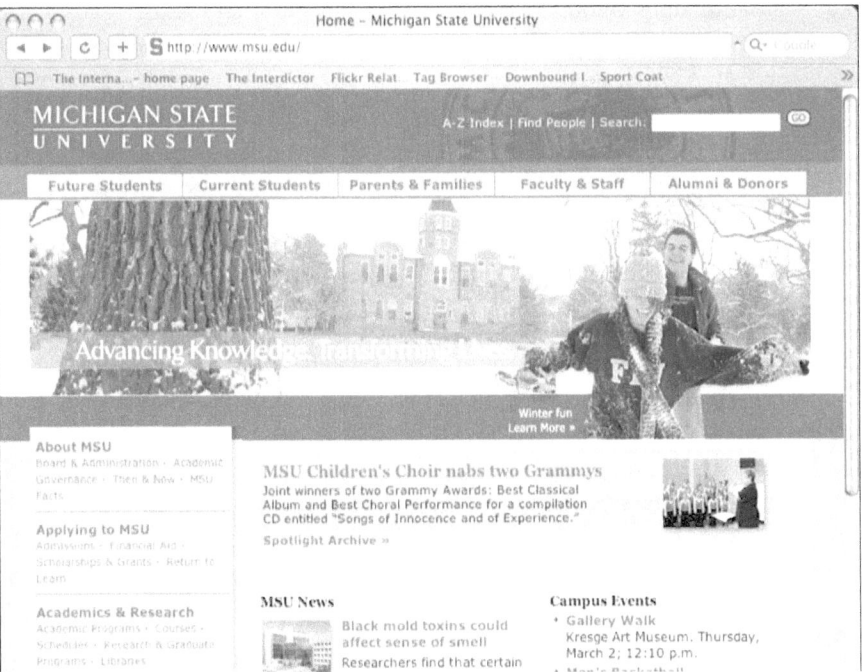

Figure 2: First instance of university appropriation, main webpage (March 2, 2006).

proach—writing with the tools that winter provided, snow itself. as Maggie recalls: "We got dye to write things in the snow and we wrote with our footprints very large in the snow 'W. R. C' so it was visible from very high up." Arguably, both the broader campaign and this specific action were a complete success, and the rhetorical goals Maggie and the others intended to achieve were reached. Due to a constant and steady stream of protests, media, and publicity, the student activists' objective was achieved on April 8, 2005, when MEXA and SEJ learned that President Lou Anna K. Simon intended to join the WRC. By the end of the summer, President Simon had kept her promise, and the university formally joined the WRC.

But that is not the end of the story, at least not for one participant in the WRC spring 2005 campaign. In November of 2006, the university used an image of Maggie from the March 2005 protest for advertising purposes (see Figures 1 and 2). According to Maggie, this appropriation wasn't something she had anticipated when the action was initially conceived. She describes how the image was captured during the action:

> I was wearing like a sweatshirt and some other people in Students for Economic Justice were playing in a snowball fight and there was a photographer during the snow fight who was really kind of sketchy scaling up the buildings to take pictures and it was really weird. And then about maybe eight months later the picture appeared on maybe the front page of the Michigan State University and the title of it was "students having fun in the snow."

Although the protest itself was far from serious, there is no doubt for Maggie what the political intentions of the assembly were. Despite the lack of seriousness associated with the action, the appropriation of Maggie's image (see Figures 2, 3, 4, 5) without her consent is indeed a strange and unanticipated occurrence with serious consequences.

Maggie Ryan's image was first used as the main focal point on the MSU Web site in 2006 (see Figures 2 and 3), but this would not be the last time the university would use her image. Even after Jim Ridolfo conducted his interview with Maggie Ryan in 2007, an additional example of appropriation took place in 2008, when the university used her image as part of a major bulk mailing effort (see Figure 5).

Maggie Ryan's case exemplifies the surprising distance that possible strategies for delivery can travel. Although the desired press coverage of the March 3 action was achieved (see Figure 2), Maggie had no way of anticipating how

Rhetorical Velocity and Copyright

Figure 3: Sub-page of main webpage (March 2, 2006).

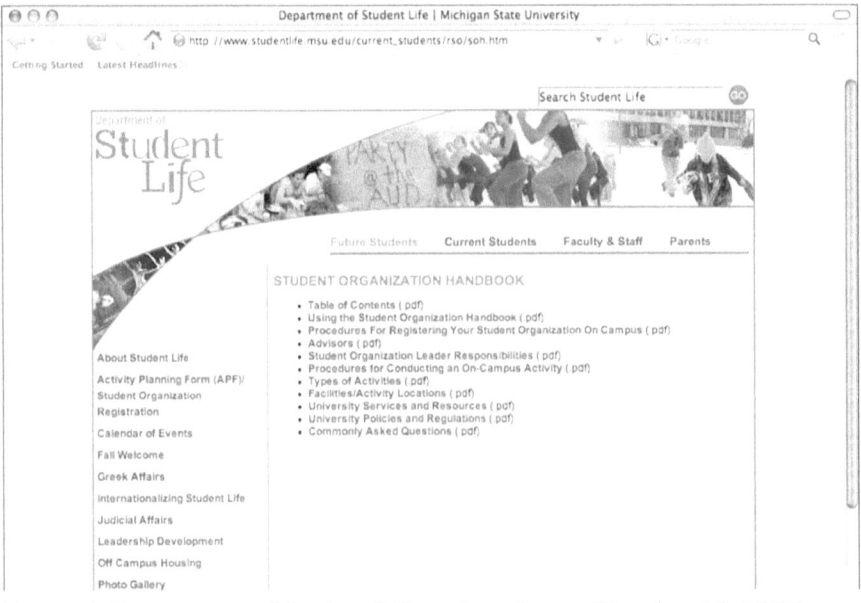

Figure 4: Department of Student Life main webpage (October 24, 2007).

the university would later use an image of her from the event to promote the Department of Student Life and the university itself. In addition to directly appropriating her image, the university also remixed her image. In Figure 2, it's clear that not only did the Web team (staffed primarily by employees of the University Relations department) take a picture of Maggie out of context but they also repurposed it by adding the caption "winter fun learn more." In Figure 1, they also cropped Maggie out of the less-scenic background of the MSU Administration Building, and put her image on a more picturesque and iconic backdrop of a recognizable campus landmark. When Maggie talked about the action after these first two acts of appropriation and remixing had taken place, she called attention to the way the university used her image without any attempt to attribute it to her:

> They [the university] didn't contact me. Nobody ever got my name. Nobody ever asked anything. The reporters I don't think even got it but university officials definitely didn't. They didn't get my name or the name of the other person in the picture. And I was like the main person, focal point of the picture.

Although Maggie never consented to or approved of the university using her image for these large-scale advertising purposes, she talked about what she could have done differently to curtail the appropriation of her image. She says that it might have been "a good idea to have more prominent posters or things with you or have things with you so people know what's going on." In articulating the options she didn't initially exercise, Maggie strategized how to resist certain forms of appropriation. These examples raise serious questions about the limitations of how far one can inductively anticipate future recomposition.

RHETORICAL VELOCITY: COMPOSING FOR STRATEGIC RECOMPOSITION

Ridolfo and Dànielle Nicole DeVoss (2009) explored the intersections of rhetorical velocity and theories of remixing. Ridolfo, drawing on his research in rhetorical delivery (see Ridolfo, 2005), and DeVoss, working from her knowledge of remixing and digital delivery, theorized that today's digital delivery is different because:

> A new element, however, enters the mix when we situate remix in today's digital culture; more elements and oth-

ers' elements become much more readily available to mix, mash, and merge. And, in fact, processes of mixing are valued across these spaces, where savvy mixers are recognized as their YouTube channels hit the top ten and as their videos become streamed across hundreds of servers. What is obvious here is that composing in the digital age is different than traditional practices of composing. Rhetorical practices in a digital age are different than traditionally conceived. Electronic copying-and-pasting, downloading, and networked filesharing change the dynamics of writing and, importantly, of delivery.

We want to expand on this conversation of examining "mix, mash, and merge" by exploring how elements of rhetorical delivery intersect with copyright concerns.

In the protest plans related to the Maggie example, there was a considerable degree of concern for how the action might be picked up by the press. The event was designed by the student activists to produce other texts; the objective was to facilitate the composition of news coverage. This strategic concern for delivery is best described by the concept of *rhetorical velocity* (Ridolfo, 2005; Ridolfo & DeVoss, 2009). Rhetorical velocity is a strategic concept of delivery in which a rhetor theorizes the possibilities for the recomposition of a text (e.g., a media release) based on how s/he anticipates how the text might later be used. The rhetorician theorizes how certain newspapers, blogs, or television stations may recompose and re-distribute the release both as and in other media. In thinking about re-composition and re-distribution as a complex multimodal strategy, the rhetorician also considers how the release may be recomposed in ways advantageous or disadvantageous to the rhetor's goals and objectives. For example, how might moving from one media to another affect the message? How might the text of the release be remixed in ways that might harm the rhetor's goals? If the rhetor composes and distributes a video release, what is the optimum format to encourage strategic remixing?[2]

In Maggie's example, she worked with other student activists to design a visually intensive protest to achieve a particular type of broadcast press coverage. Even though the protest and activist campaign were ultimately successful, in the years that followed, a series of images were used in ways neither Maggie nor the other activists could have plausibly predicted. Although the activists succeeded in their rhetorical goal of achieving third-party media coverage for their campaign, Maggie's ethos was drawn into the spotlight in questionable ways for years after the initial events took place.

Clearly, ethical questions of group rhetorical strategy in the digital age emerge from this case. In the age of remix, to what extent should groups theorize visually intensive campaigns in terms of the potential impact on future ethos for individual participants? To what extent should participants in visually intensive protests be conscious of how the images they co-produce may be used in the future? Should the university have asked Maggie for permission before making her a sort of poster child for the university? Should the Department of Student Life have asked Maggie's permission before using her image? Should the Admissions Office have asked Maggie's permission before mailing her image out as a recruiting tool? How could Maggie have realistically anticipated this latent reappropriation of her work, if at all?

Figure 5: Panel from print bulk recruitment mailing (February–March, 2008).

THE LEGAL, ETHICAL, AND CONCEPTUAL ISSUES RELATED TO THE MAGGIE CASE

In this section, we untangle some of the legal, ethical, and conceptual issues regarding the use of Maggie's image by the university. How should one "anticipate" the rhetorical appropriation of their work, and what role should knowledge of copyright play? When leveraging the tenants of Ridolfo's theory of rhetorical velocity, what laws, concepts, or set of ethical considerations might arise as one imagines one's creations, images, or cultural properties being appropriated by others?

The Appropriation of Images and Bodies

To give specific context to our discussion, we need to define exactly what was appropriated by the university: a digital image of Maggie, more broadly speaking, an image of a human body. Admittedly, a concrete and well-defined understanding of propertied ownership is likely unattainable in this instance. Human bodies, as well as products derived from those bodies (such as digital images like the one of Maggie) evade ownership in any traditional sense; on the one hand, the question of property rights in the human body lacks a clear answer. On the other hand, the question is over-determined in legal theory: there is a plethora of conceptual and legal regimes that seek to analyze and regulate the function and meaning of "ownership" in this area. (Flessas, 2008, p. 388)

Tatiana Flessas discussed some of the complicated issues surrounding claims to ownership of aboriginal bones (see also Holder & Flessas, 2008). We draw from her work although we admit that the digital image of Maggie and aboriginal bones are in some ways quite dissimilar. However, Flessas's analysis of the various arguments on the ownership of human bones, we think, is very useful for shedding new light in the area of rhetorical velocity, copyright, and the digital image of Maggie.[3] Flessas states that "'indigeneity' is an *ongoing discussion* about common values and common identity and a *strategy* for ownership claims" (p. 402). For the purposes of this chapter, we draw on the notion of radical symmetry from actor-network theory (Latour, 1998, 2005; Law, 1992), and posit that the image of Maggie and human bones are in some respects symmetrical: both are bodies over which allegations of appropriation and claims to ownership have arisen. In turn, these allegations of appropriation also invoke issues of free speech and privacy.

Free Speech and Right to Privacy

As TyAnna Herrington (1998) noted, copyright and first amendment issues are intertwined. Issues of free speech arise in Maggie's case, but not in the way that such issues are normally considered. Of course, at a public university, Maggie has a first amendment right to free speech on campus as she works towards raising awareness of the WRC cause; that's not disputed here. The right to privacy problem in this case arises from tensions between Maggie's right to privacy and the institution's right to free speech.

When someone appears in a public space, as Maggie did, the general legal standard asks whether or not a reasonable person would have a right to privacy in such a space (Rife, 2007)—this is the rationale that photojournalists rely on to report the news. When Maggie engaged in a protest in a public space—a physical commons, open to public view at a public institution—the argument is very strong that she had *little right to privacy*. Because Maggie was aware of the photographer's presence and continued with her activities nonetheless, the argument that she had any reasonable expectation of privacy would be weak. Furthermore, an argument against the institution's appropriation based on a legal right to privacy would likely fail, while an argument supporting the institution's right to "free speech" has some plausible support in this context. The institution's free speech argument is especially strong in the context of the initial appropriation if the intent was to document the protest.

In fact, an argument based on privacy rights and asserted by Maggie conflicts with the purpose of the protest, which was to draw attention to the WRC campaign. As activists, this group of students tried to design their discourse so that it *would be* appropriated to call attention to the political issue in which they were involved. The problem here is that their discourse was appropriated in unanticipated ways. In this sense, a rhetorical understanding of the possibilities for appropriation are complimentary to the legal understanding.

Copyright and Orphan Works

A recently proposed copyright law, the Orphan Works Act of 2008 (S. 2913: Shawn Bentley Orphan Works Act of 2008), was introduced in 2008, and passed the Senate later that year; however, a House vote did not occur. (Bills that have not passed during a session of Congress are cleared; however, it is likely the bill will be reintroduced in the future.) Testimony to the house subcommittee regarding this law took place on March 13, 2008, and is a continuation of a study the U.S. Copyright Office began in 2005. The study examined "issues raised by 'orphan works'—copyrighted works whose owners may be impossible to identify and locate" (Peters, 2009). Because of concern about possible copyright liability, subsequent creators and users like libraries are discouraged from appropriating such orphan works; the fear keeps potential users from making orphan works available to the public.

This proposed law, if ever adopted, attempts to wrangle with some of the issues presented in Maggie's case and provides another example of how problematic it is when a creation becomes disconnected from its origins, which is exactly what happened here. In Maggie's case, she was protesting in the WRC campaign, against the institution, but instead of the protest image event traveling solely in the way she intended, it was appropriated by the institution and subsequently inverted in order for the institution to promote itself in ways directly contrary to the protest's purpose.

The proposed Orphan Works Act, if adopted, will make it easier for users to appropriate texts, images, and sounds that have no owner. Technically they have no creator because their creator cannot be found (Curtis, 2008; Zimmerman, 2009). The concept of orphan works acknowledges that things people make can detach from their creators and take on meaning and power that was never anticipated. The idea that artifacts like Maggie's picture are orphans, and how such an idea might intersect with our rhetorical theories of production and appropriation, is something worthy of further research and examination in composition and rhetoric. In the case of Maggie's political activity, her photograph was taken. As a simple action, the image taking was a goal of her political activity. There was a desire of the student protestors that their activity would receive media attention to further their cause. However, at some point after the picture was taken and then moved from camera to computer, Maggie lost control in a very real way. And, so, the agency—the power that she engaged in her political protest—was undermined, inverted, and her image took on a life of its own. It became, in a sense, an orphan. (These issues are worthy of further discussion in our field, but due to the limitations of space in this chapter, and the breadth of ideas we wish to cover, here we can only issue a call to others for further exploration in this area.)

In Loco Parentis

One cannot conjure up the image of orphans without conjuring up the image of parents. JoAnne Podis and Leonard Podis (2007) might describe the university's actions here as evidence of the lingering presence of *in loco parentis*. According to *Black's Law Dictionary* (1979), the term means "in the place of a parent; instead of a parent; charged, factitiously, with a parent's rights, duties, and responsibilities" (p. 708). Podis and Podis localized the term, usually discussed at the broad institutional level, and discussed the possibilities of its presence in the composition classroom:

> we argue that pedagogical *in loco parentis* is a deeply embedded but often overlooked principle within the teaching of composition, one that merits more attention than it has received, especially since, in one form or another, it is likely to remain an influential pedagogical model. (p. 122)

Although many scholars thought the concept was abandoned during the 1960s, Podis and Podis cited a number of sources invoking the parental authority of the institution with respect to residential life, and argued that the "killing [of] student freedom" (p. 122) is experiencing a resurgence. Prior to the counterculture revolution, academic institutions exerted a parental-like authority by having curfews, regulating dorm visitation, instituting dress codes, etc. More recently, this authority surfaces as regulations or actions related to eliminating binge drinking and illegal substance abuse and regulating student speech, including "hate speech." Podis and Podis focused on how this parental authority can influence power relations in the writing classroom with respect to form and content of writing. Our concern is with the possibility of an even more subtle exercise of the parental "rights" of the institution. We sense a casual attitude by the university in its appropriation of Maggie's image, something akin to, "she's ours—of course we can do whatever we want with her picture." This is a similar attitude to the kind we imagine parents have when taking and circulating pictures of their child. Of course they can do this; this child is "theirs."

The ownership of such images of the human body is something we think writing students should take a critical view of, and Maggie's case study provides fertile ground for discussion. Ownership and control of such images relate to copyright law and the appropriation of Maggie's image, because copyright law makes intellectual creations "property" with assignable rights, similar to the "rights" parents have over their children. It is undeniable that in the U.S. children are propertied. This becomes extremely visible when a child's married parents divorce, when parental rights are terminated, or in any kind of custody dispute. In such cases, U.S. courts have to decide who "owns" the child. Let's say that when these kinds of issues involving children arise, the state's propertied interest in that child also arises—thus the state ultimately gets to be the arbiter of how the "property" of the child is assigned (in terms of, for instance, visitation rights, tax deductions, primary custodianship, and health insurance). These ownership issues in the case of the child and the case of Maggie's image drive the relationship between the creation and its owner, and so, ultimately, what such an examination of appropriation entails is an examination of institutional relationships. In this case, the institution has a special relationship with Maggie, because she is its student, and so the appropriation must be understood in that context.

Right to Publicity and Contractual Rights

How can the institution be permitted to take Maggie's image without her consent and then use that image for profit? According to Lloyd Rich (2008), "The right of publicity is generally defined as an individual's right to control and profit from the commercial use of his/her name, likeness and persona." The right of publicity is a matter of state law. The purpose is to protect someone like Maggie from losing the commercial value of her likeness due to an unauthorized appropriation. Cases like this are usually seen in the context of celebrities such as sports stars, whose images are appropriated without authorization by companies in order to sell a particular item. Although the institution's appropriation of Maggie's image was unauthorized, because Maggie is not a celebrity it would be difficult to argue that she is losing money due to the institution's appropriation. The institution's argument is stronger here because it features Maggie as "any female student" rather than as "Maggie." In some of the images her identity is not the rhetorical focus—the focus is instead on any female student playing in the snow.

The level and types of protection in this area vary from state to state. Michigan is the only sixth circuit state that does not have a right of publicity statute (Richardson, 2007). The root of the right of publicity is privacy law, and although Michigan has no statute, the courts developed some rights for the citizens of Michigan. Yet, without a clear statute, the probability of litigation around these matters is great in the event a conflict arises. The development of the right of publicity can be traced in Michigan by tracing its major cases in this area. In 1899, in *Atkinson v. Doherty & Co.,* Colonel John Atkinson's widow brought suit because a company produced and distributed cigars with her deceased husband's likeness attached. At that time, the Michigan Supreme Court stated "it is one of the ills that, under the law, cannot be redressed" (Richardson, 2007, p. 27). In a case more similar to Maggie's, in 1948, *Pallas v. Crowley*, a retail establishment selling cosmetics used a young woman's portrait photograph. The woman had not given her consent for the publication of her photograph. In this case, the court did recognize a legal claim in that the use of the woman's photograph might be considered "as an invasion of such person's right of privacy" (Richardson, p. 27).

An illustration of how the right of publicity often arises when celebrity names or likenesses are used without permission is the 1983 Michigan case of *Carson v. Here's Johnny Portable Toilets, Inc.* In this case, the court recognized that Johnny Carson's persona was being used without his permission, and, subsequently, "Carson's right of publicity was invaded because appellee intentionally appropriated his identity for commercial exploitation" (Richardson, 2007, p. 27). Due to space constraints of this chapter, we will not delve into a deeper analysis of Michigan's right of publicity law, but we raise these issues as worthy of further exploration in our field, especially with the turn to digital writing, remix, and the power of the Internet to disseminate appropriated images instantly.

We might contextualize Maggie's political activity as one worthy of a news story, because that was its intent. And with respect to the intersecting considerations of privacy, free speech, and the right to publicity, in news stories, as long as there is a relationship between the image used and the story, the newsmaker will be protected. As Rich (2000) argued: "An individual cannot use the right of publicity to claim a property right in his/her likeness as reflected in photographs that were taken in a public place to illustrate a newsworthy story." We imagine, then, that the university could plausibly argue that its use of Maggie's image was not to make a profit, but was instead to illustrate the joys and experiences of campus life.

Students may agree to specific, certain, yet often fine-print clauses when they sign various admission forms for entering a specific college. When students enroll in college, they also commit to institutional policies such as academic honesty, residence hall regulations, regulations for student groups, and university ordinances. A contract is a legal agreement and does not have to be strictly labeled "contract" to be enforceable; as Herrington (2003) informed us, "if you have bought a car, rented a house, or even rented a video, you have entered into a contract" (p. 53). Further, contracts do not have to be written. In the Maggie case, what must be explored is whether students, upon enrollment and agreement to institutional policies, give some type of blanket consent to have their photographs taken for institutional use. Upon examination of the 136-page Michigan State University (2009) *Student Life Handbook and Resource Guide*, we did not locate any contractual agreement that Maggie implicitly agreed to that might provide the institution the legal right to take images of Maggie and use those images in promotional materials. However, this is something to take into consideration when examining practices at other institutions, both public and private, and when discussing these issues with students who will be or are employed. It is possible that their internship, on-campus, or off-campus employment contracts give the employer explicit rights to take pictures and use those pictures in promotional materials.

Section 107 Fair Use

As is evident, the issues that arise regarding this case go far beyond the issue of copyright; copyright is, however, a factor here. U.S. copyright law protects items that are fixed and original, but that fixation must be authorized. To determine whether the institution has the copyright in Maggie's image, in this case the "fixation" was not authorized by her. It might thus occur that any person or entity could re-appropriate Maggie's image, as the institution did for promotional materials. If the institution objected to this use, it, in turn, could argue that something about this particular photograph is original and, subsequently, the institution could (ironically, in this case) attempt to stop others from using Maggie's image. The institution could argue it took this image out of the commons, if we think of the commons as a place where what is or once was owned can be re-owned by another.

The founder of Creative Commons, a Web site that provides pre-drafted licenses for creators to attach to their work in an attempt to control how their work is appropriated by others (in the spirit of rhetorical velocity), Lawrence Lessig (2005) characterized the legal battles over copyright law's reach to Web spaces to be a battle between old and new. If information is locked down, he argued, creativity is stifled: "Free cultures are cultures that leave a great deal open for others to build upon; unfree, or permission, cultures leave much less. Ours was a free culture. It is becoming much less so" (p. 30). To illustrate his points, Lessig listed 17 movies where Disney, Inc. took stories in the public domain, or the commons: "In all of these cases, Disney (or Disney, Inc.) ripped creativity from the culture around him, mixed that creativity with his own extraordinary talent, and then burned that mix into the soul of his culture" (p. 24). In Maggie's case study, the institution stands in the place of Disney: an appropriator of another's creativity, in this case an innovative protest. Like Disney, the institution took another's creativity and locked it down in the form of a variety of broadly disseminated promotional materials.

Although it might appear that the institution's use of Maggie's image is a fair use, that section of Title 17 does not really apply, because Maggie didn't create the photograph of herself. In the case of Disney, its use of stories in the public domain were not technically a fair use, because those stories were not copyright protected; the uses were legal, but that is because the stories were in the commons. It would be different if Maggie had taken the picture of herself and then the institution appropriated the image Maggie took. Section 107 applies to items that are copyright protected and, in situations like this, human bodies are not considered original and fixed in the sense that texts and artifacts are. Other laws, such as privacy laws and laws around rights to publicity, protect individuals from having their images appropriated.

But let's say for the sake of argument that fair use did come into play here. The university could potentially have fair use allowance because of its non-profit status; this is part of its institutional or organizational identity. The master narrative surrounding universities contextualize these institutions as bettering human kind, of promoting good citizenship, and as doing good generally not for profit, but as a good steward in the larger society. Yet, we all know that dollars matter a great deal to universities, like any revenue-reliant business. At the university, profitable ventures are sought after and appreciated just like in any other for-profit corporate structure. But we think, perhaps, universities-as-organizations sometimes "get away" with appropriating the work or image of others—in this case a student—because of their standing in the larger culture as not-for-profit. Rhetorical analysis and examination of the narrative around non-profit organizations in general—an examination containing a more critical stance than that which generally exists in our field—is in order. Research is needed in this area; here, however, we simply provide one small step in the effort to unpack how an organization, like an educational institution, can slide by while appropriating the image of a student and inverting the original meaning of that image.

Deciding What is in the Commons

In the context of illicit trafficking of cultural artifacts, Claudia Caruthers (1998) asserted that the commons provides a unique lens with which to understand the "increasingly inefficient conceptual framework of cultural property protection in this area" (Caruthers qtd. in Flessas, 2008, p. 392). None of the legal or conceptual frameworks we have set forth above fully address the right and wrong of the institution's appropriation. Flessas (2008) correctly asserted that the aspect of Caruthers's argument based on aligning cultural properties with natural resources is flawed, because cultural properties—unlike natural resources—are not exhaustible, and in fact depend upon appropriation to survive. But, Caruthers' idea that the commons debate can only be resolved by norm driven models that "employ a strategy of ethical imperatives and exhortations" rings true (qtd. in Flessas, p. 393). When rhetorical velocity and copyright converge, one has to define the commons, because designing documents or discourse to be appropriated ultimately means placing creations in the commons, which is a place reliant on the appropriation of things with no owners (i.e., orphaned work) and of things previously owned (as in the case of human bones).

The term *appropriation* then needs unpacking, and here we rely on Flessas' (2008) use of the Lockean concept of labour-mixing, because Maggie's image, as an object, will have rights somewhere at the intersection of property-based rights and knowledge-based rights (p. 394). Maggie's image can be an artifact, a religious relic, an ancestor, a documentation of a student protest, an object of scientific study, a political icon, or a representation of the good life on a college campus. Whether her image is in the commons such that the institution's appropriation is entirely acceptable is a context-specific, norm-driven, value judgment. When the photographer took the picture, s/he mixed labor with the natural, the purpose of which was use. This is the basis for the Lockean understanding of private property as valorized in U.S. law:

> This raises the question of commonality generally, and proposes that cultural property analysis, like intellectual property analysis, occurs on a field of endlessly shifting and reforming "commons." (Flessas, p. 394)

Seeking common values—in this case, the common values between the student protesters and the institution—is crucial in articulating the commons in this case. The commons, as defined in this situation, will depend on how the participants in this debate decide to set the boundaries of the commons, a place of re-appropriation (and this re-appropriation could take place infinitely). Creative commons licensing, for example, composes a commons with clearly marked boundaries defined by those who implement these licenses in their creations, and, subsequently, this defined commons offers artifacts that can be appropriated infinitely by others. As Flessas pointed out, the discourse of the commons can be used to argue either for protection of resources or for the legitimate taking of resources. For example, the discourse around creative commons asserts that this regime is needed to protect creativity and the public domain. In contrast, the discourse of the commons is used by museums to argue for the taking of indigenous bones. Ultimately then, when designing discourse in the spirit of rhetorical velocity or when designing for appropriation, the answer to the question of whether or not the institution *acceptably* appropriated Maggie's image will, in effect, define the commons. As we discuss in the last section, we think this kind of analysis—with all of its complexities and entanglements—proves useful in the composition classroom.

IMPLICATIONS FOR PEDAGOGY

We see Maggie's story as one that invites students to interrogate issues of appropriation and copyright with a 360-degree view of major ethical, cultural, and other issues in copyright, intellectual property, and rhetoric. Maggie's story is rich with possibilities for classroom activities and discussion. Here we offer a few suggestions for leveraging Maggie's case study in the writing classroom. Some questions for classroom activities and inquiry—which we invite others to remix, use, and build upon—include:

- If Maggie wanted the university to stop using her image, what action could she take and when? After collaborating and researching this issue, write a document in the proper genre, addressed to the proper university official, requesting that the university stop using the image.
- In her interview, Maggie states that "in innovative actions it might be a good idea to have more prominent posters or things with you." What could Maggie have done differently when designing this protest that would have possibly prevented the university's appropriation of her image? Design either a protest plan or one document that Maggie could have used to effectuate this change.
- Imagine that Maggie asks the university to stop using her image and they refuse. List one to three legal actions Maggie could take to cause the university to stop using her image. If you decide that she could institute a lawsuit, for instance, be specific about what legal grounds she could use to make her argument. Write a short argument based on one

action you think Maggie could take. Be sure to include an outcome as far as whether you think Maggie would be successful in her argument or not.
- From a moral or ethical perspective, do you think what the university did was wrong or right? Why or why not? Write a short discussion setting forth your stance as well as your reasons.
- Based on Maggie's case as well as class discussions and readings, how would you define the commons? Explain your answers and provide concrete examples of items that are definitely in or not in the commons.
- How should short-term rhetorical concerns (in this case, the campaign goals) be weighed against long-term, more distant, rhetorical concerns of Maggie's ethos over time?
- In Maggie's case, which genres of writing are in use? How does each genre cross medium? How does medium relate to genre?
- How do economics and economies of value factor into Maggie's process of delivery? How do the short-term economic interests of the media relate to the long-term economic interests of the university? \

Studying case examples of intellectual property and rhetorical delivery as situated, local practices is conducive to both areas of study. In the same way lawyers study case law, we advocate for the study of rhetorical delivery as a form of case law, a key question being: How do practitioner examples overlap, compliment, or contradict the legal and rhetorical concerns of all parties involved? This combination of concerns is increasingly important for students, teachers, and practitioners to consider. In addition, the legal delimitations of the commons are learnable and will become an increasingly strategic site for rhetors to compose and deliver into.

CONCLUSION: RHETORICAL VELOCITY REVISITED

Ridolfo and DeVoss (2009) defined rhetorical velocity as "the strategic theorizing for how a text might be recomposed (and why it might be recomposed) by third parties, and how this recomposing may be useful or not to the short- or long-term rhetorical objectives of the rhetorician." In Maggie Ryan's example, even though the protest and activist campaign were ultimately successful, in the years that followed, a series of Maggie's images were used in ways that neither Maggie nor the other activists could have plausibly predicted. Although the activists succeeded in their rhetorical goal of achieving third-party media coverage for their campaign, Maggie Ryan's ethos was affected undesirably well after the initial events took place.

The rhetorical implications for a case such as this one are complex because they necessarily include the legal realm; equally complex, however, are considerations of how legal concerns will increasingly figure into a rhetor's future practice. The intellectual property implications for Maggie are directly connected to the practice of a rhetorical theory of delivery, and both areas of study have something significant to say to the other. Putting into conversation the intellectual property implications of texts, broadly speaking, and rhetorical theory, particularly stories such as Maggie's, has the potential to provide more illustrative examples, but also more theoretically rich examples for researchers, students, and policy makers.

Such practitioner examples are able to more acutely explain how the commons may be rhetorically theorized as strategic. In other words, we need to stop thinking about copyright law in terms of what isn't possible, but also in terms of what is possible—that is, how rhetors can strategically compose for the recomposition of their own intellectual property. Conversely, for intellectual property law, these examples of how rhetorical practice and intellectual property connect are deeply important examples not only for teaching the potentialities of the commons to students, but also for arguing for better social and legal policy around the commons. A story such as Maggie's has the potential to function as a scary story; the pedagogical challenge for rhetorical theory is to teach these complex legal and rhetorical issues without alarming people so much that they're unable to act (in this case, chilled so much that they might be unable to move activist meeting agendas forward). Rather, we might focused on facilitating informed action. We thus argue that such case examples have the ability to argue lucidly for how copyright can function as a vehicle for strategic rhetorical use, and not simply as pejorative protection against public use.

Although we think that connecting copyright law and its implications to the anticipation element of rhetorical velocity is an important connection for scholars of both areas, we also argue for something we think is more methodologically significant for research and the classroom. The study of rhetorical delivery needs to be more closely connected to the stories and work of practitioners, not simply because such a study produces more illustrative, tangible examples, but also because it presents delivery as a situated practitioner strategy and not simply as an ecology or rhizome of texts. The challenge for rhetoric researchers is to find additional practitioner stories of delivery and longitudinal circulation; we need more contrasting stories to teach.

NOTES

1. An earlier version of this summary appeared in Sheridan, Michel, and Ridolfo (2009).

2. Rhetorical velocity also means anticipating strategic remixing—that is, theorizing how the media (e.g., a video) might be remixed by others in ways ultimately advantageous to the rhetor's goals and objectives. Rhetorical velocity also means theorizing how to release a image (e.g., with a watermark) to curtail the future appropriation of the image.

3. The repatriation debate is filled with arguments developed over many years by indigenous peoples worldwide, and we want to first acknowledge the importance of this issue in general, but also state that our use of Flessas's and others' theories on repatriation are not meant in any way to minimize the importance of the plight of indigenous peoples with respect to retrieving cultural artifacts.

REFERENCES

Atkinson v. Doherty & Co. 121 Mich. 372, 1899.

Black, Henry Campbell. (1979). *Black's law dictionary with pronunciations* (5th ed.). St. Paul, MN: West Publishing Company.

Carson v. Here's Johnny Portable Toilets, Inc. 698 F.2d 831, 1984.

Caruthers, Claudia. (1998). International cultural property: Another tragedy of the commons. *Pacific Rim Law and Policy Journal, 7*(1), 143–169.

DeLuca, Kevin Michael. (1999). *Image politics: The new rhetoric of environmental activism.* New York: Guilford Press.

Flessas, Tatiana. (2008). The repatriation debate and the discourse of the commons. *Social & Legal Studies, 17,* 387–405.

Herrington, TyAnna K. (1998). The interdependency of fair use and the first amendment. *Computers and Composition, 15*(2), 125–143.

Herrington, TyAnna K. (2003). *A legal primer for the digital age.* New York: Pearson Longman.

Holder, Jane B., & Flessas, Tatiana. (2008). Emerging commons. *Social & Legal Studies, 17,* 299–310.

Latour, Bruno. (1988). Mixing humans and nonhumans together: The sociology of a door-closer. *Social Problems, 35*(3), 298–310.

Latour, Bruno. (2005). *Reassembling the social: An introduction to actor-network theory.* Oxford, U.K.: Oxford University Press.

Law, John. (1992). *Notes on the theory of the actor network: Ordering, strategy, heterogeneity.* Lancaster: Centre for Science Studies

Lessig, Lawrence. (2005). *Free culture: The nature and future of creativity.* New York: Penguin.

Michigan State University. (2009). *Spartan life: Student handbook and resource guide.* http://www.vps.msu.edu/SpLife/index.htm

Pallas v. Crowley. 322 Mich. 411, 1948.

Peters, Marybeth. (2008). The importance of orphan works legislation. http://www.copyright.gov/orphan/

Podis, JoAnne, & Podis, Leonard. (2007). Power and parental authority in the writing classroom. *College English, 70*(2), 121-143.

Rich, Lloyd. (2008). Right of publicity. *The Publishing Law Center.* http://www.publaw.com/rightpriv.html

Richardson, Jeffrey. (2007). Michigan needs a statutory right of publicity. *Michigan Bar Journal, 86*(9), 26-30.

Ridolfo, Jim. (2005). *Rhetoric, economy, and the technologies of activist delivery.* Unpublished Masters Thesis. East Lansing: Michigan State University.

Ridolfo, Jim. (2005, May). Rhetorical veloooocity!!!: The economics of the press advisory and tactics of activist delivery. Paper presentation at the Computers & Writing Conference, Stanford, CA.

Ridolfo, Jim, & DeVoss, D-nielle Nicolle. (2009). Composing for recomposition: Rhetorical velocity and delivery. *Kairos: A Journal of Rhetoric, Technology, and Pedagogy, 13*(2). http://www.technorhetoric.net/13.2/topoi/ridolfo_devoss/

Rife, Martine Courant. (2007). Technical communicators and digital writing risk assessment. *Technical Communication, 54,* 157-170.

S. 2913: Shawn Bentley Orphan Works Act of 2008. http://www.govtrack.us/congress/bill.xpd?bill=s110-2913

Sheridan, David; Michel, Tony; & Ridolfo, Jim. (2009). Kairos and new media: Toward a theory and practice of visual activism. *Enculturation: A Journal of Rhetoric, Writing, and Culture, 6* (2). http://enculturation.gmu.edu/6.2/sheridan-michel-ridolfo

Zimmerman, Traci A. (2009). "It's a hard knock life": The plight of orphan works and the possibility of reform. In Clancy Ratliff (Ed.), *College Composition and Communication IP Caucus: Top intellectual property developments of 2008.* http://www.ncte.org/cccc/committees/ip/2008developments/hardknocklife

13 FOLLOWING THE FRAMERS: CHOOSING PEDAGOGY TO FURTHER FAIR USE AND FREE SPEECH

TyAnna Herrington

Previously I have written that fair use and free speech are interdependent and necessarily work together to support the functions of the democratic process (Herrington, 1998). In this chapter, I broaden my argument that fair use makes free speech possible and assert that there also exists an interdependency among the precepts of fair use, the First Amendment, and transactional pedagogy in composition classrooms. James Berlin's (1987) philosophical inquiries, extended by Fred Kemp (1984), make clear that this pedagogy can be enacted.

Fair use is a legal mechanism within the U.S. copyright statute that reflects the constitutional support of public access to knowledge, allowing individuals to use other creators' materials for certain purposes without legal violation, even when those materials are copyrighted and would be otherwise unavailable for use. Fair use makes free speech possible, because fair use allows access to the information that embodies the content with which to engage. Although the fair use doctrine, as included in the 1976 Copyright Act, speaks directly to use rather than access to authored works, support for access to intellectual products is implied in that an individual cannot make use of a work without accessing it. I expand this reasoning when I argue that the ability to access content is necessary if a nation's citizens are to participate in democratic endeavors.

My treatment of access in this chapter does not explicitly include discussion of "fair access," and its growing support among those who argue that new laws such as the Digital Millennium Copyright Act should provide fair access provisions that would allow users to reverse engineer digital work protected by encryption code. I do not explicitly address other facets of access, such as those regarding limitations on viewing digital work controlled by a third-party provider. Although these and other complex concerns regarding access beg for arguments that support the Framers' intention to maintain a robust public domain, addressing these matters requires extensive treatment more appropriate to a separate work outside the focus of this chapter. My intention here is, nevertheless, to underscore the importance of access, even in its more generic sense, to cultural content in its multiple formats. In this chapter, I further explore the importance of pedagogical choice as a means to support or inhibit a world view that enables free speech and the fair use that accompanies it. I contend that pedagogy supporting fair use goals can be significant both for preparing students to meet the challenges of an information society, and, more important, for helping them develop skills for participating in democratic processes. I examine these hypotheses: Some pedagogical choices foster a learning atmosphere that supports free speech rights provided by the Constitution; students who learn within these pedagogical spaces have greater opportunity to find their voices, learn to interact in democratic processes, and prepare to make well-considered choices regarding intellectual property issues. While Berlin (1987) explained the value of a *transactional belief system* for supporting a negotiated, socially developed knowledge base, rhetorically situated in the midst of interactions among those in dialogue, I argue that without access to the information that is the subject of dialogue, a democratic, egalitarian interaction would be impossible. The inhibition of access to knowledge and information by way of protectionist interpretation and application of intellectual property law hinders and could even eliminate the democratic dialogue made possible by fair use and free speech. Kemp (1984) pointed out that a social constructionist pedagogy is consistent with a transactional ideology; choosing a transactional pedagogy that underscores student legal use of copyrighted work and supports free speech is, I argue, consistent with the general goals of preparing students for engaged citizenship in a democratic society.

Examining the intricacies of the law to connect between free speech and access of intellectual products shows that there can exist a conflict between copyright and the First Amendment (Patterson, 1987; Yen, 1989). Further, fair use has, at times, been employed as a limiting structure to what the constitutional provision creates (Herrington, 1998). Regardless, fair use implies a structure that supports public access to copyrighted work (Lemley, 2000; Travis, 2000) and as the law is developing today, interpretation and application of fair use are strengthening it as a force to provide information access (note Bill *Graham Archives v. Dorling Kindersley, Inc.* and *Kelly v. Arriba Soft Corp.*). I use the term *fair use* to denote an enabling force for access to copyrighted work. In addition, because most of the intellectual products that composition instructors and their students use and create is copyrighted, and because fair use applies only to copyrighted work, I focus on copyright.

I begin by explaining how the constitutional intellectual property provision provides a foundation for free speech, learning, and access to democratic dialogue. I then provide two summaries: One of the interdependency of fair use and the First Amendment; the other of the interdependency of ideology and pedagogy. Building from this base, the section that follows illustrates how choices in pedagogy and ideology can affect student patterns of learning and interaction, some of which are consistent with constitutional goals enabled by fair use and the First Amendment. I argue that the constitutional intellectual property provision, unique to U.S. law, forms the base for democratic activities. I conclude with an argument that fair use, the First Amendment, and pedagogy can be interdependent, and can support student interaction in the democratic process.

THE CONSTITUTIONAL INTELLECTUAL PROPERTY PROVISION: THE FOUNDATION FOR FAIR USE

Before widespread use of digital communication structures became part of everyday life, intellectual property law was virtually ignored by the average citizen and even by many lawyers and legislators. In the past, intellectual property law had more direct impact on commercial entities than on individuals. But even before the general public began to understand its importance in affecting interchanges through public and semi-public Web communication venues, the intellectual property clause of the U.S. Constitution, when interpreted in favor of the constitutional intent and support for free speech, provided a solid foundation in policy for the lifeblood of democracy. The constitutional intellectual property provision, unique to U.S. law, ensures public access to information with the explicit goal of advancing learning by supporting a public domain of information from which to draw. On this basis, democracy is made possible. At the core of the democratic effort are the rights to free speech, egalitarian access to the democratic process, and the support of self-actualization that enables the pursuit of happiness.

The Framers, in the intellectual property provision, made the benefit to an author secondary to and merely supportive of the primary goal that benefits the public—to advance learning. American law prioritizes society's goals of educational advancement and the correlative need for democratic access to information. To help ensure that society would have a public domain to further knowledge advancement, the Framers fashioned a means to motivate authors by providing an incentive to benefit from the work they create. But the Framers also mandated a time limit on authors' right to control their work, and, as a result, fashioned a limited monopoly for managing creative products. The provision allows creators to benefit from the work, but also provides public access to the work by means of the time limitation.

To enter a discourse community, members of the public must have access to the information that constructs their world—in essence, their reality. Without that information, free speech would be impossible because there would be no basis from which to draw to enable it. As L. Ray Patterson (1987) argued, "learning requires access to the work in which the ideas to be learned are embodied. Because there can be no access without distribution, encouraging distribution is vitally important" (p. 7).

Students who wish to engage with the materials and ideas that shape their world must be supported in their use of these materials. My students have created interesting statements based on others' original work, and of these, many have made clear and important cultural commentary. A former student, Yury Gitman (1998), used an image of Joseph Stalin depicted on a bookplate as "Boekbinder Stalin" in a parody in which he repurposed the image to depict Stalin "writing" a different reality than that which was shown in the original. Gitman added the statement, "10 million killed, 130 million wounded" in his version of the work. He pointed out in his textual explanation that he understood the original image of Stalin as a bookbinder with power to create the printed word, where his recontextualized version depicts Stalin as one who "binds reality" and "binds the fate of hundreds of millions of people."

Another former student, Leah Mickens, used the premise of L. Frank Baum's version of *The Wizard of Oz* to parody the Walt Disney Company's aggressive protectionist stances in treating intellectual property issues, in part, by appropriating Baum's work. She created the character of Oswald the Lucky Rabbit, whose adventures almost led to his being held captive in a protectionist land called "Disneyana." Other students have used and written about digital video materials, music, art, and other forms of communication and supplied portions of these works as a basis for criticism, illustration, and other forms of parody. And students have also used original work in more standard ways—for instance, as a basis of research from which to develop ideas, to support arguments, and to counter the claims of original authors.

These students' creative contributions were dependent upon the cultural statements made by the original creators of the works they used. Their use and treatment of these original works as a basis for making new statements about related cultural interests allowed them to converse with the authors of the originals; the students used the original authors' work as a means to enter the cultural discussion, to participate in its conversation. They created new knowledge based on that which came before. The summary below provides the foundation for a structure of learning, using, and speaking about information.

Summary: Interdependency of Fair Use and the First Amendment

Examining the interdependency of fair use and the First Amendment leads to many avenues of complex analysis; this intricate subject is treated at length in other sources. For purposes of this work, which shares a legal and pedagogical emphasis, I summarize the relationship between fair use and the First Amendment. (For more detailed treatment, please see Herrington, 1998; Patterson, 1987; Patterson & Birch, 1996.)

The First Amendment free speech clause is well known to most Americans: "Congress shall make no law ... abridging the freedom of speech, or of the press." Although legal interpretation of free speech is complex and arguments about what free speech is and what it encompasses are broad, most Americans understand that free speech rights are essential to our ability to define ourselves, to shape the course of our country's direction, and to enable us to participate in democracy. Fewer Americans understand the impact of the Constitution's intellectual property provision, reflected in the fair use language of the Copyright Act of 1976. Fair use is the political core of the support of teaching; it grants access to intellectual work that forms the basis for creating new knowledge.

Fair use is an affirmative defense promulgated in the Copyright Act of 1976. A user who employs the fair use defense would admit to using a copyrighted work, but claim the excuse of fair use under guidelines laid out in the doctrine. Much like the support provided for free speech, commonly allowed fair uses include news reporting, critical commentary, parody, research and education, and scholarship. Fair use enables public access to subjects of national dialogue; in turn, the public has a means to speak about the content that it accesses. The Supreme Court has supported fair use and free speech in recent cases in which creators have used parody to comment on those whose works form the base of their own. *Suntrust Bank v. Houghton Mifflin Co.* (2001) dealt with Ann Randall, who created a parody of Margaret Mitchell's classic *Gone With the Wind*. Her version, *The Wind Done Gone*, depicted the slaves' point of view of life at Tara and the "Old South" during the Civil War. In *Mattel Inc. v. MCA Records* (2003), the Court allowed the rock band Aqua to parody Mattel's Barbie brand in their song "Barbie Girl," which depicted Barbie in what Mattel claimed was an unfavorable light. The Supreme Court also allowed the rap group 2 Live Crew to use Roy Orbison's song "Pretty Woman" as a basis for their version that, through changed lyrics and musical delivery, provides critical commentary of a banal white society and the music used to represent it (*Campbell v. Acuff Rose*, 1994).

Like fair use, the First Amendment provides no monetary benefit, but instead underwrites the advantages of self-actualization and participation in the cultural construction of the nation. Similarly, although it is possible to benefit monetarily by creating a work that extends from a copyrighted work (a derivative work), the policy benefits intended by the Framers are not economic in nature. Access provided for by the intellectual property provision and by fair use creates a benefit in non-monetary terms—support of and access to knowledge, leading to the ability to participate in the democratic system. When copyrighted works "constitute the expression of ideas presented to the public, they become part of the stream of information whose unimpeded flow is critical to a free society" (Patterson, 1987, p. 5). The First Amendment and fair use work together, Patterson argued, where "the promotion of learning is inherently antithetical to censorship" (p. 13). Hannibal Travis (2000), extended Patterson's arguments by noting that

> the Framers explicitly sanctioned judicial suspicion of laws that inhibit the exercise of constitutional rights to free expression. The Supreme Court has repeatedly held that these "choicest privileges," first and "transcendent" among all our natural rights in the American tradition, are not to be "sacrificed ... for too speculative a gain." (p. 846)

Both the First Amendment and fair use make democratic dialogue possible within a society dependent upon information. Both promote self-realization, knowledgeable participation in self-government, and societal advancement; the former, by creating possibility for people to speak, the latter, by enabling access to cultural content people may want to speak about. Without fair use, there would be no free speech because access to cultural content would be limited. Of course, some materials and information are available in the public domain and do not require fair use for access. Mostly, these include non-current materials and government works. In addition, some copyright holders choose to provide open licenses to their works. And, where possible, users may obtain releases or licenses for use of others' work. But the great majority of materials likely to be significant and meaningful as a basis for critical commentary require fair use by those who desire to enter public dialogue. Public domain materials provide only a portion of information important for understanding issues as a whole. For dialogue to occur, access to copyrighted work as well as to work in the public domain is necessary. Generally speaking, fair use allows a reach to materials that would otherwise be unavailable for speaking meaningfully to timely and significant issues.

Individuals' epistemological frameworks can influence whether they will accept or reject a law that allows access to copyrighted work or one that supports greater control over works by creators. Instructors making pedagogical choices can influence the efficacy of those choices in their pairing of pedagogy with epistemology. By extension, some epistemologies and pedagogies are supportive of fair use and free speech goals, while others are not. In the following section, I summarize Berlin's (1987) and Kemp's (1984) assessments of epistemology and pedagogy as a basis for relating them to the interdependency of fair use and the First Amendment.

Summary: Interdependency of Epistemology and Pedagogy

Berlin (1987) and Kemp (1984) provide a useful basis for understanding how epistemological framing, combined with pedagogical choice, can have broad effects on student learning processes. Berlin outlined a set of epistemologies that form a base for truth-seeking among composition instructors and students. I focus on three that I find most applicable to this chapter: the objective, subjective, and transactional. Berlin explained that those who follow an objective epistemology believe that truth exists prior to knowledge—that it is determined inductively, exists outside the individual, and is certain. For those who follow a subjective epistemology, truth is located within the individual or within a realm that s/he understands internally; truth transcends the material world, resisting expression. For subjective epistemology adherents, truth can be represented only by metaphor because it cannot exist materially; it must be discovered by the individual in a private act. Alternatively, subscribers to transactional epistemology believe that truth arises from rhetorically situated interactions—that it is contingent, must be negotiated, and is always subject to change. Truth does not exist in an absolute, objective form within the transactional epistemology.

Kemp (1984) applied these epistemological structures to pedagogical choice. He explained that when pedagogical preference is consistent with epistemological choice, a composition instructor is able to support student learning effectively. He describes a structure of consistent pairings: current traditional, foundational teaching supports an objective worldview; expressivist structures support subjective epistemology; and social constructionist actions are consistent with the transactional epistemology. Kemp asserted that when instructors use pedagogies inconsistent with epistemological beliefs, their choices can be counterproductive and lead to breakdown in the learning process. For instance, if an instructor's intent is that students learn rote information and provide a set of correct answers to an exam (an objectivist-oriented activity), then asking them to learn through interaction in blogs and class discussion promoting negotiation of ideas (transactional processes) would likely debilitate the instructor's goals. Or, if an instructor intends that students learn introspection in a search for truth and to express themselves in poetry or creative prose (a subjectivist goal), then using a current–traditional lecture format to provide students with facts (objectivist) rather than letting them explore introspectively would be counterproductive (for further application of Berlin and Kemp, see Herrington, 2005).

Here I focus on transactional pedagogy because it most appropriately supports free speech and fair use goals; I do not, however, discount that there can be an appropriate time and place for each of the other pedagogical choices I described above. I do not intend to claim that other pedagogical choices are not useful, but, instead, I focus on social constructionist pedagogy because it is particularly supportive of fair use and free speech goals. Epistemological and pedagogical choices can be supportive or destructive of the constitutional intellectual property provision and fair use goals; pedagogical choice can either support or inhibit instructors' intent for student learning as it relates to intellectual property issues.

ANALYSIS: EPISTEMOLOGY, FAIR USE, AND PEDAGOGY

Some pedagogical choices can broaden and deepen learning by encouraging students to use and understand fair use, and, in turn, the learning process can help build a foundation that enables free speech. By supporting speech and access, these choices can also sustain the intent of the Framers in their development of the Constitution's intellectual property provision. Other pedagogical choices, in contrast, can hinder fair use as a base for free speech, can inhibit or limit learning processes, and can create a model that encourages students to accept static knowledge rather than pursing a process of learning that enables them to synthesize information and make new knowledge—the primary goal of the constitutional intellectual property provision.

The Framers' objectives of supporting a public domain, knowledge advancement, and egalitarian access to a democratic process are made possible at the intersection of the First Amendment and fair use. These goals—based on the ideals furthered by dialogue, free speech, and access—are supported by a transactional epistemology. The transactional epistemology mandates interaction in dialogic processes. The copyright clause, reflected in fair use, makes interaction possible by enabling the right to use information and ensuring that free speech about that information is supported. Composition students who learn by way of transactional or social constructionist pedagogy, effective as a means to extend a transactional worldview, are supported in their dialogic interactions. Fair use extends their interactions beyond the classroom when it allows them to use and respond to source materials that might otherwise be outside their realm of access. Their communicated responses in the forms of class papers, blogs, digital films or art, music, and more can also be bolstered by the First Amendment and, in turn, responded to by others who could employ fair use and their own supported speech as a way to further interact.

Employing a contrary structure (such as a current–traditional pedagogy, which is consistent with objective epistemology) would support a culture that does not prize fair use and free speech, but instead intends to organize its citizens through control of information and their access to information; this pedagogy could inhibit processes of seeking truth. For example, a government of dominance would do well to employ an objective epistemology. An authoritarian source would impart "truth" by demanding that its citizens believe what the government desires. The pedagogical choices required for supporting this kind of structure are clear; students would prepare rote answers in line with expectations, relayed by their instructors. There would be no room or support for negotiated searches for truth/s or for democratic interaction within the learning process, because these activities would most likely lead to "wrong" or disallowed answers. As a result, there would also be no need for students to seek new knowledge or pursue free speech efforts.

Although an expressivist pedagogy would support introspection and would allow individuals the freedom to search for truth that could lead to a form of self-realization, it does little to further the democratic interaction reflecting U.S. goals of free speech, the constitutional intellectual property provision, and fair use. In fact, consistent with the subjective epistemology would be a protectionist viewpoint of intellectual property law. As noted above, U.S. intellectual property law encourages educational advancement (and access to the democratic process) as its primary goal. But a focus on expressivist truth leads to a Romantic concept of authorship more consistent with a European "moral rights" view of intellectual property protection, which supports the author's rights to intellectual products as a primary interest (see Howard, this volume). A moral rights approach would lead to a structure in which authors maintain near absolute control of creative works (or, more precisely, one in which publishers—who hold authors' copyright licenses—would have greatest control of creative works). This configuration would do little to support the interactive use and response to cultural information that the U.S. intellectual property provision and fair use allow and that is required for pursuing a democratic enterprise.

Clearly, a transactional epistemology, furthered by a social constructionist pedagogy, would most closely align with the Constitution's intellectual property provision and fair use. These concepts can be pragmatically applied in three broad forms: teaching about fair use and free speech as a content area in itself, bolstering access to and use of copyrighted work, and providing pedagogical support for fair use and free speech development within composition classrooms. In particular, instructors may use copyrighted materials in educational settings to advance learning, and students may make use of copyrighted work to develop creative products. In addition, instructors and students may also use student work to support activities that develop free speech tendencies among participants within composition classrooms.

PRAGMATIC CONCERNS

Communication, teaching, and intellectual property concerns are often pragmatic in nature; this section offers suggestions for how composition instructors might incorporate more practical activities involved with fair use and First Amendment issues in the classroom.

Teaching Access, Fair Use, and Free Speech

Composition instructors do not expect and are not expected to teach legal content as regular course material. To avoid potential problems stemming from misuse or inhibition of use of copyrighted work, instructors would be aided by understanding basic issues in copyright—just as they are by understanding issues in plagiarism (see Rife, 2007). In the same vein, explaining basic expectations of students as they work with copyrighted materials could facilitate efforts in the composition classroom. Instructors use copyrighted work in their classrooms to support student work, and most research using others' intellectual products. As well, students use copyrighted work in their research and should understand their choices in treating copyrighted work to develop a sense of their expected behaviors as students.

Current pedagogical practice incorporates activities that encourage students to combine multiple sources and modes of communication in their assignments. Johndan Johnson-Eilola and Stuart Selber (2007) described their process of "putting two rather conventional terms—*plagiarism* and *originality*—into conversation with a third, potentially controversial term—*assemblage*—in order to comment on the nature of writing in a remix culture" (p. 380), noting that the term *assemblage* can also be substituted with "remix," and "collage." In a parallel move, Dànielle Nicole DeVoss and Suzanne Webb (2008) described an actively synthetic means of communication in pursuing prosumer practices where information consumers are engaged in both the design and creation processes of works they consume. Mathew Barton (2005) noted that composition instructors are regularly embracing the use of blogs, wikis, and online discussion boards, all of which can involve using digital tools to synthesize texts, visuals, audio, and more elements. Even with text materials, as Rebecca Moore Howard (2007) noted, "if both writers and readers have ready access to the same set of texts, textual culture has suddenly become a much more shared phenomenon" (p. 5). These stances are clear acknowledgements that instructional goals should reflect the developing nature of source and idea remix as a basis for composition. Those who remix, incorporate, respond to, and synthesize materials from sources must understand intellectual property law to avoid non-supported uses—and more importantly for the advancement of knowledge—to find support in fair use and free speech for the communicative actions they undertake.

Compositionists have long called for content-area materials treating intellectual property, noting that reviewing and discussing basic tenets of intellectual property law could be helpful both for instructors and students (Herrington, 2001; Rife, 2007). This call is of particular importance in light of developing research by Martine Courant Rife and William Hart-Davidson (2006), which indicates that students misunderstand copyright law. Among issues of importance as a basis of instruction are:

- The constitutional basis for intellectual property law is the goal to advance learning.
- Creators are granted rights to their work as an incentive to encourage innovation and knowledge advancement.
- Without a balance between the public need for access and creators' needs for control of their work, the system will fail.
- Students do have copyrights in their work, even without copyright registration.
- Students and instructors should respect the copyrights of others.
- Notwithstanding the tenets above, students and instructors can access otherwise protected work when supported by fair use, personal use, and the First Amendment.

- Copyright and plagiarism are not the same thing, and must not be conflated.
- Without access to cultural information that makes up society, free speech and engagement in the democratic process would be impossible.

Granted, learning about and understanding the intricacies of the issues noted above is not easy. But knowing about intellectual property and its effects can be important as well as interesting for composition instructors and students.

Sources for learning about the tenets above are plentiful today. The Conference of College Composition and Communication's (CCCC) Intellectual Property Caucus Web site and email list provide up-to-date treatment of intellectual property issues that affect composition instructors, and the Intellectual Property Committee that advises the body of the National Council of Teachers of English examines issues of interest in intellectual property and educates the NCTE constituency. In addition, Web-based sources such as Lawrence Lessig's Creative Commons blog, the Electronic Frontier Foundation's (EFF) site, and the Chilling Effect Web site provide broad resources. Beyond these, there is a growing number of helpful books and articles directed to composition and technical communication.

Using, Not Abusing, Copyrighted Work

Fair use can allow instructors to employ copyrighted work both for teaching and research purposes, and can advance student learning processes. If instructors are afraid to use materials that *can* be used legally as provided by fair use and the First Amendment, not only could they inhibit the potential for learning in their classrooms, but they might, for example, discourage students from making use of materials that would otherwise be legally allowed. It is no minor issue that laws that grant benefits, if unused, are interpreted eventually as prohibitive in nature, at worst, and, at best, fail to function as a basis for providing rights and privileges. When these rights and privileges are so important that they form the basis for democratic interaction, the "use it or lose it" mandate is particularly significant.

Although access to information forms a foundation for education and free speech, students also benefit from understanding the limitations on using copyrighted or otherwise protected intellectual products. The more they understand the balance and the goals within the constitutional provision and fair use, the better they will be able to make judgments regarding their use of others' works, the circumstances under which their use is likely to be supported, and the potential societal impact of choices they make. The composition classroom provides a valuable venue for considering the ways that intellectual products reflect the characters and efforts of their creators. Although a "moral rights" treatment of intellectual products protects creators beyond the extent that U.S. law provides in support of our democratic system, students who learn the conceptual base could take a step toward understanding the ways that their work represents them as individuals and could draw from that base to value their work as an embodiment of who they are. Students who learn experientially, in this way, to assimilate the concept of authorship, might be more likely to accept a vision of the importance for avoiding plagiarism and might consider carefully the potential to violate copyright as well.

In many instances, neither students nor their professors and academic administrators are aware of or acknowledge that students retain copyrights to their work. Some professors and administrators, thinking that the quality of student work is lower than the work of others at the institution, misunderstand copyright law and treat the work as if it is not copyrightable. Others are unaware that since the Copyright Act of 1976, there is no need to register a copyright to obtain and retain it. Because composition courses, by their nature, demand that students develop copyrightable products, consideration of these aspects of copyright are particularly helpful. (Although this issue is of great importance as students are authoring a wide variety of copyright-protected work, both in hard copy and digital forms, the detail required to explain it is outside the scope of this chapter. For detailed treatment of students' rights and responsibilities in regard to intellectual property, see Herrington, *iProp*.)

CONCLUSION: THE INTERDEPENDENCY OF PEDAGOGY, FAIR USE, AND FREE SPEECH

Composition classrooms can be powerful forums that allow students to exercise speech rights; learn to voice their ideas; interact with the ideas of others; and read and examine issues with critical, analytical insight. The broader inquiry is how epistemological choice and the pedagogy that accompanies it can foster a means to support the Constitution's goals for the country, extended through fair use and free speech structures that support democratic development. The clear directive is a social constructionist pedagogy that supports these efforts most pointedly. This kind of pedagogy—which focuses on student-based interactions, highlights student choices, and validates their work—creates a kind of participatory pedagogy. Pedagogues such as Jean Lave and Etienne Wenger (1991) and Seymore Papert and Idit Harel (1991) have supported teaching practices that allow students to learn experientially, assimilating learning as a participatory event. When students are learning not only communication and writing skills, but practicing interaction in a dialogic process that eventually leads to competence in participatory democracy, the classroom becomes a powerful forum for supporting the goals of the U.S. Constitution.

Once instructors choose a pedagogy that focuses on student learning, they must have the strength to see it through—participatory pedagogy is not easy and does not hold immediate or clear rewards for the instructor. But this pedagogy's ability to foster and use fair use and free speech goals as a way to further pedagogical intention only underscores efforts in the very activities that form the base for constitutional goals and a democratic effort. Employing fair use—and especially teaching fair use principles to composition students—can help to support dialogic interaction within writing classrooms, and thus affect students' experiential understanding of the dialogic value of their communicative expressions in participatory government. Shuba Ghosh (2003) noted that "the hallmark of democracy is the liberalization of the arts and a movement away from the promotion of a national, uniform culture as in the former Soviet Union or Nazi Germany" (p. 390). And, as noted above, remix of sources and communicative interactions forms a basis for truly interactive democratic practice. Ghosh provided a scenario to explain the benefits of interaction:

> Many cultural products are valuable precisely because they are consumed by other people. While I may enjoy reading Thomas Pynchon or Margaret Atwood by myself, I benefit from knowing that others have also read their works. These benefits include the ability to converse about the works to gain deeper insights, and the possibility of communicating new insights and understandings that I may have missed in my private reading. Sharing does not mean that there is a unity of interest or understanding; my reading of *Gravity's Rainbow* or *The Blind Assassin* may be radically different from yours. It is the communal aspects of reading and consumption that create important values for cultural products. (p. 409)

Information is valuable capital and fair use allows access to it—but free speech is a means by which to use information and reflects what is even more valuable than information capital. That is the skills to use information along with the ability to think, to synthesize, and to adapt to a changing world. Composition instructors can potentially shape the future with the choices they make. We have a choice of pedagogy; we can choose one that supports free speech and fair use, or we can choose another that inhibits it. The power of language and rhetoric to create reality—particularly in a digital world—can be of extreme importance in communication classrooms. To prepare students to interact in a remix culture requires a pedagogy that allows interaction, encourages fair use, and supports free speech. Teaching from this perspective is effectively supportable by a social constructionist pedagogy and transactional worldview.

Instructors do not only teach, but also provide opportunities and guidance; in doing so, they also participate in creating a future, not just for the students themselves, but for the country in which they interact. This is particularly important today, as we use digital prosumer creations that effectively merge use and speech into one creative product. In these situations, more than ever, speech and use become mixed activities and are tied closely together—in a remix of ideas and sources that help enable participatory democracy. Employing a pedagogy that encourages students to learn within the realm of participatory democracy allows instructors to support a training ground, of sorts, for the country's future, as well.

If we are to prepare students to face the challenges of the 21st century, we cannot ask them to engage only in rote memorization of static "facts," especially when knowledge keeps changing at an ever-quickening pace. The Framers' genius was in creating a set of goals for advancing democracy through learning and access to the dialogic process by reflecting these goals in an intellectual property provision that creates the base of our ability to interact. Democracy requires creativity and innovation; these are made possible through free speech, fair use, and a pedagogy that supports their use. Our democracy is not static, but thrives on fluidity, accommodating change to allow a country that can grow and develop, hopefully, into a smarter, more innovative, more inclusive union. Choosing an appropriate pedagogy to support the mechanisms of fair use in free speech can go a long way to prepare students to engage in participatory democracy and thus to influence the shape of the country.

REFERENCES

Barton, Matthew D. (2005). The future of rational–critical debate in online public spheres. *Computers and Composition*, 22, 171-190.
Berlin, James. (1987). *Rhetoric and reality: Writing instruction in American colleges*, 1900-1985. Carbondale: Southern Illinois University Press.
Bill Graham Archives v. Dorling Kindersley, Ltd. 448 F.3d 605 (2006).
Campbell v. Acuff-Rose. 510 U.S. 569 (1994).
DeVoss, Dànielle Nicole, & Webb, Suzanne. (2008). Media convergence: Grand theft audio: Negotiating copyright as composers. *Computers and Composition*, 25, 79-103.

Ghosh, Shuba. (2003). Deprivatizing copyright. *Case Western Reserve Law Review, 54*, 387–501.

Gitman, Yury. (1998). Examining how I recontextualized. *Kairos: A Journal of Rhetoric, Technology, and Pedagogy,* 3 (1). http://endora.wide.msu.edu/3.1/coverweb/ty/myty.html

Herrington, TyAnna. (1998). Interdependency of fair use and the first amendment. *Computers and Composition*, 15, 125–143.

Herrington, TyAnna K. (2001). *Controlling voices: Intellectual property, humanistic studies, and the Internet.* Carbondale: Southern Illinois University Press.

Herrington, TyAnna. (Under review). *iProp: Students' rights and responsibilities in intellectual property.* Carbondale: Southern Illinois University Press.

Herrington, TyAnna. (2005). Linking Russia and the United States in Web forums: The Global Classroom Project. In Carol Lipson & Michael Day (Eds.), *Technical communication and the World Wide Web* (pp. 167-192). Mahwah NJ: Lawrence Ebaum Associates.

Howard, Rebecca Moore. (2007). Understanding "Internet plagiarism." *Computers and Composition*, 24, 3–15.

Johnson-Eilola, Johndan, & Selber, Stuart A. (2007). Plagiarism, originality, assemblage. *Computers and Composition*, 24, 375–403.

Kelly v. Arriba Soft Corporation. (280 F.3d 934 (CA9 2002) withdrawn, re-filed at 336 F.3d 811(CA9 2003).

Kemp, Fred. (1984, February). Lecture. Lubbock: Texas Tech University.

Lave, Jean, & Wenger, Etienne. (1991). *Situated learning: Legitimate peripheral participation.* Oxford: Cambridge University Press.

Lemley, Mark A. (2000). The constitutionalization of technology law. *Berkeley Technology Law Journal*, 529, 529–535.

Mattel Inc. v. MCA Records. 537 U.S. 1171; 123 S. Ct. 993; 154 L. Ed. 2d 912; 2003 U.S. LEXIS 920; 71 U.S.L.W. 3503.

Papert, Seymore, & Harel, Idit. (1991). *Situating constructionism.* Mahwah, NJ: Ablex.

Patterson, L. Ray. (1987). Free speech, copyright, and fair use. *Vanderbilt Law Review*, 40, 1–66.

Patterson, L. Ray, & Birch, Stanley. (1996). Copyright and free speech rights. *Journal of Intellectual Property Law*, 4, 1–23.

Rife, Martine Courant. (2007). The fair use doctrine: History, application, and implications for (new media) writing teachers. *Computers and Composition*, 24, 154–178.

Rife, Martine Courant, & Hart-Davidson, William. (2006). *Is there a chilling of digital communication? Exploring how knowledge and understanding of the fair use doctrine may influence Web composing.* WIDE Research Center Report. http://papers.ssrn.com/sol3/papers.cfm?abstract_id=918822

Suntrust Bank v. Houghton Mifflin Co., 252 F. 3d 1165 (11th Cir. 2001) per curiam, opinion at 268 F.3d 1257.

Travis, Hannibal. (2000). Pirates of the information infrastructure: Blackstonian copyright and the first amendment. *Berkeley Technology Law Journal,* 777, 777–864.

Yen, Alfred. (1989). A first amendment perspective on the idea/expression dichotomy and copyright in a work's total "concept and feel." *Emory Law Journal, 393,* 393–437.

14 RESPONSE TO PART II—BEING RHETORICAL WHEN WE TEACH INTELLECTUAL PROPERTY AND FAIR USE

James E. Porter

Let's start with the obvious: Language is a shared resource.

I wrote that five-word phrase—"language is a shared resource"—all by myself. I swear I did, or I thought I did. But then I did a phrase search in Google and discovered that the phrase is not original! It was said before, in a 2002 book by Tor Nørretranders called *The Generous Man*. Well, that's not quite true—actually, the phrase is the English translation by Jonathan Sydenham of a phrase Nørretranders expressed in Danish. The English phrase also appeared in a 2006 article by J.C. Spender in a business journal, so he must have plagiarized it from Nørretranders—or, rather, Sydenham. What a trail of deceit; it's all very dense and confusing.

Things get even worse. The more egregious act of plagiarism in paragraph one is actually the phrase "let's start with the obvious," a journalistic cliché of the first rank. Don't even bother to Google search that one—it's ubiquitous in sports and entertainment features, in editorials, in advertising.

I thought what I wrote as paragraph one was my own, but clearly it is not. I must have plagiarized it, the entire first two sentences of my paper. The textual evidence is conclusive, incontrovertible, damning. Am I to be charged with academic dishonesty, along with Steve Westbrook, who admits to stealing a phrase from Raymond Carver for the title of his chapter? Or else ...

Maybe I'm just unoriginal. Maybe I think in clichés. Maybe I am prone to ignorantly parroting phrases from my linguistic discourse community—like

Thomas Jefferson did when he wrote the Declaration of Independence, which repeated verbatim

> traces from a First Continental Congress resolution, a Massachusetts Council declaration, George Mason's "Declaration of Rights for Virginia," a political pamphlet of James Otis, and a variety of other sources, including a colonial play. The overall form of the Declaration (theoretical argument followed by list of grievances) strongly resembles, ironically, the English Bill of Rights of 1689, in which Parliament lists the abuses of James II and declares new powers for itself. Several of the abuses in the Declaration seem to have been taken, more or less verbatim, from a *Pennsylvania Evening Post* article. And the most memorable phrases in the Declaration seem to be least Jefferson's: "That all men are created equal" is a sentiment from Euripides which Jefferson copied in his literary commonplace book as a boy; "Life, Liberty, and the pursuit of Happiness" was a cliché of the times, appearing in numerous political documents. (Porter, 1986, p. 36)

Thomas Jefferson is a plagiarist, too, and one of the worst ever! Or else...

Perhaps most of what we say, in speech and writing, is "plagiarized" in the sense that it echoes, it reproduces, verisimultitudinously, phrases that we have read, heard, or felt somewhere else before. But *plagiarism* is such a negative term. Let's call it *intertextuality*, as Steve Westbrook does: The texts we create, in speech or in writing, are always comprised of others' texts—because fundamentally language is a shared resource and because fundamentally we are always speaking and writing in conversation with others, which often entails reproducing their speech/writing, even when we do not always explicitly acknowledge those piracies.

We might go further, in fact, and say that reproducing other people's speaking and writing—without attribution—is the most effective kind of rhetoric, because echoing what others think, feel, believe, and say is a legitimate rhetorical strategy for establishing rhetorical common ground with an audience. The power of the Declaration of Independence came about precisely because it was an *assemblage*—to use a key term from TyAnna Herrington's chapter—of existing political phrases, beliefs, attitudes, and ideas of the time. Assemblage is not plagiarism, because it involves strategically collecting and organizing phrases into new configurations for a new context and audience—a process that in classical rhetoric was called *compilatio*. We might also call it *re-mixing*—and this act is fundamental to how rhetoric works, not just in the digital age but in all ages (DeVoss & Porter, 2006).

The contributing authors to Part II of this collection recognize that intertextuality and assemblage, so fundamental to literacy production, raise important questions about intellectual property and fair use. It is impossible to write without doing some unattributed copying. We can't get through our day without it. We "plagiarize" all the time, in the sense that we are borrowing bits and pieces of language from other sources and repeating these fragments, echoing them, inserting them in new contexts, appropriating them, and redistributing them. And, of course, this is not always plagiarism.

And, of course, sometimes it is. Understanding that dividing line between "sharing" and "stealing"—to borrow Westbrook's language—is critical to ethical (as well as legal) composing.

The Part II essays address this all-important distinction between sharing and stealing and offer strategies for helping student writers understand the difference, make smart decisions, and become wise and ethical users of others' language—"language" defined broadly to include audio, video, and graphic, as well as textual language (speech and writing). These essays emphasize the importance of teaching intellectual property and fair use, and overall I could not agree with the authors more: We absolutely need to be teaching copyright issues as an integral part of all composition courses, but particularly in first-year composition. I agree with Ashley Hall, Kathie Gossett, and Elizabeth Vincelette that our focus as instructors should not be "lament[ing] ... the immoral and unconscionable actions of our students." Rather, our focus should be on teaching the ethics and politics of copyright and on teaching students to be advocates of fair use as well as of copyright. So, we all agree, we should be teaching students about intellectual property. The tougher question, though, is the how question: *How* should we teach intellectual property and fair use accurately, responsibly, effectively?

Thus far, we composition teachers haven't done a very good job teaching copyright accurately. Both Janice Walker and Steve Westbrook point out that many textbooks and style guides in our field still misrepresent copyright issues and/or do an inadequate job of explaining their intricacies and nuances (e.g., Walker's discussion of the 2009 *MLA Handbook*). TyAnna Herrington says that "misperceptions and inaccuracies regarding intellectual property law are both extreme and ubiquitous in this age of digital communication." Alas, especially among composition teachers, it seems.

Westbrook points to some confusions in our composition textbooks—including in some big-name, big-selling textbooks; textbooks often do not acknowledge that "the conditions for determining fair use are independent of documentation." This is a key distinction, and one that our field has not fully addressed. Citing the authors of a work may satisfy the conditions for academic integrity, but that is not the same as satisfying the conditions for fair use. Westbrook suggests that composition teachers themselves need to understand these realms better than they do.

Sometimes when we teach intellectual property and fair use, we slip into fallacies of oversimplification. One fallacy that Westbrook discusses errs on the side of excessive liberty—that is, the assumption that merely citing your sources is good enough. That fallacy confuses the realm of academic integrity and citation practices with the realm of copyright. But another fallacy exists in excessive constraint: The guideline that insists we should "always ask permission" is bad advice, too. As Westbrook says, "it oversimplifies the complexity" of how fair use operates and has the secondary effect of "obfuscat[ing] or even eras[ing] the concept of fair use." "Always ask permission" is a bad guideline because it contributes to the erosion of the Fair Use doctrine—and this also can impede our First Amendment rights as well. Powerful interests have used the threat of copyright infringement as a way to block the exercise of free speech, as both Herrington and Westbrook discuss. Westbrook cites the example of how Diebold used the threat of copyright infringement to stifle journalistic information about the unreliability of Diebold voting machines. This is a great example, first, because it highlights the importance of protecting the Fair Use provision of U.S. Copyright Law as integral to First Amendment rights, but also because Judge Fogel's decision in the case (*Online Policy Group v. Diebold, Inc.*, 2004) models the kind of step-by-step reasoning that is fundamental for writers making a fair use determination. As Westbrook says, it is that form of reasoning and analysis we should be teaching in composition.

So, first, we need to recognize that there are two different systems in play here: the realm of intellectual property/infringement and the realm of academic integrity/plagiarism. The first is a legal realm, the second an ethical realm. If a student buys a research paper from a term paper mill and submits it as his own, that is pretty clearly an act of academic dishonesty (plagiarism), but probably not a copyright infringement (if the paper purchased has been licensed for reuse). Conversely, if a student makes a YouTube video using music and images from copyrighted sources, she can uphold the standards of academic integrity (and avoid the charge of plagiarism) by citing those sources in her video. But that has nothing to do with the question of copyright: the student's academically appropriate video could still infringe upon copyright. We need to be teaching both realms—explaining their differences and identifying their points of overlap.

Second, in talking about the realm of intellectual property, we need to make sure to teach that realm as having two sides—a fundamental tension be-

Response to Part II

| UNACCEPTABLE | ACCEPTABLE |

Figure 1: The ethics of using others' texts—the simplistic view.

tween "the property side" (the author's or creator's side) and "the use side" (the user's side, the social good side):

> Copyright law ... is essentially characterized by a *balance*: between (a) creating a system of incentive by rewarding the author's labor and (b) encouraging benefits to society from the flow of information that can stimulate new ideas, inventions, and creations. (DeVoss & Porter, 2006, p. 185)

Questions of intellectual property always involve balancing the rights of the creator with the rights of the user (and the rights of society at large). So in talking about this realm, I believe we should refer to it not just one-sidedly as "intellectual property" or "copyright,"[1] but rather we should be sure to acknowledge the duality in our description: Let's always label it "intellectual property and fair use"—a binary phrase that acknowledges the tension fundamental to the area. Give both sides their due.

Third, we need to teach that this realm is not a simple binary, black-and-white world of clear rights and wrongs (as Figure 1 represents).

Rather, the realm consists of some cases and practices that are clearly acceptable, others that are clearly not acceptable, and a whole host of practices and uses of others' material where the decision is complicated, uncertain, unclear, and gray. In short, the realm is contextually complicated (as Figure 2 represents).

As writers, we face complicated decisions regularly—probably every day. For the really important stuff, we should seek expert advice. But because we can't afford to email our IP lawyers about every decision, we typically answer

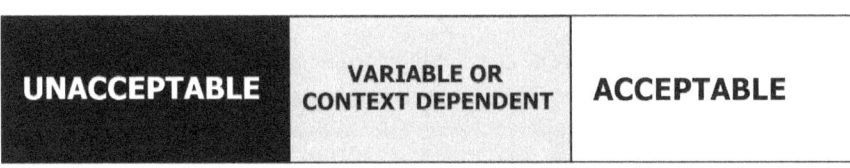

Figure 2: The ethics of using others' texts—the rhetorically complicated view.

267

these questions on our own and decide upon some reasonable course of action. We assess the circumstances and make a judgment call. Hopefully, an informed call.

Jim Ridolfo and Martine Rife provide an interesting case that falls within the gray area, I would say: Michigan State University's appropriation of Maggie Ryan's image for their own marketing purposes. As Ridolfo and Rife say, "none of the legal/conceptual frameworks we have set forth ... fully address the 'right' and 'wrong' of the institution's appropriation." Exactly. What their detailed analysis shows is the complexity of copyright law *vis-à-vis* privacy considerations and the vital importance of context in determining right and wrong. Here is where rhetoric has much to contribute to copyright law: That is, rhetoric understands the complexity of language use *vis-à-vis* context, audience, and purpose. Rhetoric "as the productive art of creating effective discourse ... is highly attuned to audience and context—that is, to the particular circumstances of a scene or situation" (McKee & Porter, 2009, p. 25).

I understand that most people would prefer a world in which there are clear answers, clear villains and heroes, tried-and-true guidelines, and a world where sharing and stealing, and right and wrong are firmly determined. But that is not the world of intellectual property, and that is why I am worried about Janice Walker's list of "clear-cut guidelines." Yes, I can accept that list as *guidelines*, but I worry that they will be used as—and become—rules. And that would be dangerous.

For instance, Walker proposes: "For print, generally the rule of thumb has been that use of ten percent or less of a work constitutes fair use." The so-called "10% guideline" is an example of a copyright guideline that has been promulgated by publishers, has been widely adopted by libraries, and has received a kind of formal authorization through the CONFU (1996) process. Yes, it is an established *guideline*. But it does not have a basis in copyright law and it should not function as a legal standard. As the U.S. Copyright Office (2009) tells us:

> There are no legal rules permitting the use of a specific number of words, a certain number of musical notes, or percentage of a work. Whether a particular use qualifies as fair use depends on all the circumstances.

Although I understand the desire for clear-cut quantitative guidelines, they don't exist—particularly not in regards to quantity of copying. (As Westbrook points out, in these litigious days, even minimal sampling of a piece of copyrighted music can be considered infringement.) Likewise, for another guideline, Walker cites: "For work to be distributed outside the classroom (for instance, to be published on the World Wide Web), it is imperative you at least make an attempt to acquire permission." No, it is not required that you do so—and doing so may have the unintended consequence of eroding fair use, for the reasons Westbrook discusses. Another guideline from Walker: "graphics, audio, or video files should not be downloaded without permission." Again, no, I disagree heartily with that advice: Always seeking permission is a practice that further contributes to the erosion of fair use. Publishers and content creators would like us to believe they have that level of control over their copyrighted works; in actual law, they don't and they shouldn't. Users (writers) have rights.

Ultimately, an algorithmic approach to copyright issues doesn't help writers because (a) "the law" is not a clear or firmly established entity, but is rather a messy, moving target; and (b) every application of law requires understanding the circumstances of a particular composing context (involving the purpose of the use, the quantity of material used, etc.). Further, we need to recognize that U.S. Copyright Law is not the only or highest authority in this realm; we need to avoid being U.S.-centric in our approach to intellectual property. When students borrow material from the Internet and then post their own creations to the Internet, they may or may not be under the authority of U.S. Copyright Law. Their writing may be governed by the copyright policies of another nation, or may fall into the vastly gray area of international copyright treaties and policies (see McKee & Porter, 2010).

So don't try to teach "the law." What is needed, I would argue, is a rhetorical frame of thinking about context and a heuristic methodology—that is, a critical procedure for making ethical and legal judgments about the use of others' intellectual property. This type of ethical reasoning is what Aristotle called *phronesis*, or the art of practical judgment. Such an approach would include some broad principles and guidelines, some heuristic questions, and some case examples—of clear-cut fair uses, clear-cut infringements, and the vast gray area in between.

In a sense, then, we have to teach students some basic legal reasoning—which is also a kind of rhetorical reasoning. We should teach not just (a) what the law says or what guidelines tell us, but also (b) how law has been or could be applied in particular cases, so that (c) students can learn a form of reasoning useful to making their own prudent judgments about intellectual property and fair use. We should resist the urge to promulgate publisher folklore or "clear-cut guidelines" such as "the 10% rule" or "always ask permission."

A more promising pedagogical approach is to examine and discuss problematic cases, and in this regard I very much like Westbrook's discussion of Judge Fogel's legal reasoning in the *Diebold* case and Ridolfo and Rife's analysis of the Maggie case (i.e., Michigan State University's continued use of Maggie's image for marketing purposes, without her permission). Cases can be elaborate, detailed, and lengthy—like the two just mentioned—or they can be short and simple examples. Here are several mini-cases I use to get students discussing and pondering the intellectual property implications of their writing practices, to help them understand the difference between the realms of academic integrity and intellectual property, and to help them think critically about context of use:

> Heping, a graduating Miami University senior, pastes a version of the Miami University logo as a graphic on his resume (both the print version and the electronic version), which he sends out to potential employers. Is this an intellectual property infringement and/or an act of academic dishonesty?

> Jim, a graduate student in English, recycles his senior undergraduate thesis paper for use in a graduate course. The original paper was his own work; Jim, however, submits the paper in nearly its original form, with only minor editorial revisions. Is this academic dishonesty?

> A teacher asks students to create a web page of annotated sources on a given historical topic. Jane locates a web page with an interesting and distinctive layout and uses that web page as a template for her own assignment. She collects and annotates the historical sources on her own, but she "borrows" the HTML coding for the format and typography of the page. Is this plagiarism? What if she did the same thing in a web-authoring course?

In their chapter, Hall, Gossett, and Vincelette focus on YouTube videos—and that is a great example case because YouTube and similar sites represent an increasingly important venue for multimedia writing. Producing remixed multimedia writing and posting such creations to sites like YouTube is an activity rich with intellectual property implications. However, Hall, Gossett, and Vincelette focus on the genre of parody, which is one of the more highly protected forms of fair use, especially if the parody is political. Parody is more likely to represent a stronger transformative effect and, therefore, is more likely to be protected under fair use (see *Campbell v. Acuff Rose*, 1994, and *Suntrust Bank v. Houghton Mifflin*, 2001). For pedagogical purposes, I wish that Hall et al. had addressed a different genre, or a wider variety of genres.[2] What if, say, a student uses video clips from a television show for a promotional video posted on YouTube for a non-profit organization?

As we contemplate how to teach issues of intellectual property and fair use, we also have to reflect humbly on our limitations. What credibility do we have—as rhetoricians and composition instructors—speculating about intellectual property and fair use? That's a legal area; shouldn't we leave it to IP lawyers? Of course some of us, like Rife and Herrington, have the requisite legal credentials, but the rest of us are, well, amateurs in this realm.

This activity—the act of making fundamental decisions about copyright ... literally, *the right to copy* something, to repeat it, to use it (with or without attribution)—is fundamental to literacy production and to composition. And so, like it or not, it falls to us, as writing teachers, to address the matter in our composition classes. However, we must take care to delineate our area of expertise. We should not be teaching intellectual property and fair use as if we were lawyers or law professors—even if we were capable of that. Our job is to teach copyright issues from the point of view of the writer who must make these decisions regularly, daily, and repeatedly in the ordinary course of composing—and without recourse to legal opinion. Our job is not to teach Fair Use (upper case), as if we were teaching law students. Rather, our job is to teach fair and ethical use (lower case) of others' work to help student writers develop critical consciousness of the issues and a pragmatic heuristic inquiry procedure they can apply across different contexts to make prudent judgments. We should teach rhetorical, case-based reasoning as it applies to the practice of borrowing, reproducing, and redistributing others' material. In this regard, the essays in Part II of this collection, indeed the entire collection, represent an important contribution to our pedagogical efforts.

NOTES

1. We need to recognize, too, that "intellectual property" and "copyright" are not synonymous. Copyright is one facet of the larger realm of intellectual property law, which also includes other matters (such as trademark and patent law).

2. The focus on YouTube does allow Hall, Gossett, and Vincelette to develop the argument—a compelling one—that YouTube exists primarily for social purposes, not for infringement purposes. Their argument is that YouTube falls into the category of Web 2.0 publication, where a "new and different cultural logic is at play." This is a very interesting argument about genre and context that merits further consideration regarding intellectual property issues.

REFERENCES

Campbell v. Acuff-Rose. 510 U.S. 569 (1994).

CONFU Conference on Fair Use. (1996). Fair Use guidelines for multimedia. Retrieved July 7, 2010, from http://www.utsystem.edu/ogc/intellectual-property/ccmcguid.htm

DeVoss, Dànielle Nicole, & Porter, James E. (2006). Why Napster matters to writing: Filesharing as a new ethic of digital delivery. *Computers and Composition, 23*, 178-210.

McKee, Heidi A., & Porter, James E. (2009). *The ethics of Internet research: A rhetorical, case-based process.* New York: Peter Lang.

McKee, Heidi A., & Porter, James E. (2010). Legal and regulatory issues for technical communicators conducting global Internet research. *Technical Communication, 57*, 312-329.

Nørretranders, Tor. (2002). *The generous man: How helping others is the sexiest thing you can do* (Trans. Jonathan Sydenham). New York: Thunder's Mouth Press.

Online Policy Group v. Diebold, Inc. 337 F.Supp.2d 1195 (2004).

Porter, James E. (1986). Intertextuality and the discourse community. *Rhetoric Review, 5*, 34-47.

Spender, J.C. (2006). Getting value from knowledge management. *TQM Magazine, 18* (3), 238-254.

Suntrust Bank v. Houghton Mifflin Co. 252 F. 3d 1165 (11th Cir. 2001) per curiam, opinion at 268 F.3d 1257.

U.S. Copyright Office. (2009, October 6). Can I use someone else's work? Can someone else use mine? http://www.copyright.gov/help/faq/faq-fairuse.html

PART III: THE PEDAGOGY

15 TOWARD A PEDAGOGY OF FAIR USE FOR MULTIMEDIA COMPOSITION

Renee Hobbs and Katie Donnelly

These days, it's inevitable: writing and composition teachers are becoming media literacy teachers. As the Internet and computing technologies have created new forms of expression and communication that are multivocal, multimodal, collaborative, public, instantaneously accessible, and sometimes anonymously authored, anyone in the business of helping students develop the capacity for self-expression and communication bumps into key concepts of media literacy education. As Brian Morrison (qtd. in Yancey, 2004) pointed out, in the 21st century, composition is "the thoughtful gathering, construction or reconstruction of a literate act in any given media" (p. 315). Writing teachers, typically tuned in to issues of identity, voice, and power, require sensitivity to how form and content interact when symbolic forms include not only printed language, but also sound, including the spoken word and music to name only a few, and still and moving images. These messages come to us through diverse forms that are variously commodified or non-commodified in an increasingly dense digital environment where economic, political, and social contexts shape both the creation and reception of messages.

Composition educators recognize the rapidly shifting tectonic plates we are now facing in education. Kathleen Yancey (2004) recommended that writing and composition educators must develop a new curriculum for the 21st century, one that expands beyond its roots in the intense and personal tutorial relationship between the teacher and the writer. According to Yancey, students need to consider how their compositions relate to "real world" genres; what the best medium and best delivery might be and so create and share different forms of communication via different media to divergent audiences; and how to adapt ideas across different media genres and technological forms. Within this changing landscape, as forms of expression make use of appropriation and sampling, and as authorship becomes increasingly collaborative, issues concerning ownership and intellectual property arise.

People now use multiple forms of representation to convey ideas, using "cutting and pasting, drawing, talking, playing, audio tracks, video interfaces and other media to achieve different perspectives on their world, solve problems, make plans, and communicate with others" (Tierney, 2008, p. 101). These multimedia environments enable literacy practices to easily travel across space and time, in and out of school. Through the use of do-it-yourself practices that enable (almost) anyone to be an author in a socially situated context, Doreen Piano (2008) found that those who create zines and other alternative publications rely on the "innovative uses of scraps and cutouts from discarded newspapers and magazines" in ways that demonstrate how popular culture contributes to literacy practices that move beyond basic, functional skills to ones "invested in personal, familial and communal meaning" (p. 315).

Many educators—at all levels and in many disciplines—rely on the ability to use copyrighted materials to help students develop the skills and knowledge to understand, analyze, and create multimodal texts. Although some educators tend to conceptualize video and multimedia compositions differently from print ones, there are important parallels between traditional compositions and 21st-century multimodal texts (Bruce, 2008). Media literacy education applies concepts such as purpose, genre, audience, tone, and point of view to strengthen critical thinking and communication skills, particularly in response to mass media and popular culture. Students learn through both close reading and analysis activities as well as creative composition practices (Costanzo, 2007). Just as it is important for students to share their print compositions, students need to be able to share their digital and multimedia compositions with authentic audiences to deepen their reflection on their editorial and creative choices. Because students and teachers need to use, quote from, and share copyrighted digital texts as part of media literacy education, we need a robust interpretation of fair use.

But old paradigms die hard. Consider the case of the college professor at a school of education, involved in preparing young people to be high school English teachers. In the course, students develop activities and lessons that help demonstrate the connection between media literacy, language arts and literature. As part of this work, students create a short video production, working in teams to develop a compelling message using images, language, and sound. The professor usually puts together a DVD of student media work at the end of each semester, but he doesn't feel comfortable screening these works or sharing them with colleagues at professional conferences. He would never think of posting them online. Why? He's concerned that he may face legal risks, because some of his students make use of copyrighted images found on Google, as well as excerpts from popular films, television programs, and You Tube videos. Many students use samples from popular music in their productions.

What is the impact of this kind of fear on the development of multimedia composition? Because our colleagues rarely see the quality of work that students can produce using multimedia texts and tools, they're sometimes not too interested in adopting innovative approaches to teaching pre-service English teachers. The uncertainty and doubt this professor experiences stems in part from a lack of knowledge and lack of confidence in understanding how copyright and fair use applies to the practice of media literacy education. Copyright confusion—a widespread misunderstanding of the purpose and scope of copyright law and a lack of understanding of the doctrine of fair use—is a situation created in part by the various outdated "educational use guidelines" misunderstood as law (Crews, 2001).

With the support of the John D. and Catherine T. MacArthur Foundation, the media literacy community recently attempted to reduce copyright confusion through the development of a code of best practices. As part of this larger project, we first conducted long-form interviews with 63 educators from K–12 institutions, universities, and with leaders in the youth media community, resulting in the report, *The Cost of Copyright Confusion for Media Literacy* (Hobbs, Jaszi, & Aufderheide, 2007).[1] Following this, we held 4-hour-long focus group meetings with 150 individuals in ten cities across the U.S. to explore various hypothetical situations regarding the use of copyrighted materials for media literacy education, looking for evidence of consensus and shared norms. This work resulted in the development of the "Code of Best Practices in Fair Use for Media Literacy Education" (Center for Social Media, 2008). In this chapter, we examine the ongoing dialogue among educators about fair use as it applies to the practice of media literacy education, with particular attention to student media production and multimedia composition activities. We begin by presenting evidence about core values among educators concerning copyright and fair use, collected through intensive interviews with educators in the first phase of developing the code. Then we consider how remix practices support the goals of media literacy education and examine how copyright and fair use apply. Finally, we discuss the views of educators concerning instructional practices that specifically relate to student multimedia composition: student use of copyrighted materials in their creative work and the types of sharing with authentic audiences part of the teaching and learning process.[2]

CORE VALUES ABOUT COPYRIGHT AND EDUCATION

Educators share a set of core beliefs about the use of copyrighted materials for teaching and learning. In our interviews with educators, the following themes emerged:

Cultural criticism is essential to democracy.

Media literacy educators value cultural criticism as an essential tool for self-actualization and democracy. "A literate citizenship cannot be created if the people who control images don't allow them to be used," one educator explained. Another teacher said that "it's important that users of media participate in it and don't just receive it." In contemporary culture, students are trained to be consumers of media, and as another teacher explained, that is why "it's important to go beyond this role."

Mass and digital media are the heart of the cultural environment.

Media literacy educators see mass media and popular culture as part of the cultural landscape, deeply connected to students' sense of personal and social identity. "Copyrighted materials are like our cultural landscape—you need to be able to use and analyze media," said one teacher. Sharing our interpretations and understandings of the diverse works of expression and communication around us is an important part of learning to make sense of the world. Digital media is a part of our lives in a way that it wasn't 20 or 30 years ago, pointed out a media educator and video artist: "We should have access to our culture and be able to talk about it and comment on the world around us. If we don't comment on it, then it feels like information is being controlled."

Effective use of copyrighted materials enhances the teaching and learning process.

A college professor who teaches pre-service teachers talked about the importance of using copyrighted works in educational settings because they provide more current examples than offered in most textbooks. Contemporary mass media materials hook attention and interest, and help teachers connect new ideas to students' existing knowledge. "Teaching is just better when we can pull from a lot of different sources," said one teacher. A number of educators pointed out the value of modeling as a tool in the learning process. "Imitation is a way to learn," explained one teacher, "so if students can't take and use the most highly developed messages that society creates, it's a handicap for them and the whole society."

Appropriation of cultural materials promotes creativity and learning.

Teachers believe that there is significant educational value in the process of juxtaposition and recombination of existing materials. A number of educators described the process of creating mashups, where existing copyrighted works are juxtaposed and recombined with original materials to create new works. One teacher described the work of an art teacher who asks students to select a famous painting of the 17th or 18th century and use image-manipulation software to "put themselves into the image." The assignment engages student learning because it connects learning about art to learning about technology to reflection on personal and social identity. Appropriation is a powerful instructional tool for student learning. As one teacher explained, "mashups are an opportunity for students to really look at the media they consume—to take it and give it their own spin. It helps show kids how they can present their own point of view." However, a number of teachers talked about the limits of appropriation, pointing out that "it shouldn't be a free-for-all, but a thoughtful process" in which students take material they can re-contextualize and make their own.

MEDIA LITERACY, REMIX, AND FAIR USE

Educators from many fields and disciplines depend on fair use, but media literacy educators perhaps have the most acute appreciation of fair use because of their reliance on copyrighted materials produced by the major corporations that control the production of mass media news, entertainment, and popular culture. In reflecting on the dominance of media and technology as a cultural force, media literacy educators are often motivated by their awareness of the well-funded and highly choreographed cultural production system, where audiences are constructed to be passive and ritualistic in their consumption of media messages. The mass media's role in constituting the public sphere has been widely criticized for narrowing the range of ideas presented, concentrating ownership in the hands of a few, and the tendency of advertising-supported media to reduce quality by focusing on ratings and advertising revenue (Gitlin, 2001). As a result, "concentrated media must structure most 'participants' in the debate as passive recipients of finished messages and images" (Benkler, 2007, p. 209). However, the rise of digital media has contributed to greater levels of awareness and sensitivity because "the practice of making one's own music, movie or essay makes one a more self-conscious user of the cultural artifacts of others," as media literacy education is part of a broad practice of learning by doing that "makes the entire society more effective readers and writers of their own culture" (Benkler, p. 299).

Increasingly, composition educators have begun to incorporate media literacy concepts into their educational practices. William Costanzo (2008) pointed out that there are many similarities between writing and producing other media:

> Filmmakers, television producers and web designers, like writers, must make decisions about purpose, audience, content, format, arrangement and style. They follow codes and conventions, observe time-honored rhetorical strategies and create visual texts for many of the purposes that motivate writers: to recollect the past, describe the present, make proposals for the future, investigate issues, or take a stand. (p. xix)

Just as students quote from other authors in their written text, they need to be able to use, sample from, and manipulate copyrighted works in learning various skills associated with media literacy, including exploring image–language relationships, considering point of view, and analyzing framing aspects. In particular, remix is a dimension of teaching media literacy that depends upon student ability to transform the meaning of an existing text by manipulating the form, structure, and/or content to explore how meaning is shaped through symbol systems that operate in a complex cultural, historical, political, and economic context (Jenkins, 2006).

In their survey of young online remixers, Patricia Aufderheide and Peter Jaszi (2007) found that video creators believed integrating various copyrighted materials into their own work was part of the creative process: "I think part of our generation is that we take and mix things together," one respondent said. "We're very much a mixed-media generation." Interviewees reported making use of copyrighted materials in new and creative ways, for instance, by setting slides of original art to popular music and incorporating television clips into original online sketch comedy shows. As Aufderheide and Jaszi maintained, "They regard existing popular culture as available raw material for new work" (p. 5). There is a clear social component to remixing as well: respondents in Aufderheide and Jaszi's study felt that the shared experience of popular culture inspired them to build upon and remix existing copyrighted works.

Appreciation of remix practices is developing among educators, but it is still contested among those who fear that it promotes shallowness and a lack of creativity. Composition educators have long conceptualized writers as lone creators of original texts: Anything that is not originally produced is typically devalued, and relying too heavily on others' resources is considered plagiarism. But the act of remixing existing materials is in itself educationally valuable, because when "students are encouraged to make explicit their borrowings and appropriations," it can stretch their ability to address specific issues, readers, and students (Johnson-Eilola & Selber, 2007, p. 380). Johndan Johnson-Eilola and Stuart Selber explained that, for composition educators, remixing "inhabits a contested terrain of creativity, intellectual property, authorship, corporate ownership and power" (p. 392). In this view, remix cannot supplant traditional composition, but it can complement it.

When it comes to considering legal issues, many of the instructional processes, curricula and multimedia products now at the very core of media literacy education fall under the provisions of the doctrine of fair use. When assessing whether a particular use of copyrighted materials is a fair use, lawyers and judges always consider the expectations and practices within a creative community (Madison, 2006). In weighing the balance at the heart of fair use analysis, judges refer to four types of considerations mentioned in the law: the nature of the use, the nature of the work used, the extent of the use, and its economic effect (referred to collectively as the "four factors"). This still leaves much room for interpretation, especially because the law is clear that these are not the only necessary considerations. In reviewing the history of fair use litigation, judges return again and again to two key questions: First, did the unlicensed use "transform" the material taken from the copyrighted work by using it for a different purpose than that of the original, or did it just repeat the work for the same intent and value as the original? And, second, was the material taken appropriate in kind and amount, considering the nature of the copyrighted work and the use? (Joyce, Leaffer, Jaszi, Ochoa, & 2003). Of course, transformativeness is not absolutely necessary for a finding of fair use. But the creation of transformative works directly supports the purpose of copyright as stated in the U.S. Constitution, which is to promote the spread of knowledge and creativity.

The "Code of Best Practices for Fair Use in Media Literacy Education," a project (as described earlier in this article) funded by the John D. and Catherine T. MacArthur Foundation (Center for Social Media, Media Education Lab at Temple University, Washington College of Law, American University, 2008) was created by gathering and synthesizing the beliefs of the media literacy community about how fair use applies to five common instructional practices. In this process, 150 participants in ten cities across the United States discussed hypothetical scenarios involving the uses of copyrighted materials in media literacy education to identify the principles and limitations articulated in the Code. Following this, the Code was reviewed by a committee of legal scholars and lawyers with expertise in copyright and fair use.

The Code identifies five principles, each with limitations, representing the community's current consensus about acceptable practices for the fair use of copyrighted materials. As stated in the Code, educators can, under some circumstances, (1) make copies of newspaper articles, TV shows, and other copyrighted works, and use and keep them for educational use. They can (2) create curriculum materials and scholarship with copyrighted materials embedded. Educators can (3) share, sell, and distribute curriculum materials with copyrighted materials embedded. Learners can, under some circumstances, (4) use copyrighted works in creating new material. They can (5) distribute their works digitally if they meet the transformativeness standard. In the next section, we review the perspective of educators concerning the two principles that address student use of copyrighted materials and the sharing of that work with authentic audiences.

STUDENT USE OF COPYRIGHTED MATERIALS FOR MEDIA COMPOSITION

In both K–12 and university settings, student media compositions are undertaken for a wide variety of purposes. Some of these purposes might not qualify as "composition" as understood by composition educators. For example, most readers know that it is now common to document student public speaking or athletic activities on video to provide students with opportunities for sustained feedback and review. In many high schools and colleges, students may take a video-production course where they learn to create news, documentary or talk show programs about local community events and issues (Hobbs, 2006). In some of these courses, the purpose of media production activities is to learn concrete skills associated with the use of the technology. These courses often use a step-by-step approach that emphasizes the gradual accretion of a fixed repertoire of skills and techniques (Buckingham, 2003). In other courses, there is more explicit focus on the process of multimedia composition, with an emphasis on the creative and collaborative skills associated with open-ended exploration and self-expression. In these courses, media tools are often seen as simply a wider palette for "conveying the 'authentic voice' of young people" (Buckingham, p. 131).

Because the current generation of young people has grown up with digital and video cameras and rapid technological advances, media composition activities are beginning to be more widely used as "alternative" assignments in secondary English education (Hobbs, 2007), where English teachers do not explicitly teach production practices but offer creative project-based learning assignments that students can choose to accomplish in print, video, or multimedia formats. At Concord High School in New Hampshire, where English teachers developed a mandatory Grade 11 course in Media/Communication as the required English course, students used video production to develop literary adaptations of a scene from Faulkner's *As I Lay Dying* (Hobbs). At the University of Pennsylvania, undergraduate English faculty use video-production assignments to enable students to demonstrate their understanding of rhetorical and semiotic concepts (Weigel Information Commons, 2007).

The key elements from the "Code of Best Practices in Fair Use for Media Literacy Education," depicted in Table 1, show the principles and limitations that relate to student use of copyrighted materials in their academic and creative work. It highlights the diverse range of purposes for which students may wish to excerpt copyrighted material, including comment and criticism, illustration, or stimulation of discussion. The principle behind student use of copyrighted materials for media production is identified as fostering and deepening awareness of the constructed nature of all media, which is one of the key concepts of media literacy (Thoman & Jolls, 2005).

The media literacy educators in our focus groups affirmed that students have the right to use copyrighted materials in their compositions, but they acknowledged that fair use must be considered within each specific teaching and learning context.

Learning Context and Situation

Because some media literacy educators are training future professional media makers to adhere to vocational standards and others need to allow for wide experimentation to build creative skills, the application of fair use will vary by context and setting. Some educators felt that editing exercises that make use of copyrighted materials were appropriate for classroom use, but not appropriate for distribution. One college professor pointed out that students need to be made aware of professional norms, arguing, "they get to college and know nothing about professional behavior."

Commentary and Critique

Although educators felt that in some instances, it is educationally valuable for students to go through the permissions-seeking process, they were in agree-

Table 1: Student Use of Copyrighted Materials in Their Academic and Creative Work.

Description	Principle	Limitations
Students strengthen media literacy skills by creating messages and using symbolic forms such as language, images, sound, music, and digital media to express and share meaning. In learning to use video-editing software and in creating remix videos, students learn how juxtaposition re-shapes meaning. Students include excerpts from copyrighted material in their creative work for many purposes, including comment and criticism, illustration, stimulation of public discussion, or in incidental or accidental ways (for example, when they make a video capturing a scene from everyday life where copyrighted music is playing).	Because media literacy education cannot thrive unless learners themselves have the opportunity to learn about how media functions at the most practical level, educators using concepts and techniques of media literacy should be free to enable learners to incorporate, modify, and re-present existing media objects in their own classroom work. Media production can foster and deepen awareness of the constructed nature of all media, one of the key concepts of media literacy. The basis for fair use here in embedded in good pedagogy.	Student use of copyrighted material should not be a substitute for creative effort. Students should be able to understand and demonstrate—in a manner appropriate to their developmental level—how their use of a copyrighted work re-purposes or transforms the original. For example, students may use copyrighted music for a variety of purposes, but cannot rely on fair use when their goal is simply to establish a mood or convey an emotional tone, or when they employ popular songs simply to exploit their appeal and popularity. Material incorporated under fair use should be properly attributed wherever possible. Students should be encouraged to make careful assessments of fair use, and should be reminded that attribution, in itself, does not convert an infringing use into a fair one.

ment that educators and learners should not have to ask permission when using copyrighted materials for the purpose of critical analysis. Educators saw this use of copyrighted materials as deeply associated with First Amendment rights. For example, one filmmaker defended his right to use copyrighted material in a critical analysis, stating, "When *The New York Times* does negative reviews, how is that any different? They don't ask the author's permission to review the book." A college professor agreed: "I don't have to ask permission from Ray Bradbury to use three paragraphs of *Fahrenheit 451*." Another educator took the argument one step further, maintaining that "you have to be able to critique materials without permission from the author—the Ku Klux Klan is not going to give you permission to do an analysis!" This example was powerful for many of the educators who held print and multimedia compositions to different standards. In fact, the standard is the same across the board: Just as a student has the right to deconstruct Ku Klux Klan materials in a written report without the Klan's permission, she has the right to use the Klan's materials in her own multimedia compositions. The social benefits of such an analysis are evident, regardless of the form in which the analysis takes place.

Sensitivity to Message Genre and Developmental Needs of Learners

All of the educators in our focus groups agreed that attribution in multimedia compositions is desirable and appropriate, as a component of ethical behavior. However, there are some instances in which attribution should not be required because of developmental and genre-specific expectations. For example, one technology educator explained that she had a student who created a 90-second video project on sex in the media that incorporated images from hundreds of different sources. It was not feasible or appropriate to this particular montage-style production for the student to list every source in the context of that specific project. Nor is it reasonable to expect the same level of detailed citation from a third grader as from a twelfth grader. However, for multimedia compositions, attribution should be taught and discussed as an important ethical dimension of creative work.

Parallels of Fair Use Across Media Forms

Like Costanzo (2007), the media literacy educators we spoke to saw many parallels between media productions and written assignments. Using copyrighted works without permission (but with attribution and generally in small amounts) was seen as a normative practice with deep parallels to the writing process. As one college professor put it: "There is a good model that is already used in writing. The thesis statement should not be found in the particular aspects that you've borrowed." A high school English teacher agreed: "Using the analogy of scholarly texts, you are framing analysis around it, not just hanging it out there like an ornament. Then I would say it is fair use." Although each situation is different, educators agreed that students and teachers should generally be sensitive to the length or amount of copyrighted materials they use as well as their purpose and intended audience. Students can learn to reflect on the transformative use of copyrighted materials, asking: "In what ways does my use of the copyrighted work add value or re-purpose the work?" Reflective consideration of how and why they are using copyrighted materials deepens student understanding of their own rhetorical, technological, and editorial choices.

Many of the educators in our focus groups maintained that students are more motivated to work on projects when they are allowed to incorporate images and sounds that are meaningful to them. Educators need to help encourage students to make reasoned choices about the ways in which they use copyrighted materials, but students should be allowed reasonable access to the cultural artifacts that they wish to examine. In our meetings, we heard countless examples of innovative student projects that had been curtailed due to copyright concerns. For example, in Philadelphia, one teacher had students retell the story of *Beowulf* by making a comic featuring images of popular actors as Beowulf. In Chicago, one teacher had students create digital videos using "The Simpsons" to tell the story of Romeo and Juliet, and another had students use voiceover, music, and pictures to discuss their responses to the book *To Kill a Mockingbird*. Some of the innovative projects were stopped all together due to copyright concerns, but, more commonly, the activities were allowed to take place but not allowed to be shared beyond classroom walls. Students need to be able to make reasoned choices about the distribution of their compositions, including the option of posting their work online.

DEVELOPING AUDIENCES FOR STUDENT WORK

Whether working from the disciplinary frame of composition, education or media studies, educators share a common belief that "the existence of a real audience can qualitatively change how students conceptualize a production work and what they learn from it" (Buckingham, 2003, p. 187). The Internet provides new ways for authors and audiences to interact with each other in ways that can be very powerful for the teaching and learning of self-expression, creativity, problem-solving and communication skills. Of course, it is important to note that, even apart from the context of educational settings, students have fair use rights as independent creative authors themselves. As we discovered in our research, *The Cost of Copyright Confusion for Media Literacy* (Hobbs et al., 2007), most educators were unaware that the doctrine of fair use supports the use of copyrighted material in all manner of creative work, not just those activities that occur in the context of teaching and learning. As stated in the Code, "If student work that incorporates, modifies, and re-presents existing media content meets the transformativeness standard, it can be distributed to wide audiences under the doctrine of fair use" (Center for Social Media, 2008).

Authentic audiences are a means to increase student ability to analyze and reflect upon the content, form, and effectiveness of their messages—whether that means showing it to a city council or placing it online. In addition to deepening student reflection, authentic audiences help students see themselves and their communities as worthy of attention, encourage students to become active as citizens in addressing community issues, support the possibility of social change, and enhance student motivation and engagement in ways that increase their investment in the process.

Audience Response to Multimedia Composition is Part of the Process

The process of peer review, critique, and redrafting is essential for reflecting on creative and editorial choices in compositions of all kinds. Composition educators have long recognized that students learn about writing from seeing how audiences respond to their work. According to Buckingham (2003), student creations should not be viewed as end products, but as "a starting point for reflection or a basis for redrafting, rather than a summation and a demonstration of what has been learned" (p. 136). Students need to have some genuine motivation to step back from their productions, and to reflect upon their theoretical implications: "Reflection or self-evaluation of this kind has to be driven by something more than abstract requirements of examiners—and it too should be recursive, part of an ongoing cycle of action and reflection" (Buckingham, p. 136).

Student Work Must be Seen as Worthy of Attention

Sharing student work intensifies student motivation and promotes deeper reflection. For adolescents and young adults, this process can have powerful psyc4hological effects on self-esteem and identity development. Steven Goodman (2003) described the ways in which students at the Educational Video Center in New York City were able to reflect upon their choices when they screened their documentary, *The Young Gunz,* in public. He noted that being pressed to answer questions about their production choices and thoughts about the problem of youth violence was a powerful experience for students. Sharing their work with wider audiences can provide students with the kind of external validation they may not receive elsewhere in their lives. Goodman also described the ways in which sharing their documentary with wider audiences helped students see themselves and their communities as worthy of attention when they heard their own voices and saw their own faces projected on a screen in community settings. When students are able to tell their stories to audiences that include not only their teachers and peers but also parents, community leaders, and other adults, the results can be powerful and long lasting. As Goodman wrote, "carried from the margins into the screening rooms of mainstream institutions, these stories of anger, confusion, and sadness reverberated in lasting ways" (p. 46).

Access to Authentic Audiences Supports Civic Engagement

Sharing their work with public audiences can help students become active members of a community. Not only are students able to engage in dialogue that encompasses a greater range of viewpoints than those they might find in a typical classroom, but, also, by interacting with larger audiences, students are able to take on greater responsibility for the messages projected in their work. Goodman (2003) described how students took on the role of experts in their community screenings:

It was also strange for the Doc Workshop students to be up onstage in front of adults and peers, presenting their ideas as journalists and artists and answering questions as experts. This was a role that they had never had before. Even though some claimed their thinking about gun violence hadn't changed, their *talking* about it had. That is, the crew was becoming practiced in public dialogue about public problems. They were getting used to the open and intergenerational exchange of ideas about issues in their community, and the idea that in this public conversation, their ideas and experiences really mattered. After all, their video was at the center of it all. They may not have had all the answers. But by re-presenting a slice of life as they saw it—as raw and imperfect as it may be—back to the community from which it was taken, they were posing a problem that demanded a response.

Audiences can provide students with valuable feedback that can become platforms for social change. Instead of merely showing their work to their peers in a classroom setting, when students are invited to show their work in the community—or online—they are more likely to interact with community leaders and others who can influence public policy or other forms of community activism. Because many youth media production projects deal with issues important to teens (e.g., drugs, school violence, sexuality, stereotypes, dating) it is imperative that their messages reach the eyes and ears of people who can collaborate with youth to create social change. Clearly, the benefits of the civic dialogue that can occur from sharing these types of works should outweigh concerns about the incorporation of copyrighted materials.

Increased Investment in Learning

The promise and potential of an authentic audience can enhance student motivation and engagement in ways that increase their investment in the learning process. William Kist (2005) relayed a conversation he had with an 8th grader named Teri, who created an online advertisement for a class project. When he asked Teri what she thought of this type of project, she answered: "It's more exciting and you learn more stuff, I think, because you're doing something you like to a certain extent and ... then you can learn more stuff, because you want to research it, so you can get a good mark on your webpage, so you can show everyone else" (pp. 55-56).

Media literacy educators in our focus groups recounted stories of low-performing students who were able to shine when they felt genuine ownership and pride and were able to share that work in screenings, readings, or on the Internet. As one high school teacher argued: "The kid is not making any money. The kid's not harming any one. What harm is being done by putting it out there? Versus how much good is being done by motivating the kids and giving them a real audience so they will spend 30 hours on something they would otherwise spend 40 minutes on if I was the only one who was going to see it?"

Pressures to Look "Professional"

In some cases, the ease of posting student productions to Web sites has also intensified pressures that student work look "professional," by adhering to genre conventions and norms of framing, shot composition, sound quality, and more. This reflects the dynamic tension between the "vocational" and "expressive" wings of the media literacy community (Hobbs, 1998). Multimedia composition activities, constructed without sensitivity to this important tension, may encourage students to mimic professionals, resulting in the loss of creativity and of a critical, analytical perspective (Davies, 1996). Video-sharing Web sites like YouTube have contributed to expanding student exposure to various hybrid and amateur genres, including non-narrative and experimental forms. For educators who showcase their students' in-class productions on sites like Teacher Tube (http://www.teachertube.com), video-sharing Web sites may also interfere with the important instructional balance between process and product. Widespread distribution can contribute to over-valuing the formal qualities of a production, sometimes at the expense of message content or the learning process. This focus can contribute to hierarchically organized often teacher-centered productions, where students play roles as production assistants who support the implementation of adult creative energies. In these experiences, students do not get a chance to experience the genuinely messy challenge of collaborative creative work.

Distribution of Student Work is Fundamental

Educators in our interviews and focus groups believe that a reflective pedagogical stance is required to determine when it is appropriate to distribute student work and that there are a number of situations where student work should not be shared widely. As stated in the Code (Center for Social Media, 2008), "educators should work with learners to make a reasoned decision about distribution that reflects sound pedagogy and ethical values" (p. 13). The educators in our focus groups recognized the need for students to distribute their creations to wide audiences, but they were sensitive about matching audience to purpose. For example, most did not feel that skill-building exercises (e.g., a video-editing assignment that makes use of copyrighted materials) require the same amount of distribution as a creative project. Many educators felt that the consideration of audience needs to be strategic and purposeful and that educators need to work with students to arrive at appropriate distribution choices. According to one college professor: "This is part of media education—helping kids figure out audience, purpose, expectations, and ramifications." A youth media educator elaborated on the need for educators to think carefully and critically about the purpose of widespread online distribution of student-produced creative work:

I would have to make an ethical decision about whether to make something like that further available. The rush of noncommercial media makers to make things public is something that I have problems with. There is an assumption that the value lies in the mass audience. Our belief is that youth media can have a purposeful audience that can be very targeted and that this is part of what the young people think about when they are creating the work. If the goal is to build media literate young people, the question is: who is the audience? There are many situations in which the young people can decide for themselves who they want to be the audience. If we make a video about a city ordinance and show it at the city council meeting I think that it is more powerful than putting it on YouTube... I think that the main point is not to teach young people to imitate and replicate mainstream formula and norms. The value is not in the number of hits but in the content.

Clearly, there are many circumstances where students benefit greatly from engaging in the process of sharing their compositions with real audiences. They also learn from the process of considering their target audience and the potential ramifications of distributing work broadly.

CONCLUSION

When students appropriate mass media and popular culture texts, they engage a process that involves analysis, commentary, and creation. Composition teachers should recognize that student response to mass media is an important component of their identity formation, as students sort out their reactions to the complex, paradoxical, and very real forms of cultural power depicted in contemporary music, television, video games, and movies. However, in many school arts and writing programs, there is some hostility to overt signs of repurposed content that comes from mass media and popular culture materials. Educators who create rigid rules about the (non) use of such copyrighted materials sacrifice the opportunity to help young people think more deeply about ethical and legal issues of repurposing, even as most of the classic works of literature used in schools are themselves the product of appropriation and transformation. As Erin Reilly and Alice Robison (2007) argued, "sampling intelligently from the existing cultural reservoir requires a close analysis of existing structures and uses of this material; remixing requires an appreciation of emerging structures and latent potential meanings" (p. 99).

By educating themselves about copyright and fair use and developing a code of best practices, composition and media literacy educators are at the point of the spear in leading a user rights movement that helps all educators reclaim their fair use rights. As we see it, the "Code of Best Practices for Fair Use in Media Literacy Education" has a number of intended outcomes. First and foremost, it is a tool designed to educate educators about copyright and fair use. It will help persuade leaders, librarians, and publishers to accept well-founded assertions of fair use. It will be useful for promoting revisions to school policies regarding the use of copyrighted materials used in education. It may discourage copyright owners from threatening or bringing lawsuits; in the unlikely event that such suits are brought, the Code will provide the defendant with a basis on which to show that her or his uses were both objectively reasonable and undertaken in good faith.

As writing and composition educators connect their pedagogical practices to a deeper understanding of copyright and fair use, they help students make connections between school and society. When students, with encouragement from their teachers, take on higher-level thinking skills and make their own judgments about fair use, they end up engaging in a process that forces them to consider their purpose and rationale for using copyrighted works, considering both the rights of owners and the rights of users. When they incorporate copyrighted materials into their compositions in new and transformative ways, these practices should be recognized as part of the creative process. When students share their works with authentic audiences, they are able to enter a dialogue about social, political, economic, and cultural issues related to their roles as consumers and producers of mediated texts. These are the social benefits that the doctrine of fair use was crafted to support.

NOTES

1. Research methods for phase one of this project are described in *The Cost of Copyright Confusion for Media Literacy* (Hobbs et al., 2007). The interview consisted of open-ended questions organized into three broad categories: (1) how teachers use copyrighted materials in the classroom or other educational settings for educational purposes; (2) how their students use copyrighted materials in their own creative work; and (3) how teachers use copyrighted materials in their curriculum development, materials production or other creative work.

2. Research methods for phase two of this project are more fully described in the "Code of Best Practices for Fair Use in Media Literacy Education" (Center for Social Media, 2008). Ten focus groups were held in various U.S. cities. Focus groups participants were recruited through national membership organizations, including the Alliance for a Media Literate America (AMLA), the Action Coalition for Media Education (ACME), the Student Television Network (STN) and the National Council of Teachers of English (NCTE), and organizations such as National Alliance for Media Arts and Culture (NAMAC) and Youth Media Reporter (YMR).

REFERENCES

Aufderheide, Patricia, & Jaszi, Peter. (2007, April 3). *The good, the bad, and the confusing: User-generated video creators on copyright.* Washington, DC: Center for Social Media, American University.

Benkler, Yochai. (2006). *The wealth of networks.* New Haven: Yale University Press.

Bruce, David. (2007). Multimedia production as composition. In James Flood, Shirley Bryce Heath & Diane Lapp (Eds.), *Handbook of teaching literacy through the visual and communicative arts, Volume II* (pp. 13-18). Mahwah, NJ: Lawrence Erlbaum Associates.

Buckingham, David. (2003). *Media education: Literacy, learning and contemporary culture.* Malden, MA: Polity Press.

Center for Social Media, Media Education Lab at Temple University, and Washington College of Law. (2008). "Code of best practices in fair use for media literacy education." http://www.ncte.org/positions/statements/fairusemedialiteracy

Costanzo, William. (2007). *The writer's eye: composition in a multimedia age.* New York: McGraw Hill.

Crews, Kenneth D. (2001). The law of fair use and the illusion of the fair-use guidelines. *Ohio State Law Journal* 62, 599-702.

Davies, Maura Messenger. (1996). *Making media literate: Educating future media workers at the undergraduate level.* In Robert Kubey (Ed.), Media literacy in the information age (pp. 263-284). New Brunswick, NJ: Transaction.

Gitlin, Todd (2001). *Media unlimited: How the torrent of images and sounds overwhelms our lives.* New York: Henry Holt.

Goodman, Steven (2003). *Teaching youth media: A critical guide to literacy, video production, and social change.* New York: Teachers College Press.

Hobbs, Renee. (1998). The seven great debates in media literacy education. *Journal of Communication,* 55, 865-871.

Hobbs, Renee. (2006) Multiple visions of multimedia literacy: Emerging areas of synthesis. In David Reinking, Michael McKenna, Linda Labbo, & Ronald Kieffer (Eds.), *Handbook of literacy and technology: Transformations in a post-typographic world* (pp. 15-28). Newark, DE: International Reading Association.

Hobbs, Renee (2007). *Reading the media: Media literacy in high school English.* New York: Teachers College Press.

Hobbs, Renee; Jaszi, Peter; & Aufderheide, Patricia. (2007). *The cost of copyright confusion for media literacy.* Washington, DC: Center for Social Media, American University.

Jenkins, Henry. (2006). *Convergence culture: Where old and new media collide.* New York: New York University Press.

Johnson-Eilola, Johndan, & Selber, Stuart A. (2007). *Plagiarism, originality, assemblage. Computers and Composition*, 24, 375-403.

Joyce, Craig; Leaffer, Marshall; Jaszi, Peter; & Ochoa, Tyler. (2003) *Copyright law* (6th ed.). Newark, NJ: LexisNexis.

Kist, William. (2005) *New literacies in action: Teaching and learning in multiple media.* New York: Teachers College Press.

Madison, Michael. (2006). *Fair use and social practices.* In Peter Yu (Ed.), Intellectual property and information wealth (pp. 177-199). Westport, CT: Greenwood Publishers.

Piano, Doreen. (2008). Exchanging life narratives: The politics and poetics of do-it-yourself practices. In James Flood, Shirley Brice Heath, & Diane Lapp (Eds.), H*andbook of research on teaching literacy through the communicative and visual arts, Volume II* (pp. 309-318). New York: Lawrence Erlbaum Associates.

Reilly, Erin, & Robison, Alice J. (2007). Extending media literacy: How young people remix and transform media to serve their own interests. Youth Media Reporter, pp. 96-101.

Thoman, Elizabeth, & Jolls, Tessa. (2005). *Media literacy education: Lessons from the Center for Media Literacy.* In Gretchen Schwarz & Pamela U. Brown (Eds.), *Media literacy: Transforming curriculum and teaching* (pp. 180-205). Malden, MA: Blackwell Publishing.

Tierney, R. (2008). Learning with multiple literacies: Observations of lives exploring meanings, identities, possibilities and worlds. In James Flood, Shirley Brice Heath, & Diane Lapp (Eds.), *Handbook of research on teaching literacy through the communicative and visual arts, Volume II* (pp. 101-108). New York: Lawrence Erlbaum Associates.

Weigel Information Commons. (2007). Thinking creatively about video assignments. A conversation with Penn faculty. University of Pennsylvania, Philadelphia, PA. http://wic.library.upenn.edu/mashup/facvideo.html

Yancey, Kathleen. (2004). Made not only in words: Composition in a new key. *College Composition and Communication*, 56, 297-328.

16 INTELLECTUAL PROPERTY TEACHING PRACTICES IN INTRODUCTORY WRITING COURSES

Nicole Nguyen

How will today's undergraduate writers be confronted with copyright and intellectual property (IP) issues once they leave the safety of the composition classroom? As an undergraduate professional writing student at a land-grant, Big 10, research-extensive institution, I came across the challenges of working within the bounds of IP issues, particularly in presenting my work online. Many of my professional writing classes involve a Web-related element, including several courses that required a final digital portfolio with examples of work done for that particular class. Inside the classroom, I had few questions as to what I could post online and who would be able to see it—I considered these Web postings as existing in a vacuum, with the instructor and the class as my audience.

However, when I purchased my own domain name and bought my own Web space, created my personal Web site and digital portfolio, and began telling people about it (via word of mouth and posts on social-networking sites like Facebook and Livejournal), I realized that my work no longer existed in a vacuum. Conceivably, anyone with Internet access could get to my Web site and see—and potentially take from or use—my work. When I searched for ways to protect my material, I was unsatisfied with the options available to me, such as Creative Commons licensing. Putting a copyright symbol at the bottom of every page was the most straight-forward way to protect my intellectual property, but if I did find that someone had infringed on my copyright, how would I be able to enforce my rights? And, more importantly, why hadn't I been exposed to these kinds of issues in my professional writing classes? This question is the driving force behind my research.

In the fall of 2008, I conducted a study on copyright issues in first-year writing curriculum. What I found was that the challenges I experienced are not limited to me, but are common among college students and will become even more common as we move out of the university setting. In my experience, college classes do not sufficiently address IP/copyright issues. Here I report the findings of my study, which concerns what first-year writing students learn about IP and copyright, and whether these students feel prepared to use that knowledge outside of the university setting.

From what I could find, limited research has been done concerning IP or copyright and academics (other authors in this collection report on the limited existing work; see, for example, Amidon and Galin), and no research has been done to find out what students are actually taking away from their instruction in these issues. I decided to conduct this research in an attempt to fill this void. My research project goes into the classroom: first, I investigated if and how teachers of first-year writing classes teach IP and/or copyright through surveys, and then defined a target audience of classes whose professors have given instruction on IP and/or copyright. These students were surveyed as to how prepared they felt about IP and how effective they felt the instruction was. From these surveys, I further narrowed the pool of students and interviewed several students about their experiences. The interview questions focused on the effectiveness of the teaching, how confident they were about utilizing their IP knowledge outside of the university setting, and the issues for which they feel they need more instruction.

Casual observation has shown me that instruction on IP and copyright issues in the university is lacking and that students do not know the options for protecting their work. Here, I present the findings of my empirical study that informs these casual observations. Ultimately, I hope the audience will be able to use my research to inform first-year writing curriculum and pedagogy as it intersects with the teaching of IP/copyright.

BACKGROUND RESEARCH

My main research question was: Are students learning enough about IP/copyright in their first-year writing classes to feel confident that they can be successful in their future writing endeavors, both inside and outside of the university setting? Additionally, my research questions include the following:
- Are teachers of first-year writing courses teaching intellectual property (IP) and copyrights?
- How much time is being spent teaching IP/copyright?

- Are students utilizing what they have learned about IP/copyright in their first-year writing courses?
- Are students only using this information for in-class assignments, or for assignments in other classes as well?
- Are students using this information for projects outside of school?
- After learning about IP/copyrights in class, do students feel that they have sufficient knowledge to make informed decisions about IP/copyright in the future?

To this end, I designed and implemented a mixed-method study using both a survey and interviews, drawing upon the work of John Creswell (2003), Huiling Ding (2007) and Martine Courant Rife (2008). I also draw upon the research of William Fisher et al. (2006); Marjorie Heins and Tricia Beckles (2005); Renee Hobbs, Peter Jaszi, and Patricia Auferheide (2007); and Rife (2008) in presenting the results of an IRB-approved, one-year study wherein I examined how and if teachers of first-year writing classes teach intellectual property and/or copyright.

Intellectual Property in the Writing Classroom

As curriculum of college writing classes grows to include more digital components, there is a growing need to educate students about basic copyright law as well as fair use (Logie, 2006; Rife & Hart-Davidson, 2006) and the challenges and problems associated with it. Of particular importance is situating these issues in the digital realm, because writing for the Web is increasingly becoming more common, especially in light of the fact that many Professional Writing (PW) courses (at Michigan State University and elsewhere) emphasize creating a digital portfolio, both for specific classes and to prepare seniors for representing their undergraduate work at graduation. Digital portfolios serve as purposeful collections of student work that allow students from various backgrounds to demonstrate their strengths on a more even playing field than more traditional methods of assessment would (Georgi & Crowe, 1998).

One scenario to consider is that of adding images to a digital portfolio required at the end of a class term. Particularly in lower-level classes, where students have less of their own work to display, many students may go to the Web to find images and other visual embellishments to add interest to their digital portfolios. Often, this is done by simply typing in a keyword to a search engine, then choosing an image from the search results, and inserting that image directly into a portfolio (perhaps in a banner image, or as a visual element in the content). Google image search results all come with a standardized warning about copyright protections: "Image may be subject to copyright." However, one must do additional research to find out whether or not each image is, indeed, copyrighted and how to get permission to use it. It is hopeful, I think, to assume that the average student will do little more than glance over this warning before appropriating the image for their own uses. In a class project, taking an image from an online source is generally considered fair use, so there is little problem. But if students are not informed about how the transition from student to non-student affects their ability to use Internet images, then we risk sending students the message that they can use images they've found online for anything, at any time.

Current scholarship indicates that fair use is not properly understood by teachers or writing students (Rife, 2008). Additionally, Hobbs et al. (2007) reported that because of a lack of understanding of fair use and copyright, "teachers use less effective teaching techniques, teach and transmit erroneous copyright information, fail to share innovative instructional approaches, and do not take advantage of new digital platforms" (p. 1). The study, conducted by the Center for Social Media at the School of Communication at American University, is an important one because it explores the relationship between teaching practices and beliefs about copyright.

John Logie (2006) asserted that educators have an obligation to teach intellectual property and copyright and to make transparent to students the challenges teachers face when dealing with copyright in the classroom. Particularly in disciplines involving digital communication and composition, there is an implied "awareness of and engagement with copyright questions" (p. 2). However, Logie pointed out that legislation such as the TEACH Act (or Technology, Education and Copyright Harmonization Act of 2002) creates a divided system, in which one tier presumably applies to non-networked classrooms, and a different, more complex set of rules applies to classrooms that engage in "distance delivery." Logie described how many classroom instructors "have a tradition of selective non-compliance with copyright laws," such as those set forth in the TEACH Act, of which students are often unaware. He suggested that actually introducing students to copyright laws—to the frustrations inherent in attempting to follow the laws or in composing and communicating peacefully alongside them—is an "important step toward eventually recalibrating copyright for the Internet era" (p. 3).

Why First-Year or Introductory Writing Classes?

For my research, I chose to concentrate on the IP/copyright instruction in first-year or introductory writing classes for several reasons. First, given the size of the student body and range of subjects offered at MSU (more than 46,000 students and over 200 programs of study), concentrating only on writing classes would give me a manageable subject pool. Second, every student at MSU is required to take two writing classes: one "Tier I" (or first-year) class and one Tier II class (taken at the upper-level, in the major). Tier I classes are usually taken in the first year of university study, and because the class is a university requirement, these classes contain students of various backgrounds and majors. Tier I writing classes at MSU are offered with many different themes, including (among others) science and technology, law and justice, and women in America. Students may choose which class to take, and many will choose a particular 100-level writing class that corresponds in some way to their major. For instance, students interested in a legal career might take the law and justice themed course, while students interested in women's studies might take the class focused on women in America. Third, from a student's perspective, it makes sense to include basic copyright/IP instruction in the curriculum of an introductory writing class so that students can continue to use and build upon that knowledge as they progress toward their degrees. Intellectual property and copyright knowledge is especially important for Professional Writing students as they become communicators in the workforce—performing usability tests, developing web content, managing communication projects, suggesting communication strategies, performing content management, etc. (see DeVoss & Julier, 2009, for an overview of the MSU PW program). According to Rife (2008), professional and technical writers "may easily become leaders among their peers; therefore, we might hope the information and ways of knowing they bring with them from academia are accurate and useful" (p. 11).

I visited and surveyed three writing classes—WRA 110 Writing: Science and Technology; WRA 115 Writing: Law and Justice in the U.S.; and WRA 202: Introduction to Professional Writing. Readings in the two 100-level courses were derived from their themed subject areas. As in many writing classes, the goals were to develop skills in narration, persuasion, analysis, and documentation. The science and technology and law and justice themes of the writing classes were two of eight theme options for the 100-level writing classes offered that semester, and there were no prerequisites for enrolling in any of these classes. The Introduction to Professional Writing class, however, is a 200-level class intended for students in the beginning of the Professional Writing major. The only prerequisite for taking WRA 202 is the completion of the Tier I writing course. The focus of the upper-level class is less on narrative or persuasive writing skills and more on professional style and studies of rhetoric. In accordance with the three focus options in the major (editing and publishing, digital and technical writing, and writing in communities and cultures) students are exposed to many different aspects of professional writing, in particular, writing across media and writing for the Web. The technological components of these classes ensure that the students have some engagement with digital intellectual property concerns, which I saw as an important aspect of my research.

FINDINGS

Teacher Survey

In early fall 2008, I sent a call for survey participants to an email list of teachers of WRA classes, directed at teachers of Tier I writing or introductory Professional Writing classes. This list included all of the teachers in the program (including graduate teaching assistants); the email request contained a brief description of the research and invited teachers who had an IP or copyright component to their class to respond. From this call for participants, I received four responses (which may or may not be indicative of the number of classes that include IP in the curriculum). Of those four, two actually participated in the survey, and both agreed to let me visit their classes to recruit student participants.

Both teachers spent 3 weeks or more on IP/copyright issues during the semester, and their instruction methods were very different. One teacher, Jessica,* used an article about the history of fair use in two ways: first, to introduce the issues and present information to students, and, second, as a writing tool. The students had to read the article and remix it into a two-page press release. The second teacher, Brian, integrated IP/copyright discussions into the coursework throughout the semester and had a guest lecturer visit the class.

Student Survey

The student survey contained several brief questions asking how the students had learned about IP/copyright in their writing class, as well as whether they had received any instruction in IP/copyright before. About 78% of the students in the Introduction to Professional Writing class stated that they had received instruction in this subject before, and their previous experiences varied. Most of the previous instruction the students listed dealt with plagiarism and using citation when writing papers. One student mentioned learning about Creative Commons licensing in a Web-authoring class. Responses to one question were particularly interesting: When asked how long their current writing class had spent on IP/copyright, answers varied from one or two class sessions

(42.9%), 1 or 2 weeks (35.7%), to 3 weeks or more (21.4%). As mentioned earlier, Jessica, the instructor for this class, responded that her class spent 3 weeks or more on IP instruction. This may indicate a pronounced difference in perspective for the definitions of intellectual property and copyright. When paired with the student responses to the question about previous IP instruction, it appears that unless the subject matter is explicitly labeled as pertaining to IP or copyright, students may not associate the material as fitting into that category. More than three-fourths (78.6%) of students stated that they had the opportunity to put their knowledge about copyright/IP to use for a class assignment. The majority of these students indicated that they used this knowledge for the class in question, though two students wrote in detail about projects for other classes in which they were using their IP knowledge.

The law and justice themed class had similar results, despite my expectations that students in this class might be more informed in copyright or intellectual property because of my assumption that students who chose to take this class would be more interested in the subject matter. Two-thirds of the participants said that they had previous instruction on copyright and intellectual property, though none elaborated on what kind of instruction. The responses regarding how much time the teacher spent on IP varied mainly between two answer choices: 57.1% indicated that they spent one or two class sessions, while 33.3% said that they spent 1 to 2 weeks on the subject. About 57.0% of the participants for this class indicated that they had the opportunity to put their knowledge about copyright/IP to use for a class assignment.

Only about half (52.9%) of those in the Writing: Science and Technology class said that they had no previous experience learning about IP/copyright, and those who had learned about it in the past said that they learned about IP in high school, rather than other college classes. In response to how long their current writing class had spent on IP/copyright, answers were similar to those for the law and justice course: one or two class sessions (58.8%), 1 or 2 weeks (35.3%), to 3 weeks or more (5.9%).

Identifying and Explaining Trends in Survey Results

Across the survey results from the three different classes, there is a trend of under-estimation of the amount of time that teachers spent teaching intellectual property/copyright. "I use, mainly, a journal article on the history of the fair use doctrine. Students read it and remix it into a two page press release. We grapple with this project for two weeks (plus revision time)," Jessica said about the inclusion of IP in her syllabus. Students, however, did not list the journal article or the remixed press release. Instead, they noted that their teacher used slides to give them instruction on IP. Again, this shows a marked difference between the perception of subject matter for students and teachers. Because this is present in all three of the classroom student surveys, it represents a general trend in student perception. What is not evident from these surveys, however, is whether or not there is any overlap in what the students listed as the tools used to teach them intellectual property and what tools the teachers actually intended to use in instruction.

Student Interviews/Vignettes: Caroline's Vignette

Caroline is a Professional Writing (PW) junior who, at the time of the interview, was enrolled in the introductory PW class (WRA 202). During her interview, Caroline displayed a view of intellectual property and copyright confined to experiences writing research papers for classes and different methods of citation. When asked how long her PW class had studied copyright, she indicated that this instruction was minimal and consisted of 3 hours, total, throughout the semester. Despite her restrictive definition of IP and copyright, Caroline expressed curiosity about other aspects of copyright and had questions beyond those asked and discussed in class. However, these questions still dealt specifically with writing research papers and primarily with issues of source use and plagiarism: for example, how much can be paraphrased before you should include a citation? When I asked Caroline if she had any concerns about protecting her work, she asked for an example of a situation where her work would *need* protecting. Until that point, she had not considered her work in any other context than a hard copy turned in to a teacher. I described a hypothetical situation in which she would put examples of her work on a personal Web site or portfolio, which is a requirement for graduating PW students at Michigan State University. She grasped the idea immediately, expressing concerns about people taking whole work (or parts) that she published online. She drew on her knowledge of how easy it is to simply use something from a Web site without including attribution, consulting a copyright or use statement, or contacting the author for permission. When asked if she felt that she had enough knowledge about copyright or IP to make a judgment about an issue concerning copyright/IP outside of the university setting, she said that she was more confident in her ability to research and find answers than in her actual knowledge. She said that if she was faced with a situation relating to copyright, she would know how and where to look to find the appropriate response.

Caroline's responses to my interview questions suggest that she is knowledgeable enough about copyright and IP issues to recognize where there may be cause for concern, but only if prompted. She indicated that her definitions and views of IP and copyright have been shaped by writing classes—English classes in high school and PW classes at MSU. It can be inferred from her responses that because these writing classes frame copyright and IP only in terms of research papers, that students do not naturally make a connection between copyright and their rights as creators, or between copyright concerns and the growing availability and easy access to work on the Internet.

Student Interviews/Vignettes: Alice's Vignette

Alice is a PW sophomore enrolled in the introductory Professional Writing course (WRA 202) at the time of the interview. She also is pursuing graphic design as a hobby. She seemed very comfortable with the idea of intellectual property and copyright in the classroom, and was willing to volunteer her concerns about these issues. Alice said that she had been first exposed to copyright issues in a Web-authoring class at MSU, where her instructor talked about copyright and IP in terms of images on the Web. Alice recognized that copyright concerns are present everywhere because "everybody's always worried about what's copyrighted." She also said that studying rhetoric and the use of visuals helped her realize that she has not observed much originality in visuals (this point raises multiple questions and issues worthy of research and discussion, but these questions and issues are beyond the scope of this chapter).

When asked if she felt confident about making copyright judgments outside of the classroom, Alice responded that her confidence depended on the area. She would be more confident working with copyright for images because that's where she initially learned about copyright. She said she would be less confident about video copyrights, though her discussion of the ideas presented in *Bound by Law*, a comic about copyright in documentary films, shows that she has a good handle on basic concepts. Alice also said that she does not think that copyright is common sense, and that important copyright/IP issues should be dealt with by someone who has studied the issues, like a copyright or intellectual property lawyer.

Her class instruction on copyright made Alice more conscious of copyright in her graphic design work, as it pertains to using images from the Web, taking source code from a Web site, or observing Creative Commons licensing (especially when using Flickr images). Having been exposed to copyright and IP concerns in another class, Alice expressed that she wanted to know more about why copyright is important. Her Web-authoring class only touched on the rules to observe when looking for images on the Web, but her introductory PW writing course concentrated a bit more on "why copyright and citation is such a big deal." She implied, though, that this instruction was not sufficient, and said that she would like someone to explain what people can and cannot do in terms of copyright, and then explain why. Alice's responses seem to show curiosity and awareness of copyright and IP issues beyond what was presented in her classes.

Identifying and Explaining Trends in the Interviews

The student interviews did not really exhibit many trends, in part because I was only able to do two in-person interviews (despite having six total volunteers; four of the six did not respond to my follow-up email asking to schedule a time and place to conduct the interview). Caroline and Alice's responses to the interview questions were so different in nature that it is difficult to say whether or not their responses are representative of the complete range of student experiences with intellectual property instruction. One thing that these two interviews do suggest, however, is that a student's prior interest in the subject is a key factor in how well they receive the instruction in class. The curiosity that Caroline showed towards the end of her interview seemed to indicate that she would be receptive to more instruction on the subject and would likely be able to put knowledge to use with a push in the appropriate direction. Alice's curiosity, however, seemed to be in and of itself a driving force for endeavoring to learn more about intellectual property on her own time.

CONCLUSIONS

Answering the Research Questions

Are teachers of first-year writing courses teaching intellectual property (IP) and copyright? Based on the survey results from the initial teacher–participant recruitment survey, it might appear that teachers of first-year or introductory writing classes are not teaching IP/copyright. These results, however, are by no means definitive. Non-participation does not necessarily mean that teachers are not including IP/copyright in their curriculum. Teachers of introductory writing classes may have chosen not to participate in this survey for a variety of reasons, including the fact that it was conducted by an undergraduate student as independent research. In response to the initial recruitment email, at least one teacher responded to me with a number of questions concerning why I was conducting this research and how it pertained to my studies as an undergraduate. After receiving my responses, this teacher declined to participate in the study. Additionally, one must consider that a low response rate for online surveys is not unusual (Andrews, Nonnecke, & Preece, 2003).

How much time is being spent on teaching IP/copyright? For the two teachers who did participate, it can be concluded that teachers who do include IP/copyright in their curriculum do so for a significant amount of time—3 weeks or more in the cases of Jessica and Brian. Their attitudes toward the importance of teaching intellectual property/copyright in writing classes may correspond to the amount of time that they spend teaching the subject. On a scale from 1 to 5, with 5 as "extremely important," both teachers ranked teaching IP/copyright to first-year writing students as a 4 or 5.

Are students utilizing what they have learned about IP/copyright in their first-year writing courses? Over half of the students surveyed (59.6%) said that they have had the opportunity to put to use the knowledge gained from instruction about intellectual property/copyright during their writing class. I would speculate, though, that for students *interested* in learning about IP/copyright, the answer would be yes more often than for students not interested in the subject.

Are students only using this information for in-class assignments, or for assignments in other classes as well? Are students using this information for projects outside of school? For the most part, the students indicated that they used what they learned for in-class assignments. Those who defined copyright/IP instruction as information about plagiarism and citations said that they used their knowledge for other classes where they had to write papers. Very few participants described using the information for projects outside of school. My suspicion here, however, is that, at this point in their academic careers, few students think that they are taking part in projects outside of school. One flaw in this question is that I did not specify what constitutes an outside project. The word "project" carries a school-related connotation that I did not recognize when I created the surveys. Web-related social activities such as Facebook, Flickr, MySpace, and maintaining a personal Web site or blog that I generally consider to be part of an outside project are likely not included in the participants' definitions of "projects outside of school."

After learning about IP/copyrights in class, do students feel that they have sufficient knowledge to make informed decisions about IP/copyright in the future? This is a tricky question to answer after such a small study. After two in-depth interviews, I received such different pictures of how students received and used instruction on IP that I cannot really come to a conclusion. To get a fuller picture of how and what students learn would require a much larger study. Still, though, based on my experience, coupled with the research I have done here, I say no, students do not feel sufficiently prepared based on the knowledge gained in their introductory writing class. Even Alice—who had received previous instruction in the subject, is very interested in the subject on her own, and has been able to incorporate what she's learned so far—does not feel that her instruction has been sufficient. However, this leads to another question: Can one ever really be sufficiently prepared? Copyright and intellectual property law is very complicated and continues to evolve in tandem with digital communication. The nature of the subject is constantly changing, so basic principles learned in the first year of college may never be wholly sufficient. The goal here, I think, is to instill a spirit of curiosity, awareness, and ethics that would lead a responsible student to, at least, think about whether or not there are IP/copyright considerations to make in their work—and to continue to think about these issues once they graduate and are part of the work force.

NOTE

1. Student and teacher names in this chapter are pseudonyms.

REFERENCES

Andrews, Doreen; Nonnecke, Blair; & Preece, Jennifer. (2003). Conducting research on the Internet: Online survey design, development and implementation guidelines. http://www.ifsm.umbc.edu/~preece/Papers/Online_survey_design_IJHCI04.

Aoki, Keith; Boyle, James; & Jenkins, Jennifer. (2005). *Tales from the public domain: Bound by law?* http://www.law.duke.edu/cspd/comics/

Creswell, John W. (2003). *Research design: Qualitative, quantitative, and mixed methods approaches* (2nd ed.). Thousand Oaks, CA: Sage Publications.

DeVoss, Dànielle Nicole, & Julier, Laura. (2009). Profile of Professional Writing at Michigan State University. *Programmatic Perspectives,* 1 (1), 71-87.

Ding, Huiling. (2007). Confucius's virtue-centered rhetoric: A case study of mixed research methods in comparative rhetoric. *Rhetoric Review,* 26 (2), 142-159.

Fisher, William; Palfrey, John; McGeveran, William; Harlow, Jackie; Gasser, Urs; & Jaszi, Peter. (2006, August). The digital learning challenge: Obstacles to educational uses of copyright material in the digital age. A Foundational White Paper. The Berkman Center for Internet & Society at Harvard Law School. Research Publication No. 2006-09. http://cyber.law.harvard.edu/publications/2006/The_Digital_Learning_Challenge.

Georgi, David, & Crow, Judith. (Winter, 1998). Digital portfolios: A confluence of portfolio assessment and technology. *Teacher Education Quarterly,* 25 (1), 73-84.

Heins, Marjorie, & Beckles, Tricia. (2005, December). Will fair use survive? Free expression in the age of copyright control. A public policy report. Brennan Center for Justice. http://www.fepproject.org/issues/copyright.html.

Hobbs, Renee; Jaszi, Peter; & Aufderheide, Patricia. (2007, October). The cost of copyright confusion for media literacy. http://www.centerforsocialmedia.org/resources/publications/the_cost_of_copyright_confusion_for_media_literacy/.

Logie, John. (2006). Copyright in increasingly digital academic contexts: What it takes. Writing in Digital Environments (WIDE) Paper #7. http://www.wide.msu.edu/widepapers.

Rife, Martine Courant. (2008). *Rhetorical invention in copyright imbued environments.* Unpublished doctoral dissertation. East Lansing: Michigan State University. Rife, Martine Courant, & Hart-Davidson, William. (2006). Digital composing and fair use: exploring knowledge and understanding of fair use among teachers and students in a university professional writing program. Pilot study report. SSRN Working Paper Series. http://papers.ssrn.com/sol3/papers.cfm?abstract_id=918822

17 MOVING BEYOND PLAGIARIZED / NOT PLAGIARIZED IN A POINT, CLICK, AND COPY WORLD

Leslie Johnson-Farris

My journey from ordinary, average community college composition instructor to intellectual property rights pedagogical philosopher began during spring semester in 2005. Working in class one day, students prepared mini-presentations on a logical fallacy they were assigned to teach their classmates. I had done this lesson many times before, but this time students could use Microsoft PowerPoint because we were scheduled in a computer-equipped classroom. Two students stood up to give their presentation on "equivocation." They started by projecting a picture of President Bill Clinton, his finger wagging in the air. With a click of the mouse, the famous words also appeared on the screen: "I did not have sexual relations with that woman."

I walked away from that class session impressed not only by students' efforts, but also by how easily the ability to point, click, and copy was necessarily changing my classroom. The picture of Bill Clinton was undoubtedly copyrighted by the Associated Press or some similar organization, so I began asking myself some important questions: "Why shouldn't my students have the same right to use such materials in educational settings that I have?" and "Wouldn't it be overkill to ask students to fully document such uses in perfect MLA style?"

At semester's end, the point, click and copy world came crashing into my pedagogy in a more unwelcome way. In the blind read part of our portfolio assessment process, I received an essay that I had already seen. Unmistakably, the essay was the same work a current student had submitted to me in her portfolio—a rough draft from earlier in the semester, but clearly the same essay. I made copies of my student's essay and the essay I read in the assessment process, and delivered them to our portfolio coordinator, who passed them on to the other instructor involved.

Two days later, I confronted my student with what I had discovered. The student broke down in my office, cried profuse tears, and swore her innocence. I had little reason to doubt her: I had read numerous drafts of the essay, beginning with the initial paragraphs; I had also seen her work on that very essay several times with peer assistants in our writing center. My trust in her was not misplaced. When confronted by my colleague, the other student involved in the situation confessed: Overwhelmed by many factors, he had discreetly helped himself to a friend's essay while supposedly resolving her computer problems.

From there, I began searching for answers. I searched for college copyright, fair use, and plagiarism policies on the Internet. Plagiarism policies were plentiful, but many were vague like my own college's policy:

> Each student is expected to be honest in their own work ... When producing work for a course, students are expected to present their own ideas and to appropriately acknowledge the incorporation of another person's work. Not doing so is dishonest. (Lansing Community College)

Most were better, giving at least some specifics about the types of activities considered plagiarism; a few laid out specific consequences. However, copyright and fair use policies specifically directed at students creating academic work were difficult to find. The preamble to such polices often reads like that of my institution:

> In the educational setting faculty and staff often have the need to use or incorporate, in whole or in part, existing works, information or materials in connection with course preparation, course presentation or course materials. (Lansing Community College)

Students, even as employees of the college, seem not to be considered end users of the policy. A few, like the copyright and fair use policy of Butler Community College, include student employees in the mix, but don't specifically include student classroom activities:

> All Butler Community College faculty, staff, and students are expected to act as responsible users of the copyrighted works

of others ... This policy applies to Butler faculty, staff, students, and other entities performing collaborative work or service for the college, whether compensated by the College or not.

In short, college policies that clearly acknowledged student fair use rights in preparing academic assignments—especially for media materials—were virtually non-existent.[1] In my first forty-six tries, I found only one college that specifically mentioned student work in its fair use statement. Colleges seem to produce only one explanation of copyright and fair use directed at students: warnings about and prohibitions against peer-to-peer file sharing, specifically using any college resources to do so.

College policies concerning intellectual property seem to focus on economic rather than educational issues. Our official statements sometimes address students as quasi-professionals developing content in their student employee positions or as consumers of college resources. When it comes to students as the most junior members of the academic community, we provide dire warnings of copyright violation, but we provide little backing for students as creators of their own intellectual property. Our official policies often fail to acknowledge the applicability of copyright and fair use to student academic work. If we examine our college webpages, we will probably find help for students negotiating copyright issues—with perhaps a small mention that student work is automatically copyrighted once it's put into some tangible form. As instructors, we expect students to contribute to our academic discourse (on a level appropriate to their development), but we give little recognition to student rights in such situations and overwhelmingly focus on their responsibilities. Worse yet, we tend to focus on one sub-issue concerning intellectual property: plagiarism. Yet, if students are not taught the inherent value of their own work in educational settings, we cannot expect them to understand the value of others' work.

I find this situation especially troubling in community college settings with their often intense focus on career training and an over-dependence on adjunct faculty. At my institution, we are seeing a heavy influx of students returning for job training, and nearly all pass through our transfer composition or business/technical writing courses. These students will join a workforce and produce documents using a variety of sources and images available with the click of a mouse. Unfortunately, our transfer composition courses don't always reflect or address this reality. Newly trained adjunct faculty do enter our classrooms with pedagogy that more accurately faces this changing world; they tend to believe that students should, at the very least, be including images in their written work and should consider the implications of using a variety of others' intellectual property. However, in our intensive exit competency assessment, our students often face trouble when images are included, because "we are teaching *writing*." Our faculty discussions of student competency are too often limited to white pages of black, printed text and our discussions of intellectual property are limited to plagiarism and source usage. Because 80% of our faculty are poorly paid adjuncts (many of whom finished their advanced degrees 10 or more years ago), they have little chance for professional development outside of the college's Center for Teaching Excellence, which, in serving a broad spectrum of faculty needs, is not going to address the latest issues in composition and professional writing. Too often, community colleges are meeting the future head-on with 20th-century, if not 19th-century, ideas about written communication and intellectual property. How are we supposed to train 21st-century workers if we are not teaching them to communicate effectively in the 21st century?

Inspired by Jim Porter, Kate Latterell, Dànielle Nicole DeVoss, Johndan Johnson-Eilola, and Stuart Selber (2006) and their call to recognize much of the student use of digital materials as fair use and not plagiarism in its most classic sense, I went to our Curriculum and Instruction Council, the body charged with making such decisions. At that point, in 2006, I asked for two things: First, a more well-defined definition of plagiarism with some clear consequences for those students who intend to deceive, and second, a clear statement of student fair use rights. When it came to the issue of blatant academic dishonesty, some council members supported a change, but others did not. The idea of a student fair use statement met with confusion. Reactions varied from those who saw no need for such a policy, to those who thought students would be covered under the faculty fair use statement, to those who didn't know what I was talking about.

In the end, only the plagiarism policy was changed. Our current statement considers plagiarism as including "but not limited to the use, by paraphrase or direct quotation or the inclusion of electronic sources, of the published or unpublished work of another person without full and clear acknowledgment." Unfortunately, I think my efforts resulted in a step backwards. If an instructor chooses to do so, the current policy could be used against students who use a cartoon or photograph from the Web in a PowerPoint presentation but only give minimal acknowledgement—even if the student avoided complete documentation for sound rhetorical purposes, such as not distracting too greatly from the presentation's visual design.[2]

Still, the next semester, students in my classes continued to weave borrowed media materials into great classroom projects with little formal documentation (in what many of my colleagues would consider incidences of plagiarism or copyright violation). And at the semester's end while reading portfolios as an external reader, I found that a former student, who previously failed a course with me, gave his essay to a friend when they re-took that class together. At the time, I also served as our college's Writing Across the Curriculum coordinator. When our Center for Teaching Excellence asked for workshop suggestions, plagiarism made its way high on the list, and I got the call. Instructors largely wanted to know "how do I catch the villains?" not "how do I help students become good, independent thinkers and ethical researchers?"

Now, over three years later, I still present the plagiarism workshop on a regular basis. If faculty members have suspicions that a student has submitted a plagiarized essay, someone tells them my name and I talk with them about the problem. Much of the conversation revolves around how to respond to the situation because of the institution's near silence on the issue. My college's official outlook on the issues of copyright, fair use, and plagiarism has changed little, but I feel as if I've changed immensely. Despite somehow finding myself as the college's *de facto* plagiarism expert, I encourage my Children's Literature students to borrow pictures of book covers from Internet booksellers when completing various projects. We've had many instructors and even a dean call for the purchase of a plagiarism-detection service, and my opinion is usually asked. I always give a vehement "no," pointing out student rights to their own work.

DONE, NOT DONE

My experiences call to my mind T.H. White's retelling of the Arthurian legends, *The Once and Future King*. In the book, Merlin sends young Arthur to live as an ant. Once there, the future king learns the ants' way of thinking: "done" or "not done." College composition instructors (as well as college policy makers) too often view plagiarism as something a student has "done" or "not done." In reality, though, the inclusion of others' intellectual property into our own work takes on myriad possibilities, where, like all good writing, audience and purpose influence how the writer must handle the situation. I have come to realize that in our discussion of intellectual property our focus is too narrow, our vocabulary too limited, and our pedagogy too restricted. And so, after my failed attempts to change college policy, I began to consider all of the questions that no one seemed to answer: Isn't intellectual property, not plagiarism, the true overarching issue? How can we talk about plagiarism when we don't talk about the value, both philosophically and monetarily, of someone's creative works and ideas? How can we emphasize the need for student research when we don't mention that their ability to include part of another's work in their own is protected by the fair use doctrine? How can we even expect students to understand why we have plagiarism policies and require documentation if we don't discuss the value that the academy places on original thought? How can we prepare them for a world of work where the issues will expand to copyright infringement and not just plagiarism? Instead of confining copyright and fair use to a sign by the departmental copier, shouldn't I be bringing these issues into my classroom, helping my students understand the complicated world in which they must create?

In answering these questions for myself, I decided that a "done, not done" mentality will no longer serve students—if it ever truly did. If a structure and policies do not exist within the college to address these issues, real change would have to start on the ground, in my classroom. I could begin helping students to think about how they use the intellectual property of others and their responsibilities in using those materials. Furthermore, if, as Porter and DeVoss (2006) argued, the ability to "remix" using digital works may help create economic growth, then those who can successfully negotiate that terrain will be in demand as employees. The ability to include all kinds of graphics and media in many different kinds of communication has eliminated the days of grey pages of texts in nearly all contexts; the digital environment in which our current students will work requires them to include, not just refer to, the intellectual property of others—and they must be prepared to consider their rights and obligations in doing so.

Community college instructors, especially, might see such an addition to their pedagogy as a drain on already precious time. After all, our teaching load is heavy. Although College Composition and Communication guidelines state that a teaching load should be limited to 60 students per semester, a 2007 survey by Two-year College English Association found that the average load was 94 students; over 20% of community college writing faculty reported teaching between 111 and 130 students each semester (Jaschik, 2007). Kami Day (2008) acknowledged that

> when community college teachers think about teaching source citation, they think often about teaching students not to plagiarize or about what the consequences should be for plagiarism, partly because they do not have much time to spend learning about and problematizing plagiarism and are not aware of its complexities and gatekeeping functions. (p. 44)

However, as community college instructors, the needs of students to negotiate the various uses of others' intellectual property in various digital environments can no longer be ignored. According to the American Association of Community Colleges (2008a), students at two-year schools make up 46%

of the undergraduate population and 41% of first-time freshmen. Of those students, 63% intend to eventually complete four-year degrees (2008b). As De-Voss and Annette Rosati (2002) pointed out:

> Admittedly, most first-year writing courses and curricula are already packed, perhaps overloaded—testament to the importance of first-year writing. But as we work toward acculturating students into the processes and function of academic writing *and* engaging them in appropriate academic processes, we must make room for addressing new research and writing spaces. (p. 201)

Knowing that I could no longer overlook these complex and pressing needs, I set out to change how I discuss intellectual property within my classroom. Specifically, I wanted students to understand their rights and responsibilities and to learn to think critically about the multitude of ways those rights and responsibilities will influence the work they produce in my class and in the future. My goal, overall, was to integrate discussions about intellectual property into our everyday activities as much as possible. When composition teachers explore the issues surrounding intellectual property, we perhaps limit that conversation to the "plagiarism and source usage day" and fail to see how these issues fit into the other subjects we must cover. Consequently, it's little wonder that when we look at adding to our burden a more comprehensive pedagogy about intellectual property, we may want to say "no more." However, by addressing the issues in small pieces at the appropriate times, perhaps we can weave the necessary discussions into our everyday classroom experiences, with little or no need to give up course time.

In its final report on plagiarism, the U.K.'s Joint Information Systems Committee (JISC) for higher education found that encouraging academic honesty requires that institutions provide students

> with clear explanations of what is valued (integrity, honest, wide-ranging research, choosing and using others' ideas etc.) and why academic conventions are important. Students should encounter the information in printed material, discuss it with teachers, and see staff treating each other in accordance with the principles (Carroll, 2004)

In small doses throughout each term, I attempt to do just that: Put the expectations in writing, encourage discussion about such issues (both in the outside world and in their own writing for the class), and model my decision-making processes when it comes to borrowed intellectual property. In this way, I've added very little to my workload, but I have extended the breadth and depth of our deliberations about these issues. The purpose in describing the work in my classroom here is to demonstrate that it is possible to expand the discussion of intellectual property well beyond the "done, not done" mode of teaching plagiarism in the first-year composition classroom—without detracting from important tasks already at hand. Instead, by changing how we present our course documents and cover topics such as the conventions of documentation, research, and source usage, we can begin to prepare students to negotiate the digital environment in which they must work and produce written communication.

EVERYDAY WORK WITH INTELLECTUAL PROPERTY CONCERNS

Course Policies and Documents

The first day of any class is usually spent in course logistics, such as reviewing the syllabus and grading policies. I include definitions of intellectual property, copyright, fair use, and plagiarism in my syllabus. Even if I point out those particular policies with my class and direct students to Web sites that define copyright and fair use and provide resources for avoiding plagiarism, I can't just say "go and look." I have also had to teach myself to express the various definitions in everyday terms, understandable to students fresh out of high school as well as those who have been out of school for many years. Intellectual property, I try to tell students, is much like real estate: It is property a person can own. Although the ideas behind creative works—such as books, songs, and paintings—can't be touched and manipulated like physical property, they still belong to the creator. Copyright is a law that guarantees creators of such materials control over how their works and ideas are used in the future. Copyright law, I try to explain, prevents others from making money off the creator's ideas; in other words, copyright holders can charge or require permission for someone to use their original work. If someone unethically uses that work without the creator's permission or paying for such use, we call that infringement. Luckily, I tell my classes, the fair use doctrine provides exceptions to copyright control for educational and other creative purposes. Plagiarism, I try to point out, is a very different—but still unethical—use of someone else's intellectual property. Plagiarism is claiming (or giving the appearance of claiming) someone else's intellectual property as one's own, especially in academic settings.

I attempt to set the discussion within the context of the academic world and the world they will enter as professionals. We talk about how plagiarism (taking credit for work not their own) will be their main concern while in college. In submitting papers using outside sources for college credit, they're using parts of another's work and not attempting to make money; therefore, fair use protects them from copyright infringement. Unfortunately, if they submit someone else's work as if it were their own, they are attempting to receive that college credit dishonestly. In this case, they have committed plagiarism. In completing their course work, they may not be faced with decisions about using copyrighted materials outside those fair use principles. Someday, however, such decisions could affect their job, their employer, and the financial and legal standing of all involved. If they don't examine who owns an idea or creative work and don't analyze their motives in using all or part that original work, they could be asking for trouble. In my class, in future classes, and in their careers, they absolutely must consider audience and purpose (as well as personal motive) if they hope to make the best decisions they can about the uses of others' works.

My students also begin the semester learning a simple truth they've probably never deeply considered: They own the rights to the work they produce in my class—and indeed the work they produce in any class. I spell out those rights along with my limited rights to read and respond to their work in my syllabus. On the very first day, students complete, only if they so choose, an "Informed Consent for Use of Student Work" that reinforces their ownership of their work and gives me the ability to use their work in certain settings.

If administrators, instructors, and copyright holders wonder why students hold so little respect for the intellectual property rights of others in a digital age, we should probably look no further than how we view student work. To catch the students who knowingly and unknowingly plagiarize, more and more colleges require students to submit every essay to a plagiarism-detection service. Plagiarism-detection services require that students sign releases, essentially acknowledging that the service has "the right to 'reproduce, display, disclose, and otherwise use' student work for their business purposes" (CCCC IP, 2006). The underlying message here is, of course, that their original work holds little value in comparison to the need to catch others who submit unoriginal work. Although most students probably never consider that their work has any creative value, they need to begin somewhere, understanding that their ideas and thoughts hold value and that they deserve authorial and legal credit for them. We should start that understanding in our composition classrooms. We cannot expect them to make good decisions about the ownership and credit of others' work until they see themselves as authors who must make decisions about how they will allow others to use their intellectual property.

Leslie Johnson-Farris

The Philosophy and Mechanics of Documentation

In the reflections my students complete throughout the semester, they regularly vent their frustration at the mechanics and seemingly arbitrary rules of the MLA documentation system. To combat such resistance, I used to fall back on the "do it or it's plagiarism" mentality—clearly just another version of that "done, not done" mode of thinking. Now, I realize the importance of explaining to students the rationale behind documentation and citation, no matter what system a student is required to use in an essay. In a sense, I attempt to answer the question so many students ask about documentation: "Why do we have to do this?" To answer that question, we begin by referring back to the syllabus and to information about copyright, fair use, and plagiarism. When I ask them about the audience and purpose of their college essays, students reliably respond with "you, my other professors" and "to show that I'm learning something." Students and I, therefore, work under the assumption that what we do is for the sake of education and not for economic gain—that what they're doing falls under fair use. Still, that recognition alone doesn't answer their "why do we have to do this?" question when it comes to documentation. Consequently, we need to discuss certain values in the academic world, touching on three important points.

First is that those in a college or university setting value original thinking. Students create knowledge. Very importantly, though, that original thinking and newly created knowledge doesn't just come from nowhere, but from careful consideration of what others have said. As members of the academy, we include the basis for our new knowledge and ideas within our written work. When we incorporate such source materials in an educational setting, we do not need to ask for permission, but we do need to fulfill our responsibility to recognize the creators of those materials, thus avoiding plagiarism. Because we place equal value on original thinking and positioning ourselves within the ideas of others, we have an exceptionally high responsibility to fulfill in formal essays. To demonstrate that we have included the ideas and knowledge of others as well as added to the larger academic discussion, college writers need to clearly distinguish their own ideas and knowledge from the ideas and knowledge of others. Citation signals to readers that "the borrowed materials end here." Looking at professional essays and sample student essays helps students to understand that even the most rudimentary citations help to distinguish the writer's research from their own knowledge.

Second, we discuss how educators value knowing the dependability of a source. We also have our own credibility or ethos to maintain. The more authority our sources have, the better we look as writers. Along those same lines,

I tell students that they just might inspire someone to find and read one of their sources. I've demonstrated how an idea presented in an article I read on plagiarism led me to yet another article and that article led to yet more and varied reading. I point out how I discovered the second article by tracing the references in the first article I read and how the same scenario played out in the works cited of the next article.

Third, people in the business of creating and disseminating knowledge—particularly college professors and students—largely want acknowledgement for their ideas. My students admit readily that they want their work acknowledged with a good grade. I hope to build on that point and explain that college professors want to have their ideas acknowledged by others—whether those others agree with them or not. In considering such intellectual property issues, Laura Murray (2008) argued that "plagiarism and copyright infringement are transgressions against two distinct but overlapping economies of knowledge: citation systems and market systems" (p. 174). With this in mind, I now attempt to guide student use of others' work in a way that will make them think in both their academic and professional careers. Borrowing Murray's notion of citation as "the currency of our research," I tell students that we really should recognize others' ideas, even if they're covered under the doctrine of fair use in their school work. Consequently, we must always ask ourselves a question, "must I pay with the currency of citation or the U.S. dollar?" In the essays they write during their college career, I hope students consistently answer that they must pay with the currency of citation. I also hope that when the question of paying for intellectual property comes up in their professional lives, they will again give careful consideration to audience and purpose and decide on the proper pay: recognition or financial payment, as needed.

Even with their understanding the need for citation, students balk at paying attention to the details of MLA documentation style. To impress upon students the value of well-done documentation, I've returned to the "pay with citation currency" idea: I've been holding Works Cited auctions. I bring in samples of several works cited pages from real student essays, including both poor and excellent examples. Students are then assigned to role play the author of one source on any one of the works cited. The question, of course, becomes, "were you happy with the 'citation pay' you received for your intellectual property?" We can set an "exchange rate" for each sample works cited by reversing the process and have some students "bid" on the work cited they want for their essay. The monetary analogy seems to work; students come to understand that poorly done documentation is worth very little in the currency of citation, so we set out to learn and use the mechanics of documentation to the best of our ability.

Leslie Johnson-Farris

Research and Source Evaluation

My institution emphasizes library research, and many of my colleagues view the Web as the enemy—the tempter, seducing students into plagiarism and poor choices about materials used in their essays. DeVoss and Rosati (2002) pointed out, however, that "to make the Web a better research space—a space where students will be doing critical, thoughtful, thorough research instead of searching for papers to plagiarize—we must engage students in tasks appropriate to the complexity of the online space" (p. 201). Most of us, in our undergraduate composition courses, were taught to look up a source in references such as *Periodicals for College Libraries* to determine its appropriateness for our essays. In our current digital environment, the Web can be used to provide students with a much deeper and richer view of the sources they are using. My students begin the process of evaluating sources with exactly what they're supposed to be using in their essays, a periodical found on and downloaded from the library subscription databases. Unfortunately, that span of several gray pages provides very little context for the student to reach any conclusions about the source, but browsing the publication's Web site provides more insight into a source's value than any reference work.

When researching and evaluating sources, students and I look at their sources through the same lens of intellectual property and academic values. Students take a source—from *The Nation* or *The National Review*, for instance—and first find the homepage for the publication. Immediately, the headlines and political cartoons clue students into any potential biases in the source. When they visit the sites for *Time* or *Newsweek*, they are annoyed by the pop-up ads, but they are absolutely clear that the purpose of these publications, on some level, is to make money. In visiting the online presence of scholarly journals, students see the editorial boards, submission guidelines, and intended audience for these publications. They learn to follow important links like "About Us," where they can learn whether the authors of the source are journalists or experts on some level. Side searches can help them find the curriculum vitae of the "expert" authors in journals and how the publications stack up against a variety of Web sites dedicated to their topics. All along, we ask the same questions students should always be asking about the value of these sources, framing our discussions and reports in the terms of academic values and intellectual property we have already discussed:

- Does the source reference and integrate the work of others?
- Does the source say something new or intriguing about the topic?
- Does the source pull from a plurality of ideas or just a few?

- Does the source pay with "the currency of citation" for the ideas of others?
- Is the authorship of the source clear? If not, is the ownership of the source clear?

In 15–20 minutes of surfing, students instinctively learn more about the value of authorship and ownership of intellectual property (and how it can enhance their own work) than I could teach in days of lecture.

The Requisite Plagiarism Discussion

When presenting the general topic of plagiarism, the discussion must center on what constitutes both proper use and misuse of others' intellectual property. The goal, as Porter and DeVoss stated in a 2006 conference presentation, is that "instead of becoming plagiarism police, our role should be to teach students how to make ethical decisions regarding copying and the re-use of others' text." The U.K. Joint Information Systems Committee (JISC) found that plagiarism must be explained to students in "everyday language" in conjunction with examples of both acceptable and unacceptable behaviors (Carroll, 2004). If ethical decision-making is indeed the goal, then, necessarily, the discussion centers on two variables familiar to all first-year composition instructors: audience and purpose. Appropriate to this goal is a problem-based learning approach in which students must make decisions for themselves about the motives behind utilizing others' works. I have tried several versions of this task: the latest involves students examining a variety of works regarding the use or misuse of others' intellectual property, some of it clearly copyrighted material. These works include:
- an essay purchased from an online paper mill;
- an essay filled with ideas cut and pasted from sources, improper paraphrases, and missing citations;
- a church bulletin, featuring the famous picture of a sailor kissing a nurse on Times Square during V-E Day celebrations (with no recognition of the photographer or copyright holder), to commemorate Veteran's Day;
- a PowerPoint presentation, submitted for an assignment in an online class, in which borrowed pictures are referenced only with the photographer's name and URL;
- a YouTube video, usually a mash-up, such as Monty Python's "Camelot" playing against scenes from the original *Star Trek* series; and
- a television commercial featuring a popular song as background music.

Students are told only that the works utilize the intellectual property of others. Working in groups, they research and discover the original source materials; locate definitions and policies concerning copyright, fair use, and plagiarism (including those of our own institution); make a determination as to the appropriate use of the intellectual property; and pose recommendations for further action. Students are told they must examine the purpose and intended audience for the work they scrutinize, and they report their findings to the entire class.

In the discussion that follows, I have to give the warning that all good composition teachers must: Misrepresenting the works of others as your own will most likely result in failure. At this point, I have tried to expand the vocabulary I use, hoping to move beyond simply a monolithic offense of plagiarism. Although "everyday language" is important, students need to know that plagiarism is not just a blanket offense. For example, when I present prohibitions against buying, borrowing, or stealing an essay, I make sure to use the word *collusion*, the term used in British and Australian universities for such an offense. Similarly, when students piece together parts of other works to make themselves sound better, I refer to it as *mosaic plagiarism*. I explain how this type of plagiarism, like collusion, is intended to deceive readers into thinking the writer created something new. My experience working with other faculty members has taught me that our vague college policy and the lack of clear policies and consequences in individual syllabi lead to a great deal of the worst instances of plagiarism on campus. Therefore, students and I refer back to the syllabus and the policy I noted to them at the semester's start, and I make clear the consequences for this worst of offenses: If students are caught intentionally misrepresenting another's work as their own, they will receive a 0.0 in the course.

Our discussion eventually leads us to inadvertent plagiarism, that offense committed by students who do not yet have adequate skills in documentation and source integration. To assist students in learning how to correctly and ethically integrate sources, they submit copies of the actual sources to me along with their essays and they are expected to revise to eliminate poor source integration. If they still are not correcting plagiarism that's the result of poor source integration or documentation in revised essays (especially after they've been warned about the problem), they should not expect a 2.0—the grade that will make the course acceptable as a core, transferable class—because they have not met the course learning objectives. Time and opportunity to learn must be given to students as they learn these academic conventions; they will not grow as authors unless we clearly distinguish between the various types of plagiarism for them and provide them with the methods to adjust to the standards of authorship in academia.

Intellectual Property in Digital Realms

Because our program's outcomes are still firmly anchored in print-based production, finding methods to teach students about intellectual property in digital and online environments has been difficult. However, even for such text-heavy classes, composition teachers can find some means for teaching about digital rights management. My students maintain a wiki that they pass onto future generations of students. They leave written advice on a variety of topics for making it successfully through Composition II. They illustrate their ideas with photographs they take themselves, short videos on topics of interest, and add screen shots of essays to illustrate points. Before they start adding to the wiki, we click on the Creative Commons Attribution Share-Alike 3.0 License link that appears at the bottom of our page. They explore the Creative Commons site and learn what rights we are retaining for our work. In addition to learning where they can find "free" resources, students have also had to make the difficult decision not to use "the perfect" cartoon or picture because they do not have the rights to do so.

MOVING FORWARD, IF ONLY A STEP AT A TIME

As composition instructors, we can no longer ignore that communication is changing. Students are already heavy consumers of multimodal texts, not only taking in the written word that appears on their computer screen, but also the video, pictures, and graphic materials that surround it. We need not doubt that they have the ability to copy and paste or otherwise embed what they find on the Web into their work. Moreover, the 21st-century workplace will probably demand that they do so—and that they do so ethically. No one, especially in an academic environment, would argue that we should allow students to dishonestly take credit for the work of others; however, we need to prepare students to make the best, most creative use of what the digital world has to offer and do so in a way that appropriately recognizes others' intellectual property. As Kathleen Henning (2003) posited: "Teaching must integrate the best of technology with the best of the 'old' ways, accepting inevitable change even if it doesn't seem better at first" (p. 311).

Compositionists understand reading and writing as basic literacies. However, if we carefully examine current pedagogy, we will find that we have long been imparting another kind of literacy—the literacy of intellectual property—even though we never saw it as such. We have always taught about plagiarism and the proper citation of source material. Like it or not, the onslaught of the digital realm has increased the urgency and scope of that literacy. We must now think about issues of copyright, fair use, and digital management rights in addition to plagiarism. Deborah Brandt (1995) noted that literacy has two ways of expanding. First, a literacy can increase *vertically* as we learn and accumulate of a certain kind of literacy; for example, we can expand our written or spoken vocabulary. Second, literacy can increase horizontally by adding on new types of literacies. Once, we only had a spoken vocabulary, but eventually we learned to read and write as well as do math. We need to expand intellectual property rights literacy both vertically and *horizontally* in our first-year composition classrooms.

Such an expansion will no doubt be uncomfortable for many of us, and we surely will only be scratching the surface of that new literacy. Fortunately, we need not overturn everything we are currently doing. Instead, writing instructors simply need to examine what they are already teaching and find methods for including a deeper discussion of intellectual property use and abuse. Through my experience, I've learned that by making intellectual property part of our regular discussions, students are beginning to ask questions as they go. After reading a sample student essay, one young woman asked, "She used the exact word I wanted for my essay, but I didn't know so until I read it. If I use that word, is it plagiarism?" The class overwhelmingly decided no; it was not plagiarism. She was not stealing the writer's ideas; she was simply realizing that she had found the exact word she was searching for. While doing his research, another student found an article title, based on a pun, and he wanted to use that same pun for his title. His peer reviewers, before I could even give input, had already decided that he could probably use a similar pun but couldn't "steal" the exact title. They, too, have now expanded the discussion of intellectual property beyond a "done, not done" view of plagiarism. Hopefully, they also now care more about the precedents for and originality of their own work.

In a point, click, and copy world, writing instructors must be called to become intellectual property pedagogical philosophers. We must advocate for clear but strong policies against the misuse of intellectual property, including the abuse of student rights to their own work. As we stand up for our own rights to fairly and ethically use others' intellectual property in our academic pursuits, we must also insist on students having those same rights in their academic pursuits. Although the work of expanding the literacy of intellectual property begins with infusing it into many facets of our first-year composition courses, it cannot end there.

NOTES

1. As an example, Chris Boulton's (2007) master's thesis analyzed print advertisements for designer children's clothing. However, unable to clear the copyright on many of the advertisements he examined, the University of Massachusetts-Amherst, based on their graduate school's Guidelines for Master's Theses and Doctoral Dissertations, forced the removal of the ads from bound copies and versions available through university's Web site. UMass guidelines fail to even mention fair use exceptions for its students pursuing any research that might involve commenting on copyrighted materials. For more information, refer to Open Access resources at http://www.openstudents.org/2008/07/08/fair-game/

2. To my knowledge no student has yet to face serious disciplinary action for such source usage. Similarly, the policy has had little effect on those who commit truly serious infractions. In fall semester 2008, a developmental writing student submitted a purchased essay as part of his portfolio for exit competency assessment, and was caught. When his instructor awarded him a 0.0 for his efforts, he told her, "I didn't get much for my $45, did I?" The student then simply retook the placement test and received the bare minimum score needed for entrance into our transfer-level composition course.

REFERENCES

American Association of Community Colleges. (2008a). CC stats. http://www2.aacc.nche.edu/research/index.htm

American Association of Community Colleges (2008b). Degree attainment. http://www2.aacc.nche.edu/research/index_students.htm

Boulton, Chris. (2007). *Trophy children: A textual analysis of print ads for designer children's clothing.* Unpublished Masters Thesis. Amherst, MA: University of Massachusetts.

Brandt, Deborah. (1995). Accumulating literacy: Writing and learning to write in the twentieth century. *College English*, 57, 649–668.

Butler Community College. Copyright policy. http://is.butlercc.edu/policy_copyright.pdf

Carroll, Jude. (2004). *Institutional issues in deterring, detecting and dealing with student plagiarism.* Joint Information Systems Committee. http://www.jisc.ac.uk/publications/publications/pub_plagiarism.aspx

Conference on College Composition and Communication Intellectual Property Caucus. Recommendations regarding academic integrity and the use of plagiarism detection services. http://ccccip.org/files/CCCC-IP-PDS-Statement-final.pdf

Day, Kami. (2008). Time is not on our side: Plagiarism and workload in the community college. In Rebecca Moore Howard & Amy E. Robillard (Eds.), *Pluralizing plagiarism: Identities, contexts, pedagogies* (pp. 43-61). Portsmouth, NJ: Heinemann.

DeVoss, Danielle Nicole, & Rosati, Annette C. (2002). "It wasn't me, was it?": Plagiarism and the web. *Computers and Composition*, 19, 191-203.

Henning, Kathleen. (2003). Writing 2003: Shifting boundaries and the implications for college teaching. *Teaching English in the Two Year College*, 30, 306-316.

Jaschik, Scott. (2007, March 27). The overflowing composition classroom. *Inside Higher Education*. http://www.insidehighered.com/news/2007/03/27/workload

Lansing Community College. Policies and procedures. http://www.lcc.edu/policy/policies_3.aspx

Murray, Laura J. (2008). Plagiarism and copyright infringement: The costs of confusion. In Caroline Ross & Martha Vicinus (Eds.), *Originality, imitation, and plagiarism: Teaching writing in the digital age* (pp. 173-182). Ann Arbor: University of Michigan Press.

Porter, James E., & DeVoss, Dànielle Nicole. (2001). Rethinking plagiarism in the digital age: Remixing as a means for economic development. Paper presentation at the WIDE Research Center 2006 Conference, East Lansing, MI. http://www.wide.msu.edu/widepapers/devossplagiarism

Porter, James; Latterell, Catherine; DeVoss, Dànielle Nicole; Johnson-Eilola, Johndan; & Selber, Stuart. (2006). Why plagiarism makes sense in the digital age: Copying, remixing, and composing. Panel presentation at the Conference on College Composition and Communication, Chicago, IL.

18 *COUTURE ET ÉCRITURE*: WHAT THE FASHION INDUSTRY CAN TEACH THE WORLD OF WRITING

Brian Ballentine

> "Fashion has always been about inspiration. Designers are inspired by nature, by culture, by events, by other designers. But there is a difference between inspiration and plagiarism."
>
> stopfashionpiracy.com

In "Framing Plagiarism," Linda Adler-Kassner, Chris Anson, and Rebecca Moore Howard (2008) stated that "plagiarism is *hot*. Nor is that heat limited to the popular media; colleges, faculty, and students are equally consumed by the notion that plagiarism is widespread and uncontrollable" (p. 231). Plagiarism has now found application and resonance in the world of fashion. The above epigraph is taken from the opening narration of an approximately 10-minute video decrying the ills of fashion piracy and advocating increased intellectual property protection, specifically copyright, for clothing design. Indeed, the use of the word "plagiarism" to describe copied fashion design should be viewed as rhetorical and deliberate. As Moore Howard (2007) reminds us elsewhere, "plagiarism is a discourse developed with that of copyright;" and although it is an ancient term, it was not until the rise of the printing press and its "monetary opportunities" in the 18th century did the term become common (p. 7). As such, it is the perfect word selection for those wishing to excoriate pirates in the name of "protecting" originality when profits are concerned. However, as Jessica Litman (1994) argued, "the model suggesting that production and dissemination of valuable, protectable works is directly related to the degree of available intellectual property protection is much too simplistic. In fact, history teaches us a more equivocal lesson" (p. 46).

Delving into that history and intellectual property's ambiguity, law professors Kal Raustiala and Christopher Sprigman (2006) argued convincingly that the "fashion industry flourishes despite a near-total lack of protection for its core product, fashion designs" (p. 1762). The absence of protection runs counter to how we typically understand the role intellectual property "should" play when a creative work such as design is involved. Cutting-edge designs parading down a fashion runway in Paris or New York are digitally photographed and emailed off to design houses where they are reverse engineered (or perhaps more appropriately, reverse designed) and then mass produced at a discounted rate for the general public. Celebrities showing off exclusive *haute couture* on the red carpet generate the same results. However, rather than stifling innovation, the missing copyright protection for fashion designs creates what Raustiala and Sprigman called a "piracy paradox" where the rapid proliferation of copied artifacts actually benefits designers by making trends obsolete faster, thus pushing innovation and increasing sales. The process of shortening the shelf-life of new designs and quickening what is known as the "fashion cycle" is called "induced obsolescence" in the fashion industry (p. 1722). Fashion design thrives in this largely unexplored "negative space" within intellectual property law (Raustiala & Sprigman, p. 1776).

This chapter details my experience in this negative space—teaching a business and professional writing course where the student body was comprised almost entirely of Textile, Apparel, and Merchandizing (TAM) majors. When we arrived at the portion of the course that dealt with the intersections of writing, intellectual property, and ethics, the students took a keen interest in learning more about copyright law's minimal sway within fashion design. In the academic setting, students receive constant reminders regarding the ills of plagiarism and copying and the importance of citing sources as inherent to upholding academic integrity. The opportunity to explore academic integrity and issues of intellectual property by pairing them with the current debates from the world of fashion was, I thought, too good of a teaching opportunity to let go by. In the middle of the semester, I adjusted the course readings and assignments and asked student groups to prepare to argue for or against fashion "piracy."

The trouble with "teaching" plagiarism is that "many cases of so-called plagiarism occur at the borders where one set of (typically academic) values and practices blurs into another (typically public) set of values and practices"

(Adler-Kassner et al., 2008, p. 239). Along with Adler-Kassner and her colleagues, I do not condone blatant plagiarism of another writer's work, but I do believe the world of fashion stages an effective teaching environment by contrasting an academic context with this unique professional space. In this chapter, I argue that the deliberate introduction of intellectual property issues and this specific fashion debate offer an effective means of reaching the goals and objectives for a business and professional writing course. In the first section, I briefly introduce course goals and examine class dialogue surrounding intellectual property. This beginning portion of the chapter serves as a backdrop for untangling some of the relationships knotting together plagiarism, copyright, and trademark. That untangling also necessitates a brief overview of the protection that intellectual property law provides for the world of fashion and how those protections are minimal in the United States as compared to Europe. I then examine a bill introduced twice to the U.S. Congress, the Design Piracy Prohibition Act, written to extend Title 17 of U.S. Code to grant copyright protection to fashion designs for 3 years. After discussing several student projects that argued for and against the passage of the bill, I claim ultimately that students left the writing class with more than just a set of rules regarding what they cannot do and instead developed more nuanced conceptions of intellectual property and plagiarism.

EXPLORING "NEGATIVE SPACES" IN THE WRITING CLASSROOM

Maybe not in large enough quantities, but curriculum yoking writing instruction and intellectual property exists; this chapter is just one small exploratory offering (Howard, "Syllabi"; see, also, other chapters in this volume). The course and curriculum discussed here relate to a business and professional writing course enrolling juniors and seniors from a wide range of majors. Because the course satisfies a university general education requirement, it is not uncommon to find science, engineering, and humanities majors of all kinds taking the course. This particular semester happened to enroll a large majority of TAM majors—19 of 22 students.

Course goals for business and professional writing classes emphasize fostering critical thinking skills as students evaluate rhetorical situations, assess audience needs, and compose and revise work (see Herrington, 1981; Knoblauch & Brannon, 1983; Odell, 1980). A persistent challenge to any number of writing courses, but especially courses like business and professional writing or technical writing, is that they attempt to prepare students for communicative contexts governed by value systems and protocols often much different from academic standards. According to Jessica Reyman (2008), "a division between workplace practices and academic expectations distances our classrooms from the workplace and presents students with an unclear picture of what is allowable and in what contexts it is allowable" (p. 64). In reflecting on my own professional experience as a software engineer responsible for a great deal of writing, much of the work our team produced was highly derivative and, by academic standards, "plagiarized." For a group of software engineers developing new applications for the medical market, our company had established a particular professional ethos and its technical and promotional documentation helped support that ethos. It would have been presumptuous, if not foolish, for each of us to compose materials in such a fashion that strove to demonstrate "authenticity" or "original authorship." The goal was to appear as a unified front of products and services; for our writing to accomplish that goal, we borrowed and patch wrote. Indeed, George Pullman (2005) suggested that technical and professional communicators would be wise to become accustomed to "thinking about text as reusable chunks of information" (p. 50).

Responding to these variances in professional writing contexts and practices, one of Reyman's (2008) proposed curricular solutions integrates "discussion of legal definitions of authorship" explicitly into her course (p. 64). Rather than just preaching plagiarism guidelines, Reyman advocates expanding on the legal guidelines for what constitutes work-for-hire as well as examining the fair use doctrine. Finally, she is a proponent of pushing students to apply critical thinking skills to intellectual property and authorship:

> Introducing scenarios, both in the classroom and in textbooks, that ask students to wrestle with understandings of the legal and ethical implications of copying and re-use allows for exploration of plagiarism as a context-specific concept. Scenarios addressing such concerns might include nontraditional acts of composition, such as ghostwriting, work-for-hire, collaboration, and using boilerplates, that challenge the single-author model. (p. 65)

Her solution is admirable, but for many of us it may mean stepping outside our classroom comfort zones. That said, addressing what Moore Howard (2007) called the "widespread hysteria" over Internet plagiarism will require facing these challenges. Again, this is no easy task; from legal scholars like Litman we do not exactly get words of encouragement. Litman noted, "the moral of the story: some things are easier to teach than others. The current copyright statute has proved to be remarkably education-resistant. One part of the problem is that many people persist in believing that laws make sense" (p. 50).

My attempt to introduce students to a more nuanced understanding of intellectual property and its relationship to writing was by way of using the current debates within the fashion industry as a scenario. The scenario is fortuitous in that we are witnessing the law while it is attempting to make sense of itself. Or, rather, we are witness to industry executives and their legal teams lobbying for greater protection for an industry that may or may not be best served without that protection. My approach was to prepare students to take part in that discussion with short readings and research and then ask them to argue for or against the Design Piracy Prohibition Act.

The first step was to select readings that would outfit students with the necessary vocabulary to participate in a conversation about intellectual property. Common textbooks used in business and professional writing or technical writing courses will often have sections dedicated to ethics and writing and some may even quickly cover fair use or the fundamentals of copyright. Textbooks, however, do not typically take the opportunity to provide students with an adequate overview of intellectual property, or a discussion that even begins to parse its complexity. To compensate, I supplied students with the introductory chapter from *The Law of Intellectual Property* (Nard, Barnes, & Madison, 2006). Although this book is designed for law students and contains a dense offering of legal cases in later chapters, the first chapter is an excellent overview of the mainstays of intellectual property: copyright, trademarks, patents, and trade secrets.[1] Even better for my purposes, the section of the introduction dedicated to trademark law contains a news story on a police raid in New York City's Chinatown confiscating counterfeit merchandise by Louis Vuitton, Kate Spade, and Fendi, and a quick overview of a logo infringement case. I also asked students to read the details of the proposed Design Piracy Prevention Act on the Open Congress Web site. The site traces the progress of the bill and shows members of Congress backing the proposal. Students also watched the 10-minute video supporting the bill on the Web site stopfashionpiracy.com. Finally, there is a useful, although very brief, summation of Raustiala and Sprigman's (2006) article available from *The New Yorker* online titled "The Piracy Paradox" (Surowiecki, 2007).

Student groups were allotted 12–15 minutes to argue their cases in front of the class. Presentations surpassed my expectations regarding overall quality and insightfulness, but also surprised me in that the dominant stance argued *against* the passage of the Design Piracy Prohibition Act. The class was divided into six teams comprised of three to four students. Of those six teams, only one advocated for the passage of the bill. As I kept reminding students, I was not there to judge right or wrong on the bill, but to assess the rhetorical maneuvers made within their arguments. I also reminded them that in addition to demonstrating their abilities to conduct research and analyze data, the goals for the course insist that they demonstrate their aptitude with comprehending and evaluating potential ethical and legal dilemmas associated with writing and research. While I am not suggesting these goals are in any way exceptional for a writing course, asking students to address the dilemma posed by a pairing of intellectual property law and the fashion industry's plea for protection did provide a unique learning scenario for students. More importantly, it changed the subjects of intellectual property and plagiarism from lecture-driven segments of the course to a dialogic one where students were engaged with critiquing the present and future reach of the law. As a class, we set out to make sense of this "negative space."

UNTANGLING INTELLECTUAL PROPERTY AND FASHION

Trademarking Fashion

Protection for fashion comes primarily from trademark law and not copyright. Under the Federal Trademark Act, otherwise known as the Lanham Act, a trademark is "any word, name, symbol or device or any combination thereof used by a person...to identify and distinguish his or her goods, including a unique product, from those manufactured or sold by others and to indicate the source of the goods, even if that source is unknown" (15 U.S.C. sec. 1127). These provisions benefit both the consumer and the trademark holder. First, consumers are spared confusion between brands. Consequently, the time required to identify a particular product and make a decision regarding its associative quality is shortened. That is, it is easy to distinguish Coca-Cola from other competing colas because trademark law prohibits other companies from assimilating Coke's appearance. Coke consumers have come to rely on a particular quality, consistency, and taste associated with its brand identity. As a result, consumers receive a second benefit in that companies have an incentive to maintain these levels of consumer expectations. Companies can spend a great deal of time and money developing what is known as "good will" with their consumers; although good will is intangible, for many companies it is often valued at "millions of dollars" (Nard et al., 2006, p. 2). Finally, companies use trademark protection to prevent competitors from abusing or trading on their established consumer good will. A competitor's sub-par offering that uses, for example, a counterfeit trademarked logo to create an incorrect brand association, can lead to a dilution of the original brand.[2]

Trademark goes into effect as soon as an individual or company uses a mark to "identify goods or services for sale to the public. Therefore, federal or state registration of a trademark is not necessary in order for a company to own, use, or even enforce a trademark" (ASME, 2001, p. 32). Most individuals and companies serious about protecting their trademarks, however, do register with the U.S. Patent and Trademark Office. Unlike copyrights and patents, trademarks can be held in perpetuity so long as the trademark holder continues to use their mark. Registering with the U.S. Patent and Trademark Office helps signal the desire for continued protection and serves as a warning to others wishing to compete in the same market. According to the Lanham Act, violations constitute the following:

> Any person who shall, without the consent of the registrant—(a) use in commerce any reproduction, counterfeit, copy, or colorable imitation of a registered mark in connection with the sale, offering for sale, distribution, or advertising of any goods or services on or in connection with which such use is likely to cause confusion, or to cause mistake, or to deceive; ... shall be liable in a civil action by the registrant for the remedies hereinafter provided. (15 U.S.C. sec. 1114)

Despite the real threat of litigation, counterfeit products have plagued the fashion industry for years; perhaps the most common form of abuse is the replication of trademarked logos.

Logo misappropriation is one of the easiest methods to capitalize on an established brand's good will. Counterfeit or "knock-off" goods are a cheaper—often both in terms of price and quality—impersonation of a desirable, higher-end consumer product. For example, Gucci and Louis Vuitton handbags and purses bearing the company's respective logos are valued by consumers because their ownership suggests or even confers a particular social status: "These are goods whose value is closely tied to the perception that they are valued by others" (Raustiala & Sprigman, 2006, p. 1718). As Brian Hilton, Chong Ju Hoi, and Stephen Chen (2004) argued, "who is buying and from whom is what gives a product its credibility. In the absence of a means to assess quality directly people use 'surrogate' indicators of quality" (p. 347). However, there is an even better reason that these designs are so quickly copied: Trademark rarely succeeds in protecting fashion designs when a logo or product-differentiating mark is not part of that design. Raustiala and Sprigman pointed out instances where designers strived to integrate their logo pervasively into a complete product design; Louis Vuitton or Coach handbags that have their logos repeated all over the bag in a wallpaper-like pattern are examples. There are other unique instances where protection is upheld, such as Burberry's trademarked plaid, but on the whole, the uses for trademark law in the world of fashion are "quite limited" (Raustiala & Sprigman, p. 1701).

Copyrighting Fashion

The limitations of trademark law have led advocates for fashion design protection to explore copyright as an alternative method. Currently, the wide array of creative works that copyright protects—including art, sculpture, and other pictorial works—does not extend to any item that may be classified as a "useful article." Title 17 of the U.S. Code elaborates on what may and may not qualify as a copyrightable work:

> Such works shall include works of artistic craftsmanship insofar as their form but not their mechanical or utilitarian aspects are concerned; the design of a useful article, as defined in this section, shall be considered a pictorial, graphic, or sculptural work only if, and only to the extent that, such design incorporates pictorial, graphic, or sculptural features that can be identified separately from, and are capable of existing independently of, the utilitarian aspects of the article. (17 U.S.C. sec. 107)

Raustiala and Sprigman (2006) clarified that a fashion designer's sketch would qualify for copyright protection as an artistic work. However, the final product (whether it be a jacket, shirt, skirt, or pants) that emerges as a result of the sketch does not retain any protection, as that final product is deemed "useful." Similarly, utilitarian designs cannot be protected within the scope of trademark law either. According to U.S. law, therefore, the cuff of a shirt or the shape of a lapel can almost always be associated with some functional aspect of a garment, which results in those designs being left open for copying.

As advocates for increased fashion protection will point out, the European community does possess legal means to deter copying designs. Arguing for increased protection for U.S. fashion designers, Karina Terakura (2000) recounted a 1994 lawsuit where Yves St. Laurent sued Ralph Lauren in a French court for copying. The garment in question was a sleeveless tuxedo gown. The

Yves St. Laurent version sold at a much higher price point of approximately $15,000, where the Ralph Lauren version was a $1,000 offering. Models wore the gowns in the courtroom for the judge, who, after examining them, said, "clearly there are differences ... [Lauren's] buttons aren't gold, while Mr. St. Laurent's are. The St. Laurent dress also has wider lapels and I must say is more beautiful, but of course, that will not influence my decision" (Terakura, pp. 613-614). Ironically, and without mention of a potential conflict of interest, Terakura reported that the judge herself owned two fashion boutiques in Paris. The original ruling dictated that Ralph Lauren pay a fine of $411,000, but that fine was later reduced to an undisclosed sum. Although Terakura judged the original sum as "relatively low," she did find the ruling in favor of Yves St. Laurent "comforting" (p. 614).

Terakura's (2000) stance is set on a traditional incentive model that predicts more protection begets more innovation; she worried that "without the original creators of fashion styles, the world would not be provided with an array of beautiful clothing" (p. 618). And according to the traditional model, the only way to ensure that these "original creators" keep producing is to provide protection for their work. Terakura continues, "Imitation is a form of flattery, but when imitators continuously benefit from other's work, creativity diminishes. Creators need protection from imitators" (p. 618). Indeed, this is what Jonathan Barnett (2005) referred to as the "standard incentive thesis that pervades much academic, judicial, and policy discussion of intellectual property" (p. 1381). It is also this line of thinking that is the backbone of the Design Piracy Prohibition Act.

THE DESIGN PIRACY PROHIBITION ACT

The Design Piracy Prohibition Act was a twice-proposed bill that would have amended Title 17 of the U.S. Code to extend copyright protection to fashion designs. The bill "excludes from such protection fashion designs that are embodied in a useful article that was made public by the designer or owner more than three months before the registration of copyright application" (Open Congress). The bill would have provided copyright protection for 3 years and it would have been the responsibility of the Register of Copyrights to evaluate the originality of a design. The bill had sponsorship from several well-known Senators including Barbara Boxer, Hillary Clinton, and Charles Schumer. At the time of this writing, the Design Piracy Prohibition Act had been introduced in the 109th and the 110th Congress; in both instances, the bill lapsed without a vote. Given the current economic climate, it is uncertain whether or not the bill will be re-introduced into the 111th Congress and, even if it is, whether or not Congress will take time to address the bill.

In the bill's first instantiation, labeled H.R. 5055, it was referred to the House Subcommittee on Courts, the Internet, and Intellectual Property. Committee members heard expert testimonies from fashion designers, lawyers, and the United States Copyright Office. Serendipitously, many of these statements are available online and there was no shortage of fodder for students as they built cases for or against the bill. Students found the U. S. Copyright Office's statement on the bill with ease. The final paragraph concludes:

> The Office does not yet have sufficient information to make any judgment whether fashion design legislation is desirable. Proponents of legislation have come forward with some anecdotal evidence of harm that fashion designers have suffered as a result of copying of their designs, but we have not yet seen sufficient evidence to be persuaded that there is a need for legislation. (U. S. Copyright Office)

However, students discovered just as quickly that there was no shortage of bill defenders. For example, Susan Scafidi is a law professor who has written on fashion and intellectual property and also keeps a blog called Counterfeit Chic. In her opening statement on H. R. 5055, delivered to the House Subcommittee on Courts, the Internet, and Intellectual Property, she advocated for the bill's passage:

> At this point in our history, America should not be a safe haven for copyists. The failure to protect fashion design is both inconsistent with our international policy and a disadvantage to our own creative designers—especially the young designers who represent the future of the American industry and who are particularly vulnerable to copying.

The stopfashionpiracy.com Web site has also amassed testimonials from American and European designers representing major corporations like Armani, Chanel, and Hermès, all advocating for the Design Piracy Prohibition Act. The U.S. and U.S. design houses, they argue, are at a severe disadvantage in a growing global economy without fashion copyright. Many of the testimonials warn that this multi-billion dollar industry could atrophy in the U.S. and that the decline would come, at least in part, as a direct result of technology and globalization. Before the days of the Internet, copying a design could take months or as long as a year to perfect. Designers are now working and showing their wares in environments where they know little can remain secret for long. According to a testimonial by Giovanna Ferragamo, a member of the board of directors for the well-known Italian designer Salvatore Ferragamo, copied designs appear in stores at the same time and in some cases *prior to*, the release of the originals. In an effort to promote awareness for the dilemma and the Design Piracy Prohibition Act, designers have started describing design piracy as "counterfeit without the label". Proponents argue that so long as the model, shape, and overall design cannot be protected, then their hard work will continue to be "stolen in plain sight" (Stop Fashion Piracy).

In addition to technology's influence on design piracy and the fashion cycle, the global economy brings inescapable competitive realities. For example, Eastern countries have undeniably lower production costs. Many of the companies producing pirated fashion take advantage of these lower costs, which, in turn, lowers the costs to consumers enticed to buy the cheaper imitated designs. Short of inspecting a garment's label for its authenticity, a consumer would need to be a fashion expert in many cases to distinguish the copy from the original design. Frustrated and fearing the potential of huge profit losses, design houses are turning to copyright to protect designs and hold onto a competitive edge. Copyright's protective reach, as noted in this collection's introduction, has been extended significantly over the last several decades, to a degree where copyright reform activists and legal scholars question whether or not the law in its current form continues to serve its original purpose.

COPYRIGHT'S PURPOSE: THE POWER TO PROMOTE PROGRESS

More important than the need to protect, if copyright law was derived from the Constitution granting Congress the right "to promote the progress of science and the useful arts," it is difficult to imagine *more* law doing a better job than the fashion industry's existing system. Despite the compilation of testimonials advocating for fashion's right to copyright protection, it is also hard to ignore the evidence of a thriving fashion industry whose gross U.S. revenues exceed $173 billion and globally are estimated at over $784 billion annually (Raustiala & Sprigman, 2006). With a tongue-in-cheek delivery, Litman (2008) imagined what our lives would be like if we did *not* have copyright for fashion designs:

> Imagine for a moment that some upstart revolutionary proposed that we eliminate all intellectual property protection

> for fashion design. No longer could a designer secure federal copyright protection for the cut of a dress or the sleeve of a blouse...The dynamic American fashion industry would wither, and its most talented designers would forsake clothing design for some more remunerative calling like litigation. And all of us would be forced to either wear last year's garments year in year out, or to import our clothing from abroad. (pp. 44-45)

Litman does eventually remind her readers that, "of course, we don't give copyright protection to fashions...We never have" (p. 46). For those in opposition to the Design Piracy Prevention Act, the rampant copying of competing designs appears only to spur more innovation and more revenue for an industry that is constantly rolling out new merchandise to the public. Some legal scholars, such as Barnett (2005), have gone so far as to make arguments that even *trademark* infringement behooves a brand. Barnett contended that introducing counterfeit goods allows designers to charge what he called a "snob premium" to fashion-conscious consumers who desire to set themselves apart from the "non-elite" (p. 1384). The result is a hyper-inflated popularity for the brand that has more consumers setting their sights on acquiring the "real" item. Although there is not a major initiative afoot to strip fashion of its trademark protection, legal scholars are questioning the efficacy of applying copyright to an industry that survives by blending and borrowing ideas from a rich history of past designs. Representing a rare "negative space" within intellectual property law, fashion's missing copyright protection counter-intuitively promotes huge levels of productivity, innovation, and profit.

Legal scholar Lawrence Lessig has written extensively on copyright law's stifling effects on cultural progression and argues that the law has expanded to the point of deterring its original purpose of promoting innovation. In *Free Culture: The Nature and Future of Creativity,* Lessig (2004) recounted a legal anomaly similar to fashion's missing intellectual property protection from the world of Japanese comics. He described the phenomenon of *doujinshi* comics, which are a kind of "copycat" work created based on existing, often mainstream, comics. *Doujinshi* comics are clear violations of copyright law in that they are derived from other works. Even though *doujinshi* works have come to take up a large portion of the Japanese comics market, there is no active effort to shut them down. Similar to Raustiala and Sprigman's (2006) argument against fashion copyright, Lessig cited research that suggests the copycat comics actually make the entire market "more wealthy and productive" (p. 27). In an effort to understand why, exactly, the comics are allowed to exist in the first place, Lessig himself seemed most satisfied with the reality that there simply are not enough lawyers to enforce what would amount to an overwhelming number of cases. He posited that "regulation by law is a function of both the words on the books and the costs of making those words have effect" (p. 27). To rephrase a cliché, then, the so-called cure for fashion's perceived illness may be much worse than the illness itself.

WRITING INSTRUCTION AND PLAGIARISM

Plagiarism Detection

Fashion's anxiety over the perceived illness of rampant copying in the age of the Internet and globalization resembles what Moore Howard (2007) described as a "sense of impending doom" brought on by a perceived technological threat poised to "undo the entire educational enterprise" (p. 3). Moore Howard provided examples from scholars and critics whose work she believes advances the less-than-critical assumption that there is a causal relationship between technology and plagiarism. While the fashion industry is lobbying for extending copyright to protect designs from plagiarism, many instructors (or at least their institutions) are resorting to protectionist methods by purchasing licenses for plagiarism-detection services such as Turnitin.com. Among the many critiques leveled at such services is Lisa Emerson's (2008) concern that in the wrong hands, "Turnitin becomes a blunt instrument to accuse those struggling to grasp a complex intellectual skill of moral failure—with huge repercussions for those students" (p. 190).

To a great degree, embracing plagiarism-detection services has been the response of my institution. As part of an effort to promote "Digital Literacy" on campus, the university library posted a number of learning modules and tutorials on their Web site. One of those tutorials is dedicated to stopping plagiarism. The introductory page informs students and instructors that "the word plagiarism comes from the Latin *plagiarius* meaning 'kidnapper'" and offers a cartoon rendering of a thief in a black mask making off with a sack full of "writing," "words," "knowledge," and "ideas" (WVU Libraries Plagiarism Tutorial). A second cartoon depicts a student being literally kicked out of the dean's office with a paper labeled "plagiarized" having fallen to the floor. (In the tutorial's defense, it does offer some useful basics on paraphrasing and citing source materials.) It closes, however, with yet another cartoon image, this one of a gold badge with the words "plagiarism detective." This portion of the tutorial reads:

> Plagiarism detection services, such as Turnitin.com, use specialized technology to compare student papers with information found on the Internet as well as their own databases of previously submitted papers. Your professor may ask you to submit your papers electronically to Turnitin.com. Turnitin.com will create an "originality report" that shows how much of your paper is original and how much, if any, is plagiarized. (WVU Libraries Plagiarism Tutorial)

The computer-generated originality report brings George Landow's (1997) "Ms. Austen's Submission" immediately to mind—a dystopian tale of a future where "Amateur Authors" submit their work to an all-knowing computer called the Evaluator that serves as the arbiter of authorship at the Agency of Culture. This machine has the power to advance an Amateur to the status of "Author" or even a "Mass" or "Serious" author. Although the story concludes with a hypertextual array of possibilities for Ms. Austen, ranging from worldwide success to complete rejection, Landow ends by providing a somber reflection: "machine intelligence necessarily reproduces *someone's* ideology" (p. 296).

Buried not too deeply in plagiarism-detection software is an ideology that the kidnappers are our students, who will remain guilty until verified as adequately "original." Subtle and not-so-subtle encouragement to use Turnitin comes in surprising forms. For example, I just completed a university-mandated audit for one of the English department's writing courses. These audits offer "proof" to the university curriculum committee that a course meets set guidelines for what constitutes a writing-intensive course. The paperwork asks for a sample syllabus and assignments, and requires that the instructor respond to a series of questions. Among the many questions is: "How do you ensure that written work does in fact reflect the student's own work? (i.e. Turnitin or Safe Assign)." Given all of the opportunities to elaborate on course goals and how writing is integral to those goals, I was surprised by the question and the suggested possibility of Turnitin. It is as if integrating multiple drafts and revisions along with peer and instructor evaluations would not begin to serve as a satisfactory answer to this question. Why couldn't the question instead suggest, "i.e. demonstrably innovative curriculum and engagement with students?" I view my university's prompt as a signal that the field of writing has come to a point where it must evaluate what role technology's "protection" plays in the instruction of writing. Rather than flashing the badge of "plagiarism detective," students may be better served with curriculum that employs a deliberate introduction of intellectual property law and its many ambiguities to set a stage for a dynamic writing classroom. I am suggesting that any writing classroom will benefit by shifting from offering lecture-based coverage of plagiarism "laws" to a student and teacher dialogue probing intellectual property and its more ambiguous and negative spaces. Giving students the opportunity to research and formulate their own ideas regarding intellectual property produced thoughtful presentations and conversation in my own class.

Creating Dynamic Dialogue

Again, in my class, it surprised me that there was little support for copyright protection for fashion designs. The one and only group that made an argument for the passage of the Design Piracy Prohibition Act took the position that as fashion design majors they had hopes of working not for a big design house but striking out on their own with small, boutique-like labels. The group made a convincing case that without protection, the big design houses could appropriate or "steal" (as they put it) their designs and bring them to market faster and with more marketing-driven attention. They also made the point that unlike writing, they do not have the option of citing sources of inspiration. The group was uncomfortable with the idea that it becomes the consumer's responsibility to be informed about fashion to the degree that he or she could recognize a pirated design and then make an informed decision on whether or not to buy. The Design Piracy Prohibition Act not only gives entrepreneurial designers a fighting chance in fashion, they argued, but copyright for new designs would improve on trademark law by serving as another marker of authenticity to would-be consumers.

The five remaining groups did not support the bill. All of the groups did, however, make a point to include a short reaffirmation for trademark law and its very necessary role in fashion. One of the groups began their presentation by circulating two Coach wallets—one authentic and one a counterfeit. Taking a cue from Barnett (2005), I asked if instead of being a problem for the world of fashion, that perhaps the presence of the fake wallet increased the value or desirability of the original. A student responded that it may be possible for a fake to have the reverse effect, however. She classified the counterfeit wallet as "true plagiarism" but did add that, "all the people that I care to impress do know the difference anyway." The remainder of their presentation was an informative side-by-side comparison of the shape and style of the wallets' designs which demonstrated subtle differences and near exact similarities between the two. The group maintained that they were against trademark infringements, such as the Coach knock-off, but concluded it would be detrimental to the progress of the industry if Coach could, for example, copyright the wallet's closure strap or overall shape. They pointed to the language of the proposed Design Piracy Prohibition Act, which states it would be the responsibility of the Register of Copyrights to process and pass judgment on the applications submitted for a registered copyright. That task alone, they speculated, would take many experts from the field and an enormous amount of time. Indeed, those wishing to litigate would use an enormous amount of resources to do so. Although we did not have time to read selections from Lessig (2004), the deductions by this student group appear to coincide with Lessig's observations of the *doujinshi* comics phenomenon mentioned earlier and the number of lawyers it would require to prosecute all of the so-called violations.

It is worth noting that the student group that was not comprised of TAM majors also opposed the Design Piracy Prohibition Act, but approached their case with a much different example. The students enjoyed sampled or remixed music and all of them remembered the controversy surrounding the release of DJ Danger Mouse's (2004) *The Grey Album*. The tracks on this album were a combination of an a cappella recording of Jay-Z's *The Black Album* and instrumental tracks from the Beatles' *The White Album*. Shortly after the release of *The Grey Album* in 2004, the record label owning the rights to the Beatles' music served cease and desist orders to DJ Danger Mouse and all stores and Web sites selling his album. The student group played excerpts from *The Grey Album* and argued that what the class was hearing was actually an original work that distanced itself adequately from both of the other albums it sampled. In short, copyright was impeding music's progress. The group suggested to the fashion majors in the room that they felt the music industry should serve as a warning for the world of fashion and that the Design Piracy Prohibition Act would be equally stifling.

CONCLUSION

In many respects, the worlds of fashion and writing instruction are undeniably different. Fashion's seasonal design cycles guarantee a fast-paced industry that moves today's most desired clothing to a store's sale rack tomorrow. Yet, the quest to identify, validate, and lay claim to originality feels remarkably familiar to a writing instructor. Naturally, copying makes many of us anxious, and according to the testimonials from major designers, copy-prevention policies should be written into U.S. code. Raustiala and Sprigman (2006), however, seem to suggest that fashion houses should recognize an exercise in futility when it is in front of them:

Original ideas are few, and the existence of fashion trends typically means that many actors copy or rework the ideas of some originator (or copy a copy of the originator's design). Some may originate more than others, but all engage in some copying at some point—or as the industry prefers to call it, "referencing" (pp. 1727-1728)

Conversely, if not ironically, perhaps Raustiala and Sprigman would find the academic discussions from the world of rhetoric and composition found in the scholarship of Lisa Ede and Andrea Lunsford (2001), Cheryl Geisler et al. (2001), and James Porter (1996) on the subjects of intertextuality and authorship useful for their research. In his "Intertextuality and the Discourse Community," Porter (1986) suggested that "referencing" is an inescapable condition of text: "Not infrequently, and perhaps ever and always, texts refer to other texts and in fact rely on them for their meaning. All texts are interdependent: We understand a text only insofar as we understand its precursors" (p. 34). For fashion, the problem is what to do when a garment's interdependence is instead utterly dependent on past work. That is, what is an appropriate response when referencing moves to blatant copying? As writing instructors, we call it plagiarism, and fashion has now taken up the term. For both fashion and writing, degrees of acceptable "referencing" remain a hot debate. In a very real and practical sense, the challenge to arrive at an acceptable equilibrium is an arduous task (if not more so for writing instructors), as writing contexts vary greatly between academic to professional settings. Reflecting on the need to understand these variances, especially as they pertain to business and professional writing and technical communication, John Logie (2005) posited that, "teachers have a special obligation to encourage students to engage with, examine, and critique the policies that will intersect with and impinge on their professional work" (p. 224). For the TAM majors in my business and professional writing course, proposed legislation in the form of the Design Piracy and Prohibition Act stood poised to implement major changes to industry policies and practices; another iteration of the bill is certainly possible.

Although I am willing to confess my bias against the Design Piracy Prohibition Act, this chapter is not necessarily an argument for or against its reintroduction and passage. Instead, the controversy within the fashion industry about whether or not copyright protection should be afforded to fashion designs presents a window of opportunity for students to explore the reach and limits of intellectual property law in a manner that goes beyond simplified discussions of plagiarism policies. These overt introductions and discussions of the law and its effect on other professions and industries outside of the classroom need to become more of the norm than the exception. Plagiarism policies, academic integrity, research methods, and source citations are all important to writing instruction. However, once students enter the workforce and the academic values of the writing classroom collide with a different professional context, the real question will be whether or not students possess the critical thinking skills to assess their situation and respond in an appropriate, professional fashion.

NOTES

1. For courses like technical writing that more often enroll students pursuing science and engineering degrees, I have recommended elsewhere (Ballentine, 2008) using the American Society of Mechanical Engineers' handbook, *Intellectual Property: A Guide for Engineers*. Despite its title, this 70-page text is useful for a range of audiences.

2. Related to the concept of dilution are trademark blurring and tarnishment. Blurring is the "diminution of the uniqueness and individuality of the mark caused by another's use of the same or similar mark" (Nard et al., 2006, p. 190). Tarnishment is a trademark infringement in which the violator creates a "negative association" by employing a deceptively similar mark or slogan. See *Chemical Corp. of America v. Anheuser-Busch, Inc.*, 306 F.2d 433 (5th Cir. 1962) and *Dallas Cowboys Cheerleaders, Inc. v. Pussycat Cinema, Ltd.*, 604 F.2d 200, 205 (2d Cir. 1979).

REFERENCES

ASME/American Society of Mechanical Engineers. (2001). *Intellectual property: A guide for engineers*. New York: ASME Press.

Adler-Kassner, Linda; Anson, Chris; & Howard, Rebecca Moore. (2008). Framing plagiarism. In Caroline Eisner & Martha Vicinus (Eds.), *Originality, imitation, and plagiarism: Teaching writing in the digital age* (pp. 231-246). Ann Arbor, MI: University of Michigan Press.

Barnett, Jonathan. (2005). Shopping for Gucci on Canal street: Reflections on status consumption, intellectual property, and the incentive thesis. *Virginia Law Review*, 91(1381), 1381-1423.

Ballentine, Brian D. (2008). Professional writing and a 'whole new mind': Engaging with ethics, intellectual property, design, and globalization. *IEEE Transactions on Professional Communication*, 51(3), 328-340.

Ede, Lisa, & Lunsford, Andrea. (2001). Collaboration and concepts of authorship. *PMLA*, 116(2), 354-369.

Emerson, Lisa. (2008). Plagiarism, a Turnitin trial, and an experience of cultural disorientation. In Caroline Eisner & Martha Vicinus (Eds.), *Originality, imitation, and plagiarism: Teaching writing in the digital age* (pp. 183-194). Ann Arbor, MI: University of Michigan Press.

Geisler, Cheryl; Bazerman, Charles; Doheny-Farina, Stephen; Gurak, Laura; Haas, Christina; Johnson-Eilola, Johndan; et al. (2001). IText: Future directions for research on the relationship between information technology and writing. *Journal of Business and Technical Communication*, 15(3), 269-308.

H.R. 5055—109th Congress (2006): To amend Title 17, United States Code, to provide protection for fashion design, GovTrack.us (database of federal legislation). http://www.govtrack.us/congress/bill.xpd?bill=h109-5055

H.R. 2033—110th Congress (2007): Design Piracy Prohibition Act, GovTrack.us (database of federal legislation) http://www.govtrack.us/congress/bill.xpd?bill=h110-2033

Herrington, Anne. (1981). *Writing to learn: Writing across the disciplines.* College English, 43(4), 379-387.

Hilton, Brian; Hoi, Chong Ju; & Chen, Stephen. (2004). The ethics of counterfeiting in the fashion industry: Quality, credence and profit issues. *The Journal of Business Ethics*, 55(4), 345-354.

Howard, Rebecca Moore. (2007). Understanding "Internet plagiarism." Computers and Composition, 24, 3-15.

Howard, Rebecca Moore. Rebecca Moore Howard's syllabi. http://wrt-howard.syr.edu/syllabi.html

Knoblauch, C. H., & Brannon, Lil. (1983). *Writing as learning through the curriculum.* College English, 45(4), 465-474.

Landow, George. (1997). *Hypertext 2.0: The convergence of contemporary critical theory and technology.* Baltimore: The Johns Hopkins University Press.

Lessig, Lawrence. (2004). *Free culture: The nature and future of creativity.* New York: Penguin Books.

Litman, Jessica. (1994). The exclusive right to read. *Cardozo Arts & Entertainment Law Journal,* 13(29), 13-54.

Logie, John. (2005). Parsing codes: Intellectual property, technical communication, and the World Wide Web. In Carol Lipson & Michael Day (Eds.), *Technical communication and the World Wide Web* (pp. 223-241). Mahwah, NJ: Lawrence Erlbaum Associates.

Nard, Craig; Barnes, David; & Madison, Michael. (2006). *The law of intellectual property.* New York: Aspen Publishers.

Odell, Lee. (1980). The process of writing and the process of learning. College Composition and Communication, 31(1), 42-50.

Open Congress. (2007, August 2). The design piracy prohibition act. http://www.opencongress.org/bill/110-h2033/show

Porter, James. (1986). Intertextuality and the discourse community. Rhetoric Review, 5(1), 34-47.

Pullman, George. (2005). From wordsmith to object-oriented composer. In Carol Lipson & Michael Day (Eds.), *Technical communication and the World Wide Web* (pp. 43-59). Mahwah, NJ: Lawrence Erlbaum Associates.

Raustiala, Kal, & Sprigman, Christopher. (2006). The piracy paradox: Innovation and intellectual property in fashion design. *Virginia Law Review*, 92(8), 1687-1777.

Reyman, Jessica. (2008). Rethinking plagiarism for technical communication. *Technical Communication*, 55(1), 61-67.

Scafidi, Susan. (2006, July). Opening statement on H. R. 5055. http://www.counterfeitchic.com/Images/HR 5055 opening statement given 7-27-06.pdf

Stop Fashion Piracy. http://www.stopfashionpiracy.com

Surowiecki, James. (2007, September 24). The piracy paradox. *The New Yorker*. http://www.newyorker.com/talk/financial/2007/09/24/070924ta_talk_surowiecki

Terakura, Karina. (2000). Insufficiency of trade dress protection: Lack of guidance for trade dress infringement litigation in the fashion design industry. *Hawaii Law Review*, 22(645), 569-619.

U. S. Copyright Office. (2006, July). Statement of the United States copyright office before the subcommittee on courts, the Internet, and intellectual property, committee on the judiciary. http://www.copyright.gov/docs/regstat072706.html

WVU Libraries Plagiarism Tutorial. (2008). http://www.libraries.wvu.edu/instruction/plagiarism/

19 THE ROLE OF AUTHORSHIP IN THE PRACTICE AND TEACHING OF TECHNICAL COMMUNICATION

Jessica Reyman

Writers working as technical communicators, whose primary role is to communicate complex technical information to the audiences who need it, face unique challenges in their roles as authors. Technical communicator concerns about issues of authorship and textual ownership derive from their dual roles as creators of works and users of others' works. Therefore, their questions tend to be either "do I own this work?" or "can I use this work that someone else has authored?" Often the reason for asking such questions is to avoid claims of copyright infringement. Writers want to establish ownership of works that they've composed so that they know how they might reuse them, and they want to establish their rights to incorporate the work of others into their own projects when it is useful. Conscientious writers seek to establish who owns a work (either their own or another's) so that they can proceed legally and ethically. Often technical communicators cannot easily determine ownership themselves, and the question soon becomes "should I ask my legal department about this?" Technical communicators who work within a corporate setting can rely on legal counsel for sound advice on whether or not they, as employees of a given organization, are authorized to claim ownership to or make use of copyrighted material. This advice aims to inform writers whether a particular activity is legal and to allow them to proceed without concern for liability. A question that technical communicators may not ask as frequently, however, is *why* the answers to questions about intellectual property are not always obvious. Why aren't the lines between who owns what—between legal and illegal, ethical and unethical activity—clearly demarcated for writers working as technical communicators?

Instructors who teach technical communication at both the undergraduate and graduate levels have a responsibility to inform students about potential legal constraints related to what they can claim ownership of and what they can make use of in their writing on the job. By educating future technical communicators on what copyright law says regarding ownership of works, instructors can help students participate in future workplace discussions that seek to answer the question "is this legal?" Technical communication instructors should discuss issues of textual ownership with students both in terms of legal authorship (or what author status allows legally) and rhetorical authorship (or what author status allows regarding agency and status within the profession). My treatment of technical communication authorship is limited to a corporate model of the writer, or the technical communicator whose job title might be "technical writer" or "content specialist," but not necessarily all writers who may communicate specialized information to specific audiences on the job who also do not work as technical communicators within a corporate environment (e.g., lawyers, researchers, freelancers).

In this chapter, I address the tension between industry models for legal ownership of intellectual property as supported through copyright law and the concept of authorship—a concept that informs technical communicators' understandings of textual ownership, as discussed in technical communication scholarship. I begin by describing legal conceptions of authorship that apply to industry professionals working as technical communicators in corporate environments. I then move to contrast that model with how authorship has been conceptualized among technical communication researchers and practitioners within the existing literature in the field. I close by arguing that instructors should address questions of legality and related implications. In doing so, instructors can more fully acknowledge the complexity of making legal and ethical decisions about textual ownership in the workplace. The aims of such an approach are to support ethical writing practices as well as to aid future technical communicators in establishing greater autonomy and increased professional status by becoming more active participants in discussions about intellectual property in their work environments.

THE PERPLEXING CIRCUMSTANCES OF AUTHORSHIP

The legal standards for ownership and use of copyrighted materials are not always in line with writers' understandings of textual ownership and use of others' materials as formed through their academic experiences. Technical communicators, particularly those who have recently moved from the academic to the corporate world, are faced with perplexing circumstances. For instance, while technical writers and editors are held accountable for composing innovative, usable, and compelling documents in the workplace, they often do not legally assume authorship of that work; instead, works are usually owned by the corporation they work for under the work-for-hire doctrine of copyright law. Another example is the way in which many technical communicators rely on existing materials in their writing, including templates and boilerplates, but also existing content composed by other writers, which runs counter to the concepts of originality and plagiarism learned in academic contexts.

Because of this unique role of the technical communicator as *non*author, situations in which questions about copyright and ownership arise are common for technical communicators. These situations often involve more than one writer and several variables that affect textual ownership. Consider these two cases:

> **Case #1:** A technical communicator has recently joined a team responsible for writing user documentation to explain to customers how to install, maintain, and repair telecommunications equipment. She was asked to review existing documentation for a quality assessment and to revise the documentation as needed. As part of the assessment, she discovered that parts of the documentation were identical to that found in user manuals that you could access freely online from a well-known, industry-leading competitor's public Web site. Further, a search on related topics revealed that other material in the documentation was copied from public online forums where users posed questions and other users responded with solutions. How should this technical communicator proceed with revising the documentation at her company?

> **Case#2:** A technical communicator who works for a small software company created, largely independently, the user manuals for a new software program. A larger corporation then purchased third-party rights to use the software program in a product of its own. As part of the program that was purchased, the corporation acquired electronic copies of the user manuals. Because the product development and customization project is on a fast track and because the user manuals are high quality, the technical publications department at the corporation determined that if they use the software company's

existing manuals, they can drastically reduce their document development time. The technical publications department is not sure whether the corporation has the rights to not only the software product, but also the user guides.

In each of these cases, legal counsel, if available, would be able to assess the situation and arrive at a recommended course of action, often with the primary goal of mitigating risk for the corporation. Because of the variables involved (number of writers, different organizations involved, varying modes of accessing materials), the situations become too complex for most writers to analyze and arrive at a comfortable decision independently. However, technical communicators have much at stake in assigning authorship. Issues of textual ownership have great bearing on their work, determining not only how they will proceed on a given project but also the recognized value of their contributions within a workplace environment. Therefore, technical communicators should be informed enough to become active participants in the decision-making process, either collaborating with legal counsel or collaborating with their team and others involved to arrive at a satisfactory model for textual ownership. Such participation requires that technical communicators understand what the law says and also the implications of models of textual ownership for their roles and status within the workplace. With this understanding, they can more confidently and soundly respond to difficult intellectual property related situations.

LEGAL NON(AUTHORSHIP) FOR TECHNICAL COMMUNICATORS

As evidenced in other chapters in this collection, the field of rhetoric and composition has addressed concepts and troubles related to authorship at some length in its scholarship. Technical communication scholars, however, have engaged in rather dispersed discussions of the concept and often borrow from the growing body of scholarship on intellectual property studies among compositionists. While it is outside the scope of this chapter to summarize the scholarship on authorship in rhetoric and composition, one particularly useful source for this discussion is Rebecca Moore Howard's (1999) *Standing in the Shadow of Giants*, which offers an argument for rethinking modern conceptions of authorship that have implications for teaching writing. In the opening chapters, Howard offers a review of scholarship on the history of the concept of authorship. Based on this history, she asserted that notions of authorship are "culture-specific, arising not as a description of foundational facts about writing, but as cultural arbitraries that support larger social trends" (p. 76). Further, and most useful here, Howard described what she called "properties" of contemporary authorship that writing students and instructors commonly rely on. Although she focused largely on plagiarism and authorship in terms of its association with morality among composition instructors and students, the other three properties she identified—autonomy, proprietorship, and originality—are more pertinent to a discussion of authorship in technical communication. Howard noted that modern conceptions of authorship posit its *autonomy* (composing individually), *proprietorship* (a "natural right," in the Lockean sense, to own what one has produced through writing), and *originality* (the notion that writing comes from inner genius; pp. 76-85).

Many written texts—and particularly those prepared in academic settings—are valued among instructors and other readers for these properties. As Howard (1999) recognized, we need only look to discussions of plagiarism in the writing classroom or university plagiarism policies to see how prevalent these assumptions are. Howard's description of the properties of authorship creates an appropriate springboard for a discussion about authorship and technical communication: As she noted, a disparity exists between composition student "patchwriting" practices and these properties of authorship. Technical communication scholars might note the differences between technical communication student assumptions about ownership of texts and the properties of authorship that apply in workplace settings. Authorship as applied in technical communicator professional practices is a far cry from the concept of authorship purported in the academic environment. In a professional context, technical communication is rarely considered an *individualized* activity; it is not something to which we assign *ownership* by an individual writer; and it typically does not produce something valued most for its *originality*. Although the treatment of authorship in most university writing curricula (both composition and technical communication) typically continues to rely on these properties, such discussions do not reflect many of the actual practices and laws governing industry professionals working as technical communicators in corporate settings.

Technical communicators often fail to achieve author status, as understood in academic settings, due in part to the types of composing activities they regularly engage in; these activities may not resemble the activity of "authoring" as recognized in academic contexts. Namely, technical communicator activities involve collaborating with other writers, editors, or subject-matter experts as opposed to working autonomously, or reworking, building on, or reusing existing text rather than producing something entirely original. Consider these common writing tasks that may lead some to question the status of the technical communicator working in corporate environments as autonomous, proprietary, and originary:

- collaborative writing: composing with others writers, editors, or subject-matter experts;
- repurposing: taking an existing document—perhaps written by another author—designed for one purpose, form, or audience and re-working it for a different purpose, form, or audience;
- single-sourcing: "creating multiple deliverables from one unmodified source document," perhaps written by another author (Brierly, 2002, p. 15);
- using boilerplates and templates;
- corporate authorship: composing works not signed by a writer or, rather, works that are signed by a representative not the writer.

In some instances, the large number of contributors can make it difficult to determine who all of the authors of a given text are. For instance, research articles in scientific journals, which technical writers and editors often help to compose and edit, routinely have large numbers of contributors. Due to the difficulties posed when assigning textual ownership among a large group of contributors, editorial boards governing these publications have developed authorship criteria for bylines in journals. The International Committee of Medical Journal Editors (ICMJE; 2008), for instance, published criteria for determining authorship status in biomedical journals based on:

1. substantial contributions to conception and design, acquisition of data, or analysis and interpretation of data;

2. drafts of the article or critical revisions for important intellectual content; and

3. final approval of the version to be published.

Such guidelines suggest that identifying authors of a written work—where there is much collaboration in the design and completion of research, the analysis of data, and the writing and editing of the article—is not an easy task. To accommodate a large group of contributors, other forms of acknowledging individual work or assigning responsibility for content include titles such as "guarantor," "clinical investigator," "participating investigator." Interestingly, "technical writer," "medical writer," and "editor" are not listed as examples of contributors deserving authorship credit.

Legal models for authorship in corporate settings likewise do not follow traditional, academic models of original, autonomous, and proprietary authorship. The work-for-hire doctrine of copyright law and contractual agreements negotiated between writers and the companies they work for may leave individual writers and editors with nonauthorship status—with little or no ownership rights over the works they compose. The work-for-hire doctrine of copyright law (see Amidon, this volume) governs the default assignment of copyright in an employee–employer relationship. Work-for-hire applies in two circumstances: when a technical communicator has prepared a work as part of his or her employment and when a technical communicator has been commissioned by an employer to complete a work and both parties have agreed via contract that the work should be considered a work for hire. This means that the work created by a technical communicator within the scope of his or her employment becomes the sole property of the employer, even if he or she is no longer employed there. This also means that if a technical communicator is not employed permanently by the company and is working on a short-term contract, he or she still may relinquish rights to the work if agreed on through a contract with the employer. (For more on the work-for-hire doctrine, how it affects technical communicators, and its treatment in case law, see Herrington, 1999.)

Under these conditions, which are typical for technical communicators working in professional settings, writers do not assume legal authorship of a work that they compose, even when the work is a solitary and original creation, that is, even if it does not rely on existing content and is carried out individually. In some cases, such as writing or editing for an ICMJE publication, the subject-matter experts assume ownership of the written work. And, in other cases, the corporation or a named representative assumes authorship. This system of nonauthorship may prevent technical communicators from receiving recognition or credit for their work. Additionally, it may prevent them from retaining important rights—including opportunities for future financial gain from the work—as it can preclude writers from reusing or repurposing their work or from marketing their work to other audiences. These limitations are particularly restrictive when a writer intends to reuse work prepared for another employer, even if he or she no longer works for that employer. However, this system for establishing legal nonauthorship may, in fact, have some benefit for technical writers and editors, namely protecting them from liability for unintended consequences caused by misuse of technical communication products or inaccuracies presented in materials they have written or edited.

Legal guidelines for product liability include responsibilities such as "duty to warn and instruct." U.S. liability law specifies that companies must include warnings about potential dangers and misuses associated with a product and that these warnings not only be available to users but that they also be understandable. Often such warnings are distributed or reprinted in product documentation written by technical communicators who also often work as an intermediary between a company and the public. In this case, they may find themselves responsible, in part, for ensuring that their company avoids costly liability lawsuits; however, technical communicators are rarely legal experts (nor should they be expected to be). Management or any available legal counsel has the authority and knowledge to advise technical communicators on their responsibilities regarding product liability, a particularly complex area of the law; and having done so, a company may also assume liability if a legal claim arises, shielding a writer-for-hire from liability. Although the legal concept of liability may or may not directly relate to legal authorship, the common model of corporate authorship adopted in workplace settings suggests a certain level of protection for technical writers from sole responsibility. (For more in-depth discussion of liability law and the responsibilities of technical communicators, see Heylar, 1992; Manning, 1997; and Smith, 1990.)

Another form of protection for technical communicators with nonauthorship status is "guarantorship" of the accuracy and integrity of the content. The role of a "guarantor" is most commonly seen in medical writing, where technical writers and editors often compose articles that present content prepared by medical professionals and researchers. Medical writers are not identified as authors of the works they compose, and they are also often exempt from being identified as "guarantors" of the final product. Guarantors of a medical article, according to the ICMJE (2008) guidelines, are the "persons who take responsibility for the integrity of the work as a whole, from inception to published article." The names of any guarantors of an article are published, and these individuals "guarantee" the accuracy of information, taking responsibility for any safety issues that may arise based on the content. By not assuming an authorship status in the publication, technical communicators do not claim responsibility for the integrity of the material presented.

By assuming legal authorship, corporations or subject-matter experts may assume responsibility for the text in three senses: credit for contributions in terms of resources and effort devoted to producing the work; liability for product safety; and guarantorship for the accuracy or integrity of the content. While technical communicators desire credit for their contributions, they often benefit from protection against liability and guarantorship for a written work. At times, this assignment of responsibility to another party is desirable, especially when it protects writers from consequences arising from situations in which they may not fully understand whether the data is accurate (as in a scientific article) or whether an end-user has been sufficiently warned of all potential harms of using a hazardous product (as in a user manual). However, it is also important to note that, despite legal responsibility, technical communicators likely still feel compelled to consider the ethical or legal liabilities they potentially bring upon clients and end users. Technical communicators seek not merely to absolve themselves from legal responsibility, but also to contribute to safe and ethical practices within their writing environments. In an article on product liability, Pamela Heylar (1992) noted that technical communicators have a responsibility not only to write clear instructions and warnings that satisfy legal requirements for adequacy, but also to engage in practices that help their companies to work toward more safe and ethical product development practices. She advises technical communicators to work with product designers, human factors experts, and end users at all stages of the product development cycle to communicate about and gather feedback on their documentation. Her suggestions are consistent with the STC Code for Communicators, written in 1988 and included in the STC 1993–1994 annual report (see Rocky Mountain Chapter of the Society for Technical Communication, 2008), which specifies that writers "recognize [their] responsibility to communicate technical information truthfully, clearly, and economically" and that to do so they hold themselves "responsible for how well [their] audience understands [their] message." This sense of ethical responsibility among technical communicators likely will not change based on legal authorship status alone. Ethical and responsible technical communicators already follow this code, despite their nonauthorship status. What may change based on authorship status, however, is the available means through which technical communicators participate in legal and ethical decision-making on the job.

Many technical communication students will be surprised to discover that they may not retain ownership of the works they prepare on the job. Instructors who share information about work-for-hire or common contractual agreements governing textual ownership will help students make the transition from an academic concept of authorship (which characterizes authorship as proprietary, originary, and solitary) to the nonauthorship model most technical communicators will encounter after graduation. Discussions of concepts of textual ownership for technical communicators tend to focus on how copyright law and other contractual agreements affect, in practical terms, what a writer can or cannot do with a written product prepared in a workplace environment. In addition to creating limitations on how a writer might seek additional revenue for a work outside of the corporate environment it was originally prepared for, however, the denial of authorship status can also contribute to a lack of professional status and decision-making power for technical communicators.

AUTHORSHIP, AGENCY, AND PROFESSIONAL STATUS IN TECHNICAL COMMUNICATION

Rethinking the properties of academic authorship in light of the practical realities of legal authorship and common composing practices can help technical communication students better understand the different conceptions of textual ownership. Another goal in addressing intellectual property issues in the technical communication classroom is to help students develop a more complicated view of the role and status of technical communicators in the workplace. A more sophisticated understanding of nonauthorship among students will lead them to explore what disenfranchises technical communicators as authors. By discussing questions of ownership and authorship, instructors and students can address the implications of assigned roles for technical communicators—as either neutral "conduits" of objective reality and "translators" of specialized information (i.e., nonauthors), or as "meaning-makers" within rhetorical contexts (i.e., authors). In the case of the former, technical communicators are relegated to the grunt work of "documenting" an already-designed product or "writing up" information provided by a subject-matter expert. In the latter case, however, they are granted the ability to contribute to the vitality and shape of the product, the organization, and the larger disciplinary discourses of science and technology. Future technical communicators who assume a form of authorship can more easily assume the role of contributor to meaning-making, as rhetorical agent, which in turn may lead to greater professional status.

As discussed earlier, the structure of legal nonauthorship is prevalent both due to common technical communication practices falling outside what is considered "authoring" and to legal and contractual negotiations establishing corporate or subject-matter authorship of works. However, this model of nonauthorship poses problems beyond the financial realm. Denying technical communicators authorship status may contribute to harmful misperceptions about the quality of their work as well as the status of technical communicators as valuable participants in the workplace. From its inception, the field of technical communication has struggled to achieve status in both academic and industry settings as a specialized field of study and practice. Gerald Savage (2003) noted, in the introduction to *Power and Legitimacy: The Historical and Contemporary Struggle for Professional Status*, that "the technical communication field lacks the status, legitimacy, and power of mature professions" (p. 1). Johndan Johnson-Eilola and Stuart Selber (2001) addressed reasons why this is the case by focusing on the need for "a coherent body of disciplinary knowledge" (p. 408) that imbues students with a common skill set and knowledge base necessary for success in the workplace. Others have noted that the challenges of establishing the value of technical communicators in industry settings may be due in part to the fact that works produced by technical communicators are not considered ends in themselves but rather a means to an end. Further, measuring the value of technical communicators cannot easily be shown by demonstrating how technical communication products contribute to a bottom line (Mead, 1998). In a field plagued by a struggle to establish its value both within the academy and in the workplace, nonauthorship status for technical communicators may function to obscure the nature of technical communicators' work and the worth of their contributions. By assigning nonauthorship to technical communicators, academics and industry professionals outside of the field fail to fully acknowledge their contributions and recognize their value as rhetorical agents, and instead view them as conduits.

Jennifer Slack, David James Miller, and Jeffrey Doak (1993) argued that researchers and practitioners have much to gain by conceiving of the technical communicator as an author. Slack et al. applied three models of communication theory to technical communication practice: the transmission model, the translation model, and the articulation model. They argued that technical communication researchers and practitioners should embrace the articulation model, which allows technical communicators to assume the role of an author who actively contributes to the creation of meaning through their composing practices: "the articulation view allows us to move beyond a conception of communication as the polar contributions of sender and receiver to a conception of an ongoing process of articulation constituted in (and constituting) the relations of meaning and power operating in the entire context within which messages move" (p. 169). As authors, technical communicators hold increased responsibility for the content and messages they craft, and they become active participants in changes to the power relations operating in a given communication situation. Slack et al. make a compelling case for the value of technical communicators as contributors to the "articulation of meaning," in arguing that by assuming authorship status, technical communicators would be free to contribute in ways that offer more than merely conveying facts.

What is not so clear, however, is whether "author status" in a traditional sense is the most productive means for establishing or confirming the role of technical communicators as meaning-makers in rhetorical contexts. About 10 years after its publication date, Slack (2004) wrote a response to her earlier, co-authored article stating that she had become "dissatisfied" with the directive "to go out into the world and assert authorship." She later saw that "the assertion of authorship offers no guarantee to technical communicators that their work will attain a level of social responsibility they may hope for" (p. 161). Following Slack, I agree that asserting authorship, at least legal authorship, may not be all that is required for technical communicators to achieve heightened professional status as rhetorical agents. Although it does allow, perhaps, increased freedom to seek financial reward for an individual writer's contributions, it does not necessarily lead to increased responsibility for the meaning created through technical communication products. In other words, while retaining legal authorship status in a traditional sense may reward *contributions*, it does not automatically establish responsibility for communication products. A sense of *responsibility* for the integrity and quality of texts seems likewise necessary for technical communicators to achieve greater autonomy in the workplace and gain recognition as valued professionals.

Outside of the Slack et al. (1993) article, technical communication scholarship addressing the concept of authorship has been sparse. Another area of scholarship we might look to for further insight into authorship in terms of both contribution *and* responsibility includes work that has chronicled the changing definitions of technical communication and its relationship to rhetorical meaning-making throughout its recent history (Dobrin, 2004; Miller, 1979; Rutter, 2004). Two landmark essays offer definitions that challenge theories of communication that limit our understanding of the technical communicator as an author and reveal the value of establishing rhetorical agency for technical communicators. In a 1979 article, Carolyn Miller argued that scholars and instructors in technical communication should no longer privilege a positivist view of science and technology, and instead view technical writing "rather than the revelation of absolute reality, [as] a persuasive version of experience" (p. 52). Miller contended that it is useful to understand the work of the technical communicator as rhetorical, as contributing to the creation of meaning rather than merely transferring meaning (as a neutral conduit) or rendering meaning clearly (as through a windowpane). By doing so, researchers and practitioners can recognize how technical communicators participate in making rhetorical choices, as agents with responsibility for content and meaning.

Russell Rutter (2004) offered a definition of technical communication that relies on a rhetorical and historical approach:

> writing must be conceptualized as an activity that by its selection and organization of information and its assessment of audience creates its own version of reality and then strives to win the consensus of its readers that this version is valid. If technical communicators create versions of reality instead of serving merely as windows through which reality in all of its pre-existent configurations may be seen, then technical com-

munication must be fundamentally rhetorical: it builds a case that reality is one way and not some other. (p. 28)

By viewing technical communicators as creating "versions of reality," rather than as neutral conduits, researchers, practitioners, instructors, and students alike can begin to understand the role of the technical communicator as one that does more than contribute to a bottom line or neutrally convey information. By assuming a role of meaning-maker, technical communicators can contribute to the shape of workplace activities, products, and the larger discourses of science and technology in positive ways. The views espoused by Miller (1979) and, subsequently, Rutter (2004) about the rhetorical work of technical communicators have been generally embraced in technical communication scholarship, which notes the usefulness of these definitions to better understanding how communicators can more ethically and responsibly participate in real-life, dynamic, and inherently complex professional communication practices.

To write well as a technical communication professional, however, is often misperceived within the corporate setting as helping a company meet a financial goal, conforming to pre-determined genre conventions, or neutrally transmitting information. This view carries over into the classroom: a cursory glance at introductory textbooks or anecdotal evidence from instructors of courses in technical communication reveals that students do not always understand technical communicators as rhetorical agents (there are, of course, exceptions to this). Instead, works of technical communication have historically been viewed—by their readers, subject matter experts, students, instructors, and even some technical communication professionals—as authorless, both in terms of how writers contribute to content ("transparent" or "objective" or "just the facts") and how they present material stylistically ("clear," "precise," "direct," "comprehensive," and "accurate"). Although technical communicators have been valued in professional and academic settings for their efficiency or proficiency, they have not necessarily been valued for their contributions as meaning-makers. Defining technical communication according to the notion of transference of objective reality encourages defining technical communicators as, at best, translators of technical material and, at worst, neutral conduits or even invisible window panes rather than as authors with rhetorical agency.

The issue of rhetorical agency and its relationship to authorship status is not a given. Technical communicators who achieve legal authorship status may not necessarily act with agency to effect change within their workplaces, just as those with nonauthorship status may be able to participate meaningfully in important decision making. Rather, rhetorical agency, or what might be understood as the capacity of an individual to shape an audience's perception or the conditions of a situation through rhetoric, may preclude, confer, and/or be produced by authorship status. Recently, scholars of rhetoric interested in the concept of agency have begun to examine the social structures and forces that precede and facilitate rhetorical agency in particular contexts. Cheryl Geisler (2004), in an article summarizing the conversation about rhetorical agency at the 2003 meeting of the Alliance of Rhetoric Societies, noted an interest in understanding "the conditions for rhetorical agency" and "the possibilities created through the arrangement of social conditions" (p. 14). Christian Lundberg and Joshua Gunn (2005), in a response to Geisler's article, explored this understanding of agency further by asking, "what happens to the conventional rhetorical account of agency if it starts out by presuming that the agency possesses the agent, as opposed to the agent possessing agency?" (p. 97). In the case of technical communicators, we might ask under what conditions does agency possess the technical communicator? That is, although legal authorship status alone will not likely lead to increased agency for technical communicators, a workplace that values technical communicators' contributions and more fully understands their roles as generators of meaning may produce conditions that facilitate greater rhetorical agency. This workplace may, in turn, lead to socially recognized authorship status, a sense of responsibility, power, and professional status among technical communicators that may or may not coincide with legal authorship.

The rhetoricians above identify what Krista Kennedy (2009) called a "bifurcation of agent and agency" (p. 306). Kennedy noted that legal authorship status (as established in the U.S. Ninth circuit opinion in *Aalmuhammed v. Lee,* 2000) requires decision-making agency and authority over a text. She argued that corporate authorship models, insofar as they rely on work-for-hire, create a situation where the writer lacks "the ability to induce the motivating factor in producing the work" (p. 8). She asserted that work-for-hire supports the notion that rhetorical agency is a condition of legal authorship: If the employer provides impetus for a written work, the conditions under which the work is created, and the resources and supported needed for its development, then "the employer assumes ownership of the resulting work" (p. 9). Kennedy recognized the ways in which authorship status—as determined through legal authorities—requires recognition of rhetorical agency among technical communicators. Technical communicators could be granted agency, or in Lundberg and Gunn's (2005) terms, agency would possess technical communicators, only if they were able to claim the social status as meaning- and decision-makers within their writing contexts. Recognizing a form of rhetorical agency among technical communicators—that is, understanding how their writings involve more than recordings of objective reality but are instead generative acts that create meaning—may contribute to establishing legal authorship status.

Such status as authors, however, does not necessarily, or even most importantly, rely on legal authorship status. Rather, author status may be social, in which writers are recognized as rhetorical agents within their workplace environments and, perhaps, within the larger discourses of science and technology. Jim Henry (2000) noted the usefulness of a "conceptual reframing of authorship, in the academy and in the workplace, to extend it to instrumental discourse, to include multiple contributors, and to take into account the *effects* of discourse as they reverberate within and beyond local cultures" (p. 150). By recognizing the ways in which authorship is constructed differently across professional writing activities, Henry shows how we might reconstruct writers' roles as producers of organizational and cultural discourses and value systems. For instance, Henry argued that professional writers' contributory expertise includes activities that often go unnoticed in workplace environments but are nevertheless essential, including

> shaping and reshaping product development processes, document review procedures and dynamics and shaping information that will travel beyond the organization and to the larger public. These activities affect practices and considerations within the workplace and establish relationships between the organization and larger culture. (pp. 154-155)

Recognizing a new conception of the author that may be separate from the legal author highlights the rhetorical effects of the technical communicators' work, on the activities of their workplaces, their company's culture, and for the larger discourses of science and technology.

By assuming status as authors with rhetorical agency, technical communicators can attain increased professional status as potential contributors to change within their communication contexts. Such an authorship requires more than recognition for individual contributions and the ability to seek financial gain granted through legal authorship. It also requires responsibility and recognition for meaning created and acknowledgement of participation in organizational, disciplinary, and cultural discourses. This rhetorical form of authorship is more than a title that offers legal ownership; it is also the status and power as meaning-making professionals within dynamic communication contexts.

IMPLICATIONS FOR TEACHING TECHNICAL COMMUNICATION

Nonauthorship status for technical communicators remains the default structure of textual ownership from a legal standpoint. In workplace contexts, technical communicators rarely rely on traditional composing models that are autonomous and original, nor are they automatically granted proprietorship over intellectual property. Corporate authorship and the work-for-hire doctrine may impose strict guidelines on—or even prevent altogether—the reuse and repurposing of work. And because much technical communication involves this kind of reuse and repurposing, these limitations can place significant financial and logistical burdens on technical writers and the companies for which they work. In addition, nonauthorship status has implications for the professional status of technical communicators. In assuming a role devoid of responsibility and authority over meaning-making in their texts, writers run the risk of perpetuating a view of technical communicators as nothing more than neutral conduits of objective reality. Because of these implications of nonauthorship status, technical communication instructors would do well to teach students about authorship from two perspectives:

- Legal: How does copyright law affect technical communicators' intellectual property rights?
- Rhetorical: How can the status of author contribute to the professional integrity of technical communicators?

Gerald Savage (1996) asserted that in teaching ethical concerns, technical communication instructors should also help students "to reconceive the profession as one that can be practiced in alternative ways that would permit them greater autonomy and professional integrity" (p. 310, qtd. in Savage & Kynell-Hunt, p. 11). By teaching technical communication students about intellectual property issues from these two perspectives, instructors can help to achieve that goal. Such instruction will require that technical communication instruction address the difficulties posed by nonauthorship status, not only in terms of the practical and financial limitations of the work-for-hire doctrine but also in terms of the need to establish the role of technical communicators as authors with rhetorical agency. If instructors are to encourage technical communication students to participate in the profession in "alternative ways" that allow increased status and agency, then future technical communicators need to understand and assert their roles as ones of authority and responsibility.

Such an approach has implications for curricula in technical communication at both the undergraduate and graduate levels. Of course, the amount of time to focus on intellectual property issues as a content unit in a course will vary depending on educational level and need of students in the class, and on curricular design and need within a program. Addressing intellectual property from a legal perspective will involve introducing the work-for-hire doctrine and contract law to students (an excellent reference for this content is Herrington's 2003 *Legal Primer for a Digital Age*). The ways in which copyright law affects ownership of texts prepared in workplace settings will be new to most students, except perhaps those who have held jobs or completed internships in which they performed writing and editing tasks. Instructors can introduce what the law says and applications of this ownership model in terms of cases, real or hypothetical.

To address intellectual property issues from a rhetorical perspective, class discussions and activities should work to break down the dichotomy between "technical communicator" and "author" as seemingly suggested by legal doctrine. It can be useful to prepare students for the workplace by introducing them to common composing practices that are collaborative and not autonomous, building on existing work rather than originary, and nonproprietary rather than owned. And it is likewise important that students understand the limitations on legal ownership of materials as determined by the work-for-hire doctrine. However, it may be necessary for instructors to look beyond typical legal approaches to determining authorship when discussing intellectual property issues in the classroom because these approaches often fail to highlight the role of technical communicators as rhetorical agents. For instance, when attending a local Society for Technical Communication (STC) chapter meeting on "Writing and Intellectual Property Rights: Respecting Others and Guarding Your Own," a patent attorney joined the group to discuss intellectual property law and its impact on how technical communicators create and manage content in a digital age. Of note was this piece of advice: "Don't be a creatively lazy fan" (Brill, 2008). As this comment illustrates, a common perception about how intellectual property issues should be treated among technical communicators can further dichotomize technical communicators and authors. This advice suggests that reusing and repurposing materials is being "lazy," when it is common practice for technical communicators; this advice also implies that technical communicators are "users" or "fans" of existing material, but not creative meaning-makers. Rather than suggesting that technical communicators act out of responsibility or authority over their texts, they seemingly act out of either "laziness" or fear of liability. A discussion of authorship and rhetorical agency, even though it strays from discussion about typical legal structures of ownership, can help here. Instructors can discuss with students how legal ownership (what can I do with this material and not face legal ramifications?) and authorship status (what are my responsibilities as an author?) are distinct concepts, and both are useful in the work of technical communicators. Although a typical technical communicator does not work individually, creating works entirely from scratch and assuming singular ownership over texts, he or she should seek to maintain a form of authorship that grants him or her rhetorical agency. Through discussions of the competing roles of the technical communicator, students can see how authorship in technical communication can be understood from two perspectives: in terms of credit (or recognition of an individual's contribution) and in terms of authority, which can lead to increased agency as a professional.

In practical terms, the use of real or hypothetical cases that pose complex questions about intellectual property for technical communicators is a sound teaching method for instructing students about intellectual property from a rhetorical perspective. Selected scenarios and cases can be used to spark discussion, but it is important to note that they cannot teach legal behavior. Instructors and students should not seek to "solve" the cases by answering the question, "is this lawful?" Instead instructors and students should discuss the implications of different actions in terms of legal liability, ethics, and professional status. Such an approach will encourage legal and ethical activity, and it can also encourage students to actively participate in future workplace discussions on the issues. Broadly speaking, the goals for teaching about intellectual property in the technical communication classroom are to help students clarify their own thinking and judgment on intellectual property issues, gain greater confidence in addressing complex questions about intellectual property, and articulate those judgments more effectively.

Sample scenarios and cases might resemble the ones outlined in the opening paragraphs of this chapter. These cases were selected because they do not lend themselves to clear-cut answers. The first case raises questions about reusing and repurposing material. Through analyzing this case, students will see that the issue of legality ("who owns this work?") is not always simple. Although it is common for technical communicators to reuse and repurpose existing material, they must first take into account the source of such material. The work-for-hire doctrine specifies that the employer, rather than an individual writer, retains legal ownership of a work when it is prepared in the workplace. In this case, before the technical communicator can proceed with her revision of the existing documentation, she needs to determine who owns the work: her company, their competitor, the users participating in the online forum, or the party hosting the online forum? The technical communicator has discovered that portions of the work that she has been assigned to revise has been copied from two other sources for which the employer does not retain ownership rights. The first source includes the user manuals that can be accessed freely online from a well-known, industry-leading competitor's Web site. While writers feel free to reuse and/or build on materials prepared within their own company, materials prepared in other workplaces cannot likely be reused. Even though the materials are accessible to the public on a free and open Web site, they cannot be used without the permission of the company who legally owns them. The second source is material written by end-users of the product, copied from online public forums where users pose questions and respond with solutions. Even if these forums are publicly accessible and unaffiliated with another company, this text could be owned by the user who wrote it or by the party responsible for hosting the online forum, depending on whether a user agreement is in place that establishes ownership. Therefore, while the technical communicator likely will not be able to legally assume ownership over the text she has been asked to revise, some interesting questions arise concerning her ethical responsibilities based on what she has discovered. If the end-users of the product have pointed out errors in existing documentation and provided solutions for how to solve other users' problems, the technical communicator may feel compelled to share this new information. How should she do so?

The second case raises questions about receiving credit for the contributions made by a technical communicator. In this scenario, a writer has prepared user manuals for a new product, which have been packaged with the software and sold to a larger, third-party corporation. The technical publications department at the corporation determined that if they used the software company's existing documentation, they could drastically reduce their document development time. However, they are not sure whether the corporation has legal ownership over the user guides. In this scenario, the reason for wanting to reuse the material appears to be related to efficiency—both in terms of time and money. It is likely that from a legal standpoint, such reuse would be permissible. If the corporation purchased the software and its documentation as a package, then the technical communicators there may be able to reuse the software company's existing documentation. However, such use may raise some interesting questions about the relationship between professional status and author status for technical communicators. Will the technical communicators at the corporation receive credit for the work in the form of monetary compensation or increased professional status? What are the implications of packaging a software product and its documentation into a single unit? Does this model perhaps negatively affect the perception of the value added by the technical communicator to the overall quality of the product? Such questions reveal the implications of legal ownership models for the perceptions held of technical communicators by those outside of the field.

In scenarios such as these, instructors can demonstrate how questions about intellectual property for technical communicators raise deeper questions about authorship from legal and rhetorical perspectives. By teaching about intellectual property issues in the technical communication classroom from these two perspectives, instructors can help students to gain greater confidence in addressing complex questions about intellectual property and to articulate those judgments more effectively. With this background, students will be able to participate more fully in discussions about intellectual property, an important first step toward better communicating their value as rhetorical agents within their future workplace cultures.

REFERENCES

Brierly, Sean. (2002, January). Beyond the buzzword: Single sourcing. *Intercom*, 15-17.

Brill, Robert. (2008). You can be the fairest (user) of them all. http://bobbrill.net/?p=594

Dobrin, David N. (2004). What's technical about technical writing? In Johndan Johnson-Eilola & Stuart A. Selber (Eds.), *Central works in technical communication* (pp. 107-123). New York: Oxford.

Geisler, Cheryl. (2004). How ought we to understand the concept of rhetorical agency? Report from the ARS. *Rhetoric Society Quarterly*, 34 (3), 9-17.

Henry, Jim. (2000). *Writing workplace cultures: An archaeology of professional writing*. Carbondale: Southern Illinois University Press.

Herrington, TyAnna K. (1999). Work for hire for nonacademic creators. *Journal of Business and Technical Communication*, 13, 401-426.

Herrington, TyAnna K. (2003). *A legal primer for the digital age*. New York: Pearson Longman.

Heylar, Pamela S. (1992). Products liability: Meeting legal standards for adequate instructions. *Journal of Technical Writing and Communication*, (22) 2, 125-147.

Howard, Rebecca Moore. (1999). *Standing in the shadow of giants: Plagiarists, authors, collaborators*. Stamford, CT: Ablex.

International Committee of Medical Journal Editors (ICMJE). (2008). Uniform requirements for manuscripts submitted to biomedical journals: Writing and editing for biomedical publication. http://www.icmje.org/

Johnson-Eilola, Johndan, & Selber, Stuart A. (2001). Sketching a framework for graduate education in technical communication. *Technical Communication Quarterly*, 10 (4), 403-437.

Kennedy, Krista. (2009). Textual machinery: Authorial agency and bot-written texts in Wikipedia. In Michelle Smith & Barbara Warnick (Eds.), *Responsibilities of rhetoric: Proceedings of the 2008 Rhetoric Society of America Conference*. Long Grove, IL: Waveland Press.

Lundberg, Christian, & Gunn, Joshua. (2005). "Ouija board, are there any communications?" Agency, ontotheology, and the death of the humanist subject, or, continuing the ARS conversation. *Rhetoric Society Quarterly*, 35 (4), 83-105.

Manning, Michael D. (1997, May). *Hazard communication 101 for technical writers*. Presentation at the 44th Annual Society for Technical Communication Conference. Toronto, Canada.

Mead, Jay. (1998). Measuring the value added by technical documentation: A review of research and practice. *Technical Communication*, 45 (3), 353-379.

Miller, Carolyn. (1979). A humanistic rationale for technical writing. *College English*, 40 (6), 610-617.

Rocky Mountain Chapter of the Society for Technical Communication. (2008). Code for communicators. http://www.stcrmc.org/resources/resource_code.htm

Rutter, Russel. (2004). History, rhetoric, and humanism: Toward a more comprehensive definition of technical communication. In Johndan Johnson-Eilola & Stuart A. Selber (Eds.), *Central works in technical communication* (pp. 20-34). New York: Oxford.

Savage, Gerald J. (1996). Redefining the responsibilities of teachers and the social position of the technical communicator. *Technical Communication Quarterly*, (5) 3, 309-327.

Savage, Gerald J. (2003). Toward professional status in technical communication. In Gerald J. Savage & Teresa Kynell-Hunt (Eds.), *Power and legitimacy in technical communication: The historical and contemporary struggle for professional status* (pp. 1-12). Amityville, NY: Baywood.

Slack, Jennifer; Miller, David James; & Doak, Jeffrey. (1993). The technical communicator as author: Meaning, power, authority. *Journal of Business and Technical Communication*, 7 (1), 12-36.

Slack, Jennifer. (2004). Notes on "The technical communicator as author: Meaning, power, authority." In Johndan Johnson-Eilola & Stuart A. Selber (Eds.), *Central works in technical communication* (pp. 160-161). New York: Oxford.

Smith, Herb. (1990). Technical communications and the law: Product liability and safety labels. *Journal of Technical Writing and Communication*, 20 (3), 307-319.

20 RESPONSE TO PART III—FAIR USE: TEACHING THREE KEY IP CONCEPTS

Rebecca Moore Howard

My favorite part of Brian Ballentine's chapter is his calm remark about teaching a business and professional course that included a portion "that dealt with the intersections of writing, intellectual property, and ethics." It's that phrase, offered so matter-of-factly, as if every writing course contained such material.

That not every writing course does is why Part III of *Copy(Write)* is so important. Renee Hobbs and Katie Donnelly tell us that writing instructors are increasingly "incorporat[ing] media literacy concepts into their educational practices." But the movement has a long way to go. Produced by an undergraduate student, Nicole Nguyen's research underscores what professors Carol Haviland and Joan Mullin (2008) found in their cross-disciplinary, cross-institutional research: Instructors teach very little about intellectual property to their undergraduate students, and when they do, they focus on generic injunctions against plagiarism. That's a long way from the instruction that Jessica Reyman believes technical writers need, instruction that will help them understand their intellectual property rights in workplaces beyond academia.

I appreciate Nguyen's point that students may not identify the instruction they are receiving as belonging to the category of "intellectual property." Still, as I teach an advanced undergraduate course for writing majors, I hear them express their interest in intellectual property and their indignation that they have heretofore been taught nothing about their own rights. In my course, after reading Haviland and Mullin (2008), as well as Susan Blum (2009), the students deliberate on what sorts of follow-up research they want to do. Then they form collaborative research groups. Recently, one group decided to research issues of intellectual property on social-networking sites such as Facebook and

Twitter; another pursued the possibility of originality in music; a third analyzed the problems of intellectual property in the arts. These are the issues that they find fascinating, the issues they decide to research.

Academic injunctions against plagiarism are stern, admonitory. In Althusserian terms, they hail the student as feckless; through scare tactics, they demand obedience. Introduced to the range of IP issues that directly affect writers and given the choice of research topic, students in my class were not fascinated by academic plagiarism. Instead, they chose to research issues that cultural producers want to be informed about. In their research choices, they hail *themselves* as authors.

They make these choices even though, as Nguyen observes, it is in the frightening issues of plagiarism that students most often receive IP instruction. Leslie Johnson-Farris' finding is not surprising: Campus IP regulations aimed at students are obsessed with preventing those students from appropriating the work of others. These policies usually pursue that goal without addressing students' rights in copy, or the extent to which fair use guidelines allow them to use the work of others for educational purposes. In fact, as Hobbs and Donnelly note, many instructors assume that remixing is merely copying, not creating. Hence, students typically receive instruction designed to contain their potential malfeasances in the context of what many are pleased to call the "plagiarism epidemic." They are not customarily addressed as authors. They get the plagiarism half of intellectual property instruction, but not the copyright half—even when the plagiarism warnings are couched as warnings of copyright violation.

In my own teaching—including the faculty development workshops I conduct online and in person for colleagues around the country—I find that copyright and plagiarism are, in fact, rarely—if ever—differentiated. Faculty erroneously tell their students that plagiarism is a federal offense and that they could be prosecuted for it, or they say that using ideas derived from another infringes on that person's copyrights. Few people, even instructors, are clear about the fact that plagiarism is locally defined and adjudicated within a community; that it includes both words and ideas; and that it transgresses against the reader, making the reader believe that the plagiarist is the producer of the words or ideas gleaned from a source. In my experience, a fair number of instructors are also not clear about the fact that copyright violation is legally defined and adjudicated on the federal level; that copyright law typically covers only expression and not ideas; and that copyright infringement transgresses against the author, depriving that author of the cultural or monetary capital due him or her. It is a rare instructor who undertakes Johnson-Farris' task of informing herself about these issues.

It is significant, too, that Nguyen finds little instruction offered to students regarding the protection of their own rights in copy. In the field of composition studies, scholars have become accustomed to respecting and acknowledging students' intellectual property. As editor of *College Composition and Communication*, Joseph Harris (1994) took the lead in establishing this principle; as a contributor to *College English*, Amy Robillard (2006) provided a vanguard extension of it when she argued for scholars to cite student work. "To cite students," Robillard said, "is to forward the argument that writing as a mode of learning is a dialogic process; teachers teach students to write, but students, in their writing, teach teachers about more than the results of particular pedagogies" (p. 263). Robillard addressed instructor interpellation of students as errormakers, and directed our attention to the ways in which citing students moves scholars toward considering student work to be knowledge-making and not just ability-performing. Hobbs and Donnelly work from another perspective: that of the students. How do students come to think of themselves as authors and thus produce authentic texts? Certainly being published in a book like this or even being cited by their instructors are two ways, but most students will not have these experiences. Hobbs and Donnelly are right, then, to explore the effect of authentic audiences on students' authorial self-perception. Regardless of whether they are published or are being cited by others, they are being listened to and learned from. Their writing is *in circulation*. Who doesn't do their best writing in that circumstance?

Such thinking is, however, not necessarily the norm outside circles of composition scholarship. Not only are instructors willing to contribute students' intellectual property to profit-making corporations such as Turnitin.com (which Ballentine delightfully pillories), but faculty are willing to appropriate the intellectual work of graduate students (Howard, 2008). Even in its most innocuous iterations, the reluctance to accord authoriality to students can be breathtaking, as in Johnson-Farris' statement:

> The idea of student fair use statement met with confusion. Reactions varied from those who saw no need for such a policy, to those who thought students would be covered under the faculty fair use statement, to those who didn't know what I was talking about.

The foundational assumption of students as practicers rather than producers, I believe, makes it difficult to move faculty to a place where they see their students as knowledge-makers possessing valuable intellectual property, or as knowledge-makers in conversation with other texts.

Changing that foundational assumption will not come from direct argument, such as Robillard's (2006) article offers. Robillard describes the goal, but not the means. Valuable as her article is, it advocates a revolutionary practice to which most scholars will respond with reluctance or rejection. A missing piece, one essential to the success of Robillard's article, is a widespread understanding of the relevant component IP concepts: plagiarism, copyright, and fair use. Understanding these concepts makes it possible for us to see the complexities and grace of intellectual property, in which we are all implicated. As we come to recognize that all three concepts are of importance to students and instructors alike, we become positioned to understand that our students, too, are authors. Knowledge-makers. Cultural producers with a stake in culture.

It is astonishing, really, to contemplate the enthusiasm with which the professoriate pursues plagiarism, and the confusion these same educators have about the foundational concepts of plagiarism, copyright, and fair use. In many years of working for better institutional plagiarism policies, I have been continuously frustrated by administrators' insistence on all-encompassing, simplistic definitions of the term *plagiarism*. The baby-step differentiation between "plagiarism" and "misuse of sources" advocated by the Council of Writing Program Administrators has, as far as I know, become policy in no college. Policy-makers in my own university's revision of its plagiarism code took the not-so-bold step of introducing "misuse of sources" as an *option* for instructor interpretation of students' imperfect acknowledgement of influence.

It is in binary pairs that the phenomenon of plagiarism becomes clearest, as Marilyn Randall (1991) demonstrated when she differentiated plagiarism from quotation, and when Susan Stewart (1991) did the same for plagiarism and forgery. The failure to recognize the differences between plagiarism and copyright infringement thus not only blurs those differences, but obfuscates each category. It is in careful, collaborative, authoritative reports such as "The Code of Best Practices in Fair Use for Media Literacy Education" (Center for Social Media, 2008), whose genesis Hobbs and Donnelly explain, that blurred boundaries between fair use and creative remix lose their power to terrorize instructors (such as the English Education professor they describe).

Informing ourselves about IP issues does, as Ballentine acknowledges, take us out of our comfort zones. It will also, Hobbs and Donnelly point out, require us to ease up on process pedagogy as the foundational model of writing instruction. But, as Ballentine demonstrates, the effort is well worth it: Our courses become more pertinent to students' real writerly lives as they become professionals in a wide range of fields. It is irresponsible for us to send students into the workplace with as little IP information as had the technical writers whom Reyman describes.

Part III of *Copy(Write)* will be required reading in many of my future classes, and it will also inform the faculty development workshops I conduct. These chapters provide insightful, data-supported examinations of the problems we encounter when we fail to regard students as authors; when we confuse plagiarism with copyright violation; when we fail to understand the role of fair use in student and instructor work with intellectual property; and when we fail to make all of this explicit to students. We can do better, and these chapters provide good models for how we might move forward.

REFERENCES

Blum, Susan D. (2009). *My word! Plagiarism and college culture.* Ithaca, NY: Cornell University Press.

Center for Social Media, Media Education Lab at Temple University, and Washington College of Law. (2008). "Code of best practices in fair use for media literacy education." http://www.ncte.org/positions/statements/fairusemedialiteracy

Council of Writing Program Administrators. (2003, January). Defining and avoiding plagiarism: WPA statement on best policies. Retrieved October 20, 2010, from http://www.wpacouncil.org/node/9

Harris, Joseph. (1994). The work of others. *College Composition and Communication,* 45(4): 439-441.

Haviland, Carol Peterson, & Mullin, Joan. (Eds.). (2008). *Who owns this text? Plagiarism, authorship, and disciplinary cultures.* Logan: Utah State University Press.

Howard, Rebecca Moore. (2008). *Plagiarizing (from) graduate students.* In Rebecca Moore Howard & Amy E. Robillard (Eds.), Pluralizing plagiarism: Identities, contexts, pedagogies(pp. 92-100). Portsmouth, NH: Boynton/Cook.

Randall, Marilyn. (1991). Appropriate(d) discourse: Plagiarism and decolonization. *New Literary History,* 22, 525-541.

Robillard, Amy E. (2006). Young scholars affecting composition: A challenge to disciplinary citation practices. *College English,* 68, 253-270.

Stewart, Susan. (1991). *Crimes of writing: Problems in the containment of representation.* New York: Oxford University Press.

21 AFTERWORD

Clancy Ratliff

After reading this collection of important and impressively diverse examinations of copyright and intellectual property issues in writing studies, composition pedagogy, and academia in general, I have refined my position on some matters and reaffirmed my position on others. My idea of plagiarism, to start, is more nuanced than ever; I now understand more fully that "not cited" does not necessarily mean "plagiarized." Composition scholars studying plagiarism have argued that instances of "not cited but not plagiarized" are possible, especially in the writing of students from cultures with different ideas about intellectual property. But in this collection, Hall and Vincelette examine parody, noting that parody works through allusion, and that a parody will not be successful if the audience does not catch the references. This is to say that the audience must distinguish the original—the parts that are not "the author's own work"—in parody, and recognize that the author is not passing the source material off as his or her own. Moreover, citation is redundant because the audience already knows where the work came from.

Johnson-Farris, too, presents a useful "not cited but not plagiarized" example when she relays an anecdote of a student presentation, a slide from which featured a photograph of former president Bill Clinton. The photograph was not cited, but it would have been utterly unreasonable for the instructor to infer that the students had been close enough to Clinton to snap the photograph themselves, when they were likely children to boot: The students gave the presentation in 2005, and the photograph was from the Monica Lewinsky scandal in 1998. Certainly the majority of writing teachers, and almost every writing program administrator, would agree that these students did not cite but did not plagiarize. This is an easy example, but it—and others throughout this collection—help me to see that even in the citation-obsessed context of academic writing, sources sometimes do not need to be cited, and also that, for the audience, sometimes it does not matter where the source material came from or who authored it.

Another major insight I gained from this book concerns fair use. For years now, I have thought to myself that the number of articles, conference presentations, and informal discussions about fair use has been unnecessarily large. I couldn't understand why so many of my colleagues so often reiterated the need for fair use. Of course fair use is needed for freedom of speech, and, yes, it's troubling that universities are sometimes not willing to let teachers use any copyrighted material without permission and royalty payments, even when that use is fair. But I always thought that composition scholars were belaboring the point. I preferred to focus my study on alternative models of copyright: the General Public License for software, configurations of Creative Commons licenses for other work, and the Creative Commons Founders' Copyright when appropriate. I have advised students and colleagues that, when searching for materials and work to use for multimodal projects, search *first* for Creative Commons licensed and public domain content, and use all-rights-reserved work if the former is not suitable. I believed that an entire pool of intelligent, creative content exists on the Internet that composers *want* others to use, and I wanted to call others' attention to that work.

And I still believe this. I insist that these new models and new projects are crucial tools to be used in the service of innovative writing pedagogy (and art pedagogy, science pedagogy, and so forth). Open textbooks—such as *Writing Spaces: Readings on Writing*, edited by Charles Lowe and Pavel Zemliansky, and *Rhetoric and Composition: A Guide for the College Writer* on Wikibooks, written by Matt Barton and students at St. Cloud State University—are projects that deserve more of our field's attention and use. I still *do* think it is worth teachers' and students' time, when searching for source material for class work, to take advantage of the option to search Creative Commons licensed content only, which is available on Flickr, Google, and Yahoo!.

However, I was struck by TyAnna Herrington's alignment of philosophies of writing pedagogy with philosophies of copyright and authorship. By revealing the analogy among current–traditional pedagogy, objective epistemology, authoritarian government, and overbearing copyright—and by contrasting that with the analogy among social constructivist pedagogy, transactional epistemology, and democratic government—Herrington explains fair use stakes in a new and compelling way. But it was Janice Walker's explanation of the need for fair use as a middle ground that especially affected my thinking about copyright and the use of creative and intellectual content. Walker cautions us against accepting the current state of copyright as a given, lest we forfeit our rights to fair use. At the same time, she argues that we reinforce the dichotomy between copyright-heavy and copyright-light when we automatically favor Creative Commons and public domain material over copyrighted material.

Now my commitment is renewed: I insist on using everything I am entitled to use—copyright and copyleft—in the service of contributing to knowledge and culture.

In addition, my conviction that we need case studies and specific examples is strengthened after reading this collection. As Reyman and others among these chapters have maintained, the best way to highlight the legal and ethical problematics and complexities of authorship, including raising awareness among university administrators and students, is to teach using these engaging examples and to listen to others' encounters with copyright and intellectual property. Nguyen's chapter on if or how intellectual property issues are taught and how writing students digest such issues is testament to our need to continue integrating copyright into our courses, and Amidon's analysis of universities' intellectual property policies reminds us why it is in our self-interest as scholars and teachers to educate administrators about copyright. Ballentine's work with fashion merchandising students provides one such story. Wiebe's reflections about Sherrie Levine's photography and his father's "Humorous Incidents" is another. Westbrook provides an analysis of the Diebold emails, while Ridolfo and Rife pose the story of Maggie Ryan's photograph and its use. Through his analyses of an old scrapbook and his own digital image collection, Whipple shows the subtle authorship at work in the act of compiling the work of others. Dornsife uses anecdotes about Fleetwood Mac's *Rumours* and the digitally remastered version of *Star Wars* to show problems with the idea of "a copy," which suggests a certain distance from the original, a gap that no longer exists in the digital world. Galin reviews court cases involving scholars facing copyright issues, and Howard (whose example I intend to follow) listens to his students' experiences with copyright issues and presents them as scenarios for fine-grain analysis. To build upon the contributions included in this volume, I will add a few illustrative cases I have experienced and learned from.

In the course of my online life, I've gone to the sites of several feminist and environmentalist organizations, sites that usually feature information about emerging legislation affecting women or the environment, and the sites often ask users to contact their representatives in Congress. We have probably all seen these action letter interfaces: Users are asked to type their names and some contact information into designated fields on the left-side of the screen and on the right, there's a "template" letter in another field. The user can send the text as is, add to it, change some words here and there, or erase the organization's letter completely and write a letter from scratch. Often I unthinkingly click "send"—in much the same manner Barrios notes we agree to end-user license agreements. One time I realized, *I'm passing this text off as my own.* I'm taking something someone else wrote, putting my name on it, and turning it in. I now use this as a classroom example in my writing courses. I have even announced to students, projecting a web site from my laptop, that I was about to plagiarize, then submitted the action letter, to call their attention to the difference between academic writing and a variety of other situations involving writing and authorship.

In our teaching, we might also think further about possible analogies we can craft to illuminate students' and colleagues' understanding of intellectual property, plagiarism, authorship, and copyright. I posted one such analogy, which I called "Plagiarism and Parking Tickets," on my blog some years ago:

> I live in a fairly large city, and it can be difficult and time-consuming to find parking. Sometimes I park in a metered spot without putting any money in the meter. When I have quarters with me, of course I put them in the meter, but sometimes I don't have any, and that's all the meter will take. So I don't put anything in there. Most of the time I go back out to my car to find no ticket, but occasionally I do get parking tickets. I know that when I don't put money in the meter, I run the risk of getting a ticket. When I don't put money in the meter, I feel a little guilty, I guess, but I won't lose any sleep over it. I have no aspirations to go my whole life without getting any parking tickets. Keeping quarters with me and putting them in the meter isn't something I take any pride in. Plus, when I get a ticket, I pay it, and if I factor the cost of the ticket in with all those times I got free parking, it evens out. Either way I'm paying for parking; the city's going to get their money one way or another. ...
>
> I've got a packed schedule with classes, extracurricular activities, and a part-time job. Sometimes I buy essays online and turn them in for my classes. When I have the time and am engaged and motivated by the assignment, of course I do the writing myself, but sometimes I don't have the time or interest, and I have to turn *something* in. I know that when I don't do the writing myself, I risk getting turned in for plagiarism. When I don't do the writing myself, I feel a little guilty, I guess, but I won't lose any sleep over it. I have no aspirations to be a professional writer. Basically I just want to pass the course with a C or above. Plus, when I get caught, I just take the zero on the assignment, and if I factor that in with all the

time and headache I save not having to do an assignment that doesn't interest me, it evens out. Besides, sometimes I get A's on the papers I buy. The grade I get at the end is probably about the same as the grade I'd have gotten had I done all the work myself.

This analogy, I believe, puts the ethics of authorship and intellectual property into perspective. Although plagiarism is certainly a violation of academic norms, teachers often get very upset when it happens to them, perceiving the action as a personal insult. However, for the student, the act of buying a paper may be simply for expediency's sake—an act revealing only low prioritization of the assignment, poor time management, and perhaps a lack of maturity. One could make a similar analogy between writing and returning library books past the due date, which a colleague suggested to me. I plan to use these analogies as discussion prompts in the training of new teachers, but I may also use them in my first-year writing class; I expect that doing so—and encouraging students to come up with other analogues to plagiarism—could initiate an open dialogue about the ethics involved in academic writing.

The third case I would like to share concerns copyright infringement and fair use. In December 2009, Australian artist Jane Korman released a video in which she, her children, and her elderly father, a Holocaust survivor, danced to Gloria Gaynor's song "I Will Survive" at various sites associated with the Holocaust. The video, titled "I Will Survive: Dancing Auschwitz," went viral on YouTube in early July 2010. Viewers' responses ranged from expressing outrage, to finding the video mildly offensive or distasteful, to crying joyfully. Many viewers remarked, on blogs and in comments under the video, that it was an important work, and the video garnered some attention from major news outlets, including *Haaretz*. Upon seeing the video, I reflected on it as an instance of why we need a robust public domain, or commons, of creative and intellectual work to use to make new works—and what a shame it would be if the rightsholder of "I Will Survive" were to send a cease and desist letter to YouTube, employees of which would likely remove the video due to claims of copyright infringement. The next time I tried to watch the video, I saw the following notice: "This video is no longer available due to a copyright claim by APRA/AMCOS." These abbreviations stand for the Australasian Performing Right Association and Australasian Mechanical Copyright Owners Society. Although the video file has been copied and reposted by other users, the APRA and AMCOS are continuing to limit the distribution of the video as much as possible.

After the takedown of the video, some users posted comments about the use of "I Will Survive," noting that because it was not used for profit, it should be considered fair use. Also, it was used for the purpose of critical commentary; through the juxtaposition of the solemnity of the landmarks and the whimsy of the dancing, which sometimes resembled the movements of a cheerleading squad, the artist was making a statement that the Jewish people, represented by this healthy and vigorous family, have thrived in spite of devastating loss. This case could be examined in a class or other meeting for fruitful discussion about fair use and four-factor analysis, or a discussion about how the case does or does not embody the "Code of Best Practices for Fair Use in Media Literacy Education," explained in helpful detail by Hobbs and Donnelly. The whole song was used, but for critical commentary and in a not-for-profit context; the extent to which the use was transformative is thus open for debate.

Korman's work, an artistic statement of celebratory defiance of the Nazi regime, is an almost too obvious example of why fair use is essential for democracy and free speech, as this book has shown. I would like to end by turning to a 2009 article in *New Left Review* in which Slavoj Žižek identified four "antagonisms" of global capitalism:

> the looming threat of ecological catastrophe; the inappropriateness of private property for so-called intellectual property; the socio-ethical implications of new technoscientific developments, especially in biogenetics; and last, but not least, new forms of social apartheid—new walls and slums. (p. 53)

For Žižek, the first three of these antagonisms contain "an awareness of the destructive potential—up to the self-annihilation of humanity itself—in allowing the capitalist logic of enclosing these commons a free run" (p. 54). He identified these issues as evidence for the "practical urgency" of "the communist hypothesis," and more generally as evidence of the need for a cultural and intellectual commons (p. 53). What I appreciate here is the fact that Žižek situates intellectual property in the same constellation with bioethics and environmental damage. I do not mean to suggest that Žižek finds these all equally important, but I value his locating intellectual property in a system of capitalist logic alongside other major global problems. I value this collection as well for reminding us, as a community of scholars, of what is truly at stake when we talk about the right to copy.

REFERENCE

Žižek, Slavoj. (2009, May-June). How to begin from the beginning. *New Left Review*, 57, pp. 43-55.

BIOGRAPHICAL NOTES

Timothy R. Amidon is a Ph.D. student and teaching assistant in the English and Writing Departments at the University of Rhode Island, where he teaches first-year composition, the short story, and writing in electronic environments. His research interests focus on the rhetorical intersections between writing technologies and institutional/public policy, with specific emphasis on the interrelationships between literacy, invention, delivery, and ownership. He currently serves as Secretary for the Graduate Assistants United (URI Graduate Student Chapter of the AAUP) and as captain for an engine company in a local volunteer fire department.

Brian D. Ballentine, prior to completing his Ph.D. at Case Western Reserve University, was a senior software engineer for Philips Medical Systems designing user-interfaces for web-based radiology applications and specializing in human–computer interaction. Ballentine has published in *Computers and Composition Online*, *IEEE Transactions on Professional Communication*, *Across the Disciplines*, and several edited collections dedicated to issues surrounding technology and writing. Ballentine is currently an assistant professor and coordinator for the Professional Writing and Editing program at West Virginia University.

Barclay Barrios is an assistant professor and the Director of Writing Programs at Florida Atlantic University. His work focuses on writing program administration, queer composition, digital media, pedagogy, and computers and composition. He has published in *Computers and Composition* and *WPA: Writing Program Administration*, and is the author of the composition reader *Emerging: Contemporary Readings for Writers* (Bedford/St. Martin's, 2010).

Dànielle Nicole DeVoss is a professor of Professional Writing at Michigan State University. Her research interests include digital–visual rhetorics and intellectual property issues in digital space. DeVoss co-edited (with Heidi McKee) *Digital Writing Research: Technologies, Methodologies, and Ethical Issues* (2007, Hampton Press), which won the 2007 Computers and Composition Distinguished Book Award. DeVoss also co-edited (with Heidi McKee and Dickie

Selfe) Technological Ecologies and Sustainability, the first title to be published by Computers and Composition Digital Press, the only digital press with a university press imprint. In November 2010, she published—with Elyse Eidman-Aadahl and Troy Hicks—a National Writing Project book, titled Because Digital Writing Matters (Jossey-Bass).

Katie Donnelly is the Associate Director of the Tookany Tacony-Frankford Watershed Partnership. She holds a Master's Degree in Broadcasting, Telecommunications and Mass Media from Temple University. As a Research Associate at the Media Education Lab, she helped develop the Code of Best Practices in Fair Use for Media Literacy Education.

Rob Dornsife is an associate professor of English at Creighton University, where he teaches composition, including multimedia theory and practice, popular culture, film, rhetorical theory, and other courses. Rob has published in *Kairos, Computers and Composition Online*, the *Journal of Advanced Composition, Radical Pedagogy*, and other journals. He provided "Computer Connection" text for Harcourt's *Rinehart Guide to Grammar and Usage* (1993), and contributed a chapter to the NCTE book *Administrative Problem-Solving for Writing Programs and Writing Centers* (1999). At Creighton, Rob was awarded the Reloy Garcia Award for Excellence in Teaching in English, and received the Creighton College of Arts and Sciences Award for Professional Excellence in Full Time Teaching. He also received Creighton University's highest teaching honor, the Robert F. Kennedy Student Award for Excellence in Teaching.

Jeffrey R. Galin is an assistant professor of English at Florida Atlantic University and Director of the University Center for Excellence in Writing. He co-edited *The Dialogic Classroom: Teachers Integrating Computer Technology, Pedagogy, and Research* (NCTE, 1998) and *Teaching/Writing in the Late Age of Print* (Hampton Press, 2003). He has also published articles in *College Composition and Communication, Computers and Composition,* and *Kairos*. His current research interests include the history of educational reform, literacy studies, intellectual property, and the impact of computers on teaching and academic policies. He teaches courses in undergraduate and graduate composition, intellectual property, literacy theory, and literary productions.

Kathie Gossett is an assistant professor of digital humanities in the English department at Iowa State University. She has published in *Kairos: A Journal of Rhetoric, Technology, and Pedagogy* and in *Reading (and Writing) New Media* (Hampton Press, 2010). Her research interests include intellectual property, open source design, new media theory & practice, user experience design and medieval rhetoric. Kathie was a member of the NEH/CHNM-sponsored team who developed the *Anthologize* plug-in for the WordPress platform and is the project manager for the NEH-sponsored Kairos/OJS plug-in project. She received the 2008 *Computers and Composition* Michelle Kendrick Outstanding Digital Production/Scholarship Award and the 2009 Teaching with Technology University Teaching Award at Old Dominion University.

E. Ashley Hall is a teaching fellow and Assistant Director of the Studio for Instructional Technology in English Studies (SITES Lab) at the University of North Carolina at Chapel Hill. As a primary investigator for a 2009–2010 grant, she helped launch the *PIT Journal*, an open-source, online, peer-reviewed publishing platform designed to transform teaching and learning by promoting and publishing undergraduate scholarship. Hall serves as a senior editor and site administrator for the journal, and teaches an experimental first-year writing course, which she designed for her students to participate as authors/submitters, peer readers/reviewers, and peer-source publishers. She received a 2009–2010 Erika Lindemann Award for Excellence in Teaching. She is a co-author of a chapter about PIT in the collection *Designing Web-based Applications for 21st Century Classrooms*.

TyAnna K. Herrington is an associate professor in the Georgia Institute of Technology's School of Literature, Communication, and Culture. She is the author of three books: *Intellectual Property on Campus: Students' Rights and Responsibilities* (Southern Illinois University Press, 2010); *Controlling Voices: Intellectual Property, Humanistic Studies and the Internet* (Southern Illinois University Press, 2001); and *A Legal Primer for Technical Communicators* (Allyn and Bacon, 2003). Herrington, who holds both J.D. and Ph.D. degrees, was awarded a Fulbright professorship in 1999, which led to her development of the Global Classroom Project.

Renee Hobbs is a professor at the School of Communications and Theater at Temple University in Philadelphia, where she founded the Media Education Lab. She is the author of *Copyright Clarity: How Fair Use Supports Digital Learning* (Corwin/Sage, 2010) and *Reading the Media: Media Literacy in High School English* (Teachers College Press, 2007). She is co-editor of the *Journal of Media Literacy Education*, an open-access, peer-reviewed journal. She has worked for over 20 years with school districts all across the U.S. to support teacher learning in media literacy education and has developed numerous multimedia curriculum materials to help students build critical thinking and communication skills in relation to mass media, popular culture, and digital media.

Tharon Howard is a professor of English at Clemson University, where he teaches seminars in digital rhetorics, visual communication, 21st-century digital publishing,

Biographical Notes

usability testing and user-experience design, and technical writing. His most recent text is *Design to Thrive: Creating Social Networks and Online Communities that Last* (Morgan Kaufmann, 2010). He has also published *Electronic Networks: Crossing Boundaries, Creating Communities* (Heinemann, 1999) and *Visual Communication: A Writers Guide* (Longman, 2001, 2nd ed.). His often-anthologized work, "Who 'Owns' Electronic Texts" first appeared in Electronic Literacies in the Workplace (NCTE, 1996).

Leslie Johnson-Farris is a professor at Lansing Community College, where she teaches writing and children's literature and serves as the Composition II Assessment Coordinator.

John Logie is an associate professor in Writing Studies at the University of Minnesota. Logie published *Peers, Pirates, and Persuasion* (Parlor Press, 2006), focused on the role of rhetoric in the debates over peer-to-peer technologies. His research explores the Internet, intellectual property laws, and the conflicts that arise with changes in communicative technologies. His current book project, *Copyright Control: A Tragedy in Five Acts*, examines the rhetorical strategies at the heart of five recent amendments to U.S. copyright law. Logie's publications have appeared in Rhetoric Society Quarterly, Rhetoric Review, and First Monday.

Rebecca Moore Howard is a professor of Writing and Rhetoric at Syracuse University. Moore Howard has published dozens of chapters and articles, including pieces in *Composition Studies, Computers and Compositions, Writing Center Journal,* and *College English*. She co-edited *Pluralizing Plagiarism: Identities, Contexts, Pedagogies* (Heinemann Boynton/Cook, 2008); *Authorship in Composition Studies* (Wadsworth, 2006); and *Coming of Age: The Advanced Writing Curriculum* (Heinemann Boynton/Cook, 2000). Most recently, she published two textbooks—*Research Matters: A Guide to Research Writing*, and *Writing Matters: A Handbook for Writing and Research* (both with McGraw-Hill, 2010).

Nicole Nguyen is a second-year law student at DePaul University College of Law, where she is pursuing a certificate in intellectual property. Nicole is a staff writer for the *Journal of Art, Technology, and Intellectual Property*, and is secretary of the Intellectual Property Law Society.

Jim Porter is a professor at Miami University of Ohio in the Department of English and at the Armstrong Institute for Interactive Media Studies, and is Director of College Composition. Porter's recent publications include articles in *Computers and*

Composition and *College Composition and Communication*. Porter co-authored *The Ethics of Internet Research: A Rhetorical, Case-Based Process* (Peter Lang, 2009).

Clancy Ratliff is an assistant professor of English and Director of First-Year Writing at the University of Louisiana at Lafayette. Ratliff has recently published pieces in *Women's Studies Quarterly; Composition, Copyright, & Intellectual Property Law* (SUNY Press, 2009); and *Computers and Composition Online*. She is the co-editor of *Into the Blogosphere: Rhetoric, Community, and Culture of Weblogs* (2004), the first collection of scholarly essays about blogging. For the last four years, she has been editor of the *CCCC Intellectual Property Annual*.

Jessica Reyman is an assistant professor of rhetoric and professional writing in the Department of English at Northern Illinois University. Her essays on authorship, copyright, and intellectual property law have appeared in *College Composition and Communication, Technical Communication*, and in several edited collections. She is the author of *The Rhetoric of Intellectual Property: Copyright Law and the Regulation of Digital Culture* (Routledge, 2010).

Jim Ridolfo is an assistant professor of Composition and Rhetoric in the Department of English at the University of Cincinnati. His scholarship examines the intersection of practice, rhetorical theory, and the digital humanities. His work has recently appeared in *Kairos*, the *Journal of Community Literacy, Pedagogy, Ariadne, Enculturation*, and the *Journal of Advanced Composition*.

Martine Courant Rife, J.D., Ph.D., is a professor of writing at Lansing Community College, where she teaches courses in digital authorship, technical and business writing, and first-year composition. She serves as Senior Chair of the CCCC-IP Caucus and is a CCCC-IP Committee member. Her work has appeared in *Technical Communication, Computers and Composition, Kairos, Teaching English in Two-Year Colleges, Technical Communication Quarterly*, and the *Journal of Business and Technical Communication*. She has pieces forthcoming in *IEEE Transactions on Professional Communication* and *E-Learning*. Martine received the 2007 Frank R. Smith Outstanding Journal Article Award for "Technical Communicators and Digital Writing Risk Assessment."

Shaun Slattery is a strategy consultant for a social software company and has been a faculty member at DePaul University and the University of South Florida Polytechnic, where he taught technical and professional writing and new media. His research on digital writing practices has been published in *Technical Communication*

Quarterly; Technical Communication; Rhetorically Rethinking Usability: Theories, Practices, and Methodologies (Hampton Press, 2009); and *Digital Writing Research: Technologies, Methodologies, and Ethical Issues* (Hampton Press, 2007).

Janice R. Walker is a professor of Writing and Linguistics at Georgia Southern University. She has published articles and books on issues of copyright, online research, documentation, and technology. Recipient of the 2008 CCCC Committee on Computers in Composition and Communication Technology Innovator Award, she is also the founder and coordinator of the Graduate Research Network at the annual Computers and Writing conference, and co-coordinator for the Georgia Conference on Information Literacy hosted by Georgia Southern University.

Steve Westbrook is an associate professor of English at California State University–Fullerton, where he teaches courses in composition, creative writing, and cultural studies. He is editor of *Composition & Copyright: Perspectives on Teaching, Textmaking, and Fair Use* (SUNY Press, 2009). His articles on intellectual property and multimedia composition have appeared in a number of journals, including *College English*.

Bob Whipple is professor of English and chair of the department of English at Creighton University, where he teaches courses in writing and in technology and literacy. He has published books on Socratic method and American author John P. Marquand, and essays on the multimediated writing process, predicting technological change and teaching with wikis.

Russel Wiebe taught English most recently at Felician College. His areas of interest included—but were not limited—to digital theory and literary theory. Among the pioneers in digital composition theory, Wiebe published in *Kairos, Computers and Composition Online*, the *Journal of Advanced Composition*, and many other outlets. Wiebe was a regular presenter at the Computers and Writing conference. Wiebe passed away unexpectedly in 2009.

Elizabeth J. Vincelette is a lecturer at Old Dominion University, teaching courses in composition and American literature. She received the 2010 award for Outstanding Classroom Instructor from Old Dominion University for teaching undergraduate English courses in American literature and composition. She has published in *NeoAmericanist* and *The Edgar Allan Poe Review*.

Index

A

Aalmuhammed v. Lee 360
aboriginal bones, ownership 231
"acceptable" plagiarism 33
access; access to work 16, 303; fair access 245
Action Coalition for Media Education (ACME) 292
activist pedagogy 191
Adler-Kassner, Linda 327, 329, 344
Adobe Corporation 121
Adobe Flash 109
agency; distributed agency 50, 109; paradox of 52, 71; rhetorical 358, 359, 360, 361, 362, 363, 364, 366; student 174
agency law test, 13-element 57, 58
Aimster 9
Alliance for a Media Literate America (AMLA) 292
Alliance of Rhetoric Societies 360
Almjeld, Jen 101, 102, 104, 105
Ambiguous language approach 63
Ambrose, Stephen 34
American Association of Community Colleges 315, 325
American Association of University Professors 74
American Society of Mechanical Engineers 344
American University 281, 293, 298

Amidon, Timothy 49, 51, 75, 122, 150, 217, 296, 353, 377
analog technologies 131, 184
Anderson, Daniel 164, 177, 183, 200
Anderson, Nate 11, 25
Andrews, Doreen 305, 306
Anson, Chris 327, 344
Aoki, Keith 306
Apple Corporation 117, 118, 126
appropriation 38, 39, 40, 41, 44, 154, 155, 159, 164, 165, 166, 171, 174, 176, 181, 182, 184, 186, 187, 191, 196, 223, 225, 226, 228, 230, 231, 232, 233, 234, 238, 239, 242, 268, 276, 279, 291
Aqua 249
Armani 336
arrangement 116, 122, 133, 189, 196, 280, 360
articulation model 357
artistic license 132, 142, 143, 144, 145
arXiv.org 17
As I Lay Dying 283
assemblage 76, 192, 201, 255, 260, 264, 265, 294
Associated Press 309
Association of Research Libraries (ARL) 17, 26
Atkinson v. Doherty & Co 235, 242
audience 235, 242; authentic audience 289
audio cassette 137

Index

Aufderheide, Patricia 277, 280, 293, 307
authorial intention 42
authorship 33, 34, 36, 37, 38, 47, 49, 50, 53, 57, 58, 59, 61, 62, 63, 68, 70, 73, 74, 76, 77, 98, 116, 160, 179, 181, 183, 184, 189, 190, 192, 205, 253, 257, 276, 281, 321, 323, 330, 340, 343, 345, 347, 348, 349, 350, 351, 352, 353, 354, 355, 356, 357, 358, 359, 360, 361, 362, 363, 364, 366, 373, 376, 377, 378, 379; authorship criteria 352; corporate authorship 183, 352, 354, 360; university authorship 57
A.V. v. iParadigms 81, 97

B

Ballentine, Brian D. 80, 173, 175, 176, 327, 344, 369, 371, 372, 377
Barbie 162, 249, 250
"Barbie Girl" 249
Barnes, David 331, 345
Barnett, Jonathan 335, 338, 341, 344
Barrios, Barclay 30, 79, 150, 377
Barthes, Roland 159, 176
Barton, Matthew D. 255, 259, 376
Basic Books, Inc. v. Kinko's Graphics Corp. 3
Bazerman, Charles 201, 345
Beard, Joseph 110, 111, 128
Beatles 115, 342
Beckles, Tricia 297, 307
Bell, Tom W. 3, 10, 14, 24, 25
Benfer, Amy 163, 176
Benkler, Yochai 279, 280, 293
Beowulf 286
Berkeley University (CA) 117
Berkman Center for Internet and Society 5, 15, 16
Berlin Declaration on Open Access to Knowledge in the Sciences and Humanities 18

Berlin, James 245, 251, 252
Bethesda Statement on Open Access Publishing 18
Beyond Words 164
Biden, Joe 31, 34
Bielstein, Susan M. 162, 176, 215, 220
Bill Graham Archives v. Dorling Kindersley, Ltd. 259
Birch, Stanley 249, 260
The Black Album 342
Blass, Evan 80, 97
blog 17, 46, 84, 97, 109, 123, 124, 156, 185, 188, 189, 256, 305, 336, 378
Blythe, Stuart 51, 52, 55, 59, 70, 71, 72, 73, 75, 77
Boise State University (ID) 56, 75
Bolter, Jay David 86, 90, 97, 134, 135, 140, 142, 147
Boxer, Barbara 195, 335
Boyle, James 306
Boynton Cook/Heinemann/Greenwood Press 11
Bradbury, Ray 285
Brand New Day 133
Brandt, Deborah 324, 325
Brannon, Lil 329, 345
Brierly, Sean 352
Brill, Robert 363, 366
browsewrap 82
Bruce, David 276, 293
Buckingham, David 282, 286, 287, 293
2002 Budapest Open Access Initiative 17
Burke, Kenneth. *See* Pentad, dramatism; *See also* Pentad, dramatism
Butler Community College 310, 311, 326

C

Cambridge University Press 211, 260

388

Campbell v. Acuff Rose 250, 270
Caputi, Jane 4, 5, 6, 7, 8, 9, 11, 14, 24, 25
Carroll, Jude 315, 321, 326
Carson v. Here's Johnny Portable Toilets, Inc. 235, 242
Cartesianism. *See also* Descartes
Caruthers, Claudia 238, 242
Carver, Raymond 159, 160, 161, 263
Casamiquela, Ryan J. 81, 82, 83, 84, 97
Cavanaugh, Tim 12
Center for Social Media at the School of Communication 298
Chanel 336
Chan, Leslie 18, 25
cheating 29, 30, 31, 32, 39, 40, 95
Chemical Corp. of America v. Anheuser-Busch, Inc. 344
Chen, Stephen 333, 345
chilling effects 4, 15
Chronicle of Higher Education 47, 98
The Chronicle Review 31
citation 11, 14, 31, 34, 39, 109, 164, 179, 180, 189, 193, 200, 205, 206, 209, 214, 215, 222, 266, 285, 300, 302, 303, 314, 318, 319, 320, 321, 324, 373, 375
Citizen Media Law 15, 16
Civic Engagement 288
Cleveland State University 56, 75
clickwrap 80, 81, 82, 83, 84, 86, 87, 88, 90, 92, 93, 94, 95, 96, 97
Clinton, Bill 309, 375
Clinton, Hillary 335
Coach 334, 341
Coalition for Networked Information (CNI) 19
Coca-Cola 332
"Code of Best Practices in Fair Use for Media Literacy Education" 277
Cohn, Cindy A. 169, 171, 176
Colbert, Courtney 40, 46
collaborative writing 41, 352

College Art Association Committee on Intellectual Property 41, 176
College Composition and Communication 3, 25, 55, 75, 76, 77, 98, 154, 160, 201, 206, 222, 243, 256, 294, 314, 326, 346, 371, 373
College Composition and Communication Intellectual Property Caucus (CCCC-IP) 3, 4, 5, 76, 154, 326
Columbia Guide to Online Style 215
Commission on New Technology Uses of Copyrighted Works (CONTU) 4
Commonplace Book 99
commons 99
Commons 15, 16, 50, 51, 53, 55, 71, 73, 91, 92, 93, 150, 154, 165, 212, 219, 236, 238, 256, 283, 294, 295, 300, 303, 323, 376
common topics. *See also* topoi
community 22, 23, 24, 26, 42, 52, 143, 248, 263, 272, 277, 281, 282, 287, 288, 289, 309, 311, 312, 314, 315, 326, 334, 346, 370, 380
CompPile 22, 24
Concord High School in New Hampshire 283
Condi Rice Raps 181, 193, 194, 195, 196, 201
Conference on Fair Use (CONFU) 4
Consolidated Appropriations Act, 2008 18
convergence of media 108
Coombe, Rosemary J. 170, 176
Cope, Bill 200
copyright; copyright infringement 13, 41, 81, 116, 120, 125, 126, 127, 151, 161, 164, 181, 183, 187, 266, 314, 317, 319, 326, 347, 370, 372, 379; metaphorical understandings of 108, 111; "moral rights" approach to 253, 257
Copyright Act of 1909 10
Copyright Act of 1976 116, 151, 245, 249, 257

Index

Copyright Clearance Center 3, 14
Copyright for Librarians 16
corporate authorship 183, 352, 354, 360
Costanzo 276, 280, 285, 293
The Cost of Copyright Confusion for Media Literacy 277, 287, 292
Council of Writing Program Administrators 92, 97, 372, 373
Counterfeit Chic 336
The Country Wife 44
course-management systems 206
Creative Commons 15, 16, 50, 51, 53, 55, 71, 73, 91, 92, 93, 150, 154, 165, 212, 219, 236, 256, 295, 300, 303, 323, 376; Creative Commons license 91, 92, 150
Crews, Clyde Wayne Jr. 7, 25, 277, 293
Crews, Kenneth 7, 277
critical technological literacy 92
Crow, Judith 306
CSPAN 195
cultural criticism 278
CUNY–College of Staten Island 56
Curtis, Alex 232
Cushman, Ellen 49, 75
Cyberlaw Clinic 16

D

Dacome, Lucia 101, 105
Dallas Cowboys Cheerleaders, Inc. v. Pussycat Cinema 344
Dames, K. Matthew 81, 97
Dauterman, Jennie 128
Davies, Maura Messenger 290, 293
Davis, Nathan 80, 81, 82, 83, 84, 97
Day, Kami 314, 326
Day, Michael 260, 345, 346
De Castell, Suzanne 85, 98
DeLuca, Kevin Michael 224, 242
democratic process 245, 247, 252, 253, 256

derivative work 116, 117, 250
Derrida, Jacques 41
Derringer, Nancy N. 34, 46
Design, Compose, Advocate 164
Designing Documents and Understanding Visuals 165
Designing Writing 167, 168
Design Piracy Prohibition Act 329, 331, 335, 336, 337, 341, 342, 343, 345
DeVoss, Dànielle Nicole 49, 50, 54, 55, 59, 75, 76, 179, 181, 183, 185, 186, 200, 215, 221, 228, 229, 240, 243, 255, 265, 267, 272, 299, 306, 312, 314, 315, 320, 321, 326
Diebold 168, 169, 170, 171, 172, 173, 174, 176, 177, 266, 269, 272, 377
DigiRhet 180, 181, 200
digital delivery 76, 200, 228, 272
Digital Media and Composition Institute (DMAC) 55
Digital Millennium Copyright Act (DMCA) 4
digital paradigm 132, 142, 145
digital portfolios 297
Ding, Huiling 297, 306
DJ Danger Mouse 342
Doak, Jeffrey 357, 367
Dobrin, David N. 358, 366
Doheny-Farina, Stephen 345
doujinshi comics 338, 342
dramatism. *See also* Burke, Kenneth; *See also* Burke, Kenneth; *See also* Burke, Kenneth; *See also* Burke, Kenneth; *See also* Burke, Kenneth
Dreamworlds 6, 26
Duffy, Kevin Thomas 162
Dush, Lisa 160, 161, 163, 176
DVD 132, 137, 140, 276

E

Ede, Lisa 50, 76, 343, 345
Educational Video Center 288

Electronic Frontier Foundation 5, 10, 14, 15, 26, 117, 256
Eliot, T.S. 5, 11, 159, 176
elocutio. See style
email 82, 108, 120, 121, 126, 128, 142, 169, 170, 171, 172, 174, 204, 256, 267, 300, 304; public 108, 120
Emerson, Lisa 339, 345
ethos 66, 101, 146, 189, 229, 230, 240, 241, 319, 330
Everett Community College 29, 37
Everything's an Argument 165
expressivist pedagogy 253

F

Facebook 93, 183, 187, 188, 189, 206, 295, 305, 369
Fahrenheit 451 285
Faigley, Lester 165, 176
Fair Copyright in Research Works Act 24
fair use 3, 4, 5, 6, 7, 8, 9, 10, 11, 12, 13, 14, 15, 16, 21, 22, 23, 24, 25, 26, 27, 58, 98, 113, 115, 116, 117, 120, 125, 128, 151, 152, 154, 159, 160, 161, 162, 163, 164, 165, 166, 167, 168, 169, 170, 171, 172, 173, 174, 175, 176, 177, 191, 192, 201, 205, 207, 208, 209, 210, 211, 212, 213, 216, 217, 219, 220, 221, 223, 237, 242, 245, 246, 247, 249, 250, 251, 252, 253, 254, 255, 256, 257, 258, 259, 260, 261, 265, 266, 267, 268, 269, 270, 271, 276, 277, 279, 281, 282, 283, 284, 286, 287, 291, 292, 293, 297, 298, 300, 301, 307, 310, 311, 312, 313, 314, 316, 317, 318, 319, 322, 324, 325, 330, 331, 370, 371, 372, 373, 376, 379, 380
Fanning, Shawn 9, 183
Fantastic Beasts & Where to Find Them 14
fared use 14, 25

Farrar, Strauss, and Giroux 12
Faulkner, William 283
feminism 76
Ferragamo, Salvatore 337
first-year writing courses 296, 297, 304, 305, 315
Fisher, William 297, 306
Fleetwood Mac 133, 377
Flessas, Tatiana 231, 238, 239, 242
Flickr 93, 102, 109, 124, 125, 303, 305, 376
forensic rhetoric. *See* rhetoric, judicial
Fortune, Ron 35, 45, 47
Foucault, Michel 22, 32, 41, 42, 46, 84, 200
four-factor analysis 166, 167, 168, 171, 173, 174, 175, 380
Framers 245, 246, 247, 248, 250, 252, 259
Frankel, Mark S. 122, 128
free speech 124, 166, 177, 223, 231, 232, 235, 245, 246, 247, 248, 249, 250, 251, 252, 253, 254, 255, 256, 257, 258, 259, 260, 266, 380
Friend, Christy 164, 177
Frost, Robert 109, 124
Frucci, Adam 80, 97

G

Galin, Jeffrey 3, 23, 26, 53, 70, 74, 76, 154, 220, 296, 377
Gasser, Urs 306
Geisler, Cheryl 343, 345, 360, 366
George, Diana 40, 41, 97, 128, 149, 165, 176, 264, 330, 340, 345, 346
Georgia Conference on Information Literacy 211, 222
Georgia State University 211
Georgi, David 297, 306
Ghosh, Shuba 258, 260
Gitlin, Todd 279, 293
Gitman, Yury 248, 260
Gladwell, Malcolm 38, 39, 44, 46

391

Glau, Gegory R. 165, 177, 208, 222
Goeglein, Timothy S. 34, 46
Gomulkiewicz, Robert W. 80, 81, 83, 84, 88, 91, 97
Gone With the Wind 249
Goodman, Steven 287, 288, 293
Goodwin, Doris Kearns 32, 34
Google 36, 39, 80, 83, 97, 98, 102, 164, 263, 277, 297, 376; Chrome 80, 97; Picasa 102
Gossett, Kathie 124, 179, 198, 201, 265, 270, 271
Grabill, Jeffrey T. 49, 51, 75, 77
Grand Upright v. Warner 161, 174, 176
Grateful Dead 119, 120, 128, 162
The Grey Album 342
Grokster 5, 9, 13, 24, 173
Grusin, Richard 86, 90, 97
guarantorship 354
Gucci 333, 344
Guess, Andy 211, 221
Gunn, Joshua 360, 367
Gurak, Laura J. 205, 221, 345

H

Haas, Christina 345
Harel, Idit 257, 260
Harlow, Jackie 306
Harnad, Steven 17, 20, 21, 23, 24, 26
Harper's Magazine 45
Hart-Davidson, William 255, 260, 297, 307
Harvard University 21
Havens, Earle 99, 100, 104, 105
Hayles, N. Katherine 181, 200
Heins, Marjorie 297, 307
Henning, Kathleen 324, 326
Henry, Jim 200, 242, 293, 294, 361, 366
Hermès 336
Herrington, TyAnna K. 52, 57, 58, 59, 60, 61, 63, 67, 69, 76, 206, 208, 221, 231, 236, 242, 245, 246, 249, 252, 255, 257, 260, 264, 265, 266, 271, 329, 345, 353, 363, 366, 376
Hess, Mickey 189, 200
Heylar, Pamela S. 354, 355, 366
Hilton, Brian 333, 345
hiring party 57, 58, 59
Hobbs, Renee 275, 277, 282, 283, 287, 289, 292, 293, 297, 298, 307, 369, 370, 371, 372, 380
Hoi, Chong Ju 333, 345
Holder, Jane B. 231, 242
Hotmail 82, 97
Howard, Rebecca Moore 31, 32, 33, 34, 35, 36, 39, 40, 41, 42, 47, 50, 76, 107, 128, 151, 253, 255, 260, 326, 327, 329, 330, 339, 344, 345, 350, 351, 366, 369, 371, 373, 377
Howard, Tharon 31, 32, 33, 34, 35, 36, 39, 40, 41, 42, 47, 50, 76, 107, 128, 151, 253, 255, 260, 326, 327, 329, 330, 339, 344, 345, 350, 351, 366, 369, 371, 373, 377
Hsieh, Sylvia 121, 128
HTML 87, 90, 93, 270
human subjects research 128
hypermediacy 90

I

image event 224, 232
imitation 76, 77, 326, 333, 344, 345
Indiana University 52, 74, 76
induced obsolescence 328
In Loco Parentis 233
institutional; institutional agents 52; institutional authors 60, 63, 68, 69, 70, 71, 75; institutional policies 52, 56, 62, 70, 236; institutional texts 52, 75
institutionalized plagiarism 34
institutional repositories (IRs) 16
institutional review board (IRB) 122
International Committee of Medical Journal Editors (ICMJE) 366

International James Joyce Foundation Special Panel on Intellectual Property 11
invention 179, 184, 307
; as inspiration of the muses. *See also* muses
iParadigms 80, 81, 83, 88, 89, 90, 91, 94, 96, 97
iPhone 117
iPhoto 102

J

Jaschik, Scott 314, 326
Jaszi, Peter 277, 280, 281, 293, 294, 297, 306, 307
Jay-Z 342
Jenkins, Henry 183, 200, 280, 294, 306
Jenkins, Jennifer 183, 200, 280, 294, 306
Jenson, Jennifer 85, 86, 98
Jhally, Sur 4, 5, 6, 7, 8, 9, 11, 14, 15, 24, 26
John D. and Catherine T. MacArthur Foundation 277, 281
Johnson-Eilola, Johndan 49, 76, 128, 179, 187, 199, 200, 201, 205, 221, 255, 260, 281, 294, 312, 326, 345, 356, 366, 367
Joint Information Systems Committee (JISC) 315, 321
Jolls, Tessa 283, 294
Joyce, Craig 294
Joyce, James 5, 11
Joyce, Lucia 11, 13
Joyce, Stephen 11, 12, 13
Julier, Laura 299, 306

K

Kalmbach, Jim 201, 215, 221
Kane, Gordon 71, 76
Kansas State University 189
Katz, Susan M. 164, 177

Kazaa 9
Keefer, Donald 42, 46
Kelly v. Arriba Soft Corp. 162, 246
Kemp, Fred 245, 246, 251, 252, 260
Kennedy, Krista 360, 367
King Kong 126
Kist, William 289, 294
Knoblauch, C.H. 329, 345
Korn, Allen 162, 176
Krauss, Rosalind 41, 42, 46
Ku Klux Klan 285

L

labour-mixing 238
Lamanna, Carrie 198, 201
Landow, George 340, 345
Lansing Community College 310, 326
Lape, Laura G. 67, 69, 70, 76
Latchaw, Joan 21, 23, 24, 26
Latour, Bruno 231, 242
Latterell, Catherine 312, 326
Lavery, Byrony 34, 38, 39
Law, John 13, 14, 15, 16, 25, 27, 76, 97, 128, 129, 151, 159, 176, 231, 233, 242, 243, 260, 261, 266, 269, 281, 293, 299, 303, 306, 331, 344, 345, 346, 373
The Law of Intellectual Property 331
Lawrence Feldman v. Google, Inc. 83
Leaffer, Marshall 281, 294
Lemley, Mark A. 246, 260
Lessig, Lawrence 9, 10, 12, 26, 184, 201, 212, 221, 236, 237, 243, 256, 338, 339, 342, 345
Lester, Jim D. 176, 208, 221
Lethem, Jeremy 45, 46, 162, 176
Leval, Pierre 113, 128
Levine, Sherrie 35, 40, 41, 42, 43, 44, 45, 46, 154, 377
The Lexicon: An Unauthorized Guide to Harry Potter Fiction and Related Materials 14
License Analyzer 93

licensing terms 93
Lindberg, Stanley W. 111, 128
Lippincott, Joan K. 19, 26
Lipson, Carol 260, 345, 346
Litman, Jessica 10, 12, 26, 197, 201, 328, 330, 337, 338, 345
Livejournal 295
Lockridge, Kenneth 99, 100, 101, 102, 103, 104, 105
Logie, John 149, 166, 176, 179, 201, 205, 221, 297, 298, 307, 343, 345
Los Alamos National Laboratory 17
Louis Vuitton 331, 333, 334
Lovett, Maria 198, 201
Lundberg, Christian 360, 367
Lunsford, Andrea A. 49, 50, 72, 76, 165, 177, 343, 345
Lynch, Clifford A. 19, 26, 164, 177
Lynch, Dennis A. 19, 26, 164, 177

M

MacBook 102
Macintosh 89
Madison, Michael 25, 281, 294, 331, 345
Maid, Barry M. 165, 177, 208, 222
Maimon, Elaine P. 167, 168, 171, 177
Malesic, Jonathan 39, 47
Manning, Michael D. 354, 367
market effect 8
Markie, Biz 161, 162, 164
Marsh, Bill 85, 86, 98
Martin, Brian 33, 34, 36, 47, 177, 221
materiality 180, 182, 184, 185
Mattel 162, 249, 250, 260
Mattel Inc. v. MCA Records 249, 260
Mattel Inc. v. Walking Mountain Productions aka Tom Forsythe 162
Max, D.T. 11, 12, 26
May, Rollo 25, 29, 69, 149, 243, 367, 380

McCloskey, Donald. *See also* McCloskey, Deirdre; *See also* McCloskey, Deirdre; *See also* McCloskey, Deirdre
McDonald's Corporation 217
McGeveran, William 306
The McGraw-Hill Guide 165
McKee, Heidi 55, 75, 212, 221, 268, 269, 272
McLeod, Kembrew 6, 27
McQuade, Christine 163, 177
McQuade, Donald 163, 177
Mead, Jay 357, 367
Media Education Foundation 6, 26
media literacy 25, 182, 221, 275, 276, 277, 279, 280, 281, 282, 283, 284, 285, 289, 291, 293, 294, 307, 369, 373
medieval publishing 110
MGM v. Grokster 173
Michigan State University 223, 226, 236, 243, 268, 269, 297, 302, 306, 307
Mickey Mouse 126, 217
Microsoft Corporation 118, 119, 128; Explorer 88; Windows 86, 88, 119; XP 86, 88
Miles, Libby 51, 77
Miller, Carolyn 357, 358, 359, 367
Miller, David James 357, 358, 359, 367
Mitchell, Margaret 249
Mittelstaedt, Robert A. 172, 177
MLA Handbook 207, 220, 265
MLA Style Manual and Guide to Scholarly Publishing 16, 220
Monty Python's "Camelot" 322
Moore Howard, Rebecca 31, 32, 33, 34, 35, 36, 39, 40, 41, 42, 47, 50, 76, 255, 326, 327, 330, 339, 345, 350, 369, 373
Morpheus 9
Mozilla Firefox 86
"Ms. Austen's Submission" 340
MSN Photo spaces 102

MTV 6, 8, 15, 26, 194
multimedia 101, 135, 143, 160, 161, 165, 167, 179, 193, 201, 206, 208, 209, 213, 214, 215, 216, 270, 272, 276, 277, 281, 282, 283, 285, 293
multimodal texts 182, 193, 276, 323
Munger, Roger 165, 177
Murray, Laura J. 319, 326
Musiccity 9
MySpace 187, 305

N

Napster 5, 9, 12, 13, 24, 76, 183, 185, 186, 187, 188, 200, 208, 212, 272
Nard, Craig 331, 332, 344, 345
National Alliance for Media Arts and Culture (NAMAC) 292
National Council of Teachers of English (NCTE) 292
National Institutes of Health (NIH) 18
The National Review 320
The Nation 320
natural ability. *See also* natural talent
natural talent. *See also* natural ability
Nelson, Theodor H. 168, 218, 221
Neumann, David 30, 47
Newitz, Annalee 80, 98
New London Group 135, 147
Newsweek 30, 320
The New Yorker 331, 346
The New York Times 177, 285
NGO 91
nonacademic creators 76, 366
non-attribution 32
nonauthorship model 355
Nonnecke, Blair 305, 306
Northern Kentucky University 56, 76

O

Ochoa, Tyler 281, 294
Odell, Lee 164, 177, 329, 346
Old Dominion University 192
Olsen, Stefanie 121, 128

The Once and Future King 313
Online Policy Group v. Diebold, Inc. 170, 174, 176, 177, 266, 272
Open Access List 18
OpenDOAR 18
Open Society Institute 17, 25
open-source 4, 24, 53
Orbison, Roy 250
originality 33, 41, 45, 46, 76, 79, 85, 95, 127, 181, 201, 255, 260, 294, 303, 324, 327, 335, 340, 342, 349, 351, 370
originality reports 85
orphan works 223, 232, 243
ownership 20, 21, 26, 27, 37, 50, 53, 54, 57, 58, 59, 61, 67, 70, 71, 73, 74, 75, 76, 79, 97, 107, 110, 111, 114, 121, 142, 151, 153, 160, 191, 207, 217, 218, 220, 230, 231, 234, 276, 279, 281, 289, 317, 318, 321, 333, 347, 348, 349, 350, 351, 352, 353, 355, 356, 360, 361, 362, 363, 364, 365
Oxford University Press 128, 211, 242, 373

P

Palchik, Anna 165, 176
Palfrey, John 306
Pallas v. Crowley 235, 243
Palmquist, Mike 167, 168, 177, 208, 221
paper mill 36, 45, 266, 321
Papert, Seymour 257, 260
Paramount 126
paraphrasing plagiarism 33
parody 124, 125, 181, 190, 191, 192, 193, 194, 195, 196, 197, 198, 199, 200, 204, 248, 249, 270, 375
participatory democracy 113, 127, 258, 259
patchwriting 32, 33, 34, 39, 41, 351

395

Patterson, L. Ray 13, 111, 128, 246, 248, 249, 250, 260
Pavlosky, Nelson 168, 169, 170, 172, 173, 174
Peadon (Hobbs), Catherine. *See also* Hobbs, Catherine; *See also* Hobbs, Catherine; *See also* Hobbs, Catherine; *See also* Hobbs, Catherine; *See also* Hobbs, Catherine; *See also* Hobbs, Catherine; *See also* Hobbs, Catherine; *See also* Hobbs, Catherine
peer review 17, 189, 287
Peers, Pirates, and Persuasion 166
Pentad. *See also* Burke, Kenneth; *See also* Burke, Kenneth; *See also* Burke, Kenneth; *See also* Burke, Kenneth; *See also* Burke, Kenneth
Periodicals for College Libraries 320
Peritz, Janice H. 167, 177
Peters, Marybeth 232, 243
Photobucket 102
Piano, Doreen 276, 294
Picturing Texts 165
piracy paradox 328, 346
plagiarism; plagiarism-detection service 80, 313, 317; plagiarism policies 125, 187, 310, 314, 343, 351, 372
Plagiarism Stoppers 31, 47
Plagiarized.com 31, 47
Podis, JoAnne 233, 243
Podis, Leonard 233, 243
Pollstar v. Gigmania (2000) 83
popular culture 25, 162, 199, 276, 278, 279, 280, 291
Porter, James E. 50, 51, 54, 55, 59, 70, 71, 75, 76, 77, 181, 183, 185, 186, 200, 263, 264, 265, 267, 268, 269, 272, 312, 314, 321, 326, 343, 346
Portland State University (OR) 56, 77
post-Napster 12, 183, 185, 186, 188, 212
Preece, Jennifer 305, 306
"Pretty Woman" 250

Princeton University Press v. Michigan Documents Services 3
print culture 160, 167
printing press 110, 111, 327
private property 107, 113, 114, 238, 380
ProCD, Inc. v. Zeidenberg 82
professional communicators 108, 109, 330
Professional Writing major 299
proprietary content 206
proprietorship 351, 362
prosumer practices 255
public domain 10, 93, 121, 150, 151, 152, 160, 209, 210, 217, 237, 239, 246, 247, 248, 250, 251, 252, 306, 376, 379
Public Knowledge 21
PubMed 18
Pullman, George 330, 346
Purdue University 52, 54, 77
Purdy, James P. 198, 201
Putnam, George Haven 111, 128

Q

Quidditch Through the Ages 14

R

Randall, Ann 249, 372, 373
Raustiala, Kal 328, 331, 333, 334, 337, 338, 342, 343, 346
RDR Books 13, 14, 15, 24, 27
Recording Industry Association of America (RIAA) 9, 109, 217
Reedy, Tom 208, 222
Register.com v. Verio Inc. 98
Reid, Alexander 181, 201, 207, 222
Reidy, Chris 15, 27
Reilly, Erin 291, 294
remediation 86, 88, 147
repurposing 291, 352, 353, 362, 363, 364

Reyman, Jessica 77, 210, 222, 330, 346, 347, 369, 372, 377
rhetoric; as techne. *See* techne; *See* techne; *See* techne; *See* techne ; as techne. *See* techne
rhetorical velocity 223, 228, 229, 230, 231, 236, 238, 239, 240, 241
Richardson, Jeffrey 235, 243
Rich, Lloyd 234, 235, 243
Ricker, Thomas 80, 98
Ridolfo, Jim 223, 226, 228, 229, 230, 240, 242, 243, 268, 269, 377
Rife, Martine Courant 58, 70, 71, 77, 119, 120, 128, 162, 166, 173, 174, 175, 177, 179, 201, 223, 231, 243, 254, 255, 260, 268, 269, 271, 297, 298, 299, 307, 377
rights; moral rights 253, 257; natural rights 110, 113, 126, 127, 151, 250
right to publicity 235
Right to Write Fund 15
Ritter, Kelly 35, 36, 45, 47, 50, 77
rivalrous goods 184
Robillard, Amy E. 35, 45, 47, 326, 371, 372, 373
Robison, Alice J. 291, 294
Roen, Duane 165, 177, 208, 222
Rosati, Annette C. 49, 76, 200, 315, 320, 326
Ross, Caroline 326
Rowling, J.K. 13, 14, 15, 27
RSS feeds 206
Rumours 133, 134, 136, 377
Rush 132
Ruszkiewicz, John J. 164, 165, 177
Rutter, Russel 358, 359, 367
Ryan, Maggie 83, 97, 224, 226, 240, 241, 268, 377

S

Safari 89
Sage Publications 211, 306
sampling 162, 176, 180, 181, 200, 268, 276, 291
Savage, Gerald J. 356, 362, 367
Scafidi, Susan 336, 346
Scanlon, Patrick 30, 47
Schwartz, John 169, 177
Seeing and Writing 3 163
Selber, Stuart A. 50, 51, 59, 72, 76, 77, 128, 179, 182, 187, 188, 191, 201, 255, 260, 281, 294, 312, 326, 356, 366, 367
Selfe, Cynthia L. 50, 77, 92, 93, 98, 129, 165, 176, 186, 188, 200, 201
Selfe, Richard J., Jr. 50, 77, 92, 93, 98, 129, 165, 176, 186, 188, 200, 201
Seltzer, Wendy 15, 152, 153, 156, 169, 171, 176
Shakespeare, William 145
SHERPA 18
Shloss, Carol Loeb 11, 12, 13, 14, 24
shrinkwrap 82, 83, 86, 88, 90, 96
Siang, Sanyin 122, 128
Silberberg, Carol M. 4, 5, 13, 27, 154
Simpson, Carol 162, 211, 222
The Simpsons 286
single-sourcing 352
Slack, Jennifer 357, 358, 367
Smith, Herb 168, 169, 170, 172, 173, 174, 354, 367
Smith, Luke 168, 169, 170, 172, 173, 174, 354, 367
social constructionist pedagogy 246, 252, 253, 254, 257, 259
Society for Technical Communication (STC) 355, 363, 367
Sony Corporation of America v. Universal City Studios 173
Specht v. Netscape Communications Corp. 82, 98
special topics. *See also* topoi
Spoo, Robert 12
Sprigman, Christopher 328, 331, 333, 334, 337, 338, 342, 343, 346
Squier, Joseph 198, 201

Stalin, Joseph 248
Star Trek 322
Star Wars 132, 133, 136, 377
Stationers Company 111
status. *See also* stasis
STC Code for Communicators 355
Stevie Nicks 133
stewardship 142, 143, 146, 153
Sting 133
stopfashionpiracy.com 331, 336, 346
Students for Economic Justice (SEJ) 223, 226
Student Television Network (STN) 292
Suber, Peter 17, 21, 22, 24, 27
subject-matter experts 351, 352, 353, 354
Sullivan, Patricia 51, 75, 77, 108, 128, 129, 161
Suntrust Bank v. Houghton Mifflin Co. 249, 261, 272
Surowiecki, James 331, 346
Swarthmore College 168, 169

T

Taylor, Todd 215, 222
Teacher Tube 290
technical communicators 272, 347, 348, 349, 350, 351, 353, 354, 355, 356, 357, 358, 359, 360, 361, 362, 363, 364, 365, 366
technoliteracy 192
Technology, Education, and Copyright Harmonization Act (TEACH Act) 77, 153, 209, 210, 216, 222, 298
technorhetorician 81
television 132, 133, 135, 137, 142, 152, 185, 188, 229, 271, 277, 280, 291, 322
templates 349, 352
Terakura, Karina 334, 335, 346
Terms of Use 118

thesis 50, 51, 52, 53, 55, 56, 73, 74, 75, 150, 217, 221, 270, 286, 325, 335, 344
Thierer, Adam 25
Thoman, Elizabeth 283, 294
Tierney, R. 276, 294
Time 320, 323, 326
Title 17 237, 329, 335, 345
To Kill a Mockingbird 286
trademark 9, 74, 271, 329, 331, 332, 333, 334, 338, 341, 344
transactional pedagogy 245, 246, 252
transformative 7, 8, 14, 81, 119, 120, 124, 125, 128, 164, 171, 191, 219, 270, 281, 286, 292, 380
transparency 86
Travis, Hannibal 246, 250, 261
turnitin.com 97
Twitter 93, 98, 188, 206, 370
2 Live Crew 250

U

United Students Against Sweatshops (USAS) 223
University of California Academic Council's Special Committee on Scholarly Communication 19
University of California Open Access Policy 19
University of Central Oklahoma 56, 77
University of Nebraska 77
University of New Orleans 56
University of Pennsylvania 283, 294
University of Texas-El Paso 56
university policy 95; approaches toward claiming texts 66; approaches toward delineating institutional authorsinstitutional authors 69; approaches toward disclaiming texts 66; creating work-for-hire 67; uses of facilities and materials that signal institutional authorship claims 54, 55, 61, 62, 64, 65, 69
Usage Policy 83

U.S. Commerce Department 90
user-generated content 186
U.S. Patent and Trademark Office 333
U.S. Treasury Department 90

V

Valentine, Kathryn 50, 77
Vander Ark, Stephen 13, 14, 24
VHS 137, 139
Vicinus, Martha 76, 77, 326, 344, 345
video games 291
Video Pipeline, Inc. v. Buena Vista Home Entertainment, Inc. 162
video production 7, 198, 276, 283, 293
volgkarate 193, 201

W

WAC Clearinghouse 22
Walker, Janice R. 205, 212, 215, 218, 222, 265, 268, 269, 376
Wallace, Emily Lehr 18, 27
Walt Disney 126, 248
Warnecke, Michael 81, 83, 84, 98
Warner Brothers 13, 14, 15, 27
web authoring 205
Webb, Suzanne 179, 181, 200, 215, 221, 255, 259
Weigel Information Commons 283, 294
Wesch, Michael 189
Westbrook, Steve 26, 159, 176, 177, 179, 191, 201, 207, 220, 263, 264, 265, 266, 268, 269, 377
Weston, Edward 40, 41, 42, 43, 154
Whipple, Bob 99, 101, 105, 154, 377
Whitaker, Elaine 39, 47
The White Album 342
White, T.H. 313
Wichita State University (KS) 56, 77
WIDE Research Collective 136, 141, 147
wiki 218, 323

Wikipedia 144, 145, 220, 222, 367
wikis 206, 255
Williams, Bronwyn T. 84, 85, 95, 98
The Wind Done Gone 249
The Wizard of Oz 248
Woodmansee, Martha 110, 129
Woods, Denis 201
Worker Rights Consortium (WRC) 224
work for hire 57, 58, 59, 60, 61, 64, 65, 66, 67, 68, 70, 73, 74, 75, 76, 122, 353
World of Warcraft 93
Wright State University (OH) 56, 78
A Writer's Resource 167, 171
Writing in a Visual Age 164
Writing Program Administrators 92, 95, 97, 372, 373
Wysocki, Anne Frances 85, 86, 87, 96, 98, 164, 177, 181, 193, 194, 197, 198, 199, 200, 201, 204

Y

Yancey, Kathleen Blake 167, 177, 275, 294
The Year of Living Dangerously 40
Yen, Alfred 246, 261
The Young Gunz 288
Young, Jeffrey R. 81, 98
Youngstown State University (OH) 56, 78
Youth Media Reporter (YMR) 292
YouTube 115, 152, 153, 156, 180, 181, 182, 183, 185, 186, 187, 188, 189, 192, 193, 198, 199, 201, 203, 208, 209, 211, 229, 266, 270, 271, 290, 291, 322, 379
Yu, Peter 110, 129, 294
Yves St. Laurent 334, 335

Z

Zimmerman, Traci A. 232, 243
Zwagerman, Sean 84, 85, 98

www.ingramcontent.com/pod-product-compliance
Lightning Source LLC
Chambersburg PA
CBHW022007300426
44117CB00005B/66